The Participation of Victims in International Criminal Proceedings

This book argues that the expressivist justice model provides a meaningful foundation for the participation of victims in international criminal proceedings.

Traditional criminal justice theories have tended to marginalise the role afforded to victims while informing the criminal procedures utilised by international criminal courts. As a result, giving content to, shaping, and enhancing victims' participatory rights have been some of the most debated issues in international criminal justice. This book contributes to this debate by advancing expressivism, which has the capacity to create a historical narrative of gross human rights violations, as a core of international criminal justice able to provide a worthwhile basis for the participation of victims in proceedings and clarifying the scope and content of their participatory rights. The work provides an in-depth discussion on issues related to victims' participatory rights from the perspective of international human rights law, victimology, and the philosophical foundation of international criminal justice.

The book will be a valuable resource for researchers, academics, and policy-makers working in the areas of international criminal justice, international human rights law, transitional justice, and conflict studies.

Alessandra Cuppini holds a senior postdoctoral fellowship awarded by the Research Foundation Flanders Grant (FWO) to conduct research at the Programme for Studies on Human Rights in Context of Ghent University. She previously worked as an Associate Lecturer at the Open University and as teaching assistant at the University of Strathclyde where her research was funded by Campbell Burns scholarship. Her academic experience includes research stays at the University of Barcelona and the University of Maastricht. Her current research looks at narrative victimology in international criminal justice.

The Participation of Victims in International Criminal Proceedings

An Expressivist Justice Model

Alessandra Cuppini

Routledge
Taylor & Francis Group
LONDON AND NEW YORK

Human Rights In Context

First published 2023
by Routledge
4 Park Square, Milton Park, Abingdon, Oxon OX14 4RN

and by Routledge
605 Third Avenue, New York, NY 10158

Routledge is an imprint of the Taylor & Francis Group, an informa business

British Library Cataloguing-in-Publication Data
A catalogue record for this book is available from the British Library

Library of Congress Cataloging-in-Publication Data
A catalog record has been requested for this book

ISBN: 978-1-032-10455-3 (hbk)
ISBN: 978-1-032-10463-8 (pbk)
ISBN: 978-1-003-21544-8 (ebk)

DOI: 10.4324/9781003215448

Typeset in Galliard
by Deanta Global Publishing Services, Chennai, India

This work was supported by the Programme for Studies on Human Rights in Context.

To my family

Contents

Acknowledgements

This book is derived from a PhD thesis produced at the University of Strathclyde from 2013 to 2018. I am deeply grateful to my supervisor, Prof Hakeem Yusuf, for his assistance during my candidature as well as motivation, enthusiasm, and advice upon completion. My heartfelt thanks to my examiners, Prof Onder Bakircioglu and Dr Elaine Webster, who made my viva an enjoyable moment and provided brilliant comments and thoughtful scholarly guidance on the future direction of the work.

Very special thanks to the Campbell Burns Research Studentship for giving me the opportunity to carry out my doctoral research and for their financial support. I want to extend my thanks to the staff members of the Faculty of Humanities and Social Sciences of the University of Strathclyde for their unfailing support and assistance.

The editorial team at Routledge gave wonderful support to this project. I would also like to acknowledge the anonymous reviewers of the book proposal, as the final version of this manuscript has benefited from their comments.

PhD students often talk about loneliness during the course of their study but this is something that I never experienced. Unquestionably, the love and support of my friends has meant so much to me during this adventure. It is difficult to express how grateful I am to my 'Scottish family' for accepting me and loving me for exactly who I am. Thank you for being there for me whenever I needed it. You helped me through the countless problems I had trouble solving, and you reassured me that no matter what, you're always going to be there for me. Thank you for laughing with me, for all the exciting adventures we went on, and all the inside jokes we still laugh about today.

I am also thankful to my lifetime friends Teresa, Luigia, Paola, Alexandra, and Paola for always being my great supporters. Your thoughts, phone calls, e-mails, and texts meant a lot to me.

Last but not least, I must express my very profound gratitude to my parents and my brother, Luca, for providing me with unfailing support and continuous encouragement throughout my life and during the process of researching and writing this book. This accomplishment would not have been possible without them. Thank you. I dedicate this work to you, who have been a constant source of strength and inspiration. Any errors or omissions are entirely my own.

List of acronyms and abbreviations

ACHR	American Convention on Human Rights
CLR	Common Legal Representative
DRC	Democratic Republic of Congo
ECCC	Extraordinary Chambers in the Courts of Cambodia
ECHR	European Convention on Human Rights and Fundamental Freedoms
ECtHR	European Court of Human Rights
EU	European Union
IACtHR	Inter-American Court of Human Rights
ICC	International Criminal Court
ICTR	International Criminal Tribunal for Rwanda
ICTY	International Criminal Tribunal for the former Yugoslavia
IMT	International Military Tribunal (Nuremberg)
NGO	Non-Governmental Organisation
RPE	Rules of Procedure and Evidence
RS	Rome Statute
TVF	Trust Fund for Victims
UN	United Nations

1 Introduction

1.1 Victims in international criminal proceedings: a *vexata quaestio*

Gross violations of human rights have been, and continue to be, perpetrated in armed conflicts as well as during tyrannical regimes. The Preamble to the Rome Statute of the International Criminal Court (ICC) is an important reminder of the significance of the plight of victims: 'during this century millions of children, women and men have been victims of unimaginable atrocities that deeply shock the conscience of humanity'.[1] While it might have been expected that the extensive nature, seriousness, and recurrence of the atrocities committed would have triggered the operation of an effective scheme of victims' participatory rights as a response to those violations, the reality seems to have been the reverse. Early international criminal tribunals, such as the International Military Tribunal (IMT) at Nuremberg and the more recent International Criminal Tribunal for the former Yugoslavia (ICTY) and the International Criminal Tribunal for Rwanda (ICTR) did not grant victims any autonomous legal standing in the proceedings apart from the status of witnesses.

Only in recent years, due to the growing recognition of the impact of mass crimes on victims and communities,[2] have victims' right to and need for justice become important considerations in international criminal justice. The limited representation of victims of mass violence, whose perceptions and needs were frequently ignored, presumed, or misunderstood,[3] has urged for positioning

1 Preamble, Rome Statute of the International Criminal Court 1998 (2187 UNTS 90).

2 See e.g., Kristen Hagen and Sophie Yohani, 'The Nature and Psychosocial Consequences of War Rape for Individuals and Communities' (2010) 2 International Journal of Psychological Studies 14; Julie Mertus, 'Shouting from the Bottom of the Well: The Impact of International Trials for Wartime Rape on Women's Agency' (2004) 6 International Feminist Journal of Politics 110; Nicola Henry, 'The Impossibility of Bearing Witness: Wartime Rape and the Promise of Justice' (2010) 16 Violence against Women 1098; Inger Skjelsbaek, 'Victim and Survivor: Narrated Social Identities of Women Who Experienced Rape during the War in Bosnia-Herzegovina' (2006) 16 Feminism & Psychology 373.

3 Fiona McKay, 'Universal Jurisdiction in Europe: Criminal Prosecutions in Europe since 1990 for War Crimes, Crimes against Humanity, Torture and Genocide' REDRESS 1999

DOI: 10.4324/9781003215448-1

victims' participation in international criminal proceedings, wherein they bring a unique perspective on the factual and cultural elements vital to assist in the comprehension of the context of violence.[4] As such, the challenge of addressing the needs for justice of victims of international crimes has been subject to increasing normative development, evidenced by the incorporation of a regime of victims' participation as participants (the ICC, the Special Tribunal for Lebanon) and as civil parties (the Extraordinary Chambers in the Courts of Cambodia) in the statutes and rules of international and hybrid criminal courts.

Nevertheless, giving content to, shaping, and enhancing victims' participatory rights have been among the most debated issues in international criminal justice: who, when, and how victims can participate are all crucial questions that are undefined, as are questions about the appropriate stage of participation. The issue of victims' participation attracted scholarly attention to the potential detrimental effects that it may bring to international criminal proceedings. As Edwards has observed, the debate on victims' participation has often been reduced to a matter of the rights of victims against the rights of the accused that ends in 'zero-sum games, in which you are either for or against victims'.[5] Zappalà determines that the rights of the accused are 'principles of an imperative nature'[6] and, likewise, other scholars such as McGonigle Leyh[7] and Chung[8] suggest that the participation of victims is a direct challenge to the principle of equality of arms, given that the Defence must respond to additional questions and evidence.[9]

The underlying accusation that victims' participation has the potential to undermine the deliberative discourse of the proceedings is shared elsewhere. The literature explains how the large number of victims involved in proceedings before international criminal tribunals poses a number of organisational challenges. Damaška,[10] Sluiter and Zahar,[11] and De Hemptinne and Rindi[12] argue

15 <https://redress.org/wp-content/uploads/2018/01/G.-June-1999-Universal-Jurisdiction-in-Europe.pdf> accessed 21 January 2022.

4 Mariana Pena and Gaelle Carayon, 'Is the ICC Making the Most of Victim Participation?' (2013) 7 International Journal of Transitional Justice 518, 523.

5 Ian Edwards, 'An Ambiguous Participant: The Crime Victim and Criminal Justice Decision-Making' (2004) 44 British Journal of Criminology 967, 971.

6 Salvatore Zappalà, 'The Rights of Victims v. the Rights of the Accused' (2010) 8 Journal of International Criminal Justice 137, 140.

7 Brianne McGonigle Leyh, 'Victim-Oriented Measures at International Criminal Institutions: Participation and Its Pitfalls' (2012) 12 International Criminal Law Review 375, 375.

8 Christine H Chung, 'Victims' Participation at the International Criminal Court: Are Concessions of the Court Clouding the Promise?' (2008) 6 Northwestern Journal of Human Rights 459, 461.

9 Zappalà (n 6) 150.

10 Mirjan Damaška, 'Problematic Features of International Criminal Procedure' in Antonio Cassese (ed), *The Oxford Companion to International Criminal Justice* (2009) 178.

11 Göran Sluiter and Alexander Zahar, *International Criminal Law: A Critical Introduction* (Oxford University Press 2008) 75.

12 Jérôme De Hemptinne and Francesco Rindi, 'ICC Pre-Trial Chamber Allows Victims to Participate in the Investigation Phase of Proceedings' (2006) 4 Journal of International Criminal Justice 342, 348.

that victims' participation in proceedings conducted in relation to situations of mass atrocities would significantly affect the expeditiousness of the proceedings, increase its complexity, and impose an unreasonable burden on both international criminal courts' functioning and defendants. In her comprehensive examination, McGonigle Leyh suggests that victims' participation has proven to be 'cumbersome and problematic' and has led to the detriment of 'the efficient and effective functioning of the courts'.[13]

International criminal tribunals, tasked with defining the scope of victims' participatory rights, faced – and still face – the above-described fundamental tensions, as Judges wrestle with providing a coherent approach to victims' participation. In fact, while one would have expected decisions by international criminal courts to be fundamental to giving meaning to victims' participation, in reality the Judges advanced solutions to the issues concerning the scope of victims' procedural rights, which resulted in experimentalism and inconsistencies across different Chambers.[14] As a result, the lack of uniformity has meant that decisions on victims' participation in international criminal proceedings have often created as much confusion as they have clarity. In the short lifespan of the ICC, different Chambers have conducted victims' participation in different ways, showing different perceptions and understandings of the scope of victims' participatory rights and, more generally, of the role of victims and the ways to make their participation meaningful. Friman comments that the ICC has found it difficult to incorporate victims' rights, with the law often taking a back-seat to personal opinion when ruling on important issues.[15] In her interviews with staff of the ICC, Wemmers supports Friman's contentions, as she found that key figures within the Court had different views, perspectives, and attitudes towards victims' participation, due to the legal traditions they belong to, namely the common law and civil law traditions and their respective adversarial and inquisitorial procedural approaches, which almost exclusively informed international criminal law and procedure.[16]

This book is grounded in the conviction that the rationale for victims' participation is linked to the nature of the judicial mandate of international criminal justice, and, thus, the contradictions and anomalies concerning the role of victims unveil essential questions about the goals and functions of international criminal proceedings. The overall goal is to provide critical insight into the question of which criminal justice model is able to provide a meaningful foundation for the participation of victims in the international criminal proceedings and best

13 McGonigle Leyh (n 7) 493.

14 Sergey Vasiliev, 'Victim Participation Revisited: What the ICC Is Learning About Itself' in Carsten Stahn, *The Law and Practice of the International Criminal Court* (Oxford University Press 2015) 1146.

15 Håkan Friman, 'The International Criminal Court and Participation of Victims: A Third Party to the Proceedings?' (2009) 22 Leiden Journal of International Law 485, 499.

16 See Jo-Anne Wemmers, 'Victims' Rights and the International Criminal Court: Perceptions within the Court Regarding the Victims' Right to Participate' (2010) 23 Leiden Journal of International Law 629.

clarifies the scope and content of their participatory rights. As such, a great deal of rethinking is needed on the understanding of the main purpose behind the entire enterprise of international criminal justice.

The study is carried out on the basis of the growing awareness that having a coherent understanding of the rationale behind victims' participatory rights can potentially form the basis for making the international criminal justice system more meaningful to directly victimised populations by fostering their involvement in proceedings.

1.2 Towards an expressivist justice model

To understand what model of international criminal justice best clarifies the scope and content of victims' participatory rights, the analysis framework explores classical criminal justice models, namely retributive, deterrent, and restorative justice models, as well as victimological developments, which have mostly informed victims' status in the international criminal proceedings. Such analysis is instrumental in highlighting the fact that the application of the retributivist, deterrent, and restorative justice theories to the international criminal justice system is problematic, not only because these justice models do not effectively accommodate victims' participatory rights, but also because they do not fulfil the objective of delivering international justice.

The analysis of the application of domestic criminal law models in prosecuting extraordinary crimes of mass violence indicates that there is a gap between practices of criminal prosecution and punishment and their assumed penological goals of retribution, deterrence, and restoration. This critique is based on two factors. First, the high level of selectivity of prosecution, caused by financial constraints, political contingency, or simply by the decision to prosecute those cases where there was a better chance of getting a conviction, decreases the deterrent effect of punishment by lowering the chances of being punished or of getting caught. But selectivity of prosecution also limits the amount of retribution international criminal tribunals can exact, since not all persons deserving a punishment are actually punished. Second, the very serious nature of the international crimes affects the ability of the international criminal justice to serve retributive ends because it stretches the notion of proportionality, making it difficult to inflict a proportionate punishment for atrocities committed. In a similar way, the restorative justice practices and their prioritisation of victims' participation, developed to address juvenile criminality, first-time offenders, and low-level crime, are not structured to operate in the particular context of international criminal justice, which is characterised by grave harm caused to victims and communities by mass atrocity.

A well-grounded foundation for victims' participation in international criminal proceedings needs to depart from the above-mentioned criminal justice frameworks, which still relegate victims to the periphery of the criminal process. A unifying thread that runs throughout the analysis in this book is the idea that victims' participation must be based on the expressivist model of justice, which best captures the nature and priorities of international criminal justice as well as the scope and content of victims' rights in international criminal proceedings.

For expressivism, international criminal justice primarily bears a normative didactic endeavour since the trial is conceived as a site for impacting on present and future societal understandings of mass violence, promoting a particular structuring of thought. International criminal proceedings, thus, can function as communicative institutions in the post-conflict societies by conveying disavowal of the moral unacceptability of atrocity, narrating an official history of past violence, and reinforcing social norms of respect for the rule of law. On this view, international criminal proceedings foster the development of a narrative shaped by courtroom interactions, where acts and perspectives of the different actors, such as Judges, Prosecutors, Defence lawyers, and victims, get voiced throughout the proceedings on the international stage that the international criminal justice institutions provide. This book, therefore, contemplates expressivism as a key rationale for international criminal justice, able to shape and enhance victims' role as active participants in the establishment of the historical record of events and, more generally, in the quest for justice and the closure of the impunity gap.

While literature exists in the field of international criminal law regarding the ability of the international criminal justice to exhibit an expressivist value,[17] the expressivist potential for victims' participation to construct messages and narratives within the courtroom in the context of mass atrocities is underappreciated in international criminal justice scholarship. Academic debate has been quite attentive to the diversity of messages constructed by competing actors, mainly Prosecutor and Defence, as part of the struggles within international criminal courtrooms. Specifically, it has been examined whether and how prosecution and defendants might mobilise the expressive power of international criminal justice to advance the legitimation of their preferred messages and narratives. Scholars like deGuzman[18] and Drumbl[19] advance the need for an expressivist approach to the selection of the cases for prosecution before the ICC. Specifically, deGuzman argues that, when deciding whether to investigate and prosecute situations and cases, Prosecutors and Judges should aim primarily to maximise the Court's expressive impact because only an expressivist agenda can stimulate a didactic process through which social norms and values are expressed.[20] Glasius and

17 See Chapter 4.

18 Margaret deGuzman, 'Choosing to Prosecute: Expressive Selection at the International Criminal Court' (2012) 33 Michigan Journal of International Law 265, 319.

19 See Mark A Drumbl, 'The Expressive Value of Prosecuting and Punishing Terrorists: Hamdan, the Geneva Conventions, and International Criminal Law' (2007) 75 The George Washington Law Review 1165.

20 deGuzman (n 18) 319. See also Diane Marie Amann, 'Group Mentality, Expressivism, and Genocide' (2002) 2 International Criminal Law Review 93.

Meijers examine whether defendants and prosecution may harness the expressive power of international criminal trials to advance their strategic political and social agendas. The authors consider how the messaging about historical narratives and their authentication as truths are constructed in the course of the trial, by examining the discourses of both prosecution and Defence in the context of Charles Taylor's trial before the Special Court for Sierra Leone[21] and Karadžic's trial before the ICTY.[22] This study sheds light on the extent to which what is said and done by the defendants in international criminal trials confirms or disrupts the potential expressivist functions of international criminal justice. In this scenario, where international criminal proceedings convey parallel and quite often conflicting discourses, Judges play an important role in enacting the norm-expression function of the trial, as they are expected to cut through the adversarial narrative contestation of the antagonists at trial to render a single authoritative judgement. Sander advances that Judges can invalidate unpersuasive interpretations of the past, thereby combatting denial and attempts at revisionism, and, at the same time, promoting societal solidarity around the narratives they declare as authoritative.[23] McCarthy engages with the implications of expressivism for victims of gross violations of human rights, but his analysis focuses on the expressivist approach as the basis for the system of reparations for victims at the ICC. He suggests that expressivism is a meaningful paradigm of international criminal justice for understanding that reparations for victims (as the punishment of those who commit grave crimes under international law) can serve the purpose of giving expression to social norms and values, by 'providing a measure of vindication for victims and denunciation of the barbarities in question'.[24]

This book is, therefore, intended to make a contribution to the literature on victims' participation in international criminal justice, by advancing the idea that the victim's role is fundamental for expressivist purposes. This contribution suggests that the expressivist assumption that international criminal trials provide a platform for framing the narrative of gross violations of human rights urges victims to express their independent voice and bring their dimension to the proceedings. Expressivism, thus, becomes a vehicle for effectively tailoring victims' participation, which should be informed by the idea that victims act as 'participants' in criminal proceedings, whose voices are not tied to that of the parties. Reading through the expressivist approach, it becomes clear that the narratives of the victims about charged heinous events, their causes, and their consequences,

21 See Marlies Glasius and Tim Meijers, 'Constructions of Legitimacy: The Charles Taylor Trial' (2012) 6 International Journal of Transitional Justice 229.

22 See Marlies Glasius and Tim Meijers, 'Expression of Justice or Political Trial? Discursive Battles in the Karadžić Case' (2013) 35 Human Rights Quarterly 720.

23 Barrie Sander, 'The Expressive Turn of International Criminal Justice: A Field in Search of Meaning' (2019) 32 Leiden Journal of International Law 851, 856.

24 Conor McCarthy, 'Victim Redress and International Criminal Justice: Competing Paradigms, or Compatible Forms of Justice?' (2012) 10 Journal of International Criminal Justice 351, 368.

should become constitutive parts of discursive battles about how mass violence is best understood, explained, and responded to.

1.3 Bridging the gap between the adversarial and inquisitorial systems

As remarked above, one of the greatest practical challenges that international criminal courts face arises from the diametrically opposed conception of the role of victims developed by the adversarial and inquisitorial systems of criminal procedure, originating respectively in the common law and the civil law traditions. The idea of a more harmonised international procedural system is not a novelty in the academic debate;[25] however, this work aims to make a unique contribution to the need to harmonise the different legal traditions coexisting in the international criminal procedure. It calls for the adoption of the expressivist justice model to the international criminal procedure as a 'tool' that goes beyond the simple juxtaposition of common law and civil law elements, developing a common grammar that harmonises the 'accusatory grammar' and the 'inquisitory grammar'.

The adoption of the expressivist model by international criminal justice has important implications for the structure of the proceedings, which should not only be systematised with reference to common technical rules, but should also entail didactic and communicative purposes as its guiding principles. An important procedural implication of the truth-telling and didactic functions of the trial is the relaxing of the bipolar dispute resolution pressures that arise from the proceedings organised as a contest of two partisan cases. Rooting the international criminal trial in the expressivist justice model has a big impact on the articulation of the procedural role of individuals involved in the proceedings. Establishing a common grammar within the framework of the didactic role of the international criminal trial leads to a change of perspective on the role and rights of all actors involved in the criminal process, as victims' rights are intertwined with the roles and rights of the Prosecutor, Judges, and defendants. Specifically, the truth-telling and didactic aims call for a more active role for Judges and victims alike. Most importantly, expressivism as an effective mechanism that is able to bridge the gaps between adversarial and inquisitorial approaches contributes to developing a legal language and – perhaps in the future – a legal culture which are essential for the articulation of victims' participatory rights in a consistent manner.

25 Christoph Safferling, 'The Role of the Victim in the Criminal Process – A Paradigm Shift in National German and International Law?' (2011) 11 International Criminal Law Review 183, 212; Kai Ambos, 'International Criminal Procedure: "Adversarial", "Inquisitorial" or Mixed?' (2003) 3 International Criminal Law Review 1, 34–35; *Prosecutor v Dražen Erdemović* (Separate and Dissenting Opinion of Judge Cassese) IT-96–22-T, Appeals Chamber (7 October 1997), para 4.

1.4 The expressivist capacity of international criminal tribunals and regional human rights courts

The book's analysis focuses, first, on the evaluation of the trials of the IMT, the ICTY, and the ICTR from an expressivist perspective, and considers the expressivist value of the limited instances of participation of victims before these tribunals in light of the predominance of the common law adversarial model in their practices. This work aims to demonstrate that, while the Nuremberg IMT, the ICTY, and the ICTR were vested with an expressivist value, there was a corresponding expressivist 'deficit' with regard to the way the procedural role of victims is framed in their founding legal instruments and implemented in their practices. This will provide a background for the analysis of the development of the victims' participation scheme set in the ICC legal framework. At the ICC, victims can apply to become participants, a status that grants them a range of participatory rights, such as presenting 'their views and concerns' at 'appropriate' 'stages of the proceedings'.[26] This status is more extensive than that of the early Nuremberg IMT and *ad hoc* tribunals for the former Yugoslavia and Rwanda, where victims could only appear if called as witnesses. Thus, whereas the discussion contends that the practices of the Nuremberg IMT, the ICTY, and ICTR undermined the capacity of victims' narratives expressed during the trials to present their perspective on the events and to bring about a potential qualitative change in the message the trial conveys, the analysis of the case law of the ICC reveals how victims appear as participants when they are authorised to do so, and what the effects of these appearances are. This book argues that, from the ICC's case law on victims' participatory rights, expressivism emerges not only as one of the key foundations for international criminal justice, but also as a vehicle for effectively tailoring meaningful victim participation.

This work also acknowledges that one of the problems academics confront when engaging with issues related to victims is that various branches of international law (including comparative criminal law and procedure, international criminal law, international humanitarian law, and international human rights law) deal with the issue in a compartmentalised manner, as each of these disciplines pursues disparate goals, approaches, and methodologies. Bassiouni remarks that continuing to develop the notion of victims' rights with gaps and overlaps prevents such rights from being effectively addressed.[27] In view of this, this book aims to build a link between human rights, international criminal justice, and victims' rights by illustrating that human rights courts, such as the European Court of Human Rights (ECtHR) and the Inter-American Court of Human Rights (IACtHR), represent a source of relevant jurisprudence on victims' right to participate in criminal proceedings. Despite the conceptual divergence

26 Article 68(3), Rome Statute of the International Criminal Court.

27 Mahmoud Cherif Bassiouni, 'International Recognition of Victims' Rights' (2006) 6 Human Rights Law Review 203, 205.

(international criminal law is based on individual responsibility, while the ECtHR and the IACtHR are based on the State responsibility framework), common underlying principles (international crimes embody violations of human rights sanctioned under international human rights treaties) allow international criminal courts to draw from both bodies of law in developing principles and practices. At a general level, Article 38 of the International Court of Justice Statute, and, at a more specific level, Article 21 of the Rome Statute, contemplate such interplay. Because these articles, generally regarded as a statement of the sources of international law, require international criminal courts to apply as secondary sources treaties, principles, and rules of international law, whose 'application and interpretation (…) must be consistent with internationally recognised human rights', they are subject to the international criminal justice's reliance on the ECtHR and the IACtHR as a source of principles and rules that can be applied for purposes relating to the participation of victims. The analysis of the case law of the ECtHR and the IACtHR seeks to provide a valid contribution to enhancing the expressivist approach to victims' participatory rights within the criminal proceedings. Thus, the rights of victims in the jurisprudence of these two regional human rights bodies is analysed with a view to suggesting ways of operationalising victims' participation in international criminal proceedings.

1.5 Book structure

This book is divided into nine chapters. These introductory comments represent the first chapter, which consists of contextualising the book's overall purpose, arguments, analytical frameworks, and significance. By positioning the book in the existing, fast-paced literature on international criminal justice, the chapter illustrates the primary questions and arguments concerning the modalities of participation for victims in the international criminal proceedings. The chapter then outlines the book's key contribution to the scholarship on what model of criminal justice best captures the nature and priorities of international criminal justice, and, most importantly, can provide a meaningful foundation for the participation of victims in the international criminal proceedings and clarifies the scope and content of their participatory rights.

The second chapter is structured around two main themes. First, it offers an insight into retributive and deterrent theories of criminal justice to highlight how these views affect the role given to victims in criminal proceedings. The second part of the chapter is devoted to investigating to what extent victimological studies respond to the need for a better integration of victims in systems of criminal justice. Specific attention is paid to restorative justice in order to evaluate the degree to which it represents an effective response to the demands of victims' participation in criminal proceedings. The chapter concludes that the victimological response has resulted in a range of mechanisms that have relegated victims to the periphery of the criminal justice system.

The third chapter questions whether or not retributivism, deterrence, and restorative justice are eligible justifications for international criminal justice.

The discussion explores normative differences between international crimes and ordinary crimes, to understand to what extent the above-mentioned criminal justice theories, developed to be implemented in domestic criminal justice systems, can effectively be transplanted to the field of international criminal law. The chapter offers a critical evaluation of case law by the ICTY, the ICTR, and the ICC, which have grounded punishment within these criminal justice frameworks, with the objective of exposing the shortcomings of using such theories within the international criminal justice arena.

Chapter 4 contends that expressivism is the most appropriate theoretical justification for international criminal justice. It provides an outline of expressivist theories to illustrate that expressivism imposes a change in the perspective of the international criminal justice system: as opposed to punishing simply because the perpetrators deserve it or because potential perpetrators will be deterred, the expressivist potential lies in the didactic function of the trial and its capacity to create historical narratives as representations of truth and their pedagogical dissemination. For this reason, the chapter focuses its analysis on the international criminal trial as a site for impacting on present and future societal understandings of mass violence, peremptorily repudiating conducts amounting to international crimes, symbolically rejecting acquiescence to those crimes and promoting human rights.

The fifth chapter addresses the challenges originating from the ideological and structural differences between the adversarial and inquisitorial systems and, specifically, how the role of victims in proceedings is conceived. The focus is on adversarial and inquisitorial systems due to the fact that international criminal law and procedure draw almost exclusively from these two legal traditions. This chapter proposes that expressivism can be the mechanism used to bridge the gaps in language between civil law and common law systems of criminal justice. The expressivist dimension of the international criminal trial has a strong impact on the articulation of the goals and procedural role of victims. In this view, this chapter considers the change of perspective on the role and rights of all individuals involved in the criminal process, as victims' rights are intertwined with the roles and rights of the Prosecutor, Judges, and defendants.

Chapter 6 examines the case law of the ECtHR and the (IACtHR, which has been central to the elaboration of victims' rights to participate in criminal proceedings. This chapter maintains that the IACtHR and the ECtHR have developed a case law that conveys a system of values consistent with the expressivist dimension of the criminal justice system and, more importantly, with the status of victim-participant in criminal proceedings as tailored by expressivism. International criminal justice can draw relevant lessons from the case law of the IACtHR and the ECtHR on victims' participatory rights in criminal proceedings. To begin with, decisions by these regional human rights bodies concerning the participation of victims in criminal proceedings suggest ways of operationalising victims' participation in international criminal proceedings. This chapter will appraise to what extent the developments made by the IACtHR and the ECtHR can impact the call for greater rights for victims in the international criminal justice system.

In Chapter 7, the analysis of the expressivist foundation of international criminal justice is extended to the post-World War II Nuremberg IMT, the ICTY, and the ICTR. This chapter aims to identify the expressivist nature of these tribunals and explore the limitations of the development of the role of victims in these early international criminal trials. While these international criminal tribunals are vested with an expressivist value, there was a corresponding expressivist 'deficit' with regard to the way the procedural role of victims is framed in the founding legal instruments and implemented in the practices of the Nuremberg IMT, the ICTY, and the ICTR. The practices of these tribunals undermined the capacity of victims' narrative expressed during the trials to present their perspective on the events and to bring about a potential qualitative change in the message the trial conveys.

The eighth chapter elaborates upon the case law of the ICC on victims' participation in proceedings, intending to investigate whether or not, and to what extent, the Chambers have interpreted the ICC Statute provisions for victims' participation in a manner consistent with the expressivist framework. First, the chapter illustrates that the ICC represents a unique procedural system which is *sui generis* in the sense that it departs from the dominant adversarial and inquisitorial systems of justice. Subsequently, the focus of the chapter is on the analysis of the procedural rights of victims in the three main stages of the proceedings: the investigation, pre-trial, and trial stages. Then, the chapter looks to procedural issues arising out of victim participation, focusing on two main themes: the role of victims in the evidence-gathering process and victims' common legal representation.

Chapter 9, the conclusion, brings together all the major conclusions reached in the study about which criminal justice model should be adopted to ensure effective participatory rights to victims in international criminal proceedings. It highlights that, due to the specific features of international criminal justice, the retributive, utilitarian, and restorative justice models are not adequate to meet the victims' need for justice. It further argues that the expressivist model is a key rationale for international criminal justice and provides a meaningful foundation for victims' participation in international criminal proceedings, clarifying the scope and content of their rights. The chapter concludes with some considerations that endeavour to promote an effective framework of victims' participation that is able to bring about a potential qualitative enhancement to the messages the trial conveys.

References

Books and journals

Amann DM, 'Group Mentality, Expressivism, and Genocide' (2002) 2 International Criminal Law Review 93

Ambos K, 'International Criminal Procedure: 'Adversarial', 'Inquisitorial' or Mixed?' (2003) 3 International Criminal Law Review 1

Bassiouni MC, 'International Recognition of Victims' Rights' (2006) 6 Human Rights Law Review 203

Chung CH, 'Victims' Participation at the International Criminal Court: Are Concessions of the Court Clouding the Promise?' (2008) 6 Northwestern Journal of Human Rights 459

Damaška M, 'Problematic Features of International Criminal Procedure' in Antonio Cassese (ed), *The Oxford Companion to International Criminal Justice* (2009)

deGuzman M, Choosing to Prosecute: Expressive Selection at the International Criminal Court' (2012) 33 Michigan Journal of International Law 265

De Hemptinne J and Rindi F, 'ICC Pre-Trial Chamber Allows Victims to Participate in the Investigation Phase of Proceedings' (2006) 4 Journal of International Criminal Justice 342

Drumbl MA, The Expressive Value of Prosecuting and Punishing Terrorists: Hamdan, the Geneva Conventions, and International Criminal Law' (2007) 75 The George Washington Law Review 1165

Edwards I, 'An Ambiguous Participant: The Crime Victim and Criminal Justice Decision-Making' (2004) 44 British Journal of Criminology 967

Friman. H, The International Criminal Court and Participation of Victims: A Third Party to the Proceedings?' (2009) 22 Leiden Journal of International Law 485

Glasius M and Meijers T, 'Constructions of Legitimacy: The Charles Taylor Trial' (2012) 6 International Journal of Transitional Justice 229

Glasius M and Meijers T, 'Expression of Justice or Political Trial? Discursive Battles in the Karadžić Case' (2013) 35 Human Rights Quarterly 720

Hagen K and Yohani S, 'The Nature and Psychosocial Consequences of War Rape for Individuals and Communities' (2010) 2 International Journal of Psychological Studies 14

Henry N, 'The Impossibility of Bearing Witness: Wartime Rape and the Promise of Justice' (2010) 16 Violence against Women 1098

McCarthy C, 'Victim Redress and International Criminal Justice: Competing Paradigms, or Compatible Forms of Justice?' (2012) 10 Journal of International Criminal Justice 351

McGonigle Leyh B, 'Victim-riented Measures at International Criminal Institutions: Participation and Its Pitfalls' (2012) 12 International Criminal Law Review 375

McKay F, 'Universal Jurisdiction in Europe: Criminal Prosecutions in Europe since 1990 for War Crimes, Crimes against Humanity, Torture and Genocide' (1999) REDRESS 1999 <https://redress.org/wp-content/uploads/2018/01/G.-June-1999-Universal-Jurisdiction-in-Europe.pdf> accessed 21 January 2022

Mertus J, Shouting from the Bottom of the Well: The Impact of International Trials for Wartime Rape on Women's Agency' (2004) 6 International Feminist Journal of Politics 110

Pena M and Carayon G, 'Is the ICC Making the Most of Victim Participation?' (2013) 7 International Journal of Transitional Justice 518

Safferling C, The Role of the Victim in the Criminal Process – A Paradigm Shift in National German and International Law?' (2011) 11 International Criminal Law Review 183

Sander B, 'The Expressive Turn of International Criminal Justice: A Field in Search of Meaning' (2019) 32 Leiden Journal of International Law 851

Skjelsbaek I, Victim and Survivor: Narrated Social Identities of Women Who Experienced Rape during the War in Bosnia-Herzegovina' (2006) 16 Feminism & Psychology 373

Sluiter G and Zahar A, *International Criminal Law: A Critical Introduction* (Oxford University Press 2008)
Vasiliev S, Victim Participation Revisited: What the ICC Is Learning About Itself' in Carsten Stahn, *The Law and Practice of the International Criminal Court* (Oxford University Press 2015)
Wemmers J-A, 'Victims' Rights and the International Criminal Court: Perceptions within the Court Regarding the Victims' Right to Participate' (2010) 23 Leiden Journal of International Law 629
Zappalà S, The Rights of Victims v. the Rights of the Accused' (2010) 8 Journal of International Criminal Justice 137

Case

Prosecutor v Dražen Erdemović. (Separate and issenting Opinion of Judge Cassese) IT-96–22-T, Appeals Chamber (7 October 1997)

Legislation

Rome Statute of the International Criminal Court 1998 (2187 UNTS 90)

2 Victims' status under theories of criminal justice

A critical perspective

2.1 Introduction

In the modern age, the centralised and State-provided criminal justice consolidated what Shafer called the 'correctional ossification' of the criminal justice system, as the criminal law and its penal sanctions aimed at protecting the public interest and not the private interests of individual parties, leaving very little room for victims to play a role in criminal proceedings.[1] It is on this basis that retributive and deterrent paradigms of punishment, which shape the structure and values of the criminal justice system, have largely been conceived. However, just as in the 1700s the Enlightenment's developments in criminology and penology relegated victims to a peripheral role, in the mid-1900s the rise of victimology, as an academic discipline, responded to the removal of victims in the context of the domestic criminal justice system.

Against this background, this chapter is structured around two macro themes. First, it provides an insight into retributive and deterrent theories of criminal justice to offer a better understanding of their nature and primary purpose. Specifically, the first part investigates the retributive and deterrence paradigms in relation to the functioning of the criminal justice system and the role these theories grant to victims. The second part of this chapter discusses whether victimological studies have produced effective strategies to make criminal justice more responsive to the concerns of victims. The analysis aims to explore the extent to which the victimological response to calls for a better integration of victims into systems of criminal justice has effectively granted victims substantive and enforceable procedural rights in criminal justice systems. The focus is on the debate about two victim-based approaches: the rights of victims to services, which address the victims' physical, psychological, and material needs; and victims' procedural rights. Consequently, this chapter extensively discusses the restorative justice mechanism to evaluate to what degree it represents an effective response to the demands of victims' participation in criminal proceedings.

1 Stephen Schafer, *The Victim and His Criminal. A Study of Functional Responsibility*, vol 34 (Random House 1968) 37–38.

DOI: 10.4324/9781003215448-2

2.2 Criminal justice theories and the role of victims in proceedings

The political doctrines on the legitimation of the power of the State over the individual developed during the Enlightenment deeply influenced modern theories on criminal justice and punishment. In his ground-breaking pamphlet *On Crimes and Punishments* (1764), the Italian philosopher Cesare Beccaria, whose ideas on criminal justice represent the foundation of classical criminology and modern penology, advocated a reform of the criminal justice system aiming to transform it into a 'centralized and rational system of justice'.[2] In this system, where crime was conceived as a harm to society as a whole, the central authority was called to prosecute and punish criminals in order to defend the public good and prevent the dissolution of society.[3] However, this view of criminal prosecution as a means of repaying society and deterring potential offenders completely overlooked the interests of the victims to the benefit of those of the community.[4] In case of conflict between the interests of society and those of victims, the former had to prevail over the latter, because criminal prosecution was undertaken for social utility.[5] The model of criminal justice envisaged by Beccaria had positive aspects, as it contributed to the development of formal safeguards for the defendant. However, the focus on the defendant's right to due process came at the expense of the victim's role, reducing the criminal justice system to a dispute between the State and the defendant.[6]

It is on this approach, in which the victim's role is of little significance, that modern theories of criminal justice have largely been based. Traditionally the justification for punishment falls into two broad categories: retributive theories and the utilitarian or crime-control school.[7] These rationales can be roughly categorised according to their temporal orientation. The retributivist approach is backward-looking as it focuses on the wrongfulness of the crime to justify punishment as perpetrators' just deserts.[8] Conversely, utilitarian theories can be

2 Cesare Beccaria, *On Crimes and Punishment and Other Writings* (Cambridge University Press 1995) xii.

3 David B Young, 'Cesare Beccaria: Utilitarian or Retributivist?' (1983) 11 Journal of Criminal Justice 317, 319; Peggy M Tobolowsky, 'Victim Participation in the Criminal Justice Process: Fifteen Years After the President's Task Force on Victims of Crime' (1999) 25 New England Journal on Criminal and Civil Confinement 21, 26.

4 William F McDonald, 'Towards a Bicentennial Revolution in Criminal Justice: The Return of the Victim' (1975) 13 The American Criminal Law Review 649, 655.

5 Jonathan Doak, *Victims' Rights, Human Rights and Criminal Justice. Reconceiving the Role of the Third Parties* (Hart Publishing 2008) 5.

6 Schafer (n 1) 30.

7 Robert D Sloane, 'The Expressive Capacity of International Punishment: The Limits of the National Law Analogy and the Potential of International Criminal Law' (2007) 43 Stanford Journal of International Law 39, 69.

8 Mikaela Heikkilä, *International Criminal Tribunals and Victims of Crime: A Study of the Status of Victims before International Criminal Tribunals and of Factors Affecting This Status* (Institute for Human Rights Åbo Akademi University 2004) 23.

described as forward-looking because of their focus on the future benefits that punishment can produce, such as specific and general deterrence, rehabilitation, and incapacitation.[9]

2.2.1 Retributive theories

Retributive theories have a long tradition in criminal law, but they found their philosophical formulation in Immanuel Kant's characteristic discourse of 'just deserts'.[10] According to the German philosopher, the theory of retribution is that criminals should be punished because they deserve it. In this view, punishment becomes a categorical imperative.[11] Such a standpoint is reinforced by another prominent German philosopher, Hegel, who, in his *Philosophy of Right,* holds that 'as the criminal has done, so should it be done to him'.[12] Generally speaking, retribution can be defined as a form of criminal justice involving the infliction of punishment upon a perpetrator who, as result of his/her wrongful behaviour, is considered to be deserving punishment.[13] As Cottingham outlined, the etymology of the word retribution comes from the Latin *re+tribuo*, which means 'to pay back'. Criminals have taken unfair advantage from breaching the law and, therefore, their punishment is meted out to pay back their debt to society.[14] The emphasis, thus, rests on the link between punishment and wrongdoing without any regard for the possible effect or benefit that the punishment could reasonably have. The central concern is providing the offender with a consistent treatment and a proportional punishment, which is meted out based on the seriousness of the crime and the mental state of the offender.[15]

The retributivist premise that the severity of punishment inflicted upon the perpetrator should be proportional to the seriousness of the crime requires strict

9 ibid; David J Luban, 'Fairness to Rightness: Jurisdiction, Legality, and the Legitimacy of International Criminal Law' (2008) Georgetown Public Law Research Paper No. 1154117 1, 8.

10 Antony Duff and David Garland (eds), *A Reader on Punishment* (Oxford University Press 1994) 1–3.

11 Immanuel Kant, *The Metaphysical Elements of Justice. Part I of the Metaphysics of Morals* (Mary Gregor tr, Cambridge University Press 1991) 142.

12 Georg WF Hegel, *Philosophy of Right* (Thomas M Knox tr, Oxford University Press 1967) 71.

13 Brianne McGonigle Leyh, *Procedural Justice? Victim Participation in International Criminal Proceedings* (Intersentia 2011) 37; Heikkilä (n 8) 25; Robert Nozick, *Philosophical Explanations* (Harvard University Press 1981) 374–384; Andrew von Hirsch, 'Punishment, Penance and the State' in Matt Matravers (ed), *Punishment and Political Theory* (Hart Publishing 1999) 69.

14 John Cottingham, 'Varieties of Retribution' (1979) 29 The Philosophical Quarterly 238, 238–239; Heikkilä (n 8) 26; Robert Cryer et al., *An Introduction to International Criminal Law and Procedure* (Cambridge University Press 2014) 19; Bill Wringe, 'Why Punish War Crimes? Victor's Justice and Expressive Justifications of Punishment' (2006) 25 Law and Philosophy 159, 167.

15 Heikkilä (n 8) 26; Wringe (n 14) 167.

adherence to fair procedures for the accused. This explains why, at the heart of the retributive justice systems, there are the rights and due process safeguards for the accused and the concept of impartiality of the decision-maker.[16] On the one hand, the emphasis on impartiality is one of the strengths of retributive justice, but, on the other hand, a retributive approach depersonalises the judicial process because justice becomes concerned mainly with wrongs and not with persons, except for the perpetrator.[17] This focus on the offender and the wrong committed 'blinds justice to the crime's victim (…) [who] loses his central role'[18] in the criminal justice process. Although the wrongdoing affecting the victim underlies the whole retributive justice system, the defendant's conduct and not the suffering of the victim is what is examined in the trial. The seriousness of the offence and the consequent severity of the punishment depend on the act itself and the offender's state of mind, rather than on the degree of harm inflicted on the victim.[19] Few scholars have argued that the retributive justice model acknowledges the plight of the victims as punishment stems 'from the wrongdoer's denial of respect for the victims' integrity'[20] and, thus, it can be seen as the expression of society's solidarity with victims. However, by virtue of the fact that retributive justice is focused first and foremost on the offence committed and not on the victimised individual, there is a general consensus that retributive justice should be viewed as neither a victim-centred nor a victim-friendly approach.

The main argument to justify the marginal role of victims is that their participation and voice in criminal proceedings are considered to be a threat to the rights and guarantees crafted in favour of the accused, which are fundamental in retributive justice theories. It has been argued that a prominent procedural role for victims introduces arbitrariness to the process on two counts. First, the accused should be held accountable for the harm intended or at least the harm that can be objectively established. However, in everyday courtroom practice, it is difficult to assess the subjective suffering experienced by victims within the realm of reasonably foreseeable consequences to victims.[21] The unlikelihood of unequivocally establishing an objective degree of suffering can affect the disparity of treatment of the accused.[22] Second, through participation, victims can express feelings of revenge or forgiveness, which can actively influence the impartiality of the decision-maker throughout the procedure and in particular in the sentencing

16 McGonigle Leyh (n 13) 38.

17 Wesley Cragg, *The Practice of Punishment: Towards a Theory of Restorative Justice* (Routledge 1992) 19.

18 ibid.

19 Miriam J Aukerman, 'Extraordinary Evil, Ordinary Crime: A Framework for Understanding Transitional Justice' (2002) 15 Harvard Human Rights Journal 39, 54.

20 Andrew Ashworth, *Principles of Criminal Law* (5th edn, Oxford University Press 2006) 16; Randy Barnett, 'Restitution: A New Paradigm of Criminal Justice' 87 Ethics 284.

21 Heikkilä (n 8) 27; Donald J Hall, 'Victims' Voices in Criminal Court: The Need for Restraint' (1990) 28 American Criminal Law Review 233, 256.

22 Hall (n 21) 258.

phase.[23] This logic underlying retributive justice, which primarily sees victims' participation as introducing an element of arbitrariness to the proceedings, is reflected in the role assigned to the Prosecutor, who is tasked with preventing victims' subjective experiences and suffering from negatively affecting the outcome of a trial.[24]

The retributive view on punishment as a response to a wrong committed by the accused's action, rather than a response to the sufferings experienced by victims, does not grant them any procedural role in the criminal trial process other than that of witnesses. In the words of Moore, the amount of wrong done is contingent on 'how many times the norm was violated' and this is the point at which victims play the role of information providers about the norm violation.[25] In this sense, the victim serves simply as a witness among the prosecution's witnesses, enjoying very limited measures, mainly related to his/her protection and the guarantee to be treated with compassion and respect during the trial.[26]

2.2.2 Utilitarian theories

Utilitarian theories can be described as consequentialist because they consider criminal justice as a means of achieving a legitimate end and justifying punishment by linking it to the different consequences that it can produce, namely specific and general deterrence, rehabilitation, and incapacitation.[27] Despite the different consequences or objectives that a punishment may serve, the common point of utilitarian theories is their focus on the future benefits of criminal justice: the imposition of a predictable criminal sanction as a result of an offence can potentially prevent offenders and, more generally, the population from engaging in prohibited conducts.[28] International criminal tribunals have invoked as a prominent rationale for punishment the goal of deterrence,[29] while the place of rehabilitation and incapacitation is marginal.[30] Therefore, this section focuses on deterrence, both general and specific, as a justification for sentencing in criminal justice.

23 Michael Moore, 'Victims and Retribution: A Reply to Professor Fletcher' (1999) 3 Buffalo Criminal Law Review 65, 77.
24 Dennis Klimchuck, 'Retribution, Restitution and Revenge, Law and Philosophy' (2001) 20 Law and Philosophy 81, 83.
25 Moore (n 23) 71.
26 Heikkilä (n 8) 28.
27 McGonigle Leyh (n 13) 41–42; Aleksandar Fatić, *Punishment and Restorative Crime-Handling: A Social Theory of Trust* (Avebury 1995) 1.
28 Cryer et al. (n 14) 20.
29 See section 3.5.
30 Mark A Drumbl, 'Collective Violence and Individual Punishment: The Criminality of Mass Atrocity' (2004) 99 Northwestern University Law Review 539, 559–560; Gavin Dingwall and Tim Hillier, 'The Banality of Punishment: Context Specificity and Justifying Punishment of Extraordinary Crimes' (2010) 6 International Journal of Punishment and Sentencing 6, 7–8; Sloane (n 7) 71–72; Cryer et al. (n 14) 20–21.

General deterrence suggests that the goal of punishment is to dissuade the public at large from committing crimes in the future,[31] while specific deterrence seeks to avoid a particular offender repeating a criminal action.[32] The dominant model of deterrence assumes that rational members of the community's should be able to calculate whether or not the possibility and severity of punishment for a criminal action would outweigh any benefits.[33] The deterrent model infers that criminals undertake in their rational minds a cost-benefits analysis that impacts their decision about whether to commit the criminal action. This rational cost-benefit analysis is basically grounded on two parameters: the likelihood of being caught and the severity of the punishment, generally interpreted as the length of imprisonment.[34] Punishment, therefore, is meted out not simply because the perpetrator deserves it, but to fulfil its utilitarian and consequentialist effects, namely undertaking a social engineering function aimed at reducing the occurrence and gravity of crimes and building a safer world.[35]

Like retributive theories, deterrence is problematic from the perspective of a victim-friendly response to crime, as it fails to provide victims with a relevant role in criminal proceedings. In light of the fact that punishment seeks to reduce and prevent the occurrence of crimes, deterrent theories are principally focused on the interests of society and the offender.[36] Specifically, society is conceived as the victim of crime and criminal sanctions are hence 'not designed to meet the private interests of the individual victim, but rather, are imposed in the public interest (...) to provide public protection from crime'.[37] That being so, the interests of society always prevail over the interests of the victims.[38] In this scenario, the vicitim's role in the criminal proceedings is overlooked because a victim-friendly response to crime might not be sufficient to achieve an adequate level of deterrence and preventive effect.[39] For instance, the granting of amnesties or presidential pardons is a clear example of outcomes which are completely detrimental to the victims. While those decisions seek to meet the interests of society, like national reconciliation in a post-conflict context, victims lose any possibility

31 Drumbl (n 30) 560.

32 Margaret deGuzman, 'Choosing to Prosecute: Expressive Selection at the International Criminal Court' (2012) 33 Michigan Journal of International Law 265, 306; George P Fletcher, *The Grammar of Criminal Law: American, Comparative, and International: Volume One: Foundations* (Oxford University Press 2007) 247.

33 Johannes Andenaes, 'The General Preventive Effects of Punishment' (1965) 114 University of Pennsylvania Law Review 949, 964.

34 deGuzman (n 32) 306.

35 Drumbl (n 30) 589.

36 George P Fletcher, *With Justice for Some: Victims' Rights in Criminal Trials* (Addison-Wesley Publishing Company 1995) 192–193.

37 Christopher Corns, 'Criminal Sanctions: Offenders, Victims and the State' (1995) 7 Legaldate 5, 5.

38 McGonigle Leyh (n 12) 43–44; Luke Moffett, *Justice for Victims before the International Criminal Court* (Routledge 2014) 17.

39 Heikkilä (n 8) 31.

of claiming remedy for the harm inflicted by the criminal conduct and, more importantly, their status in the criminal proceedings is annulled.

2.3 Victimology: a challenge to the traditional criminal justice theories

The period immediately following the Second World War saw the birth of an academic interest in the position of victims in the reality of crime, which later on would take the term 'victimology'. It is still debated who first coined the word victimology, as some authors claimed the term should be attributed to German-American psychiatric Frederick Wertham,[40] while, according to others, the Romanian criminologist Benjamin Mendelsohn referred to victimology as a new science at his presentation at a conference in Bucharest (Romania) in 1947.[41] However, whatever the genesis of this word was, it is widely recognised that Mendelsohn and the German criminologist Hans von Hentig are the founding fathers of victimology.[42] With their early pioneering scientific studies, they profoundly contributed to the establishment of victimology as an independent academic discipline.[43] They acknowledged there is a legal, ethical, moral, and psychological link not only between the criminal and society, but also between the criminal and his/her victim. Their first research projects mainly sought to understand the individualistic criminal-victim relationship, and, specifically, to comprehend the victim's nature as a factor of the crime, the victim's physical and psychological reaction to the trauma suffered, and his/her experience of the criminal justice system.[44] In his masterwork, *The Criminal and His Victims,* von Hentig observed the sociological and psychological circumstances of crimes and concluded there is a sort of reciprocity between victim and perpetrator, which is more complex than the representation that criminal law would suggest.[45] Because of this reciprocity, the victim can paradoxically shape criminals and their crimes. Thus, it would have been a mistake to label the victim as a completely passive element, as opposed to the offender, who bore the burden of the responsibilities

40 Matthew Hall, *Victims and Policy-Making: A Comparative Perspective.* (Taylor & Francis 2012) 16.

41 Hans Boutellier, *Crime and Morality: The Significance of Criminal Justice in Post-Modern Culture* (Kluwer 2002) 52.

42 See e.g., Mike Maguire and John Pointing (eds), *Victims of Crime: A New Deal?* (Open University Press 1988); Andrew Karmen, *Crime Victims: An Introduction to Victimology* (6th edn, Wadsworth Publishing 2006); Shlomo G Shoham, Paul Knepper and Martin Kett (eds), *International Handbook of Victimology* (CRC Press 2010); Sandra Walklate and Rob Mawby, *Critical Victimology: International Perspectives* (Sage 1994); Jan Van Dijk, 'Introducing Victimology' in Jan Van Dijk, Ron GH van Kaam and Joanne Wemmers (eds), *Caring for Crime Victims: Selected Proceedings of the Ninth International Symposium on Victimology, Amsterdam, August 25–29, 1997* (Criminal Justice Press 1999).

43 See e.g., Boutellier (n 41); Maguire and Pointing (n 42); Schafer (n 1).

44 Boutellier (n 41) 50–51; Walklate and Mawby (n 42) 70.

45 Schafer (n 1) 40–41.

for the crime committed. As von Hentig remarked, 'the outcome may be profit to one party, harm to another, yet psychological interaction, carefully observed, will not submit to this kindergarten label'.[46] The American sociologist and criminologist Marvin Wolfgang further developed Mendelsohn and von Hentig's theories, introducing the concept of 'victim precipitation'. Wolfgang, recalling von Hentig's argument that the distinction between victims and offenders was not as clear-cut as it seemed, posited that some individuals were more prone to victimisation and to consciously or unconsciously precipitate the crime through their lifestyle.[47]

2.3.1 Victims' movement

Although the introduction of the concept of 'victim precipitation' by the first victimologists was meant to describe the dynamics of criminal behaviours, such a notion was used to defend the offender and partially to shift the blame on victims.[48] For this reason, early victimology theories attracted serious public attention and feminist groups, in particular, opposed 'victim precipitation', as they felt it encouraged the blaming of female victims of sexual abuse.[49] The emerging crime victims' movement was a multifaceted reality because it included groups and individuals with interests in various features of victimisation, like, for instance, groups interested in restitution or compensation, feminist groups, mental health professionals, groups promoting the welfare of children and the elderly, survivors of Nazi concentration camps or capture in Vietnam, criminologists, and State Prosecutors' offices.[50]

Of those groups, the law-and-order movement, the feminist movement, the civil rights movement, and the civil liberties movement, each with their own motives and perspectives, have contributed to an unprecedented degree of discussion about victims and action on their behalf. The law-and-order movement paid serious attention to the plight of victims of street crimes and thefts. This movement looked at dismissing those practices and the technicalities of the criminal justice system, which weakened the efforts to arrest, convict, and punish the defendants at the expense of the victims.[51] The feminist movement focused on providing protection to a specific group of victims: women who suffered harm inflicted by men. Feminist groups undertook anti-rape and anti-battering initiatives in order to awaken social consciousness to the fact that the plight of women-victims were not personal troubles, but an outgrowth of societal and institutional

46 Hans von Hentig, *The Criminal and His Victim: Studies in the Sociobiology of Crime* (Yale University Press 1948) 384.
47 See Marvin E Wolfgang, *Patterns in Criminal Homicide* (University of Pennsylvania Press 1958).
48 Van Dijk (n 42) 2–3.
49 Boutellier (n 41) 52.
50 Maguire and Pointing (n 42) 2.
51 Karmen (n 42) 28.

problems. Their principal aim was to eradicate the patriarchal tradition that put the blame for sexual abuse and violence on women.[52] In a similar way, the civil rights movement fought for the interests and rights of minority groups, aiming to oppose racist beliefs and discriminatory behaviours by the white majority, which intimidated, harassed, and attacked Afro-American people. The civil rights movement demanded an impartial administration of justice since minorities were more likely to be victims of misconduct by police, false accusations, frame-ups, and wrongful convictions.[53] The main purpose of the civil liberties' movement was to preserve constitutional guarantees and, in particular, to safeguard the due process principle, which protects suspects, defendants, and prisoners from the State's abuses. Crime victims gained a twofold benefit from the victories of the civil liberties movement. First, the improvement of police professionalism granted victims a prompter response, effective services, and more sensitive and respectful treatment. Second, by strengthening the principle of equal protection under the law, a wider range of people, including victims, could ask for help, have access to the police and to prosecutorial assistance.[54]

Thanks to the impact of the victims' movement, which lobbied for a more victim-oriented court proceedings, victimology began to move away from the archetype of 'victims' precipitation'.[55] The discourse on victims' rights focused on proposing a reform of the interrelation between victims and criminal justice is twofold: on the one hand, it advocated for victims' rights to services that State agencies have to provide to meet victims' needs; on the other hand, it argued that victims have specific procedural rights and, therefore, are entitled to see their role acknowledged in the criminal process.[56] The next section and its subsections engage with the victim's rights to services and the victim's procedural rights approaches in order to illustrate the merits of each specific method, but also to explore the limits of each in developing a valid system of participation for victims in the criminal process.

2.4 Determining victims' needs to develop a right to services perspective

The rights of victims to services aim at addressing the victims' physical and psychological needs in the period following the offence. They are designed to deal with the emotional and financial impact of the crime and to prevent or

52 ibid.

53 ibid 29.

54 ibid.

55 Jan Van Dijk, 'Ideological Trends within the Victims Movement: An International Perspective' in Mike Maguire and John Pointing (eds), *Victims of Crime: A New Deal?* (Open University Press 1988) 116.

56 Rob Mawby, 'Victims' Needs or Victims' Rights: Alternative Approaches to Policy-Making' in Mike Maguire and John Pointing (eds), *Victims of Crime: A New Deal?* (Open University Press 1988) 127.

minimise any 'secondary victimisation' resulting from exposure to the criminal process. Those rights are: the right to be treated with respect and sympathy by law enforcement agents during the investigation process; the right to be treated with respect and understanding before and during court proceedings; and the right to compensation for victims of criminal violence.[57]

Several scholars have been attracted by the powerful appeal of the rights of victims to services as a way of tackling the issues of victim-based policies within the criminal justice system.[58] However it is a thorny position, because it means justifying the role of victims by relying solely on the identification of needs that have been continuously ignored by the State in favour of other welfare needs. If it were possible to enunciate a straightforward, neutral, objective definition of needs, the goals of the social services would equally be set in an objective way, avoiding a disputable appeal to social and political values. Matching needs with social services would be a technical rather than an ideological issue.[59] But the problem at stake is still an ideological one, because whether or not a need exists inextricably depends on the kind of definition used and on the definer. Assuming that need is what is necessary to survive, the ideological problem is still in the picture, because there is no agreement on the quality of survival. It is even more difficult to agree on the minimum support necessary to ensure human survival.[60]

Identifying victims' needs by asking individuals how much the crime affected their life and what issues it brought about apparently provides a solution. Nonetheless, even this approach can be controversial. First, the victims can either overestimate or underestimate their needs. Second, social expectations of what the victim may need can influence the concept of needs.[61] Needs are to some degree culturally based, as they are intertwined with the expectations of victims, their knowledge of what remedies exist, and the potential effects of the offence.[62] When the criminal justice system translates individual needs to demands, the potential risk is to cope with the demands coming from the victims who have the capacity and determination to make their voices heard, but to leave unmet the needs of the most vulnerable. Grounding the definition of needs on general consensus within a society means that 'victims experience needs where the problems of crime reach levels intolerable to the majority of the citizens of a country'.[63] However, this

57 Andrew Ashworth, 'Victim Impact Statements and Sentencing' (1993) Criminal Law Review 498, 499.

58 See e.g., Joanna Shapland, 'The Victims, the Criminal Justice System and Compensation' (1984) 24 The British Journal of Criminology 131; Mike Maguire, 'Victims' Needs and Victim Services: Indications from Research' (1985) 10 Victimology 539; Mike Maguire and Claire Corbett, *The Effects of Crime and the Work of Victims Support Schemes* (Gower 1987).

59 Raymond Plant, Peter Taylor-Gooby and Anthony Lesser, *Political Philosophy and Social Welfare: Essays on the Normative Basis of Welfare Provisions* (Routledge 1980) 21.

60 Mawby (n 56) 131.

61 ibid 132.

62 Shapland (n 58) 143.

63 Mawby (n 56) 133.

perspective faces the risk of falling into relativism, as citizens are left subject to expectations based on their tolerance of the unacceptable. To rely on an expert to provide a definition of needs can be a thorny problem too, since definitions by experts, which are based on ideal norms or minimum standards, are subjective and controvertible.[64]

The difficulties of providing an indisputable definition of needs does not mean undermining their importance, it rather aims to demonstrate that criminal justice policies cannot rest in the 'comfort zone' where the needs of victims are easily identified and broadly accepted.[65] Basing the approach on victims' rights only on the matter of meeting needs can produce an individualised discretionary response to victims and likely marginalise and exclude groups of victims that do not meet the requirements of the moment.[66]

2.4.1 Victim as consumer of public services

Despite the difficulties of identifying an objective definition of victims' needs, the emphasis on victims' rights to services channelled the criminal justice mechanism towards services that individuals expect to receive.[67] The economic development of the 1980s and, specifically, the rise of consumerism, influenced the growing debate on the place of victims in the criminal justice system, questioning whether crime victims could be conceptualised as consumers of criminal justice in the same way citizens are consumers of other public services. In her attempt to answer to this question, Joanna Shapland introduced the concept of criminal justice as a public service, which is characterised by the acknowledgement of the multiple responsibilities and accountabilities of criminal justice institutions, of victims, and of offenders.[68] This new conception of justice produced some major changes, especially for victims. The model of the criminal justice system as a public service contributed to breaching the traditional concept of the criminal justice system as the owner of the conflict-solving process, by including the concerns of victims. Criminal justice would be more transparent, accessible, and visible, because there would be an obligation on the agents practising criminal justice to explain their decisions.[69] This model attempts to heal the separation between victims and criminal justice agencies. In this particular context, the implementation of the service delivery policy redefined the nature of the role of victims as 'consumers' of the criminal justice system, who have individual needs that the criminal justice

64 ibid.
65 ibid.
66 Walklate and Mawby (n 42) 178.
67 Basia Spalek, *Crime Victims: Theory, Policy and Practice* (Palgrave Macmillan 2006) 127.
68 Joanna Shapland, 'Victims and Criminal Justice: Creating Responsible Criminal Justice Agencies' in Adam Crawford and Jo Goodey (eds), *Integrating a Victim Perspective within Criminal Justice: International Debates*, vol 3 (Dartmouth Publishing Company 2000) 159.
69 ibid 161.

system has to satisfy, but, at the same time, are equally capable of choosing the service they need.[70]

Although this wider perspective on victimisation is praised for challenging the societal structures that affected crime victims, nonetheless, some criticisms can be levelled against it. The assimilation of the victim-consumer of criminal justice is controversial. Consumers have freedom of choice in the market, while the victim-consumers of criminal justice are generally captive to the use of such a service.[71] Moreover, the concept of consumer sees the individual as belonging to a politically neutral community and it does not consider the structural inequalities related to class, gender, race, and so forth. Differences within the social and political context frequently shape victims' expectations of the requirements of the services provided by the criminal justice system and deeply affect the experiences of individuals.[72] The prevailing bureaucratic and political goals of the State, being focused 'on value for money, performance measurement for individual agencies and individual services to customers/users',[73] can potentially exclude the most vulnerable members of society from the criminal justice mechanism.[74] Applying the language of liberalisation of the market economy to victims before a substructure of rights has been established means that only some victim-consumers have full access to the services they need.[75] The threat of the exclusion of the most vulnerable from the criminal justice mechanism 'has the perverse effect of emphasizing the unequal purchasing powers with respect to this service, thus seriously damaging the legitimacy of the provider, the state, which in a democracy is based precisely on the equality of citizens'.[76]

There is an ideological difference between victim-consumers of the criminal justice system and consumers of other public services, because the ancient notion of public 'authority' still informs the criminal justice system, which is 'extrinsically tied to its sovereignty and not coming under the category of public services provided to individuals'.[77]

70 Spalek (n 67) 127.

71 Renée Zauberman, 'Victims as Consumers of the Criminal Justice System?' in Adam Crawford and Jo Goodey (eds), *Integrating a Victim Perspective within Criminal Justice: International Debates*, vol 3 (Dartmouth Publishing Company 2000) 40.

72 Spalek (n 67) 123. See also Peter Dunn, 'Matching Service Delivery to Need' in Sandra Walklate (ed), *Handbook of Victims and Victimology* (Routledge 2007).

73 Adam Crawford, 'Introduction' in Adam Crawford and Jo Goodey (eds), *Integrating a Victim Perspective within Criminal Justice: International Debates*, vol 3 (Dartmouth Publishing Company 2000) 6.

74 Spalek (n 67) 130.

75 Jo Goodey, *Victims and Victimology: Research, Policy and Practice* (Pearson Education 2005) 136, 149.

76 Zauberman (n 71) 40.

77 ibid.

2.5 Advancing victims' rights at the procedural level

The changes to victims' rights demanded by the abolitionist ideology of the victims' movement, which called for a smaller role for traditional criminal justice institutions and a larger role for victims in the process, have been more 'procedural' in nature.[78] The procedural rights of victims in the criminal process are of a different nature than the rights to services, as they confer victims with the means to make an impact on the process itself. Procedural rights change the position of victims within the criminal justice system, since they enable victims to contribute to the prosecution and to obtain restitution or reparation.[79] While the rights of victims to services attempt to meet victims' needs and to ameliorate the criminal process for the victim by providing various services, the cornerstone for setting procedural rights should be the nature and goals of the criminal process as a legal and social institution, rather than the wishes of victims.[80]

The victims' procedural rights approach had an impact at the international level and paved the way to the adoption of international legal instruments, which, despite their soft-law nature, constitute an international law hallmark in enhancing victims' rights in criminal proceedings. Starting with the United Nations (UN) Declaration of Basic Principles of Justice for Victims of Crime and Abuse of Power[81] (Declaration for Victims of Crime), adopted by the UN General Assembly in 1985, international legal norms began to recognise the need 'to restore the balance between the fundamental rights of suspects and offenders, and the rights and interests of victims'.[82] Despite the Declaration for Victims of Crime being praised as a great breakthrough in the recognition of victims' rights, because it 'contains essential provisions, which, applied in practice, could be a veritable Magna Carta for victims',[83] in practical terms it made a modest contribution to the issue of access to justice for victims. In fact, if on the one hand the Declaration for Victims of Crime urges States to adopt measures to improve victims' access to justice and, concretely, their active participation in criminal proceedings, on the other hand the rights of victims enshrined in

78 Matti Joutsen, *The Role of the Victim of Crime in European Criminal Justice Systems: A Cross National Study of the Role of the Victim* (Helsinki Institute for Crime Prevention and Control 1987) 51–52; Yvonne McDermott, 'Victims and International Law: Remedies in the Courtroom?' (2009) 4 Hague Justice Journal 199, 203.

79 Helen Fenwick, 'Procedural "Rights" of Victims of Crime: Public or Private Ordering of the Criminal Justice Process?' (1997) 60 The Modern Law Review 317, 318.

80 ibid; Ashworth, 'Victim Impact Statements and Sentencing' (n 57) 499.

81 Declaration of Basic Principles of Justice for Victims of Crime and Abuse of Power, UNGA Res 40/34 (29 November 1985) UN Doc A/RES/40/34.

82 UN Office for Drug Control and Crime Prevention, 'Guide for Policy Makers on the Implementation of the United Nations Declaration of Basic Principles of Justice for Victims of Crime and Abuse of Power' (1999) UNDCP/ODCCP(09)/V642 1.

83 UN Office for Drug Control and Crime Prevention, 'Handbook on Justice for Victims: On the Use and Application of the Declaration of Basic Principles of Justice for Victims of Crime and Abuse of Power' (1999) UNDCP/ODCCP(09)/J96 105.

the Declaration are contingent on the domestic law of States.[84] According to Principle 4 of the Declaration for Victims of Crime, victims 'are entitled to access to the mechanisms of justice and to prompt redress, as provided for by national legislation (...)'. The same approach is kept by Principle 6(b), which acknowledges that the responsiveness of the judicial mechanism to victims' needs should be facilitated by 'allowing the views and concerns of victims to be presented and considered at appropriate stages of the proceedings where their personal interests are affected, without prejudice to the accused and *consistent with the relevant national criminal justice system*' (emphasis added). After almost 20 years of work, in December 2005, the UN General Assembly adopted by consensus the Basic Principles and Guidelines on the Right to a Remedy and Reparation for Victims of Gross Violations of International Human Rights Law and Serious Violations of International Humanitarian Law[85] (the Basic Principles and Guidelines). In a rather extensive way, the Basic Principles and Guidelines set an effective judicial remedy, including reparation,[86] for those who claim to be victims of such violations.[87] Under Principle 2(b), States should adopt appropriate and effective legislative and administrative procedures that provide fair, effective, and prompt access to justice to victims.[88] Additionally, Principle 11 includes the victim's right to equal and effective access to justice within the remedies for the gross and serious violations of human rights and humanitarian law suffered.[89] However, although the Basic Principles and Guidelines recognise the right of access to justice as an effective remedy for victims, they do not clarify whether this right incorporates the victim's right to participate in criminal proceedings. For instance, by affirming that satisfaction for victims should include, where applicable, judicial and administrative sanctions against persons liable for the violations, Principle 22(f) acknowledges that an impartial investigation followed by criminal prosecution and punishment of perpetrators are elements of the reparation due to victims.[90] In the event that the State fails to carry out an effective prosecution, it violates the general obligation to respect and enforce human rights, as well as the right of victims to an effective remedy.[91] Nevertheless, Principle 22 does not confer upon victims specific procedural rights.

84 Juan Carlos Ochoa Sanchez, *The Rights of Victims in Criminal Justice Proceedings for Serious Human Rights Violations* (Martinus Nijhoff Publishers 2013) 106.
85 Basic Principles and Guidelines on the Right to a Remedy and Reparation for Victims of Gross Violations of International Human Rights Law and Serious Violations of International Humanitarian Law, UNGA Res 60/147 (21 March 2006) UN Doc A/RES/60/147.
86 Art 3(d) ibid.
87 Art 3(c) ibid.
88 Art 2(b) ibid.
89 Art 11(a) ibid.
90 Ochoa Sanchez (n 84) 108.
91 Mahmoud Cherif Bassiouni, 'International Recognition of Victims' Rights' (2006) 6 Human Rights Law Review 203, 264.

In 2001, the European Union (EU) passed the Council Framework Decision on the standing of victims in criminal proceedings[92] (EU Framework Decision), the first 'hard law' international legal instrument that contributed to establishing a set of procedural rights for victims, such as: right to respect; right to receive information; right to be heard during proceedings and to supply evidence; right to protection; and right to compensation.[93] In 2012, the EU Framework Decision was replaced by the Directive establishing minimum standards on the rights, support and protection of victims of crime of the European Parliament and of the Council[94] (EU Directive on Victims), which presents a similar catalogue of victims' procedural rights in criminal proceedings, although in more detailed manner. Thus, victims have among other rights: the right to be heard, i.e. victims may be heard and may provide evidence;[95] the right to information about the case;[96] rights when making a complaint, e.g. the right to receive written acknowledgement of their formal complaint;[97] rights in the event of a decision not to prosecute;[98] the right to understand and to be understood;[99] the right to interpretation and translation;[100] the right to compensation from the offender;[101] the right to return of property;[102] and the right to protection, including protection of victims with specific needs.[103] Nevertheless, the preamble of the EU Directive on Victims acknowledges that '[t]he role of victims in the criminal justice system and whether they can participate actively in criminal proceedings vary across Member States'[104] and, consequently, it does not oblige States to grant victims the status of civil party.

2.5.1 Victims' participation in the sentencing process

The acceptance that the trial had to engage with victims' procedural rights in a positive sense expanded the 'battle' for victims' rights into areas beyond the mere

92 Council Framework Decision 2001/220/JHA of 15 March 2001 on the standing of victims in criminal proceedings [2001] OJ L82/1.
93 Arts 2–9 ibid.
94 European Parliament and Council Directive 2012/29/EU of 25 October 2012 establishing minimum standards on the rights, support and protection of victims of crime, and replacing Council Framework Decision 2001/220/JHA [2012] OJ L315/57.
95 Art 10 ibid.
96 Arts 4–6 ibid.
97 Art 5 ibid.
98 Art 11 ibid.
99 Art 3 ibid.
100 Art 7 ibid.
101 Art 16 ibid.
102 Art 15 ibid.
103 Arts 18–19 ibid.
104 Preamble, para 20 ibid.

role of a witness.[105] Mainly in the USA and Canada, the academic debate initially engaged with victims' participation at the final stage of the criminal process.[106] The focus was on the interrelation between victims and the community specifically at the sentencing stage because the shift from the fixed sentence term to an open-ended imprisonment term brought about an 'estrangement from influence by what I will refer to as the interests and values of the community'.[107] The fixed sentencing process embodied the link between the punishment inflicted by Judges and the public wishes, because the term for punishment set? in a law passed by parliament represented the expression of people sovereignty.[108] Conversely, the open-ended imprisonment term, which was defined only by a maximum statutory term, or by a non-judicial agency (such as parole commissions), granted rather broad judicial discretion in sentencing.[109] For this reason, it was argued that the operation of the open-ended imprisonment term justifies the involvement of representatives of society in the sentencing process, as a form of interrelation between the criminal behaviour and the social revulsion of it.[110] In this scenario, the role of victims 'may be viewed as a symbolic act bringing the hearing back into the context of social condemnation on a moral as opposed to a legal level'.[111] Specifically, victims' rights in the sentencing process stage represented an attempt to accommodate the interrelation between victims and the social community and, at the same time, to alleviate the social dissatisfaction because of the limited involvement of victims in the resolution of conflicts.[112] More simply, the acknowledgment of the sentencing process as the condemnation by the public of criminal conduct is embodied by the inclusion of victims' input in the courts' decisions.[113]

Eve Kunen discussed the influence of victims and the public on the sentencing process in the USA and stressed the importance of the interrelation between them. Public opinion 'often parallels the voices of those least heard by the criminal justice system: the victims'.[114] Thus, behind the demands for victims' participation, there was the demand for a broader public influence. The victim

105 Edna Erez, 'Victim Participation in Sentencing: Rhetoric and Reality' (1990) 18 Journal of Criminal Justice 19, 20–21; Howard C Rubel, 'Victim Participation in Sentencing Proceedings' (1985) 28 Criminal Law Quarterly 226, 226.

106 Lynne N Henderson, 'The Wrongs of Victim's Rights' (1985) 37 Stanford Law Review 100, 186.

107 Joseph W Little, 'The Law of Sentencing as Public Ceremony' (1983) 35 University of Florida Law Review 1, 1.

108 Rubel (n 105) 228.

109 ibid 230.

110 Eve Kunen, 'The Effect of External Pressures on Sentencing Judges' (1983) 11 Fordham Urban Law Journal 263, 266–268; Little (n 107) 7–9.

111 Rubel (n 105) 231.

112 ibid 247.

113 Erez (n 105) 23.

114 Kunen (n 110) 265.

was seen as an instrument through which the community could realise its goal of representation and participation. Indeed, because of their proximity to the criminal conduct, victims were more entitled to participate in the sentencing process than the public, but, most importantly, victims' rights at the sentencing stage were 'necessary for the victim to become a reification of the public desire to have input into and be part of the sentencing process'.[115] Kunen concluded that 'increasing judicial awareness of the impact of crime on a victim's life is one step toward giving voice to large segments of the community who are routinely targeted for specific types of crimes'.[116] Victims' participation in the sentencing process represented the public input and could contribute to the realisation of society's demands for its values to be expressed in the offender's sentencing process.[117]

Influenced by this debate, across the countries of common law tradition there have been reforms aimed at enhancing victims' status in criminal proceedings. Even if victims were not elevated to the role of civil parties, they were granted a certain degree of participation to voice their interests and concerns, but only during the sentencing stage of the proceedings. For instance, countries like the USA,[118] England,[119] and Canada[120] granted victims procedural rights in the sentencing proceedings through victims' impact statements. These statements are heard for sentencing, parole, and plea-bargaining purposes since they can only be submitted once the accused pleads or is found guilty. The victim's impact statement model does not provide victims with sufficient power to influence the prosecutorial or adjudicative process, rather it seeks to reflect the physical and emotional harm inflicted on victims as well as the loss and property damage caused by the crime.[121]

Joseph Little observed that victims' participation in the sentencing process could effectively express society's sense of abhorrence by imposing a minimum term for punishment, but, in practice, the majority of the discretion is in the hands of Judges or parole commissions.[122] Victims' interests are only one factor to be taken into account when passing a sentence and such limitation caused erratic take-up rates among victims, it raised unrealistic expectations and consequently lowered the level of victims' satisfaction.[123] The paltry impact victims' participation has in the sentencing process, which can be considered as having only a purely

115 Rubel (n 105) 231.
116 Kunen (n 110) 266.
117 Little (n 107) 28.
118 United States Federal Crime Victims' Rights Act, 18 U.S.C. § 3771.
119 See Doak (n 5) 150.
120 Criminal Code, RSC 1985, chapter C-46, section 722.
121 Renée Kool and Martin Moerings, 'The Victim Has the Floor: The Victim's Right to Be Heard in Writing or Orally in the Dutch Courtroom' (2004) 12 European Journal of Crime, Criminal Law and Criminal Justice 46, 47. Tobolowsky (n 3) 70.
122 Little (n 107) 28.
123 Doak (n 5) 152.

expressive function, eventually made the criminal justice system more distant than it should be, attenuating community values and interests and unnecessarily estranging the process from public view and, more importantly, from victims' participation.[124] Although, the inclusion of victims' standing in the sentencing process clearly represents a step forward on the path to the acknowledgement of victims' rights within the criminal proceedings, victims were still on the periphery of the criminal justice system.

2.6 A restorative response to victims

The emerging of restorative justice thinking represents a response to the issues raised by the victimological discourse that transcends the service-related and procedural rights approaches and embraces a holistic approach based on participation, protection, and reparation. Specifically, restorativism is distinct from the service-related and procedural rights approaches, as it is a theory of criminal justice.[125] Restorative justice theories call for the replacement of the traditional retributive and utilitarian paradigms with a so-called victim–offender reparation model, which, by emphasising the reconciliation between the victim and the offender, empowers the victim.[126] Restorative justice works from the premise that crime is an 'individual, relational and social harm'[127] done to victims and community members, which causes divisions in the social fabric.[128] To address these divisions, the restorative justice system is informed by a set of values and principles,[129] including: the healing of victims and society;[130] amends made by the offender;[131] reconciliation of parties and community;[132] reparation of the harm

124 Little (n 107) 28..

125 Erik Luna, 'Punishment Theory, Holism, and the Procedural Conception of Restorative Justice' (2003) 1 Utah Law Review 205, 227.

126 Heikkilä (n 8) 37.

127 Lode Walgrave, 'Restorative Justice: An Alternative for Responding to Crime?' in Shlomo Giora Shoham, Ori Beck and Martin Kett (eds), *International Handbook of Penology and Criminal Justice* (CRC Press 2008) 621.

128 Daniel van Ness and Karen Heetderks Strong, *Restoring Justice: An Introduction to Restorative Justice* (Anderson Publishing 1997) 32.

129 James Coben and Penelope Harley, 'International Conversations about Restorative Justice, Mediation and the Practice of Law' (2004) 25 Hamline Journal of Public Law & Policy 235, 240; Carrie J Niebur Eisnaugle, 'An International "Truth Commission": Utilizing Restorative Justice as an Alternative to Retribution' 36 Vanderbilt Journal of Transnational Law 209, 211.

130 Lawrence Sherman, 'Two Protestant Ethics and the Spirit of Restoration' in John Braithwaite and Heather Strang (eds), *Restorative Justice and Civil Society* (Cambridge University Press 2001) 55.

131 Daniel van Ness, 'The Shape of Things to Come: A Framework for Thinking about a Restorative Justice System' in Elmar GM Weitekamp and Hans-Jürgen Kerner (eds), *Restorative Justice: Theoretical Foundations* (Willan Publishing 2002) 4.

132 Howard Zehr, *Changing Lenses: A New Focus for Crime and Justice* (Herald Press 1990) 200–203; Chris Cunneen, 'Reparations and Restorative Justice: Responding to Gross

caused to victims;[133] and active participation of parties in the process.[134] Within this redefinition of principles shaping the criminal justice system, victims become one of 'the key stakeholders in the justice process whose needs are the primary concern'.[135] Central to restorative justice are claims about giving voice to victims, healing them through positive engagement in the process, and repairing the harm they suffered.[136]

2.6.1 Understating restorative practices

Restorative justice consists of a set of values and principles but, at the same time, it can also be conceived as a process, which involves various mechanisms, methods, or practices, aiming to 'bring together those affected to establish truth and provide a framework for reconciliation'.[137] A variety of programmes fall under the umbrella term of restorative justice practices, which broadly includes victim-focused initiatives, such as victim compensation schemes, victim–offender mediation, crime repair crews, victim intervention programmes, family group conferencing, peace-making circles, sentencing circles, community reparative boards before which offenders appear, victim empathy classes for offenders, community-based support groups for crime-victims, and community-based support groups for offenders.[138] Due to this profusion of practices falling under the rubric of restorative justice, there is still contention among academics on its precise definition.[139] The difficulty in defining restorative justice as a process can be attributed to the various elements involved in the restorative mechanisms and methods, which 'are given differing weights (…) reflecting different "sensibilities" and cultures'.[140] Against this background, Marshall has offered one of the

Violations of Human Rights' in John Braithwaite and Heather Strang (eds), *Restorative Justice and Civil Society* (Cambridge University Press 2001) 88.

133 Gordon Bazemore and Mara Schiff, 'Paradigm Muddle or Paradigm Paralysis? The Wide and Narrow Roads to Restorative Justice Reform (or, a Little Confusion May Be a Good Thing)' (2004) 7 Contemporary Justice Review 37, 41.

134 van Ness and Strong (n 128) 67.

135 Margarita Zernova, *Restorative Justice: Ideals and Realities* (Ashgate 2007) 47.

136 Mariana Pena and Gaelle Carayon, 'Is the ICC Making the Most of Victim Participation?' (2013) 7 International Journal of Transitional Justice 518, 522–523.

137 Cunneen (n 132) 88.

138 James Dignan, *Understanding Victims and Restorative Justice* (Open University Press 2004) 2; Heikkilä (n 8) 39.

139 See e.g., Ashworth, 'Some Doubts about Restorative Justice' (n 20); Luna (n 126) 227–228; Jo-Anne Wemmers and Katie Cyr, 'Victims' Perspectives on Restorative Justice: How Much Involvement Are Victims Looking For?' (2004) 11 International Review of Victimology 259, 261; Dorothy Vaandering, 'A Faithful Compass: Rethinking the Term Restorative Justice to Find Clarity' (2011) 14 Contemporary Justice Review 307.

140 Jane J Bolitho, 'Restorative Justice: The Ideals and Realities of Conferencing for Young People' (2012) 20 Critical Criminology 61, 76.

most widely accepted definitions,[141] which describes restorative justice as 'a process whereby all parties with a stake in a specific offence come together to resolve collectively how to deal with the aftermath of the offence and its implications for the future'.[142] Van Ness and Heetderks Strong have identified five basic elements of restorative practices, which are interlinked. Three of these elements relate to the restorative process, namely the victim–offender encounter; the offender's acknowledgement of responsibility and apology; and the collaborative conflict-resolution approach. The remaining two elements, notably the healing and reconciliation of victims and communities and the symbolic reparation and material compensation, are tied to the outcomes of such a process.[143]

The typical restorative process consists of an encounter (circles, conferencing, and mediation),[144] which involves a face-to-face meeting with a victim, an offender, their respective supporters, and often community members, as representatives of the community's interest.[145] However, first and most importantly, prior to the beginning of the restorative justice procedure, it is imperative for the offender to admit his/her guilt. Once the offender has done so, the restorative procedure can start. The objective of the victim–offender meeting is to encourage dialogue and negotiation between victims and offenders, since the victim has the chance to explain to what extent the criminal conduct harmed her/him, while the offender has the opportunity to acknowledge the consequences of the harm he/she provoked, and he/she sympathises and sincerely apologises to the victim.[146] This meeting is followed by a collaborative conflict-resolution approach which aims to negotiate the settlement of the case.[147] This negotiation process places the victim in an active problem-solving role, as he/she works together with the offender to reach an agreement on how to overturn the harm caused by the criminal conduct.[148] Victims and communities' involvement as decision-makers at this stage of the process is crucial because redress cannot be accomplished

141 McGonigle Leyh (n 13) 54; Patrick Gerkin et al., 'Implementing Restorative Justice Under the Retributive Paradigm: A Pilot Program Case Study' (2017) 7 SAGE Open 1, 1.

142 Tony F Marshall, 'The Evolution of Restorative Justice in Britain' (1996) 4 European Journal on Criminal Policy and Research 31, 37.

143 See Daniel van Ness and Karen Heetderks Strong, *Restoring Justice* (Anderson Publishing 1997); van Ness (n 131) 23–42.

144 Paul McCold, 'The Recent History of Restorative Justice: Mediation, Circles, and Conferencing' in Dennis Sullivan and Larry Tifft, *Handbook of Restorative Justice. A Global Perspective* (Routledge 2006) 23.

145 Dena M Gromet and John M Darley, 'Restoration and Retribution: How Including Retributive Components Affects the Acceptability of Restorative Justice Procedures' (2006) 19 Social Justice Research 395, 396.

146 Claire Garbett, 'From Passive Objects to Active Agents: A Comparative Study of Conceptions of Victim Identities at the ICTY and ICC' (2016) 15 Journal of Human Rights 40, 44; Moffett (n 38) 42.

147 Mark S Umbreit, Robert B Coates and Boris Kalanj, *Victim Meets Offender: The Impact of Restorative Justice and Mediation* (Lynne Rienner Publishers 1994) 4.

148 Aukerman (n 19) 77.

without the input from those who have suffered the most from the committed crime.[149] The outcome of the restorative process is an agreement between the parties on the appropriate terms of compensation to redress the wrongdoing and 'heal individuals, communities, and even nations after harm'.[150] In this kind of agreement, the offender offers as material restitution, monetary compensation or some services that he/she can provide to victims,[151] but, when material restoration is unable to undo the effects of the crime, the outcome of this negotiated process should include a symbolic redress seeking to restore psychological losses and the dignity of individuals and communities.[152]

2.6.2 Does restorative justice enhance victims' participatory rights?

There is a certain degree of confusion around the concept of restorative justice, which has generated a wide discussion on what practices are restorative, how restorative justice can fit within the established criminal justice system, and whether restorative justice should be conceived as a process or an outcome. First, as Dignan observed, the different definitions of restorative justice restrict themselves to the scope of criminal justice, but restorative practices have been applied beyond this context.[153] The wide range of practices include: 'diversion from court prosecution; actions taken in parallel with court decisions, and meetings between victims and offenders at any stage of the criminal process'.[154] Restorative justice practices are wrongly held as a concern of the criminal justice system. Such practices are rather in the nature of social service entitlements, because they provide practical support to victims, who have to cope with the demands of the criminal process, at a time when they are traumatised by the offence and subject to financial and emotional pressures.[155]

Second, restorative justice theories deal with several variants of the restorative process, but they do not engage with specific reference to the outcome of such process. There is a debate as to whether the negotiated outcome of restorative process should be purely symbolic and simply reparative or include punitive measures.[156] Braithwaite and Strang argue that the focus of restorative justice depends on the offence, rather than on the offender and, therefore, in

149 Gordon Bazemore and Sandra O'Brien, 'The Quest for a Restorative Justice Model of Rehabilitation: Theory-for-Practice and Practice-for-Theory' in Lode Walgrave (ed), *Restorative Justice and the Law* (Willan Publishing 2002) 43.
150 Kathrine S van Wormer and Lorenn Walker, 'Preface' in Kathrine S van Wormer and Lorenn Walker (eds), *Restorative Justice Today: Practical Applications* (Sage 2013) xv.
151 Moffett (n 38) 42; Gromet and Darley (n 145) 396.
152 Umbreit, Coates and Kalanj (n 147) 2.
153 Dignan (n 138) 2; Heikkilä (n 8) 39.
154 Kathleen Daly, 'South Australia Juvenile Justice (SAJJ) Research on Conferencing, Technical Report No. 2: Research Instruments in Year 2 (1999) and Background Notes' (School of Criminology and Criminal Justice, Griffith University 2001) 5.
155 Ashworth, 'Some Doubts about Restorative Justice' (n 20) 281–282.
156 Dignan (n 138) 3; McGonigle Leyh (n 13) 56; Heikkilä (n 8) 39.

a process aiming to repair the harm caused by the offence, there should be no place for punitive measures. Restorative justice should not respond to the hurt of the crime with the hurt of punishment, it should rather deal with healing and restoration.[157] Supporters of this view reject the idea that courts and prison sentences are a part of restorative justice, as they argue that only the negotiated processes and reparative sanctions should be included in it.[158] Other academics refuse this concept of restorative justice, claiming that, to be complete, the restorative process needs to involve punitive measures. Robinson contends that amends for the crime cannot be obtained purely by restorative mechanisms, they must be accompanied by additional punishment of the offender to demonstrate he/she has understood the wrongs he/she has committed.[159] Duff echoes this claim with his argument that a non-punitive restorative justice model addresses the harm caused by the criminal conduct, but it does not deal with the wrongdoing committed by the offender and, thus, neglects the moral reparation which requires a punishment for the offender.[160]

In the practice, some restorative outcomes can be purely reparative, but others may mete out additional obligations to the offender, which can be as punitive as the sentencing imposed by a Judge at a traditional criminal trial. This raises doubts as to the fairness and proportionality of restorative justice, because the application of two different standards relies on the arbitrary decision to refer either to a restorative justice process or to a more traditional paradigm.[161] This sort of 'twin-track'[162] system creates a diversion of cases from the formal criminal process that seems reasonable for non-serious offences committed by young offenders; nonetheless, it remains unclear whether or not the restorative justice process should also be applied to serious crimes.[163]

A third weakness of the restorative paradigm is represented by its failure to specify the level of victim participation necessary in order for it to be considered a restorative practice. In other words, it is not clear whether there is a minimum acceptable level of victims' participation or, conversely, whether there is any restriction on such participation.[164] Moreover, as stated above, restorative justice comes into play only after offenders accept and acknowledge their guilt or, at least, the wrongness of their actions. If offenders do not take this first step,

157 John Braithwaite and Heather Strang, *Restorative Justice and Civil Society* (Cambridge University Press 2001) 1.
158 Gromet and Darley (n 145) 397.
159 Paul H Robinson, 'The Virtues of Restorative Processes, the Vices of Restorative Justice' (2003) Utah Law Review 375, 377–378.
160 Antony Duff, 'Restorative Punishment and Punitive Restoration' in Lode Walgrave (ed), *Restorative Justice and the Law* (Willan Publishing 2002) 82.
161 Dignan (n 138) 4.
162 ibid.
163 Andrew Ashworth, 'Victims' Rights, Defendants' Rights and Criminal Procedure' in Adam Crawford and Jo Goodey, *Integrating a Victim Perspective within Criminal Justice: International Debates* (Ashgate 2000) 193–194.
164 Dignan (n 138) 4–5.

victims' participation within the criminal proceedings can be an effective way of expressing emotional suffering, but it is not considered sufficient to make the process restorative.[165] Procedural rights for victims and restorative systems are two very distinctive concepts. Those two concepts can overlap, but it is also possible to confer participatory rights to victims within a traditional criminal justice system without converting this system into a restorative one. In a similar way, it is possible, but probably less likely, to develop a restorative system which provides practical support to victims but does not grant substantial participatory rights to victims within the framework of the criminal trial.[166]

These remarks do not mean to undermine the contribution of the restorative theories to cope with the needs of crime victims. It is important to acknowledge that victim compensation schemes, victim–offender mediation, and many other restorative practices which address victims' emotional, practical, financial, psychological, and social needs have placed new obligations on criminal justice agencies to make their practice more inclusive of victims' concerns.[167] Nevertheless, it is extremely important to be aware of some of the shortcomings of the restorative justice paradigm at the domestic level, since such limitations are magnified when restorative practices are applied to the international criminal justice system, as will be explored in the next chapter.[168]

2.7 Conclusion

The victim-centred debate has come to light after centuries of responses to crime as an act first against the Sovereign and subsequently against the State. Following the tragic events of the Second World War, academic debate has been characterised by an ongoing discussion about the place of victims' needs and rights in the criminal justice system. Although victimological studies quickly moved away from the first pioneering work, which researched those factors that predispose an individual to become a victim, the response to the demands of victims' participation in the criminal proceedings has been only partially satisfactory. Given that the retributive and deterrent theories of criminal justice relegated the victims to a marginal role, the victimological developments were expected to challenge and break down those mechanisms which prevent victims from exercising participatory rights by radically reforming the existing procedural models and effectively reconfiguring the balance between the role and rights of the judiciary, the accused, and the victim(s). There was a general agreement on the need to give a meaningful response to the concern of crime victims; however, the victimological

165 McGonigle Leyh (n 13) 57.
166 Ashworth, 'Victims' Rights, Defendants' Rights and Criminal Procedure' (n 163) 192; James Dignan and Michael Cavadino, 'Towards a Framework for Conceptualizing and Evaluating Models of Criminal Justice from a Victim's Perspective' (1996) 4 International Review of Victimology 153, 153.
167 Spalek (n 67) 92.
168 See section 3.6.

debate showed that there was no consensus about how best to enhance victims' rights in the criminal justice system.

The systems implemented by the both the victims' procedural rights and victims' right to service approaches are limited because they have resulted in a range of mechanisms seeking to reposition the victim that have ended up relegating victims to the periphery of criminal justice. The victims' right to service approach, which justifies the role of the victim by relying on the identification of the physical, psychological, and financial needs that the criminal justice system has to satisfy, tended to divert victims away from the criminal justice system into alternative pathways to justice. Moreover, matching victims' needs with social services is rather a complex process. The notion of need is inextricably dependent on welfare ideology and, thus, it is difficult to provide a straightforward, neutral, and objective definition of need. As a consequence, it is equally difficult to set up an objective system of victims' services. There is a potential risk to fall into relativism, since the victim's right to service approach can give rise to an individualised discretionary response to victims and probably marginalise and exclude groups of victims that do not meet certain requirements. The victims based approach grounded in the victim's procedural rights, primarily directed towards influencing the sentencing, reflected the sense of reluctance in common law countries to afford victims a greater say in the criminal process.

Restorative practices have the merit of having placed new obligations on criminal justice agencies to make their practice more inclusive of victims' concerns. However, since restorative justice engages with victims, by means of a negotiated process – e.g., victim–offender mediation, peace-making circles, victims' intervention programmes – its practices go beyond the strict scope of the criminal process. Additionally, the lack of agreement on whether the outcome of restorative justice is purely reparative or punitive makes it questionable whether this model belongs to the sphere of the criminal proceedings.

Having a clear understanding of the limitations of the mechanisms elaborated by victimology to the demands of victims' participatory rights is important because international criminal justice has, in its development, relied, and continues to rely, quite substantially on the victimological experience. The next chapter will deal with the transplant of retributive, deterrent, and restorative justice mechanisms to international criminal justice in light of the constitutive differences between the domestic and the international criminal justice systems.

References

Books and journals

Andenaes J, 'The General Preventive Effects of Punishment' (1965) 114 University of Pennsylvania Law Review 949

Ashworth A, 'Victim Impact Statements and Sentencing' (1993) Criminal Law Review 498

Ashworth A, 'Victims' Rights, Defendants' Rights and Criminal Procedure' in Adam Crawford and Jo Goodey, *Integrating a Victim Perspective within Criminal Justice: International Debates* (Ashgate 2000)

Ashworth A, *Principles of Criminal Law* (5th edn, Oxford University Press 2006)

Aukerman MJ, 'Extraordinary Evil, Ordinary Crime: A Framework for Understanding Transitional Justice' (2002) 15 Harvard Human Rights Journal 39

Barnett R, 'Restitution: A New Paradigm of Criminal Justice' (1977) 87 Ethics 279

Bassiouni MC, 'International Recognition of Victims' Rights' (2006) 6 Human Rights Law Review 203

Bazemore G and O'Brien S, 'The Quest for a Restorative Justice Model of Rehabilitation: Theory-for-Practice and Practice-for-Theory' in Lode Walgrave (ed), *Restorative Justice and the Law* (Willan Publishing 2002)

Bazemore G and Schiff M, 'Paradigm Muddle or Paradigm Paralysis? The Wide and Narrow Roads to Restorative Justice Reform (or, a Little Confusion May Be a Good Thing)' (2004) 7 Contemporary Justice Review 37

Beccaria C, *On Crimes and Punishment and Other Writings* (Cambridge University Press 1995)

Bolitho JJ, 'Restorative Justice: The Ideals and Realities of Conferencing for Young People' (2012) 20 Critical Criminology 61

Boutellier H, *Crime and Morality: The Significance of Criminal Justice in Post-Modern Culture* (Kluwer 2002)

Braithwaite J and Strang H, *Restorative Justice and Civil Society* (Cambridge University Press 2001)

Coben J and Harley P, 'International Conversations about Restorative Justice, Mediation and the Practice of Law' (2004) 25 Hamline Journal of Public Law & Policy 235

Corns C, 'Criminal Sanctions: Offenders, Victims and the State' (1995) 7 Legaldate 5

Cottingham J, 'Varieties of Retribution' (1979) 29 The Philosophical Quarterly 238

Cragg W, *The Practice of Punishment: Towards a Theory of Restorative Justice* (Routledge 1992)

Crawford A, 'Introduction' in Adam Crawford and Jo Goodey (eds), *Integrating a Victim Perspective within Criminal Justice: International Debates*, vol 3 (Dartmouth Publishing Company 2000)

Cryer R et al., *An Introduction to International Criminal Law and Procedure* (Cambridge University Press 2014)

Cunneen C, 'Reparations and Restorative Justice: Responding to Gross Violations of Human Rights' in John Braithwaite and Heather Strang (eds), *Restorative Justice and Civil Society* (Cambridge University Press 2001)

Daly K, 'South Australia Juvenile Justice (SAJJ) Research on Conferencing, Technical Report No. 2: Research Instruments in Year 2 (1999) and Background Notes' (School of Criminology and Criminal Justice, Griffith University 2001)

deGuzman M, 'Choosing to Prosecute: Expressive Selection at the International Criminal Court' (2012) 33 Michigan Journal of International Law 265

Dignan J, *Understanding Victims and Restorative Justice* (Open University Press 2004)

Dignan J and Cavadino M, 'Towards a Framework for Conceptualizing and Evaluating Models of Criminal Justice from a Victim's Perspective' (1996) 4 International Review of Victimology 153

Dingwall G and Hillier T, 'The Banality of Punishment: Context Specificity and Justifying Punishment of Extraordinary Crimes' (2010) 6 International Journal of Punishment and Sentencing 6
Doak J, *Victims' Rights, Human Rights and Criminal Justice. Reconceiving the Role of the Third Parties* (Hart Publishing 2008)
Drumbl MA, 'Collective Violence and Individual Punishment: The Criminality of Mass Atrocity' (2004) 99 Northwestern University Law Review 539
Duff A, 'Restorative Punishment and Punitive Restoration' in Lode Walgrave (ed), *Restorative Justice and the Law* (Willan Publishing 2002)
Duff A and Garland D (eds), *A Reader on Punishment* (Oxford University Press 1994)
Dunn P, 'Matching Service Delivery to Need' in Sandra Walklate (ed), *Handbook of Victims and Victimology* (Routledge 2007)
Erez E, 'Victim Participation in Sentencing: Rhetoric and Reality' (1990) 18 Journal of Criminal Justice 19
Fatić A, *Punishment and Restorative Crime-Handling: A Social Theory of Trust* (Avebury 1995)
Fenwick H, 'Procedural 'Rights' of Victims of Crime: Public or Private Ordering of the Criminal Justice Process?' (1997) 60 The Modern Law Review 317
Fletcher GP, *With Justice for Some: Victims' Rights in Criminal Trials* (Addison-Wesley Publishing Company 1995)
Fletcher GP, *The Grammar of Criminal Law: American, Comparative, and International: Volume One: Foundations* (Oxford University Press 2007)
Garbett C, 'From Passive Objects to Active Agents: A Comparative Study of Conceptions of Victim Identities at the ICTY and ICC' (2016) 15 Journal of Human Rights 40
Gerkin P et al., 'Implementing Restorative Justice Under the Retributive Paradigm: A Pilot Program Case Study' (2017) 7 SAGE Open 1
Goodey J, *Victims and Victimology: Research, Policy and Practice* (Pearson Education 2005)
Gromet DM and Darley JM, 'Restoration and Retribution: How Including Retributive Components Affects the Acceptability of Restorative Justice Procedures' (2006) 19 Social Justice Research 395
Hall DJ, 'Victims' Voices in Criminal Court: The Need for Restraint' (1990) 28 American Criminal Law Review 233
Hall M, *Victims and Policy-Making: A Comparative Perspective* (Taylor & Francis 2012)
Hegel GWF, *Philosophy of Right* (Thomas M Knox tr, Oxford University Press 1967)
Heikkilä M, *International Criminal Tribunals and Victims of Crime: A Study of the Status of Victims before International Criminal Tribunals and of Factors Affecting This Status* (Institute for Human Rights Åbo Akademi University 2004)
Henderson LN, 'The Wrongs of Victim's Rights' (1985) 37 Stanford Law Review 100
Joutsen M, *The Role of the Victim of Crime in European Criminal Justice Systems: A Cross National Study of the Role of the Victim* (Helsinki Institute for Crime Prevention and Control 1987)
Kant I, *The Metaphysical Elements of Justice. Part I of the Metaphysics of Morals* (Mary Gregor tr, Cambridge University Press 1991)
Karmen A, *Crime Victims: An Introduction to Victimology* (6th edn, Wadsworth Publishing 2006)

Klimchuck D, 'Retribution, Restitution and Revenge, Law and Philosophy' (2001) 20 Law and Philosophy 81
Kool R and Moerings M, 'The Victim Has the Floor: The Victim's Right to Be Heard in Writing or Orally in the Dutch Courtroom' (2004) 12 European Journal of Crime, Criminal Law and Criminal Justice 46
Kunen E, 'The Effect of External Pressures on Sentencing Judges' (1983) 11 Fordham Urban Law Journal 263
Little JW, 'The Law of Sentencing as Public Ceremony' (1983) 35 University of Florida Law Review 1
Luban DJ, 'Fairness to Rightness: Jurisdiction, Legality, and the Legitimacy of International Criminal Law' (200)] Georgetown Public Law Research Paper No. 1154117 1
Luna E, 'Punishment Theory, Holism, and the Procedural Conception of Restorative Justice' (2003) 1 Utah Law Review 205
Maguire M, 'Victims' Needs and Victim Services: Indications from Research' (1985) 10 Victimology 539
Maguire M and Corbett C, *The Effects of Crime and the Work of Victims Support Scheme*, (Gower 1987)
Maguire M and Pointing J (eds), *Victims of Crime: A New Deal?* (Open University Press 1988)
Marshall TF, 'The Evolution of Restorative Justice in Britain' (1996) 4 European Journal on Criminal Policy and Research 31
Mawby R, 'Victims' Needs or Victims' Rights: Alternative Approaches to Policy-Making' in Mike Maguire and John Pointing (eds), *Victims of Crime: A New Deal?* (Open University Press 1988)
McCold P, 'The Recent History of Restorative Justice: Mediation, Circles, and Conferencing' in Dennis Sullivan and Larry Tifft, *Handbook of Restorative Justice. A Global Perspective* (Routledge 2006)
McDermott Y, 'Victims and International Law: Remedies in the Courtroom?' (2009) 4 Hague Justice Journal 199
McDonald WF, 'Towards a Bicentennial Revolution in Criminal Justice: The Return of the Victim' (1975) 13 The American Criminal Law Review 649
McGonigle Leyh B, *Procedural Justice? Victim Participation in International Criminal Proceedings* (Intersentia 2011)
Moffett L, *Justice for Victims before the International Criminal Court* (Routledge 2014)
Moore M, 'Victims and Retribution: A Reply to Professor Fletcher' (1999) 3 Buffalo Criminal Law Review 65
Niebur Eisnaugle CJ, 'An International 'Truth Commission': Utilizing Restorative Justice as an Alternative to Retribution' (2003) 36 Vanderbilt Journal of Transnational Law 209
Nozick R, *Philosophical Explanations* (Harvard University Press 1981)
Ochoa Sanchez JC, *The Rights of Victims in Criminal Justice Proceedings for Serious Human Rights Violations* (Martinus Nijhoff Publishers 2013)
Pena M and Carayon G, 'Is the ICC Making the Most of Victim Participation?' (2013) 7 International Journal of Transitional Justice 518
Plant R, Taylor-Gooby P and Lesser A, *Political Philosophy and Social Welfare: Essays on the Normative Basis of Welfare Provisions* (Routledge 1980)
Robinson PH, 'The Virtues of Restorative Processes, the Vices of Restorative Justice'(2003) Utah Law Review 375

Rubel HC, 'Victim Participation in Sentencing Proceedings' (1985) 28 Criminal Law Quarterly 226

Schafer S, *The Victim and His Criminal. A Study of Functional Responsibility*, vol 34 (Random House 1968)

Shapland J, 'The Victims, the Criminal Justice System and Compensation' (1984) 24 The British Journal of Criminology 131

Shapland J, 'Victims and Criminal Justice: Creating Responsible Criminal Justice Agencies' in Adam Crawford and Jo Goodey (eds), *Integrating a Victim Perspective within Criminal Justice: International Debates*, vol 3 (Dartmouth Publishing Company 2000)

Sherman L, 'Two Protestant Ethics and the Spirit of Restoration' in John Braithwaite and Heather Strang (eds), *Restorative Justice and Civil Society* (Cambridge University Press 2001)

Shoham SG, Knepper P and Kett M (eds), *International Handbook of Victimology* (CRC Press 2010)

Sloane RD, 'The Expressive Capacity of International Punishment: The Limits of the National Law Analogy and the Potential of International Criminal Law' (2007) 43 Stanford Journal of International Law 39

Spalek B, *Crime Victims: Theory, Policy and Practice* (Palgrave Macmillan 2006)

Tobolowsky PM, 'Victim Participation in the Criminal Justice Process: Fifteen Years After the President's Task Force on Victims of Crime' (1999) 25 New England Journal on Criminal and Civil Confinement 21

Umbreit MS, Coates RB and Kalanj B, *Victim Meets Offender: The Impact of Restorative Justice and Mediation* (Lynne Rienner Publishers 1994)

UN Office for Drug Control and Crime Prevention, 'Guide for Policy Makers on the Implementation of the United Nations Declaration of Basic Principles of Justice for Victims of Crime and Abuse of Power' (1999) UNDCP/ODCCP(09)/V642

UN Office for Drug Control and Crime Prevention, 'Handbook on Justice for Victims: On the Use and Application of the Declaration of Basic Principles of Justice for Victims of Crime and Abuse of Power' (1999) UNDCP/ODCCP(09)/J96

Vaandering D, 'A Faithful Compass: Rethinking the Term Restorative Justice to Find Clarity' (2011) 14 Contemporary Justice Review 307

Van Dijk J, 'Ideological Trends within the Victims Movement: An International Perspective' in Mike Maguire and John Pointing (eds), *Victims of Crime: A New Deal?* (Open University Press 1988)

Van Dijk J, 'Introducing Victimology' in Jan Van Dijk, Ron GH van Kaam and Joanne Wemmers (eds), *Caring for Crime Victims: Selected Proceedings of the Ninth International Symposium on Victimology, Amsterdam, August 25–29, 1997* (Criminal Justice Press 1999)

van Ness D, 'The Shape of Things to Come: A Framework for Thinking about a Restorative Justice System' in Elmar GM Weitekamp and Hans-Jürgen Kerner (eds), *Restorative Justice: Theoretical Foundations* (Willan Publishing 2002)

van Ness D and Heetderks Strong K, *Restoring Justice* (Anderson Publishing 1997)

van Ness D and Strong KH, *Restoring Justice: An Introduction to Restorative Justice* (Anderson Publishing 1997)

van Wormer KS and Walker L, 'Preface' in Kathrine S van Wormer and Lorenn Walker (eds), *Restorative Justice Today: Practical Applications* (Sage 2013)

von Hentig H, *The Criminal and His Victim: Studies in the Sociobiology of Crime* (Yale University Press 1948) von Hirsch A, 'Punishment, Penance and the State' in Matt Matravers (ed), *Punishment and Political Theory* (Hart Publishing 1999)

Walgrave L, 'Restorative Justice: An Alternative for Responding to Crime?' in Shlomo Giora Shoham, Ori Beck and Martin Kett (eds), *International Handbook of Penology and Criminal Justice* (CRC Press 2008)

Walklate S and Mawby R, *Critical Victimology: International Perspectives* (Sage 1994)

Wemmers J-A and Cyr K, 'Victims' Perspectives on Restorative Justice: How Much Involvement Are Victims Looking For?' (2004) 11 International Review of Victimology 259

Wolfgang ME, *Patterns in Criminal Homicide* (University of Pennsylvania Press 1958)

Wringe B, 'Why Punish War Crimes? Victor's Justice and Expressive Justifications of Punishment' (2006) 25 Law and Philosophy 159

Young DB, 'Cesare Beccaria: Utilitarian or Retributivist?' (1983) 11 Journal of Criminal Justice 317

Zauberman R, 'Victims as Consumers of the Criminal Justice System?' in Adam Crawford and Jo Goodey (eds), *Integrating a Victim Perspective within Criminal Justice: International Debates*, vol 3 (Dartmouth Publishing Company 2000)

Zehr H, *Changing Lenses: A New Focus for Crime and Justice* (Herald Press 1990)

Zernova M, *Restorative Justice: Ideals and Realities* (Ashgate 2007)

Legislation

Basic Principles and Guidelines on the Right to a Remedy and Reparation for Victims of Gross Violations of International Human Rights Law and Serious Violations of International Humanitarian Law, UNGA Res 60/147 (21 March 2006) UN Doc A/RES/60/147

Council Framework Decision 2001/220/JHA of 15 March 2001 on the standing of victims in criminal proceedings [2001] OJ L82/1

Criminal Code, RSC 1985, chapter C-46, section 722

European Parliament and Council Directive 2012/29/EU of 25 October 2012 establishing minimum standards on the rights, support and protection of victims of crime, and replacing Council Framework Decision 2001/220/JHA [2012] OJ L315/57

Declaration of Basic Principles of Justice for Victims of Crime and Abuse of Power, UNGA Res 40/34 (29 November 1985) UN Doc A/RES/40/34

United States Federal Crime Victims' Rights Act, 18 U.S.C. § 3771

3 Arguments for a change of paradigm in international criminal justice

Shortcomings of the retributive, utilitarian, and restorative models of justice

3.1 Introduction

While the previous chapter analysed retributivism, deterrence, and restorative justice to criticise the little practical impact they had in conferring on victims an effective standing within the criminal proceedings at the domestic level, this current chapter shifts the focus to the international criminal justice system. The discussion will take a broader look, since it questions whether the above-mentioned criminal justice models are eligible justifications for justice within the international arena. The transplanting of retributivism, deterrence, and restorative justice to the international field is problematic because there are constitutive differences between the domestic and international criminal justice systems. In particular, the distinctive features of the international criminal justice system raise new questions about the meaning of justice, which can eventually result in multiple and contradictory understandings and practices of justice before international criminal tribunals.[1] This scenario also undermines the consistency and predictability of victims' participatory rights. Having a clear understanding of the purposes of international criminal justice is fundamental because the adopted criminal justice framework contributes to shaping the structure of the proceedings as well as the role of all individuals involved in the criminal process. Thus, this chapter's main goal is to expose the drawbacks produced by such a transplant from the domestic to the international forum in terms of principled justification for punishment and breaks down the retributive, deterrent, and restorative approaches of the international criminal justice system. These crime-control justifications, which work reasonably well in domestic criminal justice systems, are weakened by the contingency of the process of international criminal law.

This chapter develops around a second goal, which is ancillary to the main one. It aims to provide a general understanding of the difference between the domestic and international criminal justice system. These legal paradigms originate from two distinct socio-political contexts and, consequently, the international criminal

1 Carolyn Hoyle and Leila Ullrich, 'New Court, New Justice?' (2014) 12 Journal of International Criminal Justice 681, 702.

DOI: 10.4324/9781003215448-3

justice system presents some constitutive characteristics which are unique. It is important to mark the normative differences between extraordinary crimes against the world community and ordinary crimes against local communities in order to understand the extent to which the prevailing domestic criminal justice theories can be effectively transplanted to the international criminal law field and to what degree the latter should develop its own judicial method.

3.2 Distinctive features of the international criminal justice system

This section points out the ideological and structural features of international criminal justice that have to be considered in trying to work out a clear distinction between the international and domestic systems of criminal justice. International criminal law and domestic criminal law mainly diverge in two ways that focus on the distinctive nature of the communities involved and of the crimes implicated.

3.2.1 The meaning of 'international community'

While domestic criminal law can be appraised in terms of concerning the community of a State's citizens, a system of international criminal justice intends to serve both the literal and the figurative international community because international crimes affect the interests of States and national communities and threaten fundamental values of all mankind.[2] International community in a literal sense entails multiple and heterogeneous communities composed of different ethnic or national communities that uphold competing and diverging interests which international bodies have to mediate.[3] The figurative international community conceived as a community of mankind,[4] echoing ideas of natural law, is an ambiguous concept because it hides and dissimulates the fact that there is not a world community, but rather several international constituencies, such as communities of national States (UN members, Security Council members, NATO countries, and so on), communities of non-governmental organisations (NGOs), and communities of other actors (corporations, academics, and so on).[5]

2 Robert D Sloane, 'The Expressive Capacity of International Punishment: The Limits of the National Law Analogy and the Potential of International Criminal Law' (2007) 43 Stanford Journal of International Law 39, 53.

3 ibid 41.

4 The Preamble of the Rome Statute of the International Criminal Court affirms that 'the most serious crimes of concern to the international community as a whole must not go unpunished and that their effective prosecution must be ensured'.

5 Laura A Dickingson, 'The Promise of Hybrid Courts' (2003) 97 American Journal of International Law 295, 303.

3.2.2 The nature of international crimes

The second relevant feature that differentiates international criminal law from domestic criminal law is the peculiar nature of international crimes under the jurisdiction of the international criminal justice institutions. The crime of genocide, crimes against humanity, war crimes, and crimes of aggression, known collectively as core international crimes, generally involve five features: (1) mass victimisation; (2) large-scale organised participation; (3) ideologically driven perpetration; (4) the impact of the crimes and impunity on victims and their families; and (5) State involvement.[6] International crimes often occur in situations of civil conflict that set community against community,[7] involving, therefore, a large number of victims and extensive participation of perpetrators as well.[8] Mass victimisation means that international crimes are not a single crime perpetrated against a singular individual, but generally involve a large number of criminal actions committed against a group of individuals over a protracted period of time. The collective nature of the victim is well expressed in the Rome Statute (RS) of the International Criminal Court (ICC). The norms of crimes against humanity refer to 'a widespread or systematic attack directed against any civilian population',[9] while the crime of genocide includes 'acts committed with intent to destroy, in whole or in part, a national, ethnical, racial or religious group'.[10] Article 8 of the RS on war crimes, by referring to acts against persons or property protected under the provisions of the relevant Geneva Conventions of 12 August 1949,[11] seems not to involve collective victims in the sense above discussed in respect to crimes against humanity and genocide. In fact, those conventions require the criminal action be committed against a member of one protected group, such as the wounded and sick in armed forces in the field, the wounded, sick, and shipwrecked members of armed forces at sea, prisoners of war, and civilians who find themselves under the rule of a foreign power in the event of international conflict.[12] However, the same article of the RS on war crimes, stat-

6 Luke Moffett, *Justice for Victims before the International Criminal Court* (Routledge 2014) 10.

7 Paolina Massidda, 'Retributive and Restorative Justice for Victims and Reconciliation: Considerations on the Lubanga Case before the ICC' (2015) 1 Peace Processes Online Review 1, 4.

8 Moffett (n 6) 10.

9 Article 7, Rome Statute of the International Criminal Court 1998 (2187 UNTS 90).

10 Article 6, ibid.

11 Article 8, ibid.

12 Geneva Convention for the Amelioration of the Condition of the Wounded and Sick in Armed Forces in the Field (First Geneva Convention) 1949 (75 UNTS 31); Geneva Convention for the Amelioration of the Condition of Wounded, Sick and Shipwrecked Members of Armed Forces at Sea (Second Geneva Convention) 1949 (75 UNTS 85); Geneva Convention Relative to the Treatment of Prisoners of War (Third Geneva Convention) 1949 (75 UNTS 135); Geneva Convention Relative to the Protection of Civilian Persons in Time of War (Fourth Geneva Convention) 1949 (75 UNTS 287).

ing that the ICC has jurisdiction on war crimes 'when committed as part of a plan or policy or as part of a large-scale commission of such crimes',[13] clearly expresses the need to prosecute such crimes in a systematic, rather than in an isolated way.[14]

The second specific feature of international crimes, that is large-scale organised participation, is linked to the feature of collective victims because mass victimisation can involve a highly organised number of groups or individuals who have perpetrated international crimes.[15] Indeed a collective perpetrator is not a mandatory element of international crimes, but in the vast majority of cases it represents an invariable feature because criminals act on behalf of a collective criminal project such as eliminating an ethnic, religious, national, or racial group, or undertaking systematic attacks against civilians, and so on.[16] Using the words of Dworkin, collective action 'is a matter of individuals acting together in a way that merges their separate actions into a further, unified act that is together theirs'.[17] As a consequence of that, international crimes involve a collective mental state. As a practical matter it means that the perpetrators are conscious of being part of a common project, of sharing a specific intent, and of acting as a group.[18]

The third aspect to take into consideration is that international crimes can be ideologically driven. Individuals are a target because of their race, ethnicity, religion, political beliefs, and, as part of the ideology, they are dehumanised to legitimise the violence.[19] The fourth characteristic is the impact of the crimes and impunity on the victims and their families. It goes to the core of the heinous nature of international crimes because they involve mutilations and brutal killings that cause suffering and mental trauma to the victims, but also to those who simply witnessed these events. The literature on the suffering of victims brought about by mass conflicts illustrates that victims experience a high tendency to develop depression and anxiety as a result of the internalisation of negative feelings, such as self-blame, outrage, alienation, and exclusion during any subsequent legal proceedings.[20] Victims endure particularly serious violence, not just at the individual level, but also as members of a given community, who are deeply affected by the fragmentation of their community and the social culture of segregation. Impunity is another factor that affects victims, since they are denied the recognition of their suffering and access to justice.[21] The last distinguishing

13 Article 8, Rome Statute of the International Criminal Court.

14 Sloane (n 2) 57.

15 Moffett (n 6) 10.

16 Sloane (n 2) 56.

17 Roland Dworkin, *Freedom's Law: The Moral Reading of the American Constitution* (Oxford University Press 1999) 20.

18 Sloane (n 2) 56.

19 Moffett (n 6) 11.

20 Jonathan Doak, 'The Therapeutic Dimension of Transitional Justice: Emotional Repair and Victim Satisfaction in International Trials and Truth Commissions' (2011) 11 International Criminal Law Review 263, 265.

21 Moffett (n 6) 12.

element of international crimes is that they occur on a widespread and organised scale because of the action or inaction of the State.[22] Perpetrators of international crimes operate in an instable normative framework, characterised by war, ethnic conflicts, and social deterioration. The basic social norms against violence are undermined and gradually removed to the detriment of specific ethnic, political, religious, and national groups.[23]

3.3 Plurality of goals ascribed to international criminal justice

International criminal institutions have been greatly influenced by deterrence and retributivism. These two criminal justice models have been invoked by the UN Security Council resolutions establishing the ICTY and the ICTR, which emphasise that the goals of prosecution include putting 'an end to such crimes', taking 'effective measures to bring to justice the persons who are responsible', and 'ensuring that such violations are halted and effectively redressed'.[24] In a similar way, the Preamble of the ICC Statute suggests retribution and deterrence are its main purpose, since it states that 'the most serious crimes of concern to the international community as a whole must not go unpunished and that their effective prosecution must be ensured by taking measures' and that the ICC is 'determined to put an end to impunity for the perpetrators of these crimes and thus to contribute to the prevention of such crimes'.[25]

The case law of the ICTY and ICTR demonstrates that substantial agreement exists that deterrence and retribution are important rationales when determining the sentence, supporting both approaches, at times preferring one approach to another. In several decisions, the ICTY and the ICTR pointed out an important aspect of retributivism, which is the proportionality between the gravity of the offences committed by the defendant and the punishment meted out as the primary consideration in imposing sentence.[26] Specifically, in *Zdravko Mucić et al.*,

22 ibid 11.
23 Sloane (n 2) 41.
24 Preamble, UNSC, Res 827 (25 May 1993) UN Doc S/RES/827; Preamble, UNSC, Res 955 (8 November 1994) UN Doc S/RES/955.
25 Preamble, Rome Statute of the International Criminal Court.
26 *Prosecutor v Juvénal Kajelijeli* (Judgement and Sentence) ICTR-98–44A-T, Trial Chamber II (1 December 2003), para 963. See also *Prosecutor v Laurent Semanza* (Judgement and Sentence) ICTR-97–20-T, Trial Chamber III (15 May 2003), para 555; *Prosecutor v Zoran Kupreškić et al* (Judgement) IT-95–16-T, Trial Chamber (14 January 2000), para 852; *Prosecutor v Dragan Nikolić* (Judgement on Sentencing Appeal) IT-94–2-A, Appeals Chamber (4 February 2005), para 21; *Prosecutor v Milomir Stakić* (Judgement) IT-97–24-T, Trial Chamber II (31 July 2003), para 903; *Prosecutor v Simon Bikindi* (Appeals Chamber Judgement) ICTR-01–72-A, Appeals Chamber (18 March 2010), para 145; *Prosecutor v Joseph Serugendo* (Judgement and Sentence) ICTR-2005–84-I,Trial Chamber I (12 June 2006), para 39.

better known as the *Čelebići* case, the Judges affirmed that the 'touchstone of sentencing is the gravity of the offence for which an accused has been found guilty',[27] whereas undue weight should not be accorded to deterrence as a factor in the determination of the appropriate sentence.[28] In other cases, it has been claimed that deterrence is the most important parameter to take in consideration when determining a sentence. In *Ndindabahizi*, the trial Chamber affirmed that, to decide on an appropriate sentence to be imposed on the defendant, '[s]pecific emphasis is placed on general deterrence'.[29] Another strand of decisions affirmed that deterrence and retribution have equal importance as underlying principles in the sentencing of an individual found guilty.[30]

In addition to retributive and deterrent attributes, international criminal justice is viewed as a 'technique or instrument'[31] that can be used by the international community to foster reconciliation of communities in conflict and, thus, long-term peace and security.[32] The UN Security Council provided significant support for the interconnection of restoration, reconciliation, and justice. Such determination is reflected in the Security Council's creation of the *ad hoc* tribunals, aimed to take actions to restore and promote international peace and security.[33] In its Preamble, the RS urges the ICC to contribute to 'the process of national reconciliation and to the restoration and maintenance of peace'.[34] Specifically, the innovative victim-oriented provision contained in Article 68(3) of the RS, which enables victims to present their views and concerns in the proceedings, is more

27 *Prosecutor v Zdravko Mucić et al.* (Judgement) IT-96–21-T, Trial Chamber (16 November 1998), para 1260.
28 *Prosecutor v Zdravko Mucić et al.* (Judgement) IT-96–21-A, Appeals Chamber (20 February 2001), paras 799–801. See also *Prosecutor v Duško Tadić* (Judgement in Sentencing Appeals) IT-94–1-A and IT-94–1-Abis, Appeals Chamber (26 January 2000), para 48.
29 *Prosecutor v Emmanuel Ndindabahizi* (Judgement and Sentence) ICTR-2001–71-I, Trial Chamber I (15 July 2004), para 498. See also *Prosecutor v Alfred Musema* (Judgement and Sentence) ICTR-96–13-A, Trial Chamber I (27 January 2000), para 986; *Prosecutor v Eliézer Niyitegeka* (Judgement and Sentence) ICTR-96–14-T, Trial Chamber I (16 May 2003), para 484; *Prosecutor v Elizaphan and Gérard Ntakirutimana* (Judgement and Sentence) ICTR-96–10 & ICTR-96–17-T, Trial Chamber I (21 February 2003), para 882.
30 *Prosecutor v Jean Kambanda* (Judgement and Sentence) ICTR-97–23-S, Trial Chamber I (4 September 1998), para 28. See also *Prosecutor v Georges Rutaganda* (Judgement and Sentence) ICTR-96–3-T, Trial Chamber I (6 December 1999), para 456; *Prosecutor v Zlatko Aleksovski* (Judgement) IT-95–14/1-A, Appeals Chamber (24 March 2000) para 185.
31 Brianne McGonigle Leyh, *Procedural Justice? Victim Participation in International Criminal Proceedings* (Intersentia 2011) 61.
32 Antonio Cassese, 'Reflections on International Criminal Justice' (1998) 61 The Modern Law Review 1, 5–6. See also Robert Cryer et al., *An Introduction to International Criminal Law and Procedure* (Cambridge University Press 2014) 22, 30.
33 Preamble, UNSC, Res 827 (25 May 1993) UN Doc S/RES/827; Preamble, UNSC, Res 955 (8 November 1994) UN Doc S/RES/955.
34 Preamble, Rome Statute of the International Criminal Court.

attuned to the idea of 'justice for victims',[35] urging the ICC to contribute to the process of reconciliation of conflict-affected communities.[36]

The view that the integration of victims as active participants within the ICC proceedings can contribute to reconciliation, restoration, and justice for victims has been developed into a narrative claiming that the ICC operates as a mechanism of restorative justice.[37] Wemmers[38] and Combs[39] suggested the ICC marks something of a shift towards a more expansive model of international criminal justice that incorporates elements of restorative justice. By the same token, Funk[40] and Guhr[41] advanced that enabling victims to participate in international criminal justice indicates a broader construction of justice than retribution and deterrence, towards a more reparative approach that seeks to restore victims and, more generally, connect international criminal justice to the process of social reconciliation typical of the restorative justice paradigm.[42] In the aftermath of mass atrocities, victims must not only cope with their individual suffering, but also participate in the process of social healing involving all those affected by the violence.[43] The recovery of victims is, thus, intertwined with the restoration of the socio-political fabric, as reconciliation requires not only the healing of individuals, but also of society as a whole.[44] In this view, the right of victims to actively participate in

35 Claire Garbett, 'From Passive Objects to Active Agents: A Comparative Study of Conceptions of Victim Identities at the ICTY and ICC' (2016) 15 Journal of Human Rights 40, 51.

36 Moffett (n 6) 102.

37 Emily Haslam, 'Victim Participation at the International Criminal Court: A Triumph of Hope Over Experience?' in Dominic McGoldrick, Peter Rowe and Eric Donnelly, *The Permanent International Criminal Court: Legal and Policy Issues* (Hart Publishing 2004) 315. See also Mark Findlay and Ralph Henham, *Transforming International Criminal Justice: Retributive and Restorative Justice in the Trial Process* (Routledge 2005) 275; Silvia A de Gurmendi Fernández and Håkan Friman, 'The Rules of Procedure and Evidence of the International Criminal Court' (2000) 3 Yearbook of International Humanitarian Law 289, 312; Jenia Iontcheva Turner, 'Legal Ethics in International Criminal Defense' (2010) 10 Chicago Journal of International Law 685, 695–696; Navanethem Pillay, 'Equal Justice for Women: A Personal Journey' (2008) 50 Arizona Law Review 657, 671.

38 Jo-Anne Wemmers, 'Victims' Rights and the International Criminal Court: Perceptions within the Court Regarding the Victims' Right to Participate' (2010) 23 Leiden Journal of International Law 629, 630.

39 Nancy A Combs, *Guilty Pleas in International Criminal Law: Constructing a Restorative Justice Approach* (Stanford University Press 2007) 141.

40 Markus T Funk, *Victims' Rights and Advocacy at the International Criminal Court* (Oxford University Press 2015) 4;

41 Alexandra H Guhr, 'Victim Participation During the Pre-Trial Stage at the International Criminal Court' (2008) 8 International Criminal Law Review 109, 109–110.

42 Carsten Stahn, 'International Criminal Justice and Reconciliation: Beyond the Retributive v. Restorative Divide' (2015) 36 FICHL Policy Brief Series 3.

43 Mina Rauschenbach and Damien Scalia, 'Victims and International Criminal Justice: A Vexed Question?' (2008) 90 International Review of the Red Cross 441, 451.

44 ibid 453.

proceedings at the ICC becomes an important factor in this healing process,[45] as well as an indispensable element if post-conflict justice processes are to be 'capable of building the foundations for a strong transition through empowerment of those who were victimised during conflict'.[46]

The proposition that the ICC metes out restorative justice to victims through their participation in legal proceedings was advanced by Judge Silvia Fernandez de Gurmendo,[47] Judge Sang-Hyun Song,[48] and the Registrar.[49] The 'Report of the Court on the strategy in relation to victims' (Strategy) confirmed that a key feature of the system established in the RS is the recognition that the ICC has not only a punitive, but also a restorative function, which reflects the growing importance that participation and reparations play in achieving justice for victims.[50] In the following *Court's Revised Strategy in Relation to Victims* (Revised Strategy), the ICC emphasised the key role played by victims – as participants – before the Court and the importance of the Court's restorative function.[51]

International criminal justice, like most criminal justice systems, can be rooted through a plurality of goals synergistically, including deterrence, retribution, and restoration, since it aims to protect the rights of victims and defendants alike; to

45 Assembly of States Parties, 'Report of the Court on the strategy in relation to victims' (2009) ICC-ASP/8/45, para 2. See also Yael Danieli, 'Massive Trauma and the Healing Role of Reparative Justice', in Carla Ferstman, Mariana Goetz and Alan Stephens (eds), *Reparations for Victims of Genocide, Crimes against Humanity and War Crimes: Systems in Place and Systems in the Making* (Martinus Nijhoff 2009); Mariana Goetz, 'The International Criminal Court and Its Relevance to Affected Communities' in Nicholas Waddell and Phil Clark, *Courting Conflict? Justice, Peace and the ICC in Africa* (Crisis States Research Centre 2008); Fiona McKay, 'Universal Jurisdiction in Europe: Criminal Prosecutions in Europe since 1990 for War Crimes, Crimes against Humanity, Torture and Genocide' (REDRESS 1999).

46 Mariana Pena and Gaelle Carayon, 'Is the ICC Making the Most of Victim Participation?' (2013) 7 International Journal of Transitional Justice 518, 519.

47 Silvia A de Gurmendi Fernández, 'International Criminal Court Today: Challenges and Opportunities' (2016) 4 <https://www.icc-cpi.int/itemsDocuments/1600609-Helsinki-keynote-speech-ICC-President-Fernandez.pdf> accessed 2 October 2021.

48 ICC Press Release, 'ICC President Tells World Parliamentary Conference "ICC Brings Retributive and Restorative Justice Together with the Prevention of Future Crimes"' (11 December 2012) <https://www.icc-cpi.int/Pages/item.aspx?name=pr860> accessed 2 October 2021.

49 Herman von Hebel, 'Remarks to the 15th Session of the Assembly of States Parties' (2016) 11 <https://asp.icc-cpi.int/sites/asp/files/asp_docs/ASP15/ASP15-Opening-Statement-Registrar-ENG.pdf> accessed 2 October 2021.

50 Assembly of States Parties, 'Report of the Court on the strategy in relation to victims' (n 45), para 3.

51 Assembly of States Parties, 'Court's Revised Strategy in Relation to Victims' (2012) ICC-ASP/11/38 <https://asp.icc-cpi.int/iccdocs/asp_docs/ASP11/ICC-ASP-11-38-ENG.pdf> accessed 24 October 2021, para 2. See also Assembly of States Parties, 'Report of the Court on the Implementation in 2013 of the Revised Strategy in Relation to Victims' (2013) ICC-ASP/12/41, paras 2, 28; Assembly of States Parties, 'Report of the Court on the Revised Strategy in Relation to Victims: Past, Present and Future' (2012) ICC-ASP/11/40, para 34.

provide equal measures of deterrence, punishment, and rehabilitation, and to avoid scapegoating the few, while not falling into the trap of collective guilt.[52] Although these principles are pertinent at the international level, nevertheless the theories discussed above are not entirely applicable to international criminal justice because they have been developed to be implemented at the domestic level. Retribution, deterrence, and restorative justice cannot be fully transferred to the legal and institutional context of an international criminal tribunal because such a transplant tries to match the contrasting histories, assumptions, and paradigms of two different legal branches.[53] Domestic criminal law, as a coercive body of law which concretely represents the basic values and norms of the single Nation-State,[54] is a product of continuity, while international criminal law is a product of discontinuity, of upheaval, and political rupture.[55] These core aspects of post-conflict justice situations, which are mainly absent in the domestic realm of criminal justice, pose a challenge to the successful application of these theories to cases of gross violations of human rights and other serious acts of mass violence and mass victimisation, amounting to international crimes.

3.4 Limitations of retributive justice

International criminal justice cannot be fully grounded on retributivism because it emerges as problematic when faced with some of the features of international criminal law previously outlined. The specific idea of retributivism, which holds punishment as a debt to be paid to the community by those individuals who acquire an unfair advantage through criminal acts, is particularly problematic in the context of international criminal justice because it posits a quasi-contractual relationship between the individual and society.[56] A contract model of retributive justice makes sense in the domestic criminal field, where crimes represent a deviation from generally accepted social norms in the time and place they are perpetrated. The same, however, cannot be said about international crimes, which are committed in places characterised by political and social breakdown.[57] In other words, in the scenario where international crimes are perpetrated, those who commit such crimes are conforming to social norms, while those who do not

52 José E Alvarez, 'Trying Hussein: Between Hubris and Hegemony' (2004) 2 Journal of International Criminal Justice 319, 321.

53 Steven R Ratner, 'The Schizophrenias of International Criminal Law' (1998) 33 Texas International Law Journal 237, 251.

54 Sloane (n 2) 40.

55 David J Luban, 'Fairness to Rightness: Jurisdiction, Legality, and the Legitimacy of International Criminal Law' (2008) Georgetown Public Law Research Paper No. 1154117 1, 8.

56 Sloane (n 2) 80.

57 Mark A Drumbl, 'Collective Violence and Individual Punishment: The Criminality of Mass Atrocity' (2005) 99 Northwestern University Law Review 539, 567.

are considered to have deviant behaviour.[58] A specific feature of international crimes is that perpetrators do not act individually as the offender in the domestic context, but, on the contrary, they are generally part of a collective that shares ethnic, national, racial, or religious values. In such circumstances, perpetrators are less likely to breach social values.[59] The case of Rwanda provides a valid example of this phenomenon. The genocide in Rwanda was marked by the support of the majority of Rwandans and by the suspension of pre-existing social norms that were replaced with norms that normalised ethnic elimination. In Rwanda, genocide became a civil duty.[60] The quasi-contractual paradigm of retributive justice also seems misplaced when applied to international crimes because one of the features of international crimes, outlined in the previous paragraph, requires the action or inaction of the State, which confers on individuals a collective cloak of authority. This means that international crimes usually involve States as an entity that shares culpability for the crimes, rather than an entity aimed at ensuring the proper distribution of benefits and burdens in the community.[61]

Other important criticisms about the ability of international criminal justice to serve retributive goals are mainly centred, firstly, on the selectivity of international criminal law, which punishes only a few of the alleged perpetrators, while the majority of them escape prosecution and, secondly, on the difficulty of inflicting a proportionate punishment for the atrocity perpetrated.[62] Selectivity raises a significant challenge to retributivism, which fails to justify selecting some perpetrators and not others.[63] While the imperative of retributivism requires that all persons deserving a punishment have to be punished,[64] selectivity is deeply-rooted in international criminal justice. The ICTY and ICTR have been compelled to select a small number of cases from potentially thousands. Such selectivity had a discretional nature since prosecution was exercised in those cases where there was a better chance of getting a conviction because the gravity, the planning, the brutality, and the wide scope of crimes provided greater means of evidence.[65] In this scenario, the creation of the permanent ICC seemed to reduce the selectivity which afflicts the *ad hoc* tribunals, but, as Drumbl notes, 'it is impossible to squeeze out the political contingency of criminal liability in the ICC practice'.[66]

58 Immi Tallgren, 'The Sensibility and Sense of International Criminal Law' (2002) 13 European Journal of International Law 561, 573.
59 ibid.
60 Drumbl (n 57) 569–570.
61 Sloane (n 2) 81.
62 ibid; Margaret deGuzman, 'Choosing to Prosecute: Expressive Selection at the International Criminal Court' (2012) 33 Michigan Journal of International Law 265, 302.
63 Michael T Cahill, 'Retributive Justice in the Real World' (2007) 85 Washington University Law Review 815, 870.
64 ibid 826.
65 Mark A Drumbl, *Atrocity, Punishment, and International Law* (Cambridge University Press 2007) 151.
66 ibid 152. See also Héctor Olásolo, 'The Prosecutor of the ICC Before the Initiation of Investigations: A Quasi-Judicial or a Political Body?' (2003) 3 International Criminal Law Review 87, 142.

De facto there are two main factors influencing the prosecutorial discretion. The first factor is the limited resources available, meaning that only a few crisis situations are selected for investigation and prosecution, and the second is the political consensus, which is necessary for the ICC to maintain the resource support. Such elements encourage the ICC to investigate situations involving perpetrators from politically weak countries and show to what extent the ICC's decision to investigate a situation (or not) is influenced by concerns regarding how the eventual prosecution can affect the political standing, sources, and support among States.[67] Therefore, the high selectivity, formerly of the ICTY and ICTR, and now of the ICC, undermines their capacity to achieve retributive justice and shows the inadequacy of such account of criminal justice because too few persons received their just deserts, while many powerful States and organisations have escaped the grasp of international criminal justice.[68]

The proportionality between the gravity of the offence and the severity of the punishment is another aspect that gives rise to questions about the validity of the retributive paradigm of international criminal justice. The construction of the punitive proportionality is itself highly problematic because the seriousness of the atrocities can become unintelligible and immeasurable and, from a retributive account, to truly punish such international criminals, the right punishment should exceed anything ordinary.[69] Probably in a retributive sense, pain infliction or death are the punishments which would best fit the most serious international crimes. However, allowing this sort of punishment would undermine the developments in international human rights law, which aspires to abolish the death penalty and, more generally, to emphasise rehabilitation as a fundamental goal of punishment.[70]

The severity of the punishment meted out in international criminal proceedings should be greater than that of national trials because of the extraordinary nature of international crimes; however, the sentences of international tribunals are not lengthier than the sentences inflicted by domestic jurisdictions.[71] To clarify this point, it is useful to briefly analyse the sentencing practices of the ICTY and ICTR. The maximum term in the sentencing practice of the ICTY is often a 20-year sentence, while the maximum term adopted by the States that emerged from the former Yugoslavia it is between 40 and 45 years. Very similarly, the defendants convicted by the ICTR, mainly senior officials, received a sentence which is milder than the one that would have been meted out in Rwanda, where the death penalty is still contemplated. This aspect, in the Rwandan case in particular, creates a paradox because leaders who committed international crimes

67 Drumbl (n 65) 152.
68 Drumbl (n 57) 558.
69 Drumbl (n 65) 157.
70 Sloane (n 2) 66–67.
71 Drumbl (n 57) 578; Stuart Beresford, 'Unshackling the Paper Tiger – The Sentencing Practices of the Ad Hoc International Criminal Tribunals for the Former Yugoslavia and Rwanda' (2001) 1 International Criminal Law Review 33, 90.

are punished by the ICTR with a lower sentence than the lower-level offenders prosecuted by Rwandan national tribunals.[72] Such shortcomings of the proportionality between the gravity of the offence and the severity of the punishment in the practice of domestic and international criminal institutions clearly weaken the retributive account of international criminal law.

While assessing the retributive value of the international criminal justice system, in addition to the quantitative length of the punishment meted out by international criminal institutions, the conditions of the incarceration must be considered. Looking again at the experience of Rwanda, the conditions of imprisonment at the international level are much better than those of the perpetrator sentenced at the national level.[73] This specific aspect raises a paradox that underlines the limitation of retributivism within international criminal justice with regard to victims. Such a paradox emerges in the case of many perpetrators of violence in Rwanda who were HIV-positive and deliberately infected their victims. At the ICTR, prisoners who were HIV-positive received an excellent level of healthcare and access to medication that few, if any, of the victims could ever claim. Although prosecuting and punishing these perpetrators was supposed to express retribution, in fact, punishment kept perpetrators alive and able to enjoy a quality of life that exceeded that of their victims and may also exceed the conditions in which they would live, whether or not they were sentenced to detention in their own country. In this case, it is evident why the retributive value of punishment is controversial.

3.5 Limits of deterrence

Deterrence is subject to several criticisms,[74] but there are two principal challenging arguments: the probability of being punished is too low to deter, and criminals do not rationally calculate the cost-benefit effects of criminal actions.[75] Deterrence depends on the efforts of international criminal institutions 'to communicate a credible threat authoritatively';[76] however, such aspiration is greatly limited by institutional and resource constraints that require a choice to be made between investigating and prosecuting certain defendants to the exclusion of oth-

72 See Drumbl (n 65) chapter 4.

73 ibid 160.

74 For general criticism on utilitarian theories see: Mikaela Heikkilä, *International Criminal Tribunals and Victims of Crime: A Study of the Status of Victims before International Criminal Tribunals and of Factors Affecting This Status* (Institute for Human Rights Åbo Akademi University 2004) 30–31; Erik Luna, 'Punishment Theory, Holism, and the Procedural Conception of Restorative Justice' (2003) Utah Law Review 205, 210–215; Wesley Cragg, *The Practice of Punishment: Towards a Theory of Restorative Justice* (Routledge 1992) 35–37.

75 deGuzman (n 62) 308; Drumbl (n 65) 169; Cryer et al. (n 32) 20; Gavin Dingwall and Tim Hillier, 'The Banality of Punishment: Context Specificity and Justifying Punishment of Extraordinary Crimes' (2010) 6 International Journal of Punishment and Sentencing 6, 8–9.

76 Drumbl (n 57) 590.

ers that should deserve the same consideration. International criminal tribunals fail to clearly communicate the potential prospect of getting caught, as they are culturally foreign and geographically distant and, most importantly, lack their own police force. For instance, international criminal tribunals face many difficulties in keeping the accused in custody because they are completely reliant on the cooperation of States' authorities.[77] Diane Amann provocatively affirmed that 'because [the tribunals] have no power to arrest, defendants come to them by chance'.[78] In a similar way, the scarcity of resources limits the operation of international criminal tribunals, narrowing down the breadth of the risk of being punished, which is supposed to discourage a rational perpetrator.

Against this backdrop, deterrence does not explain how to identify what crimes give rise to greater or lesser setbacks to social welfare,[79] leaving the selectivity of prosecution to a certain degree of randomness, or at least of indeterminacy. The lack of criteria to rank the value of different criminal conduct represents an important issue when it comes to allocating prosecutorial resources to make the most of deterrence. The ICC tried to address this issue and established parameters to maximise deterrence. In *Lubanga*, the Pre-Trial Chamber affirmed that the Court initiated cases against the most senior leaders because focusing on this type of individual was the only way to maximise the deterrent effects of the activities of the Court.[80] The exclusion of many perpetrators on the grounds proposed in *Lubanga* could severely hamper the deterrent role of the Court by announcing that any perpetrators other than those at the very top are automatically excluded from the exercise of the jurisdiction of the Court.[81] In contrast, for the Appeals Chamber in *Ntaganda*, it seems more logical to assume that the deterrent effect of the Court is highest if no category of perpetrators *per se* is excluded from potentially being brought before the Court. Even if the ICC acknowledges that the deterrent role of the Court is a cornerstone of its own creation,[82] it is highly controversial how a framework for selecting cases for prosecution based on deterrence should be set up.

The second basic idea underpinning general deterrence is the presumption of a certain level of rationality of perpetrators while committing gross violation of human rights.[83] However, the rational-perpetrator model of deterrence, in

77 ibid.

78 Diane Marie Amann, 'Group Mentality, Expressivism, and Genocide' (2002) 2 International Criminal Law Review 93, 116.

79 deGuzman (n 62) 308.

80 *Prosecutor v Thomas Lubanga Dyilo* (Decision concerning Pre-Trial Chamber I's Decision of 10 February 2006 and the Incorporation of Documents into the Record of the Case against Mr Thomas Lubanga Dyilo) ICC-01/04–01/06, Pre-Trial Chamber I (24 February 2006), paras 50–54.

81 *Prosecutor v Bosco Ntaganda* (Judgement on the Prosecutor's appeal against the decision of Pre-Trial Chamber I entitled 'Decision on the Prosecutor's Application for Warrants of Arrest, Article 58') ICC-01/04–02/06, Appeals Chamber (13 July 2006), paras 73–75.

82 ibid, para 75.

83 Drumbl (n 57) 590.

the chaos of large-scale violence, provocative propaganda, and overturned social order, may be unlikely in calculating the cost-benefit effects of their actions.[84] Drumbl identifies two factors that compromise such an assumption: gratification and survival. Many perpetrators want to be part of violent groups because membership of such groups provides them with a feeling of solidarity and comfort.[85] They may be hooked in by social norms inciting anger and violence or they may believe they act for the general wellbeing of the community, rather than for their personal benefits.[86] Some criminals can distort the cost-benefit calculation of their criminal conduct (on which the deterrence model depends) because they 'may be so idiosyncratically devoted to genocide or ethnic cleansing as to be undeterrable by anything short of massive military force, and maybe not even that'.[87] Megalomaniac dictators tend to show a sense of infallibility and invulnerability that make them less likely to rationally weigh the eventuality of being prosecuted and convicted against the immediate benefits of political power, territorial acquisitions, and elimination of ethnic groups.[88] Against this backdrop, where perpetrators believe that violent behaviours are morally justified, even necessary, and sometimes also gratifying, it is unlikely that the chances of being punished may deter people from committing such actions.[89] However, not every criminal necessarily belongs to such a psychosocial profile. Perpetrators responsible for mass atrocities can be also defined as 'conflict entrepreneurs' who manipulate values and the tools of State power as a means of increasing their own social, economic, or political power.[90] In this case, the value of killing oversteps the benefits of living in peace without the risk of a future punishment by a distant international criminal court.[91]

The second factor that challenges the assumption of a rational perpetrator in mass violence events is the necessity to survive. Often, individuals need to join a violent group because being isolated makes them more likely to be perceived as 'other' and to be victimised. In this scenario, committing a crime might not bring any gratification, but it may be a guarantee of survival. When individuals are acting in this way, it is unlikely they will be deterred by the chance of being punished by a distant international criminal tribunal.[92]

84 Drumbl (n 65) 171; Sloane (n 2) 72.
85 Sloane (n 2) 72.
86 Jaime Malamud-Goti, 'Transitional Governments in The Breach: Why Punish State Criminals?' (1990) 12 Human Rights Quarterly 1, 1.
87 Gary Jonathan Bass, *Stay the Hand of Vengeance: The Politics of War Crimes Tribunals*, vol 142 (Princeton University Press 2014) 294.
88 ibid 291.
89 Michael Ignatieff, *The Lesser Evil: Political Ethics in an Age of Terror* (Edinburgh University Press 2005) 121.
90 Sloane (n 2) 73.
91 Drumbl (n 65) 171.
92 ibid 172.

3.6 Limitations of the restorative justice paradigm

There is a conceptual difficulty that the restorative mechanisms have to face when entering the international criminal procedure, as it is unclear whether and to what extent the ICC considers its legal proceedings to be a practice of restorative justice as outlined above. The ICC's Strategy and Revised Strategy, which is the primary articulation of the ICC's approach to its victims' mandate, recognised restorative justice principles,[93] but failed to integrate them into the modalities of participation and reparation for victims. It is essential to point out that the ICC does not employ central practices of restorative justice, like mediation, circles, and conferencing, which bring victims and offenders together in face-to-face meetings to determine how to fix the harm caused by the wrongdoing in question.

Questions concerning the positioning of restorative mechanisms within international criminal justice should be answered looking at the specific context within which they are used. Practices of restorative justice have been developed mainly against the background of Western democratic societies and their application mainly addresses situations involving first-time offenders, low-level crime, and juveniles.[94] International crimes, on the other hand, consist of mass atrocities on a scale incomprehensible to those who have not experienced them, causing suffering and mental trauma to victims, but also to those who simply witnessed these events.[95] It would be fallacious to ignore the contrasting histories, assumptions, and paradigms of domestic and international criminal justice systems while assessing whether the ICC's justice approach is effectively structured to mete out restorative practices. The core aspects of post-conflict justice situations, which are mainly absent in the domestic realm of criminal justice, pose a challenge to the successful implementation of restorative practices into cases of gross violations of human rights and other serious acts of mass violence and mass victimisation, amounting to international crimes. The following analysis seeks to assess the extent to which the proceedings before the ICC can deliver a restorative process and whether this process has contributed to restoration, reparation, and healing for victims. It does so by framing the analysis around the five key elements of the restorative justice practice, namely (1) victim–offender encounter; (2) offender's acknowledgement of responsibility and apology; (3) collaborative conflict-resolution approach; (4) healing and reconciliation of victims and communities; (5) symbolic reparation and material compensation.[96]

93 See section 3.3.

94 Heikkilä (n 74) 37; Kerry Clamp and Jonathan Doak, 'More than Words: Restorative Justice Concepts in Transitional Justice Settings' (2012) 12 International Criminal Law Review 339, 346.

95 Moffett (n 6) 12.

96 See section 2.6.

3.6.1 The voluntary victim–offender meeting

The restorative justice process provides an opportunity for a voluntary meeting between victims and offenders, in which victims are able to ask questions, seek clarification, and informally express their feelings and emotions, while defendants accept and acknowledge their guilt or, at least, the wrongness of their acts.[97] Through the expression of emotions, both victims and offenders open up a forum for discussion, which addresses the offence, unsolved and, perhaps, undiscovered emotional consequences of the wrongdoing, and eventually develops a narrative for the healing of victims and the community at large.[98] Victims and offenders provide an account of the crime through the lens of a subjective narrative, using an emotional language, instead of the rational legal language.[99] However, this kind of meeting falls short of the symbolic element of a public trial, as victim-offender dialogue is not mediated through formal legal rules. Such encounters are not concerned with producing legal evidence that a crime occurred, they rather seek to reach a 'mutually satisfactory written restitution agreement'[100] between private participants. It is difficult to reconcile these specific features of the voluntary-based encounter with the nature of the trials at the ICC, which are a much more public affair, normatively built as an adversarial contest, constrained by rules of evidence, due process, and associated rights. Through the application of evidential rules, the adversarial format of the proceedings enables the Judges to identify the central action in the alleged crime; to make empirical connections between evidential elements based on that storyline; and then to interpret and evaluate those connections for consistency, completeness, and their collective implications for the central action.[101]

Most significantly, the ICC's Trial Chambers have limited the opportunities for a direct victim–offender encounter to take place, as very few victims have appeared in person in proceedings before the ICC. Common legal representation (CLR) has become a settled feature at the ICC, despite the fact that neither the RS nor the ICC Rules of Procedure and Evidence (RPE) considered it to be mandatory. In *Lubanga*, the Trial Chamber I decided that victims' views and concerns should have been presented through a joint presentation of views and

97 Brianne McGonigle Leyh, 'Victim-Oriented Measures at International Criminal Institutions: Participation and Its Pitfalls' (2012) 12 International Criminal Law Review 375, 380.

98 Clamp and Doak (n 94) 354.

99 Claire Garbett, 'The International Criminal Court and Restorative Justice: Victims, Participation and the Processes of Justice' (2017) 5 Restorative Justice 198, 204.

100 Paul McCold, 'The Recent History of Restorative Justice: Mediation, Circles, and Conferencing' in Dennis Sullivan and Larry Tifft, *Handbook of Restorative Justice. A Global Perspective* (Routledge 2006) 24.

101 Lance Bennet and Martha S Feldman, *Reconstructing Reality in the Courtroom: Justice and Judgement in American Culture* (Rutgers University Press 1981) 67.

concerns by joint legal representatives.[102] The Chamber's prerogative of setting groups of victims under legal teams has been confirmed in *Bemba*[103] and *Katanga and Chui*.[104] It can be said that the CLR has the task of condensing victims' personal interests into 'generalisable interests'.[105] The operation of the CLR conflicts with the emerging victims' role as active participants, sustained by restorative justice practices that supposedly prioritise direct participation in the process of all parties involved in the offence.[106]

3.6.2 The offender's acknowledgement of responsibility and apology

As previously illustrated,[107] the offender has to acknowledge his/her responsibility before the restorative process gets underway. The process of acknowledging responsibility entails, first, the offender's realisation of the full measure of his/her wrongdoing, as he/she must sincerely feel guilty, rather than formally admit his/her guilt. Defendants must apologise for their conduct, by providing an explicit manifestation and declaration of repentance and, lastly, they must express willingness to undertake steps to expiate their guilt.[108] However, in the experience of international criminal justice institutions, the expression of a fully accomplished acknowledgement of guilt and a sincere apology is rather unlikely to occur. The courtrooms of both the ICTY and ICTR have witnessed defendants who have not expressed any remorse because of their actions; instead, they showed indignation and anger for being indicted. For instance, in *Kambanda*, the defendant did not express any contrition, regret, or sympathy for the victims in Rwanda, even when given the opportunity to do so by the Chamber during the hearing of 3 September 1998.[109] Particularly symbolic is the trial of Slobodan Milošević, who showed neither signs of remorse nor attempted to apologise. Milošević, who died during his trial, appeared impassive to the atrocities inflicted on the

102 *Prosecutor v Thomas Lubanga Dyilo* (Decision on victims' participation) ICC-01/04–01/06, Trial Chamber I (18 January 2008), para 116.

103 *Prosecutor v Jean-Pierre Bemba Gombo* (Decision on common legal representation of victims for the purpose of trial) ICC-01/05–01/08, Trial Chamber III (11 November 2010), para 15; *Prosecutor v Jean-Pierre Bemba Gombo* (Corrigendum to Decision on the participation of victims in the trial and on 86 applications by victims to participate in the proceedings) ICC-01/05–01/08, Trial Chamber III (12 July 2010), para 27.

104 *Prosecutor v Germain Katanga and Mathieu Ngudjolo Chui* (Order on the organisation of common legal representation of victims) ICC-01/04–01/07, Trial Chamber II (22 July 2009), paras 10–11.

105 Sara Kendall and Sarah Nouwen, 'Representational Practices at the International Criminal Court: The Gap between Juridified and Abstract Victimhood' (2013) 76 Law and Contemporary Problems 235, 250.

106 For a comprehensive examination of victims' common legal representation at the ICC see section 8.8.

107 See section 2.6.

108 Stephen P Garvey, 'Restorative Justice, Punishment, and Atonement' (2003) 2003 Utah Law Review 303, 313.

109 *Prosecutor v Jean Kambanda* (n 30), para 51.

victims, while he strongly expressed his resentment for being indicted and constantly accused the tribunal of being the aggressor, presenting himself and the Serbians as the real victims.[110]

In only a few cases did the defendants admit their guilt, express profound regret and convincingly apologise for their wrongdoing.[111] At the ICC, the statement of admission of guilt by Ahmad Al Faqi Al Mahdi is an example of sincere acknowledgement of responsibility and apologies, which were unanimously accepted by the Trial Chamber.[112] Al Mahdi expressed his deepest sorrow for his actions, stating that:

> I am really sorry. I am really remorseful and I regret all the damage that my actions have caused. I regret what I have caused to my family, my community in Timbuktu, what I have caused my home nation, Mali, and I'm really remorseful about what I had caused the international community as a whole.[113]

A very common occurrence, instead, is the expression of what can be considered an insincere acknowledgement of responsibility. This is due to the practice of accepting statements of apology as a mitigating factor if they include expressions of sincere remorse for wrongdoing.[114] The jurisprudence of the ICTY has given an extremely broad interpretation of the legal definition of sincere remorse as a mitigating factor. In a few cases, a sincere expression of remorse did not require the admission of criminal responsibility or guilt, but only the defendant's acceptance of some measure of moral blameworthiness for personal wrongdoing.[115] In other cases, the Judges accepted as mitigating circumstances the expressions of

110 Oliver Diggelmann, 'International Criminal Tribunals and Reconciliation: Reflections on the Role of Remorse and Apology' (2016) 14 Journal of International Criminal Justice 1073, 1087.

111 *Prosecutor v Georges Ruggiu* (Judgement and Sentence) ICTR-97–32-I, Trial Chamber I (1 June 2000), paras 69–72; *Prosecutor v Tihomir Blaškić* (Judgement) IT-95–14-T, Trial Chamber (3 March 2000), para 775; *Prosecutor v Dražen Erdemović* (Sentencing Judgement) IT-96–22-T, Trial Chamber (29 November 1996), paras 96–98; *Prosecutor v Omar Serushago* (Sentence) ICTR-98–39-S, Trial Chamber I (5 February 1999), paras 40–41.

112 *Prosecutor v Ahmad Al Faqi Al Mahdi* (Judgement & Sentence) ICC-01/12–01/15, Trial Chamber VIII (27 September 2016), paras 9–10.

113 *Prosecutor v Ahmad Al Faqi Al Mahdi* (Trial hearing transcript) ICC-01/12–01/15, Trial Chamber VIII (22 August 2016) 8.

114 See e.g., *Prosecutor v Milan Simić* (Sentencing Judgement) IT-95–9/2-S, Trial Chamber II (17 October 2002), para 92; *Prosecutor v Dragan Obrenović* (Sentencing Judgement) IT-02–60/2-S, Trial Chamber I Section A (10 December 2003), para 121; *Prosecutor v Miroslav Kvočka et al* (Appeal Judgement) IT-98–30/1-A, Appeals Chamber (28 February 2005), para 715; *Prosecutor v Tihomir Blaškić* (Appeal Judgement) IT-95–14-A, Appeals Chamber (29 July 2004), paras 678, 696, 705; *Prosecutor v Stanislav Galić* (Trial Judgement) IT-98–29-T, Trial Chamber I (5 December 2003), para 579.

115 *Prosecutor v Mitar Vasiljević* (Appeal Judgement) IT-98–32-A, Appeals Chamber (25 February 2004), para 177.

remorse made by defendants who maintained their innocence.[116] Lastly, another strand of decisions by the ICTY and ICTR held that simple expressions of sympathy, compassion, or sorrow, which do not amount to remorse as such,[117] are sufficient to be qualified as mitigating circumstances.[118] Indeed, granting discounts for remorse and apology creates a strong incentive to deceive. A paradigmatic example of this phenomenon is the *Biljana Plavšić* case. During the trial, Mrs Plavšić pleaded guilty and released a statement in which she accepted her responsibility and expressed 'her remorse fully and unconditionally, Mrs Plavšić hopes to offer some consolation to the innocent victims – Muslim, Croat and Serb – of the war in Bosnia and Herzegovina'.[119] The ICTY, in the sentencing judgement, acknowledged that this step by Mrs Plavšić was 'undertaken under circumstances requiring considerable courage' and it represented 'an unprecedented contribution to the establishment of truth and a significant effort toward the advancement of reconciliation'.[120] The expression of remorse given in her guilty plea allowed Mrs Plavšić to receive a mild judgement, since the Court dropped the charge of genocide against her. However, several years later she retracted her statement of remorse, explicitly stating she still felt she had done nothing wrong.[121]

In *Karadžić*, the defendant's statements appeared calculated, carefully scripted, and exactly tailored in order to receive a milder sentence. In a Final Brief, the defendant:

116 *Prosecutor v Tihomir Blaškić* (n 111), para 775; *Prosecutor v Dragoljub Kunarac et al* (Trial Judgement) IT-96–23-T& IT-96–23/1-T, Trial Chamber (22 February 2000), para 869; *Prosecutor v Zejnil Delalić et al* (Trial Judgement) IT-96–21-T, Trial Chamber (16 November 1998), para 1279.

117 The *Oxford English Dictionary* defines remorse as 'a feeling of compunction, or of deep regret and repentance, for a sin or wrong committed'.

118 See e.g., *Prosecutor v Pavle Strugar* (Judgement) IT-01–42-A, Appeals Chamber (17 July 2008), para 366; *Prosecutor v Naser Orić* (Trial Judgement) IT-03–68-T, Trial Chamber II (30 June 2006), para 752; *Prosecutor v Milomir Stakić* (Trial Judgement) IT-97–24-T, Trial Chamber II (31 July 2003), para 992; *Prosecutor v Jean-Paul Akayesu* (Judgement) ICTR-96–4-T, Trial Chamber I (2 September 1998), para 45; *Prosecutor v Alfred Musema* (Appeal Judgement) ICTR-96–13-A, Appeals Chamber (16 November 2001), para 396.

119 ICTY Press Release, 'Statement on Behalf of Biljana Plavšić / Statement by Robert Pavich, Lead Counsel for Biljana Plavšić' (2 October 2002) <https://www.icty.org/en/press/statement-behalf-biljana-plavsic-statement-robert-pavich-lead-counsel-biljana-plavsic> accessed 2 October 2021.

120 *Prosecutor v Biljana Plavšić* (Sentencing Judgement) IT-00–39 & 40/1, Trial Chamber (27 February 2003), para 67.

121 Jelena Subotić, 'The Cruelty of False Remorse: Biljana Plavšić at the Hague' (2012) 36 Southeastern Europe 39, 48; Daniel Uggelberg Goldberg, 'Bosnian War Criminal: "I Did Nothing Wrong"' *The Local Sweden* (26 January 2009) <https://www.thelocal.se/20090126/17162> accessed 28 September 2021; Ian Traynor, 'Leading Bosnian Serb War Criminal Released from Swedish Prison' *The Guardian* (27 October 2009) <https://www.theguardian.com/world/2009/oct/27/bosnian-serb-war-criminal-freed> accessed 28 September 2021.

> expresses his deep regret and sympathy to the victims (…) and to their families. *Regardless of the issue of his individual criminal responsibility for those crimes* (emphasis added), he understands that as President of Republika Srpska, he bears moral responsibility for any crimes committed by citizens and forces of Republika Srpska.[122]

With this statement, Mr Karadžić apologised to the victims and expressed his regret and sympathy, but he did not admit his criminal responsibility or guilt. He only acknowledged he had moral blameworthiness for the conducts perpetrated by the Republika Srpska citizens, rather than for his actions. This is inconsistent with the restorative acknowledgement of the responsibility and apology process, which holds that the perpetrator has to acknowledge his/her culpability and then ask for forgiveness from the victims. In the restorative justice mechanisms, acknowledgement of responsibility and apology require sincerity and authenticity as the first step towards reconciliation. Conversely, the above-described cases revealed a remarkable gap between the dynamics of the trial in the tribunal's everyday work and the restorative practices, as the offenders failed to turn the corner from formal acknowledgement of their responsibility to a genuine experience of it. The difficulty in achieving a declaration of guilt and a sincere apology suggests that restorative justice might appear less than restorative. The level of restoration includes the degree to which the offenders are remorseful, aware of the impact of the crime on the victim, and spontaneously apologetic to the victim. The lack of a fully accomplished apology jeopardises the restoration process that should emerge in the relationship between the victim and the offender and requires a degree of empathic concern and perspective-talking.

3.6.3 Collaborative conflict-resolution approach

The collaborative conflict-resolution approach aims to achieve an agreement between the parties involved in the process, with regard to 'what should be done to achieve both material and emotional restoration'.[123] This approach does not provide any method of adjudication because restorative practices are participatory and consensually based, meaning that there is no Judge, only a facilitator, whose main function is to ensure that the victim–offender dialogue remains within the boundaries of mutual respect.[124] That said, it does not mean that the restorative process does not hold the offenders accountable, but the standard of restorative

122 *Prosecutor v Radovan Karadžić* (Public Redacted Version of Judgement Issued on 24 March 2016 Volume I of IV) IT-95-5/1, Trial Chamber (24 March 2016), para 6059.

123 Heather Strang, 'Conferencing and Victims' in Estelle Zinsstag and Inge Vanfraechem (eds.), *Conferencing and Restorative Justice: International Practices and Perspectives* (Oxford University Press 2012) 85.

124 Garvey (n 108) 314.

accountability needs offenders to acknowledge their culpability and willingness to amend for their wrongdoing.[125]

In the conflict-resolution approach, there should be no place for punitive measures, such as prison sentences.[126] Punishment is not imposed on the offender; conversely, amends arise from the accused themselves who accept the burden and recognise it as the price to be paid to expiate their guilt.[127] This view clashes with the Preamble of the RS, which, by affirming that 'the most serious crimes of concern to the international community as a whole must not go unpunished (...)',[128] demands that the ICC pursues justice through adjudication and punishment and not by means of an agreement made between victims and offenders. More specifically, the ICC Statute does not envisage any role for victims in the decision-making and sentencing process. The decision on the guilt or innocence of the defendant is issued through judgement by a Trial Chamber,[129] and, in case of a conviction, the determination of the appropriate sentence to be imposed on the convicted one is still a task of the Trial Chamber.[130] While a pure conflict-resolution approach seems reasonable for non-serious offences committed by young offenders,[131] moving towards such a paradigm in international criminal justice does not properly address the seriousness and heinousness of the large-scale violence perpetrated against civilians and communities. In the adversarial arena of the ICC, the visible punishment of perpetrators seems more likely to serve the interests of justice.

3.6.4 The healing and reconciliation outcome

The possibility of healing victims and affected societies through their participation at the ICC has been also discussed by the Court, which acknowledged the importance of understanding the devastating effect that crimes can have on victims and recognised that victims' participation in the justice process is one step on the road to healing, not only for individuals, but for affected societies as well.[132] However, neither the Strategy nor the Revised Strategy clarified how the judicial proceedings can effectively heal the individual and reunite splintered communities, given that, apart from setting objectives and principles, they do not develop

125 Miriam J Aukerman, 'Extraordinary Evil, Ordinary Crime: A Framework for Understanding Transitional Justice' (2002) 15 Harvard Human Rights Journal 39, 84.

126 See John Braithwaite, 'Restorative Justice' in Michael Tonry, *The Handbook of Crime and Punishment* (Oxford University Press 2000).

127 Garvey (n 108) 314.

128 Preamble, Rome Statute of the International Criminal Court.

129 Art. 74, ibid.

130 Art 76, ibid.

131 Andrew Ashworth, 'Victims' Rights, Defendants' Rights and Criminal Procedure' in Adam Crawford and Jo Goodey, *Integrating a Victim Perspective within Criminal Justice: International Debates* (Ashgate 2000) 193–194.

132 Assembly of States Parties, 'Report of the Court on the strategy in relation to victims' (n 45), paras 2, 10.

detailed approaches to victims' participation to be applied in the proceedings before the ICC.

At the level of individuals, the contention that there is a connection between victims' engagement in international criminal proceedings and their restoration is unverified so far, as little has been written about the cathartic and therapeutic experience of victims expressing their views and concerns before the ICC.[133] A remarkable study on the experience of victims as participants in international criminal trials and their views following such participation was conducted in the context of the trial of Kaing Guek Eav, better known as the *Duch* case, before the Extraordinary Chambers in the Courts of Cambodia (ECCC).[134] The study interviewed victim participants to examine how they perceived the participation in the trial, the work of the ECCC, and how it had affected them, if at all.[135] Generally, victims viewed the experience of participating and providing testimony positively, since 'the trial made them feel stronger mentally and increased their hopefulness about the future'.[136] However, when asked specifically whether or not the trial had an impact on forgiveness, reconciliation, and mental health, victims were more negative compared to the Cambodian population. Regarding forgiveness and reconciliation, victim participants were more negative than the general population about the trustworthiness of the defendant's apology and their readiness to reconcile with him/her after the trial. In more general terms, civil parties were more negative about the ECCC's contribution to reconciliation, rebuilding trust in Cambodia, and bringing justice to victims.[137] Considering the impact on mental health, the expected restorative effects of participation were not observed, as none of the victims described any cathartic or healing effect.[138] Victims were also less positive about the ability of the trial to help them accept the loss of loved ones and come to terms with the past.[139] Victims' participation in trials at the ECCC turned out to be of little help in contributing to the recovery of highly distressed victims. The context in which the ECCC operates, characterised by heinous and widespread crimes and an extremely violent social and institutional background where such atrocities occur, allows the building of a nexus with the participation of victims in proceedings before the ICC. The finding of this study casts doubts on the capacity of the ICC to effectively bring about therapeutic effects

133 Michael L Perlin, 'The Ladder of the Law Has No Top and No Bottom: How Therapeutic Jurisprudence Can Give Life to International Human Rights' (2014) 37 International Journal of Law and Psychiatry 535, 535; Dejo Olowu, 'Therapeutic Jurisprudence: An Inquiry into Its Significance for International Criminal Justice' (2007) 76 Revista Juridica Universidad de Puerto Rico 129, 130.

134 See Phuong N Pham et al., 'Victim Participation and the Trial of Duch at the Extraordinary Chambers in the Courts of Cambodia' (2011) 3 Journal of Human Rights Practice 264.

135 ibid 280.

136 ibid 281, 284.

137 ibid 282–283.

138 ibid 284.

139 ibid 282.

and beneficial outcomes in order to heal the harm and suffering experienced by victims. This suggests that the healing effect of international criminal proceedings for victims is not mandatory or a regular outcome, but, on the contrary, those effects are strictly individual and subject to variables that are difficult to foresee in advance.[140]

At the collective level, it is even more difficult to ascertain the extent to which the participation of the individual victim can contribute to the reconciliation and restoration of society.[141] In the aftermath of mass violence, societies are characterised by complex politicised issues and, at a basic level, prosecution can effectively remove public figures whose presence impedes reconciliation, but it is still questionable whether and how the ICC can undertake the ambitious task of providing social catharsis. The capacity of the restorative justice process to transform the relationship between victims, perpetrators, and society requires a close interaction between people responsible for such gross violations of human rights and their victims. Studies showed that the ICTY and ICTR, instead of being vehicles for public catharsis and promoting reconciliation, in some cases highlighted the contrasts within ethnically divided communities and confirmed existing biases. Akhavan reported that each Yugoslav ethnic group thought that the tribunal favoured the other and was biased against it.[142] Meernik observed that the effect of trials at the ICTY was quite the opposite of reconciliation for destabilised communities. In his study of the relationship between the trials at the ICTY and reconciliation, the author found that '[m]ore often than not, ethnic groups responded with increased hostility toward one another after an arrest or judgment'.[143]

Recently, the discussion about the reduction of Mr Lubanga's sentence[144] has given rise to issues concerning the effective contribution to peace and reconciliation of the judicial proceedings at the ICC. Consultations with victims, NGOs, community leaders, and activists illustrate that there was major disagreement about the impact on security and reconciliation of Mr Lubanga's possible resettlement in the Democratic Republic of Congo (DRC). Some expressed fear that Mr Lubanga's release from prison would undermine the peace process and destabilise the situation in the Ituri region, by reigniting tension between the commu-

140 Solange Mouthaan, 'Victim Participation at the ICC for Victims of Gender-Based Crimes: A Conflict of Interest' (2012) 21 Cardozo Journal of International and Comparative Law 619, 648.

141 Sergey Vasiliev, 'Victim Participation Revisited: What the ICC Is Learning About Itself' in Carsten Stahn, *The Law and Practice of the International Criminal Court* (Oxford University Press 2015) 65.

142 Payam Akhavan, 'Beyond Impunity: Can International Criminal Justice Prevent Future Atrocities?' (2001) 95 The American Journal of International Law 7, 16–17, 21–22.

143 James Meernik, 'Justice and Peace? How the International Criminal Tribunal Affects Societal Peace in Bosnia' (2005) 42 Journal of Peace Research 271, 287.

144 *Prosecutor v Thomas Lubanga Dyilo* (Decision on the review concerning reduction of sentence of Mr Thomas Lubanga Dyilo) ICC-01/04–01/06, Appeals Chamber (22 September 2015).

nities and fomenting reprisals for the victims.[145] Others argued that Mr Lubanga's release would contribute to reinforcing peace and consolidating reconciliation.[146] The different reactions to the prospect of Mr Lubanga being freed, which ranged from frustration and despair by victims to satisfaction by Lubanga's network, demonstrate that, in post-conflict societies, achieving reconciliation by a judicial process is a rather difficult task. In this scenario, the reconciliation and healing in the community dimension through international criminal proceedings are yet to be empirically verified.

3.6.5 Material restitution and symbolic reparation

Restoring victims and the wider community by reparation and compensation is a key feature of restorative justice. However, the ICC failed to impose a pecuniary condition on offenders to make right their wrongs, arguably undermining the restorative quality of the process to the greatest extent. The financial aspect of restoration is also affected by the selectivity. The selection of charges and victims admitted to participate operated by Judges, coupled with the limited amount of resources available for reparations, which can satisfy only a small number of victims, shows that the ICC falls short in addressing the reparative feature of the restorative paradigm.[147] In *Lubanga*, the Judges decided that the financial situation of the defendant exempted him from making any contributions to the Trust Fund for Victims (TFV).[148] Financial compensation for the harm suffered by the victims seeking reparation would be funded by the State's contributions to the Trust Fund, rather than by Mr Lubanga, who did not bear any of the financial cost. This contradicts the restorative justice paradigm, according to which the perpetrator has to offer reparation and restoration to those victimised and harmed by his/her wrongdoing.

Along with the more conventional means of material reparation, like proprietary and monetary measures, symbolic redress is widely considered to be a fundamental element of restorative justice,[149] particularly in those cases where the harm caused to victims is of a moral nature.[150] In the context of international crimes, material restoration may be unable to undo the effects of serious and

145 *Prosecutor v Thomas Lubanga Dyilo* (Observations of the V01 group of victims on the possible review of Mr Thomas Lubanga Dyilo's sentence) ICC-01/04–01/06, Appeals Chamber (10 July 2015), paras 11–13.

146 Massidda (n 7) 21.

147 Mouthaan (n 140) 649.

148 *Prosecutor v Thomas Lubanga Dyilo* (Decision on Sentence pursuant to Article 76 of the Statute) ICC-01/04–01/06, Trial Chamber I (10 July 10 2012), para 106.

149 See e.g., Howard Zehr and Bill Toews, *Critical Issues in Restorative Justice* (Criminal Justice Press 2004); Dennis Sullivan and Larry Tifft, *Restorative Justice: Healing the Foundations of Our Everyday Lives* (Willow Tree Press 2001); Susan Sharpe, 'The Idea of Reparation' in Gerry Johnstone and Daniel Van Ness, *Handbook of Restorative Justice* (Routledge 2013).

150 Clamp and Doak (n 94) 351.

traumatic events and rectify the harm caused to victims and societies.[151] Symbolic redress, therefore, can come into play to contribute to restoring victims' dignity and making it easier for them to cope with the multiple losses they suffered.[152] In this view, the TFV's Strategic Plan held that the concept of reparation is in no way limited to individual monetary or material compensation. It could also include symbolic forms of reparation, which, being focused on providing recognition of the injustices that have occurred, mark a major step towards healing and reconciliation.[153] In *Uhuru Muigai Kenyatta*, Judge Eboe-Osuji further develops the concept of symbolic reparation, by observing that the right to reparation for victims should be in step with developments in international law that lay great store on ensuring that restorative justice is delivered to the victims.[154] In this connection, an element of symbolic redress is satisfaction, which belongs to the stock list of what reparation has been accepted to mean in international law. The Judge draws on Principle 22 of the *Basic Principles and Guidelines on the Right to a Remedy and Reparation for Victims of Gross Violations of International Human Rights Law and Serious Violations of International Humanitarian Law* to explain that satisfaction includes: disclosure of the truth, verification of the facts, and a judicial decision restoring the dignity, reputation, and rights of victims.[155] Therefore, the value of satisfaction as a measure of reparation includes, among other things, the right of the victims to have their day in court to settle the truth to the extent possible.[156] In this vein, if proceedings at the ICC are understood to provide symbolic reparation, they should reasonably comprise both the recovery of facts, which relates to the victims' narration of the truth and harm suffered, and their clarification through the formal acknowledgement by the ICC of victims' experiences in the judgement rendered against the accused.

However, the ICC seems to be ineffective when addressing these features of symbolic redress for victims, as its focus remains on the proof of guilt rather than on truth-finding and acknowledgement of victims' experiences. For example, in *Lubanga*, the proceedings neither exhaustively recovered the truth of victims' harms through their truth-telling, nor did the outcome of the case adequately acknowledge the victims and their harm. The Trial Chamber limited the potential contribution of victims 'views and concerns' to the construction of the truth of the events under adjudication because, despite victims' claims, sexual violence was not included in the charges as forming an intrinsic part of the recruitment and use of child soldiers. The *Lubanga* trial provides an account of the actions

151 Naomi Roht-Arriaza, 'Reparations Decisions and Dilemmas' (2004) 27 Hastings International and Comparative Law Review 157, 159.

152 Mahmoud Cherif Bassiouni, 'International Recognition of Victims' Rights' (2006) 6 Human Rights Law Review 203, 231.

153 The Trust Fund for Victims, 'TFV Strategic Plan 2014–2017' (2014) 18.

154 *Prosecutor v Uhuru Muigai Kenyatta* (Dissenting Opinion of Judge Eboe-Osuji) ICC-01/09–02/11, Trial Chamber V(B) (27 November 2013), para 61.

155 ibid, para 61.

156 ibid, para 62.

of the accused, but it leaves the narrative of victims' harms and experiences in connection with sexual crimes outside the courtroom. Similarly, *Lubanga*'s sentencing judgement established the role and responsibility of the offender for the recruitment of child soldiers, but neither clarified nor validated the experiences of the victims of sexual violence, nor included any consideration of the effects of harm as victims understood and felt them.[157] If we follow the principle of symbolic redress as a fundamental element of restorative justice, the ICC should also function to recover and clarify the truth of the harm and experiences of victims. However, *Lubanga*'s judgement has represented the harmful act perpetrated against victims, but not the harm of the act itself experienced by victims. It appears questionable whether the ICC, by prohibiting victims from relating details about sexual violence, as this was not relevant to the charges of *Lubanga*, can live up to the promise of rendering a symbolic redress to victims.

3.7 Conclusion

International criminal justice institutions, like the ICTY, ICTR, and ICC, were established under the banner of retributive, deterrent, and restorative justice models, given that, according to their Statutes, their main goals and priorities are: ensuring effective prosecution, putting an end to impunity, preventing crimes, restoring peace, and promoting the process of national reconciliation. Nevertheless, it would be a mistake to downplay the issue of the suitability of those criminal justice theories, which have been developed to be implemented in domestic legal systems, to the context of mass atrocities in international law. The significant departures from domestic criminal law, namely the distinctive nature of 'community' and 'crimes' within the international criminal law field, demonstrate that matching the contrasting histories, assumptions, and paradigms of two different legal branches is particularly problematic. First, in domestic criminal law, the concept of community is clear as criminal law applies to the national community of a singular State, but in the scenario of international law such a concept is more ambiguous. Second, unlike domestic crimes, international crimes generally occur during wars or social breakdowns, such as ethnic conflicts, when basic norms against violence are undermined and gradually removed to the detriment of specific ethnic, political, religious, and national groups.

The foregoing observations call for greater attention to the impact that the specific features of international criminal law have on the existing theoretical framework on which international criminal justice institutions are based. The selectivity of prosecution, caused by financial constraints, political contingency, or simply by the decision to prosecute those cases where there was a better chance of getting a conviction, decrease the deterrent effect of punishment by lowering the chances of being punished or getting caught. But selectivity also undermines the imperative of retributivism that requires all persons deserving a punishment

157 *Prosecutor v Thomas Lubanga Dyilo* (Case Information Sheet) ICC-01/04–01/06.

to be punished. There is another factor that does not serve retribution, which is the lack of proportionality between the gravity of the offence and the severity of punishment. The punishment inflicted by the ICTY and ICTR has often been more modest than the punishment inflicted by domestic criminal courts and this reality has weakened the retributive aspirations of the international criminal justice system. Similarly, from the deterrent perspective, the lack of proportionality negatively influences the cost-benefit analysis undertaken by criminals because the benefits of the crime outweigh the seriousness of the punishment.

While the scholarly debate on the victim-based provisions of the RS has been marked by the contention that the ICC leans towards a restorative form of justice, this chapter has cast doubt on the pertinence of labelling the ICC as a restorative justice institution. Principles of restorative justice, like granting victims the opportunity to have their voices heard in the legal process, healing victims, repairing the harm done to them, and reconciliation of affected community, are reflected in the growing importance that participation in proceedings at the ICC plays in achieving justice for victims. However, the ICC does not align with the five core elements of restorative justice practices and their prioritisation of victims' participation because these elements, developed to address juvenile criminality, first-time offenders, and low-level crime, are not structured to operate in the particular context of the ICC, which is characterised by the grave harm caused to victims and communities by mass atrocity. Indeed, the introduction of victims' active participation in the proceedings in the ICC legal framework shows significant potential for providing new forms of justice to address and redress the harm suffered by victims; however, the attempt to clarify some of the key concepts underpinning the restorative justice process underlines the ICC's failure to set out clear parameters of its restorative function.

In conclusion, there is nothing to prevent the ICC from aspiring to the ideals of retributive, deterrent, or restorative justice; however, there is a range of objectives that criminal justice can fulfil in addition to the prosecution and punishment of individuals, significant as the latter may be. Indeed, given the particular context in which international criminal justice institutions exist, a broader and more diverse approach to the paradigm of international criminal justice may be desirable. The next chapter will discuss the critical need to reconceive and reformulate the criminal justice paradigm that underpins the international criminal justice system.

References

Books and journals

Akhavan P, 'Beyond Impunity: Can International Criminal Justice Prevent Future Atrocities?' (2001) 95 The American Journal of International Law 7

Alvarez JE, 'Trying Hussein: Between Hubris and Hegemony' (2004) 2 Journal of International Criminal Justice 319

Amann DM, 'Group Mentality, Expressivism, and Genocide' (2002) 2 International Criminal Law Review 93

Ashworth A, 'Victims' Rights, Defendants' Rights and Criminal Procedure' in Adam Crawford and Jo Goodey, *Integrating a Victim Perspective within Criminal Justice: International Debates* (Ashgate 2000)

Assembly of States Parties, 'Report of the Court on the strategy in relation to victims' (2009) ICC-ASP/8/45

Assembly of States Parties, 'Court's Revised Strategy in Relation to Victims' (2012) ICC-ASP/11/38 <https://asp.icc-cpi.int/iccdocs/asp_docs/ASP11/ICC-ASP-11-38-ENG.pdf> accessed 24 October 2021

Assembly of States Parties, 'Report of the Court on the Revised Strategy in Relation to Victims: Past, Present and Future' (2012) ICC-ASP/11/40

Assembly of States Parties, 'Report of the Court on the Implementation in 2013 of the Revised Strategy in Relation to Victims' (2013) ICC-ASP/12/41

Aukerman MJ, 'Extraordinary Evil, Ordinary Crime: A Framework for Understanding Transitional Justice' (2002) 15 Harvard Human Rights Journal 39

Bass GJ, *Stay the Hand of Vengeance: The Politics of War Crimes Tribunals*, vol 142 (Princeton University Press 2014)

Bassiouni MC, 'International Recognition of Victims' Rights' (2006) 6 Human Rights Law Review 203

Bennet L and Feldman MS, *Reconstructing Reality in the Courtroom: Justice and Judgment in American Culture* (Rutgers University Press 1981)

Beresford S, 'Unshackling the Paper Tiger – The Sentencing Practices of the Ad Hoc International Criminal Tribunals for the Former Yugoslavia and Rwanda' (2001) 1 International Criminal Law Review 33

Braithwaite J, 'Restorative Justice' in Michael Tonry, *The Handbook of Crime and Punishment* (Oxford University Press 2000)

Cahill MT, 'Retributive Justice in the Real World' (2007) 85 Washington University Law Review 815

Cassese A, 'Reflections on International Criminal Justice' (1998) 61 The Modern Law Review 1

Clamp K and Doak J, 'More than Words: Restorative Justice Concepts in Transitional Justice Settings' (2012) 12 International Criminal Law Review 339

Combs NA, *Guilty Pleas in International Criminal Law: Constructing a Restorative Justice Approach* (Stanford University Press 2007)

Cragg W, *The Practice of Punishment: Towards a Theory of Restorative Justice* (Routledge 1992)

Cryer R et al., *An Introduction to International Criminal Law and Procedure* (Cambridge University Press 2014)

Danieli Y, 'Massive Trauma and the Healing Role of Reparative Justice', in Carla Ferstman, Mariana Goetz and Alan Stephens (eds), *Reparations for Victims of Genocide, Crimes against Humanity and War Crimes: Systems in Place and Systems in the Making* (Martinus Nijhoff 2009)

de Gurmendi Fernández SA, 'International Criminal Court Today: Challenges and Opportunities' (2016) <https://www.icc-cpi.int/itemsDocuments/1600609-Helsinki-keynote-speech-ICC-President-Fernandez.pdf> accessed 2 October 2021

de Gurmendi Fernández SA and Friman H, 'The Rules of Procedure and Evidence of the International Criminal Court' (2000) 3 Yearbook of International Humanitarian Law 289

deGuzman M, 'Choosing to Prosecute: Expressive Selection at the International Criminal Court' (2012) 33 Michigan Journal of International Law 265

Dickingson LA, 'The Promise of Hybrid Courts' (2003) 97 American Journal of International Law 295
Diggelmann O, 'International Criminal Tribunals and Reconciliation: Reflections on the Role of Remorse and Apology' (2016) 14 Journal of International Criminal Justice 1073
Dingwall G and Hillier T, 'The Banality of Punishment: Context Specificity and Justifying Punishment of Extraordinary Crimes' (2010) 6 International Journal of Punishment and Sentencing 6
Doak J, 'The Therapeutic Dimension of Transitional Justice: Emotional Repair and Victim Satisfaction in International Trials and Truth Commissions' (2011) 11 International Criminal Law Review 263
Drumbl MA, 'Collective Violence and Individual Punishment: The Criminality of Mass Atrocity' (2005) 99 Northwestern University Law Review 539
Drumbl MA, *Atrocity, Punishment, and International Law* (Cambridge University Press 2007)
Dworkin R, *Freedom's Law: The Moral Reading of the American Constitution* (Oxford University Press 1999)
Findlay M and Henham R, *Transforming International Criminal Justice: Retributive and Restorative Justice in the Trial Process* (Routledge 2005)
Funk MT, *Victims' Rights and Advocacy at the International Criminal Court* (Oxford University Press 2015) <http://www.oxfordscholarship.com/view/10.1093/acprof:oso/9780199941469.001.0001/acprof-9780199941469> accessed 4 February 2019
Garbett C, 'From Passive Objects to Active Agents: A Comparative Study of Conceptions of Victim Identities at the ICTY and ICC' (2016) 15 Journal of Human Rights 40
Garbett C, 'The International Criminal Court and Restorative Justice: Victims, Participation and the Processes of Justice' (2017) 5 Restorative Justice 198
Garvey SP, 'Restorative Justice, Punishment, and Atonement' (2003) 2003 Utah Law Review 303
Goetz M, 'The International Criminal Court and Its Relevance to Affected Communities' in Nicholas Waddell and Phil Clark, *Courting Conflict? Justice, Peace and the ICC in Africa* (Crisis States Research Centre 2008)
Goldberg DU, 'Bosnian War Criminal: 'I Did Nothing Wrong'' *The Local Sweden* (26 January 2009) <https://www.thelocal.se/20090126/17162> accessed 28 September 2021
Guhr AH, 'Victim Participation During the Pre-Trial Stage at the International Criminal Court' (2008) 8 International Criminal Law Review 109
Haslam E, 'Victim Participation at the International Criminal Court: A Triumph of Hope Over Experience?' in Dominic McGoldrick, Peter Rowe and Eric Donnelly, *The Permanent International Criminal Court: Legal and Policy Issues* (Hart Publishing 2004)
Heikkilä M, *International Criminal Tribunals and Victims of Crime: A Study of the Status of Victims before International Criminal Tribunals and of Factors Affecting This Status* (Institute for Human Rights Åbo Akademi University 2004)
Hoyle C and Ullrich L, 'New Court, New Justice?' (2014) 12 Journal of International Criminal Justice 681
ICC Press Release, 'ICC President Tells World Parliamentary Conference "ICC Brings Retributive and Restorative Justice Together with the Prevention of Future

Crimes"' (11 December 2012) <https://www.icc-cpi.int/Pages/item.aspx?name=pr860> accessed 2 October 2021ICTY Press Release, 'Statement on Behalf of Biljana Plavšić / Statement by Robert Pavich, Lead Counsel for Biljana Plavšić' (2 October 2002) <https://www.icty.org/en/press/statement-behalf-biljana-plavsic-statement-robert-pavich-lead-counsel-biljana-plavsic> accessed 2 October 2021

Ignatieff M, *The Lesser Evil: Political Ethics in an Age of Terror* (Edinburgh University Press 2005)

Kendall S and Nouwen S, 'Representational Practices at the International Criminal Court: The Gap between Juridified and Abstract Victimhood' (2013) 76 Law and Contemporary Problems 235

Luban DJ, 'Fairness to Rightness: Jurisdiction, Legality, and the Legitimacy of International Criminal Law' [2008] Georgetown Public Law Research Paper No. 1154117 1

Luna E, 'Punishment Theory, Holism, and the Procedural Conception of Restorative Justice' (2003) 1 Utah Law Review 205

Malamud-Goti J, 'Transitional Governments in the Breach: Why Punish State Criminals?' (1990) 12 Human Rights Quarterly 1

Massidda P, 'Retributive and Restorative Justice for Victims and Reconciliation: Considerations on the Lubanga Case before the ICC' (2015) 1 Peace Processes Online Review 1

McCold P, 'The Recent History of Restorative Justice: Mediation, Circles, and Conferencing' in Dennis Sullivan and Larry Tifft, *Handbook of Restorative Justice. A Global Perspective* (Routledge 2006)

McGonigle Leyh B, *Procedural Justice? Victim Participation in International Criminal Proceedings* (Intersentia 2011)

McGonigle Leyh B, 'Victim-Oriented Measures at International Criminal Institutions: Participation and Its Pitfalls' (2012) 12 International Criminal Law Review 375

McKay F, 'Universal Jurisdiction in Europe: Criminal Prosecutions in Europe since 1990 for War Crimes, Crimes against Humanity, Torture and Genocide' (REDRESS 1999) <https://redress.org/wp-content/uploads/2018/01/G.-June-1999-Universal-Jurisdiction-in-Europe.pdf> accessed 21 January 2022

Meernik J, 'Justice and Peace? How the International Criminal Tribunal Affects Societal Peace in Bosnia' (2005) 42 Journal of Peace Research 271

Moffett L, *Justice for Victims before the International Criminal Court* (Routledge 2014)

Mouthaan S, 'Victim Participation at the ICC for Victims of Gender-Based Crimes: A Conflict of Interest' (2012) 21 Cardozo Journal of International and Comparative Law 619

Olásolo H, 'The Prosecutor of the ICC Before the Initiation of Investigations: A Quasi-Judicial or a Political Body?' (2003) 3 International Criminal Law Review 87

Olowu D, 'Therapeutic Jurisprudence: An Inquiry into Its Significance for International Criminal Justice' (2007) 76 Revista Juridica Universidad de Puerto Rico 129

Pena M and Carayon G, 'Is the ICC Making the Most of Victim Participation?' (2013) 7 International Journal of Transitional Justice 518

Perlin ML, 'The Ladder of the Law Has No Top and No Bottom: How Therapeutic Jurisprudence Can Give Life to International Human Rights' (2014) 37 International Journal of Law and Psychiatry 535

Pham PN et al., 'Victim Participation and the Trial of Duch at the Extraordinary Chambers in the Courts of Cambodia' (2011) 3 Journal of Human Rights Practice 264

Pillay N, 'Equal Justice for Women: A Personal Journey' (2008) 50 Arizona Law Review 657

Ratner SR, 'The Schizophrenias of International Criminal Law' (1998) 33 Texas International Law Journal 237

Rauschenbach M and Scalia D, 'Victims and International Criminal Justice: A Vexed Question?' (2008) 90 International Review of the Red Cross 441

Roht-Arriaza N, 'Reparations Decisions and Dilemmas' (2004) 27 Hastings International and Comparative Law Review 157

Sharpe S, 'The Idea of Reparation' in Gerry Johnstone and Daniel Van Ness, *Handbook of Restorative Justice* (Routledge 2013)

Sloane RD, 'The Expressive Capacity of International Punishment: The Limits of the National Law Analogy and the Potential of International Criminal Law' (2007) 43 Stanford Journal of International Law 39

Stahn C, 'International Criminal Justice and Reconciliation: Beyond the Retributive v. Restorative Divide' (2015) 36 FICHL Policy Brief Series

Strang H, 'Conferencing and Victims' in Estelle Zinsstag and Inge Vanfraechem, *Conferencing and Restorative Justice: International Practices and Perspectives* (Oxford University Press 2012)

Subotić J, 'The Cruelty of False Remorse: Biljana Plavšić at the Hague' (2012) 36 Southeastern Europe 39

Sullivan D and Tifft L, *Restorative Justice: Healing the Foundations of Our Everyday Lives* (Willow Tree Press 2001)

Tallgren I, 'The Sensibility and Sense of International Criminal Law' (2002) 13 European Journal of International Law 561

The Trust Fund for Victims, 'TFV Strategic Plan 2014–2017' (2014)

Traynor I, 'Leading Bosnian Serb War Criminal Released from Swedish Prison' *The Guardian* (27 October 2009) <https://www.theguardian.com/world/2009/oct/27/bosnian-serb-war-criminal-freed> accessed 28 September 2021

Turner JI, 'Legal Ethics in International Criminal Defense' (2010) 10 Chicago Journal of International Law 685

Vasiliev S, 'Victim Participation Revisited: What the ICC Is Learning About Itself' in Carsten Stahn, The Law and Practice of the International Criminal Court (Oxford University Press 2015)

von Hebel H, 'Remarks to the 15th Session of the Assembly of States Parties' (2016) <https://asp.icc-cpi.int/sites/asp/files/asp_docs/ASP15/ASP15-Opening-Statement-Registrar-ENG.pdf> accessed 2 October 2021

Wemmers J-A, 'Victims' Rights and the International Criminal Court: Perceptions within the Court Regarding the Victims' Right to Participate' (2010) 23 Leiden Journal of International Law 629

Zehr H and Toews B, *Critical Issues in Restorative Justice* (Criminal Justice Press 2004)

Cases

Prosecutor v Ahmad Al Faqi Al Mahdi (Trial hearing transcript) ICC-01/12-01/15, Trial Chamber VIII (22 August 2016)

Prosecutor v Ahmad Al Faqi Al Mahdi (Judgement & Sentence) ICC-01/12–01/15, Trial Chamber VIII (27 September 2016)
Prosecutor v Alfred Musema (Judgement and Sentence) ICTR-96–13-A, Trial Chamber I (27 January 2000)
Prosecutor v Alfred Musema (Appeal Judgement) ICTR-96–13-A, Appeals Chamber (16 November 2001)
Prosecutor v Biljana Plavšić (Sentencing Judgement) IT-00–39 & 40/1, Trial Chamber (27 February 2003)
Prosecutor v Bosco Ntaganda (Judgement on the Prosecutor's appeal against the decision of Pre-Trial Chamber I entitled 'Decision on the Prosecutor's Application for Warrants of Arrest, Article 58') ICC-01/04 169, Appeals Chamber (13 July 2006)
Prosecutor v Dragan Nikolić (Judgement on Sentencing Appeal) IT-94–2-A, Appeals Chamber (4 February 2005)
Prosecutor v Dragan Obrenović (Sentencing Judgement) IT-02–60/2-S, Trial Chamber I Section A (10 December 2003)
Prosecutor v Dragoljub Kunarac et al (Trial Judgement) IT-96–23-T& IT-96–23/1-T, Trial Chamber (22 February 2000)
Prosecutor v Dražen Erdemović (Sentencing Judgement) IT-96–22-T, Trial Chamber (29 November 1996)
Prosecutor v Duško Tadić (Judgement in Sentencing Appeals) IT-94–1-A and IT-94–1-Abis, Appeals Chamber (26 January 2000)
Prosecutor v Eliézer Niyitegeka (Judgement and Sentence) ICTR-96–14-T, Trial Chamber I (16 May 2003)
Prosecutor v Elizaphan and Gérard Ntakirutimana (Judgement and Sentence) ICTR-96–10 & ICTR-96–17-T, Trial Chamber I (21 February 2003)
Prosecutor v Emmanuel Ndindabahizi (Judgement and Sentence) ICTR-2001–71-I, Trial Chamber I (15 July 2004)
Prosecutor v Georges Ruggiu (Judgement and Sentence) ICTR-97–32-I, Trial Chamber I (1 June 2000)
Prosecutor v Georges Rutaganda (Judgement and Sentence) ICTR-96–3-T, Trial Chamber I (6 December 1999)
Prosecutor v Germain Katanga and Mathieu Ngudjolo Chui (Order on the organisation of common legal representation of victims) ICC-01/04–01/07, Trial Chamber II (22 July 2009)
Prosecutor v Jean Kambanda (Judgement and Sentence) ICTR-97–23-S, Trial Chamber I (4 September 1998)
Prosecutor v Jean-Paul Akayesu (Judgement) ICTR-96-4-T, Trial Chamber I (2 September 1998)
Prosecutor v Jean-Pierre Bemba Gombo (Decision on common legal representation of victims for the purpose of trial) ICC-01/05–01/08, Trial Chamber III (11 November 2010)
Prosecutor v Jean-Pierre Bemba Gombo (Corrigendum to Decision on the participation of victims in the trial and on 86 applications by victims to participate in the proceedings) ICC-01/05–01/08, Trial Chamber III (12 July 2010)
Prosecutor v Joseph Serugendo (Judgement and Sentence) ICTR-2005–84-I,Trial Chamber I (12 June 2006)
Prosecutor v Juvénal Kajelijeli (Judgement and Sentence) ICTR-98–44A-T, Trial Chamber II (1 December 2003)

Prosecutor v Laurent Semanza (Judgement and Sentence) ICTR-97–20-T, Trial Chamber III (15 May 2003)

Prosecutor v Milan Simić (Sentencing Judgement) IT-95–9/2-S, Trial Chamber II (17 October 2002)

Prosecutor v Milomir Stakić (Judgement) IT-97–24-T, Trial Chamber II (31 July 2003)

Prosecutor v Milomir Stakić (Trial Judgement) IT-97–24-T, Trial Chamber II (31 July 2003)

Prosecutor v Miroslav Kvočka et al (Appeal Judgement) IT-98–30/1-A, Appeals Chamber (28 February 2005)

Prosecutor v Mitar Vasiljević (Appeal Judgement) IT-98–32-A, Appeals Chamber (25 February 2004)

Prosecutor v Naser Orić (Trial Judgement) IT-03–68-T, Trial Chamber II (30 June 2006)

Prosecutor v Omar Serushago (Sentence) ICTR-98–39-S, Trial Chamber I (5 February 1999)

Prosecutor v Pavle Strugar (Judgement) IT-01–42-A, Appeals Chamber (17 July 2008)

Prosecutor v Radovan Karadžić (Public Redacted Version of Judgement Issued on 24 March 2016 Volume I of IV) IT-95–5/1, Trial Chamber (24 March 2016)

Prosecutor v Simon Bikindi (Appeals Chamber Judgement) ICTR-01–72-A, Appeals Chamber (18 March 2010)

Prosecutor v Stanislav Galić (Trial Judgement) IT-98–29-T, Trial Chamber I (5 December 2003)

Prosecutor v Thomas Lubanga Dyilo (Decision concerning Pre-Trial Chamber I's Decision of 10 February 2006 and the Incorporation of Documents into the Record of the Case against Mr Thomas Lubanga Dyilo) ICC-01/04–01/06, Pre-Trial Chamber I (24 February 2006)

Prosecutor v Thomas Lubanga Dyilo (Decision on the review concerning reduction of sentence of Mr Thomas Lubanga Dyilo) ICC-01/04–01/06, Appeals Chamber (22 September 2015)

Prosecutor v Thomas Lubanga Dyilo (Decision on victims' participation) ICC-01/04–01/06, Trial Chamber I (18 January 2008)

Prosecutor v Thomas Lubanga Dyilo (Observations of the V01 group of victims on the possible review of Mr Thomas Lubanga Dyilo's sentence) ICC-01/04–01/06, Appeals Chamber (10 July 2015)

Prosecutor v Thomas Lubanga Dyilo (Decision on Sentence pursuant to Article 76 of the Statute) ICC-01/04–01/06, Trial Chamber I (10 July 2012)

Prosecutor v Thomas Lubanga Dyilo (Case Information Sheet) ICC-01/04–01/06

Prosecutor v Tihomir Blaškić (Judgement) IT-95–14-T, Trial Chamber (3 March 2000)

Prosecutor v Tihomir Blaškić (Appeal Judgement) IT-95–14-A, Appeals Chamber (29 July 2004)

Prosecutor v Uhuru Muigai Kenyatta (Dissenting Opinion of Judge Eboe-Osuji) ICC-01/09–02/11, Trial Chamber V(B) (27 November 2013)

Prosecutor v Zdravko Mucić et al. (Judgement) IT-96–21-T, Trial Chamber (16 November 1998)

Prosecutor v Zdravko Mucić et al. (Judgement) IT-96–21-A, Appeals Chamber (20 February 2001)

Prosecutor v Zejnil Delalić et al (Trial Judgement) IT-96–21-T, Trial Chamber (16 November 1998)

Prosecutor v Zlatko Aleksovski (Judgement) IT-95–14/1-A, Appeals Chamber (24 March 2000)

Prosecutor v Zoran Kupreškić et al (Judgement) IT-95–16-T, Trial Chamber (14 January 2000)

Legislation

Geneva Convention for the Amelioration of the Condition of the Wounded and Sick in Armed Forces in the Field (First Geneva Convention) 1949 (75 UNTS 31)

Geneva Convention for the Amelioration of the Condition of Wounded, Sick and Shipwrecked Members of Armed Forces at Sea (Second Geneva Convention) 1949 (75 UNTS 85)

Geneva Convention Relative to the Protection of Civilian Persons in Time of War (Fourth Geneva Convention) 1949 (75 UNTS 287)

Geneva Convention Relative to the Treatment of Prisoners of War (Third Geneva Convention) 1949 (75 UNTS 135)

Rome Statute of the International Criminal Court 1998 (2187 UNTS 90)

4 Expressivism

A philosophical foundation for international criminal justice

4.1 Introduction

This chapter puts forward a potentially significant shift away from the manner in which international criminal justice has been conceptualised so far, as it advances the need to go beyond the confines of traditional criminal justice models. Chapter 3 illustrated international criminal trials should not be expected to be 'magical vessels of catharsis';[1] neither retribution nor deterrence is a fully adequate justification for international criminal justice. The present chapter builds on expressivist theories to provide a well-grounded philosophical foundation for international criminal justice, since one of the virtues of this justice model is its ability to explain and overcome some of the unique features, paradoxes, and limitations of international criminal law. This chapter discusses the nature and complexity of expressivism as it operates in national and international justice systems. The chapter introduces an outline of the contemporary expressivist discourse in criminal law, from its origins in the sociological theory of Durkheim to its modern application in the international criminal justice arena which is then examined. Specifically, the author looks at the branch of expressivism, which is not only concerned with the normative potential of criminal punishment, but also with the performative and communicative features of the adjudication process, paying attention to the didactic and storytelling functions that the international criminal trial can facilitate. It is important to highlight that retribution, deterrence, and restorative justice are not irrelevant as rationales for the action of international criminal justice. On the contrary, each of these theories remains a plausible justification largely because of the expressivist dimension of international criminal justice. With this in mind, the goal of the current chapter is to clarify the meaning of international criminal justice and to establish what goals it can and should realistically serve. An expressivist model of international criminal justice best captures the nature and priorities of international sentencing and its

1 Marc S Groenhuijsenme and Antony Pemberton, 'Genocide, Crimes against Humanity and War Crimes' in Rianne Letschert et al. (eds), *Victimological Approaches to International Crimes: Africa* (Intersentia 2011) 33.

DOI: 10.4324/9781003215448-4

potential to contribute to the goals ascribed to it, given the political and resource constraints that international criminal tribunals inevitably face.

4.2 Legal expressivism: between descriptive and normative claims

The expressivist model draws on several disciplines, including sociology, anthropology, philosophy, psychology, law, and economics.[2] Studies by Anderson and Pildes are essential to understand the core nature of expressivist theories. At the most general level, theories of expressivism 'tell actors – whether individuals, associations, or States – to act in ways that express appropriate attitudes toward various substantive values'.[3] After clarifying the nature of the term 'expression', defined as the ways an action, a declarative sentence, or a statement (speech or writing or any other vehicle of expression) manifests a cognitive state of mind (a belief, idea, theory, moods, emotions, attitudes, desires, intentions, or personality trait),[4] the authors engage with a discourse on how expressive theories figure in normative theories of conduct. Actions, by definition, express intentions, and therefore they always carry expressive meaning.[5] The normative expressivist theories of action should evaluate 'actions in terms of how well they express certain intentions, attitudes, or other mental states'.[6] In short, this theory, first, prescribes norms for regulating the adoption of certain mental states, and, secondly, requires actions and statements to express these states.

The main concern of normative expressivist theories of action is not only to reach certain ends, by prescribing or proscribing certain means (types of action), but also to establish whether or not performing act A for the sake of goal B expresses rational or morally right attitudes towards people.[7] Put more simply, expressivism acknowledges that a harmful message in itself causes harm and a good message causes good, but it does not determine what is good or bad. It is society that has to evaluate whether an action is good or bad,[8] by interpreting the way in which such action is in keeping with the practices of the community and other relevant norms. In this sense, the meaning of an action is socially constructed because it relies on the values of society. However, expressivist theorists

2 Diane Marie Amann, 'Group Mentality, Expressivism, and Genocide' (2002) 2 International Criminal Law Review 93, 118; Alan Strudler, 'The Power of Expressive Theories of Law' (2001) 3 Maryland Law Review 60 492, 492.
3 Elizabeth S Anderson and Richard H Pildes, 'Expressive Theories of Law: A General Restatement' (2000) 148 University of Pennsylvania Law Review 1503, 1503.
4 ibid 1506.
5 ibid 1508; Cass R Sunstein, 'On the Expressive Function of Law' (1996) 144 University of Pennsylvania Law Review 2021, 2021.
6 Anderson and Pildes (n 3) 1508.
7 ibid 1509.
8 Amann (n 2) 119.

do not mean that the social meaning of actions is definitive.[9] Expressivist thinkers rather acknowledge a degree of dynamism in societal norms, as they are not seen as static, but, conversely, they undergo constant change.[10] Therefore, the societal interpretation has to take into consideration the full context in which a norm is adopted, including the community practices, its shared values, and its history.[11]

The application of normative expressivist theories of conduct to the legal field posits that by manifesting beliefs, attitudes, and intentions the law, like other forms of expression, has a social meaning.[12] The identification of the social meaning of the law comes from the ways in which a community interprets and understands the law in the context of the existing social norms, in other words, it originates from the message communities get from the law.[13] Expressivism conceives law as reflecting the values of a specific society, what norms should be esteemed, and what norms should be abhorred.[14] According to this understanding, expressivism emphasises that the law triggers a communicative process, working 'by what it says in addition to what it does'.[15]

The expressivist approach to the function of the law is somewhat heterogeneous. Matthew Edwards distinguishes two branches of expressivism, which he respectively defines as revelatory and instrumental. The former affirms that the law, by expressing fundamentally normative commitments to certain pre-existing political, moral, or constitutional norms, represents only the dominant moral attitude in society.[16] The latter, instrumental expressivism, evaluates what regulatory choices can trigger desired changes in norms, social meanings, and behaviour.[17] Additionally, within the branch of instrumental expressivism, a distinction should be made between its descriptive and normative claims. The descriptive claim posits that the law can be used to transform moral attitudes in society,[18]

9 Anderson and Pildes (n 3) 1525.

10 ibid 1539, 1568; Dan M Kahan, 'The Secret Ambition of Deterrence' (1999) 113 Harvard Law Review 413, 486.

11 Anderson and Pildes (n 3) 1525.

12 ibid 1504–1505; Sunstein (n 5) 2021–2022; Amann (n 2)118–119; Margaret deGuzman, 'Choosing to Prosecute: Expressive Selection at the International Criminal Court' (2012) Michigan Journal of International Law 265, 312–313.

13 Diane Marie Amann, 'Message as Medium in Sierra Leone' (2000b) 7 ILSA Journal of International and Comparative Law 237, 238; deGuzman (n 12) 313; Sunstein (n 5) 2022–2024; Mark A Drumbl, 'Collective Violence and Individual Punishment: The Criminality of Mass Atrocity' (2005) 99 Northwestern University Law Review 539, 592.

14 Amann (n 2) 118.

15 Mark Van Hoecke, *Law as Communication* (Bloomsbury Publishing 2002) 10; Richard H McAdams, 'A Focal Point Theory of Expressive Law' (2000) 86 Virginia Law Review 1649, 1649–729, 1650–1.

16 Marlies Glasius and Tim Meijers, 'Expression of Justice or Political Trial? Discursive Battles in the Karadžić Case' (2013) 35 Human Rights Quarterly 720, 724; Matthew A Edwards, 'Legal Expressivism: A Primer' (2009) Social Science Research Network 24 <https://ssrn.com/abstract=1361101> accessed 19 June 2021.

17 Edwards (n 16) 6.

18 Anderson and Pildes (n 3) 1525.

while, according to the normative claim, transforming moral attitudes in society should be the function of the law.[19]

4.3 Expressivism and criminal law

Criminal law has been associated with the normative claim of instrumental expressivism because of its ability to transmit values and change attitudes.[20] Criminal law is a particularly strong form of expression of messages about moral or legal wrongdoing, serving as 'an articulation of the appropriate reaction to criminal act on the part of a society'.[21] Criminal law sets norms, which reflect the values of society, establishes authority over citizens, calls for law-abiding behaviour,[22] and condemns the breaches of those norms.[23] As Günther argues, criminal law is not 'detached from the real interests of individual citizens, but the result of a public deliberation about interests',[24] which seeks to influence the behaviour of individuals and speak to the members of the normative community. It would be simplistic to see the crime only as a natural act, entailing material and mental elements; it rather represents a social act which carries a specific meaning,[25] which can be understood as 'a violation of legally protected interests or goods, a harm to others which is legally prohibited'.[26]

In this view, the normative claim underlying instrumental expressivism can hold a greater importance within the international criminal justice system. International criminal tribunals should seek to provide beneficial effects to societies in transition[27] and, therefore, their normative agenda should interpret and apply the law to express a valued social message and, consequently, operate as mechanisms for altering social norms.[28]

19 Glasius and Meijers, 'Expression of Justice or Political Trial?' (n 16) 724; Sunstein (n 5) 2021; Fiona O'Regan, 'Prosecutor vs. Jean-Pierre Bemba Gombo: The Cumulative Charging Principle, Gender-Based Violence, and Expressivism' (2011) 43 Georgetown Journal of International Law 1323, 1352.

20 Kirsten J Fisher, *Moral Accountability and International Criminal Law: Holding Agents of Atrocity Accountable to the World* (Routledge 2013) 59.

21 Larry May and Shannon Fyfe, *International Criminal Tribunals: A Normative Defense* (Cambridge University Press 2017) 51.

22 Sunstein (n 5) 2021.

23 Drumbl (n 13) 592; Amann (n 2) 118,120.

24 Klaus Günther, 'Criminal Law, Crime and Punishment as Communication' 14 <https://d-nb.info/1054399557/34> accessed 20 June 2021.

25 Georg Friedrich Hegel, *Elements of the Philosophy of Right* (Allen W Wood ed, Hugh Barr Nisbet tr, Cambridge University Press 1991) 126.

26 Günther (n 24) 8.

27 Glasius and Meijers, 'Expression of Justice or Political Trial?' (n 16) 724.

28 deGuzman (n 12) 313.

4.4 The expressivist objective of punishment

The foundations for the theory of the expressivist function of criminal justice can be traced to the work of Emile Durkheim. He was one of the first thinkers that conceived punishment as a form of social expression, rather than just a display of State control. Durkheim's central claim in relation to the role of punishment has been developed from the concept of collective conscience, which represents a set of collective beliefs that can be found in all healthy individuals of a given society, as the basis for social cohesion.[29] A conduct does not shock the common conscience because it is criminal *per se*, but rather because its commission contradicts the deeply rooted and defined collective conscience. According to Durkheim, the evil nature of the crime lies in its attack on the collective belief and sentiment of a given society. Repression of crime constitutes an instrument to react to the destructive effects on common beliefs, by reaffirming social solidarity.[30] Punishment is a 'passionate reaction of graduate intensity', which indicates that the conscience of the collectivity is not changed regardless of the choice of the offender to diverge from it.[31] Thus, punishment is a tool through which a society of law-abiders disapproves and condemns deviant criminals and asserts what cannot be tolerated. In Durkheim's theory, punishment does not serve primarily to correct the culprit or to deter potential followers. Punishment's authentic function is to keep social cohesion unbroken and, consequently, to maintain a reactive common conscience.[32] The lack of reaction from the community would result in a breakdown of social solidarity. The only way to affirm the common conscience of society is to express the unanimous aversion that society has for crimes, by means of infliction of suffering upon the criminal.[33] The originality of Durkheim's work lies in the fact that his idea of punishment is more focused on the message and social meaning of punishment and less on the offender. He stressed the value of punishment as a reflection of the will of society 'to manifest itself to itself',[34] to promote the formation of a universal social solidarity.[35]

In contemporary criminal law scholarship, expressivism has gained momentum as a means of going beyond the traditional accounts of criminal justice, which seek to justify punishment either by focusing on the wrongfulness of the crime and emphasising punishment as perpetrators' just deserts (e.g., retribution) or by focusing on the future benefits that punishment can produce, such as specific and

29 Émile Durkheim, *The Division of Labour in Society* (Wilfred Douglas Halls trs, Macmillan 1984) 80.

30 Carsten Stahn, *Justice as Message: Expressivist Foundations of International Criminal Justice* (1st edn, Oxford University Press 2020) 26.

31 ibid 97–98.

32 ibid 84.

33 ibid.

34 Frédéric Mégret, 'Practices of Stigmatization' (2013) 76 Law and Contemporary Problems 287, 290.

35 David Garland, 'Sociological Perspectives on Punishment' (1991) 14 Crime and Justice 115, 125.

general deterrence, rehabilitation, and incapacitation (e.g., utilitarian theories). A number of theorists built on Durkheim's work to mitigate both approaches to the justification for punishment and emphasise its meaning and communicative dimensions, rather than its effect on retribution and crime prevention.

4.4.1 Punishment as norm expression

Several scholars justified punishment from a sociological standpoint. Garland argued the expressive value of punishment is embodied in its ability to capture the social identity of a community.[36] Such a view recognised that punishment does not derive its justification only from the wrongdoing and/or the threat of enforcement of sentences, but also from certain beneficial effects, such as norm expression. Jakobs, who advanced a communicative model of criminal justice, saw punishment as a demonstration of norm affirmation. Punishment carries an expressive function by demonstrating that society responds to the expectation to maintain and enforce norms. At the same time, punishment has a preventive function by reminding the offender and fellow citizens of the duty to abide by the law as members of society. Norm expression is inherent in punishment, since its expression of rejection of the attack on the validity of social norms is a consequence of punishment and not its goal.[37] Similarly, Mark Drumbl affirmed that the focus of expressivism is on the way punishment embodies and strengthens social norms and encourages a law-abiding attitude.[38] Punishment is considered to be a response to the wrongful expression inherent in the criminal conduct.[39]

4.4.2 Punishment as expression of censure

Another expressivist justification of punishment is the expression of censure. This account merges retributive and deterrent elements, as it holds that the justification for punishment should be related to censure rationales with respect to offenders and related to broader preventive arguments with reference to society.[40] The sanction is not only an enactment of the argument of 'just desert', it becomes a means of expressing censure and condemnation to the offender.[41] Particularly relevant to this understanding of punishment is the work of Hirsh, who looked at punishment as a primary form of expression of censure.[42] He acknowledged that

36 David Garland, *Punishment and Modern Society: A Study in Social Theory* (University of Chicago Press 1990) 287.
37 Stahn (n 30) 35.
38 Mark A Drumbl, *Atrocity, Punishment, and International Law* (Cambridge University Press 2007a) 174.
39 deGuzman (n 12) 313.
40 Stahn (n 30) 36. 6
41 Robert Nozick, *Philosophical Explanations* (Harvard University Press 1981) 363–364.
42 Awol Kassim Allo, 'The "Show" in the Show Trials: Contextualizing the Politicization of the Courtroom' (2010) 15 Barry Law Review 41, 41.

censure involves the expression of reprobation of crime and an acknowledgement of the harm caused by the perpetrator directed at the offender, victims, and the society as a third party.[43] The censure-based approach to punishment, by presenting crime as morally wrong, gives the general public reasons to avoid such conduct to.

Hirsh's reasoning was further developed in a number of works that upheld the concept of punishment as expression of censure. Sloane and deGuzman understood punishment as a social institution because the conviction of the defendant does not only mean that he/she is subjected to punishment, it also conveys a formal and public message of censure of the wrongdoing, educates society about the unacceptable nature of the actions condemned, demonstrates societal intolerance and stigmatisation of certain forms of conduct, and, ultimately, reaffirms the community's common identities.[44]

The point of punishment as expression of censure was also made by Feinberg. In his seminal *The Expressive Function of Punishment*, he argues that:

> punishment is a conventional device for the expression of attitudes of resentment and indignation, and of judgments of disapproval and reprobation, on the part either of the punishing authority himself or of those 'in whose name' the punishment is inflicted. Punishment, in short, has a *symbolic significance* largely missing from other kinds of penalties.[45]

Feinberg identifies four functions in the expressivist account of punishment. First, punishment of a criminal allows the expression of an authoritative disavowal and condemnation of the criminal conduct.[46] As such, on the one hand, punishment affirms that the criminal did not have any right to commit the criminal action and, on the other hand, represents the recognition of the violated rights.[47] Secondly, punishment also indicates a symbolic non-acquiescence to crime. Thirdly, punishment vindicates the law and encourages law-abiding behaviour.[48] Finally, when the perpetrator is part of a group, by punishing the guilty individual, the others are absolved.[49]

43 Stahn (n 30) 37.

44 Robert D Sloane, 'The Expressive Capacity of International Punishment: The Limits of the National Law Analogy and the Potential of International Criminal Law' (2007) 43 Stanford Journal of International Law 39, 71; Robert Cryer et al., *An Introduction to International Criminal Law and Procedure* (Cambridge University Press 2014) 23; Saira Mohamed, 'Deviance, Aspiration, and the Stories We Tell: Reconciling Mass Atrocity and the Criminal Law' (2015) 124 Yale Law Journal 1628, 1670.

45 Joel Feinberg, *Doing and Deserving: Essays in the Theory of Responsibility* (Princeton University Press 1970) 98.

46 ibid 101.

47 ibid 102.

48 ibid 102–104.

49 ibid 105.

It has been observed that Feinberg's four dimensions of punishment are linked to the criminal sentence and the trial as a process, but fail to offer a full explanation of the value of expressivism in relation to the punishment of the offender.[50] Feinberg's reasoning seemed to suggest that alternative ways of condemnation other than criminal punishment can effectively entail expressions of censure. An answer to this issue is provided by Anderson and Pildes, who explained how condemnation without punishment would have a reduced censure expression effect. They suppose the case of a defendant who is convicted for a heinous crime. The Judge, while sentencing, declares that the defendant's crime is horrific and wrong and that the State condemns him for it, but then he releases the convict without punishment. Society would feel outraged and would think that the Judge did not really mean what he said. A meaningful condemnation requires not simply 'a mere utterance, even in the form of a stern lecture from the bench, but a practice of punishment socially understood to express condemnation effectively (...)'.[51] Punishment is not meted out simply and only to inflict suffering on the perpetrator, to achieve deterrence, and to require the criminal to pay his/her debt to society.[52] On the same topic, Primoratz maintained that 'merely verbal condemnation is not likely to reach its immediate addressee [the criminal] and to be fully understood by him'.[53] If the expression of censure and condemnation is meant to reach the criminals and provide an understanding of the wrongfulness of their actions, it is necessary to use a language that criminals understand. In this regard, punishment translates the expression of censure 'into the one and only language they understand'.[54]

4.5 An expressivist model of international criminal justice

Providing a coherent theoretical basis for punishment in international criminal justice has proved to be highly problematic. Research on the application of retributive and utilitarian criminal law models in the context of international criminal justice indicates that there is a gap between practices of criminal prosecution and punishment and their assumed penological goals.[55] Expressivism balances out the limits met by traditional justice theories when dealing with the unique features of international criminal justice. The most valuable merit of expressivism lies in its ability to provide a justification for international criminal justice based on punishment as a communicative institution intended to affirm

50 Igor Primoratz, 'Punishment as Language' (1989) 64 Philosophy 187, 201–202; Barrie Sander, 'Justifying International Criminal Punishment: A Critical Perspective' in Morten Bergsmo and Emiliano J Buis (eds), *Philosophical Foundations of International Criminal Law: Foundational Concepts* (Torkel Opsahl Academic EPublisher 2019) 196.

51 Anderson and Pildes (n 3) 1567.

52 Sloane (n 44) 70.

53 Primoratz (n 50) 200.

54 ibid.

55 See Chapter 3.

societal norms and convey messages of censure to the offender and community at large. Expressivist theories capture the different meanings that accountability and punishment gain in the particular context of social conflicts where mass atrocities occur, which relate in some ways to the future of the affected societies, including democratic reform, societal reconciliation, search for truth, and restoration of the rights of victims. The strikingly heinous nature of crimes international criminal justice adjudicate, as well as the collective character in terms of perpetration and victimisation, and the fact that often these crimes are perpetrated during armed conflicts by governments against their own populations, firmly urge expressions of condemnation, especially because those crimes had historically been tolerated by the international community.[56] International crimes are not adjudicated for the crime's sake, but to affirm that 'their commission contradicts our deeply held believes'.[57] Echoing Durkheim, Wise posits that the role of punishment as a particularly vivid symbol of the existence of a real community applies with particular force to the RS of the ICC, which reflects the idea of an international criminal justice institution serving as a community-creating and community-maintaining device.[58] The engagement in the rituals of reprobation that punishment represents is the most striking possible way for the ICC to say that 'peoples united by common bonds, their cultures pieced together in a shared heritage'[59] are indeed a cohesive community, held together by feelings of social solidarity and a sense that everyone is a law-abiding citizen.[60] Sloan defended that punishment for perpetrators of gross violation of human rights aims to peremptorily repudiate such conduct, to symbolically reject the acquiescence of the international community to those crimes, to vindicate international human rights, and to absolve ethnic or national communities, as collectives, from guilt by punishing individual perpetrators.[61]

A thorough appreciation of how the expressivist account of punishment can represent an approach that better responds to the nature and goals of international criminal justice calls for an understanding of the place of expressivism in relation to retributivism and deterrence. Expressivism can transcend retributivism and deterrence by focusing on the inherent value of norm expression, but it can also supplement those paradigms.[62] Expressivism and retributivism share the idea that the punishment of perpetrators is the consequence of the crime they committed. However, while retributivism, being focused on the infliction of the 'just desert'

56 deGuzman (n 12) 316.
57 Mégret (n 34) 289.
58 Edward M Wise, 'The International Criminal Court: A Budget of Paradoxes' (2000) 8 Tulane Journal of International and Comparative Law 261, 267.
59 Rome Statute of the International Criminal Court (opened for signature 17 July 1998, entered into force 1 July 2002) 2187 UNTS 90, Preamble.
60 Wise (n 58) 267–268.
61 Sloane (n 44) 71.
62 Margaret deGuzman, 'Giving Priority to Sex Crime Prosecutions: The Philosophical Foundations of a Feminist Agenda' (2011) 11 International Criminal Law Review 515, 525.

on the offender, struggles to mete out a punishment which is proportionate to the extraordinary gravity of the international crimes, expressivism is less focused on this aspect. Instead it emphasises that the perpetrator deserves to be punished when his/her conduct convey disrespect for important values.[63] Punishment is a necessary societal reaction to crime, serving to express objection and legal condemnation as a response to crime. D'Ascoli relates punishment to the expression of disapproval and condemnation to the offender, as well as to encouragement of States to take responsibility to protect human rights.[64] In this view, punishment not only speaks to the offender, but to the international community at large.[65] The objective of punishment, rather than being based on the calculation of proportional penalties, should be to highlight 'the visibility and symbolic power of international criminal justice as a value of its own'.[66]

Duff has developed an account of punishment based on its communicative nature towards the offender. He stressed that punishment involves not only norm expression and censure, but also conveys messages about individual wrongdoing and responsibility allocation with the objective of influencing and fostering the perpetrator's understanding of the gravity of their actions.[67] Duff's main point is that punishment is an act of communication to the offenders, through which they can experience the norm violations and take responsibility for their conduct.[68] However, as Golash has observed, the capacity of international punishment to convey such a message to offenders depends on their acknowledgement of the legitimacy and moral authority of international criminal institutions, which many high-level perpetrators fail to recognise.[69]

Expressivist and consequentialist theories are often invoked in conjunction,[70] as they both seek to discourage future criminals, but they operate differently. Deterrence is principally focused on prescribing any means which can produce the best results.[71] In other words, deterrence targets those individuals who may

63 ibid.
64 Silvia D'Ascoli, *Sentencing in International Criminal Law: The UN Ad Hoc Tribunals and Future Perspectives for the ICC* (Bloomsbury Publishing 2011) 298.
65 Rosa Aloisi and James Meernik, *Judgment Day: Judicial Decision Making at the International Criminal Tribunals* (Cambridge University Press 2017) 167–168.
66 Harmen van der Wilt, 'Why International Criminal Lawyers Should Read Mirjan Damaška', in Carsten Stahn and Larissa van den Herik (eds), *Future Perspectives on International Criminal Justice* (TMC Asser Press 2010) 55.
67 Antony Duff, 'Penance, Punishment and the Limits of Community' (2003) 5 Punishment & Society 295, 301–302.
68 Antony Duff, *Punishment, Communication, and Community* (Oxford University Press 2011) 106.
69 Deirdre Golash, 'The Justification of Punishment in the International Context' in Larry May and Zachary Hoskins (eds), *International Criminal Law and Philosophy* (Cambridge University Press 2010) 200–201.
70 Kai Ambos, *Treatise on International Criminal Law: Vol. I: Foundations and General Part* (Oxford University Press 2013) 71.
71 Anderson and Pildes (n 3) 1511.

commit a crime in the near future and tries to dissuade them from doing so for fear of being caught and the threat of punishment. Expressivism, instead, is interested in evaluating a justification for the means-end connection encompassing two dimensions of deterrence, mainly 'negative general prevention' aimed at deterring potential offenders from committing crimes and 'positive general prevention' focused on reaffirming the validity of agreed norms and prompting law-abiding individuals to conform to them.[72] With regard to the aspect of 'negative general prevention', international criminal justice can intimidate potential offenders not only by threatening a punishment (as the deterrent approach does), but also by the expression of the moral condemnation of society.[73] According to Kahan, the engagement with past behaviour can influence future attitudes, as 'the law can discourage criminality not just by "raising the cost" of such behaviour through punishments, but also through instilling aversions to the kinds of behaviour that the law prohibits'.[74] As remarked by Stahn, this reasoning, which conceives 'negative general prevention' as a consequence rather than a goal of international criminal justice, avoids some of the pitfalls of deterrence. The fact that, so far, international criminal justice has largely failed to deter the commission of crimes should not undermine the normative function of expressivism, which aims to form and reinforce social perceptions and norms, by serving as a symbolic affirmation that repudiates criminal conduct, rejects the acquiescence of the international community, and vindicates human rights.[75]

The expressivist account of punishment is closely linked to 'positive general prevention'. Demko affirms that '[i]nternational punishment expresses with great symbolism and emphasis, and with the communicative inclusion of the elements of positive affirmative general prevention, that no human being is above the law (...).[76] Specifically, expressivism helps to explain how 'positive general prevention' operates. International criminal justice is intended to speak mainly to those individuals who are not yet in the position of committing a crime but may do so in the near future. Expressivism can serve as an intergenerational approach, as the message conveyed by the punishment can speak to those not yet assimilated in the mechanism of mass violence and prevent the indoctrination phase. In the context of international criminal justice, it can be more difficult to deter violence once it is imminent or has already started, so it seems somewhat more tenable to decelerate indoctrination of hate-mongering rhetoric and build up a social

72 Stahn (n 30) 336.
73 deGuzman (n 62) 525.
74 Dan M Kahan, 'What Do Alternative Sanctions Mean?' (1996) 63 The University of Chicago Law Review 591, 603.
75 van der Wilt (n 66) 55; Wise (n 58) 267.
76 Daniela Demko, 'An Expressive Theory of International Punishment for International Crimes' in Florian Jessberger and Julia Geneuss (eds), *Why Punish Perpetrators of Mass Atrocities?* (Cambridge University Press 2020) 184–185.

consensus regarding the moral unacceptability of mass violence. In this sense, punishment operates as a moral educator.[77]

Moreover, 'positive general prevention' can work as a process of norm expression by fostering society's internalisation and support of norms as well as moral and legal values, such as those advocated in international human rights and humanitarian law.[78] This can potentially lead to a decrease in international crimes because of the demands and incentives for individuals to display a positive attitude towards norm-abiding behaviour, mainly by demonstrating disobedience or resistance to international crimes.[79]

These features of expressivist punishment call for a shift in the centre of gravity of international criminal justice from punishment to the trial. Luban identifies a distinctive role for criminal trials, as a continuation of the purposes of criminal punishment, but is not reducible to it. Trials do not only aim to identify those who deserve to be punished they also have an independent, non-instrumental significance, which is best captured by the norm expression function of the criminal trial.[80]

4.6 The expressivist value of international criminal trials

The work of Mark Osiel has been (and still is) fundamental to developing an understanding of the expressivist feature of the legal processes (in particular criminal trials) during times of transition. Whereas Durkheim's principal philosophical inquiry focused on understanding the sources of solidarity in modern society, which he believed was threatened by the rise of individualism, the specialisation of labour, and the decline of universal religion,[81] Osiel attempted to adjust Durkheimian theories to circumstances when a State commits mass atrocities against its own citizens. In his work on the national post-conflict trials, including on the Eichmann trial (1961) and the Argentinian military trial in the 1980s, Osiel argues that prosecuting wrongdoers is a central strategy for rebuilding social values that mass violence has destroyed.[82] However, he rejects the Durkheimian view that trials facilitate collective memory and social solidarity

77 Mark A Drumbl, 'The Expressive Value of Prosecuting and Punishing Terrorists: Hamdan, the Geneva Conventions, and International Criminal Law' (2007b) 75 The George Washington Law Review 1165, 1183–1184.

78 Sloane (n 44) 44.

79 van der Wilt (n 66) 99; see also Bronwyn Leebaw, 'Justice and the Faithless: The Demand for Disobedience in International Criminal Law' (2018) 24 European Journal of International Relations 344.

80 David J Luban, 'Fairness to Rightness: Jurisdiction, Legality, and the Legitimacy of International Criminal Law' (2008) Georgetown Public Law Research Paper No. 1154117 1, 9.

81 David Garland, 'Punishment and Social Solidarity' in Jonathon Simon and Richard Sparks (eds), *The SAGE Handbook of Punishment and Society* (Sage Publishers 2013) 24.

82 Mark Osiel, *Mass Atrocity, Collective Memory and the Law* (Transaction Publishers 1997) 28–29.

by evoking shared societal indignation at a breach of universally moral principles.[83] Such a conception only works in the rare case in which members of a society share the same view on justice. Conversely, in deeply politically divided communities, where populations have been traumatised by State-sponsored atrocity, the pronouncements by courts develop an illusory consensus and solidarity, failing to recognise the reality of the possible co-existence of conflicting interpretations of history.[84] Osiel conceived criminal trials as a venue for civil discourse and, specifically, 'civil dissensus', since they can trigger the parties' opposing view on justice and past events mediated by the ritual application of legal procedure.[85] The central claim of Osiel's theory is his belief in the dramatic power of the trial, as it uses procedural and evidence law 'to recast the courtroom drama in terms of the "theatre of ideas", where large questions of collective memory and even national identity are engaged'.[86]

From his analysis, a new concept of solidarity emerges. Civil dissensus encourages a 'discursive solidarity', which is no longer based on consensus, but on 'civil engagement in disagreements',[87] and acknowledges that members of a given society can often utterly disagree over the way they understand the concepts of justice and good, but equally they can agree on the 'need to settle upon a common scheme of association and cooperation'.[88]

Osiel further argues that the debate that occurs within the courtroom, allowing parties to amplify their competing interpretations of history and to explore how society was brought to a state where the crimes under adjudication happened, encourages public discussion outside the courtroom.[89] However, Osiel's vision of trials as 'a sort of national group therapy' or 'a cathartic theatre' for a deeply divided society,[90] which becomes captivated by the public discussion about the trial,[91] is not flawless. The expressivist value of the trial depends on the existence of both democratic structures and a society willing to respect and tolerate difference, despite opposing perspectives on justice and the events of the past.[92] For instance, Aiken illustrated that, in the context of the former Yugoslavia, lack of security and ethnic or religious bias impeded the development of a discursive solidarity.[93]

83 ibid 140.
84 ibid.
85 ibid 51.
86 ibid 3.
87 ibid 48.
88 ibid 51.
89 ibid 296.
90 ibid 471–473.
91 ibid 39.
92 See David A Crocker, 'Democracy and Punishment: Punishment, Reconciliation, and Democratic Deliberation' (2002) 5 Buffalo Criminal Law Review 509; Pablo De Greiff, 'Deliberative Democracy and Punishment' (2002) 5 Buffalo Criminal Law Review 373, 375.
93 See Nevin T Aiken, *Identity, Reconciliation and Transitional Justice: Overcoming Intractability in Divided Societies* (Routledge 2014).

Several scholars interpreted the metaphor of the trial as a theatrical spectacle as carrying a pejorative connotation. Hannah Arendt warned that trials can lose their value as performances of justice if they turn into mere show or theatre.[94] The image of trials as theatre seems to suggest that the trial is illusory, insincere, and scripted, raising serious concerns in relation to international criminal justice, given its long-standing association with staged political trials.[95] More recently Sloane observed that 'when international criminal justice distracts from prophylactic strategies or excuses failure to take prompt action in the face of [human rights] crises, it emerges as no more than a cynical theatre'.[96]

Despite the fact that the notion of trial as theatre is subject to some criticisms, the idea of the international criminal trial as a performative ritual fostering a dialogue about the meaning of mass violence and its implications for the national conscience has gained modern reception in the international criminal justice discourse. As remarked by Allen, taking the theatrical analogy seriously can illuminate the potential of international courts to effect real change.[97]

4.7 International criminal trials as performance and communication

The performative and communicative dimensions lie at the core of the expressivist metaphor of the international criminal trial as a theatrical spectacle. Trials involve a visible demonstration of 'the power of the law to submit the most horrific outrages to its sober ministration',[98] as well as the creation of communicative relations that go beyond the relationship between agents in the proceedings. This inherent synergy between performance, communication, and the trial calls for an understanding of what type of performance and message international criminal trials should entail.

As Stahn illustrates, the Aristotelian features of classical drama help us to understand the performative dimension of international criminal proceedings. Trials imitate the action of life (*mimesis*) as they re-enact the crime through the mediation of actors, such as Prosecutors, Defence counsel, Judges, and victims.[99] Secondly, the proceedings embody an active process of construction (*poiesis*), given that it not only reproduces the crime, but also constructs reality, by making sense of violence and 'transforming [social conflict] into the system

94 Hannah Arendt, *Eichmann in Jerusalem: A Report on the Banality of Evil* (Penguin 1977) 8.
95 Allo (n 42) 66.
96 Sloane (n 44) 46.
97 Jessie Allen, 'Theater of International Justice' (2012) 3 Creighton International & Comparative Law Journal 121, 122.
98 Lawrence Douglas, *The Memory of Judgment: Making Law and History in the Trials of the Holocaust* (Yale University Press 2001) 41.
99 Stahn (n 30) 253.

of social representations, exchanges, surrogacies that make up the law'.[100] Lastly, the performative feature of the trial brings about a transformation (*kinesis*) that can alter society, since new information may emerge or decisions can attach new meanings to the law, and affirm or create legal authority.[101] The 'doing of justice' and the 'showing of justice' do not solely rely on the fair and expeditious application of the law to conducts, but also on the performative value of the trial, which is enacted through performative elements, such as the stage, the script, and the actors.[102] International criminal proceedings are staged in a particular space, namely the courtroom, which gives the proceedings a defined identity and visibility. The trials are 'scripted' in the sense that they are governed by legal sources and procedural rules, which give the proceedings an objectivity and authority that are conductive to persuasion and enforcement.[103] The actors in the proceedings (Prosecutors, Judges, Defence counsel, victims' legal representative) are assigned a specific role and serve different functions.[104]

The international criminal process, as an institution that produces certain 'designations of reality',[105] driven by the interaction between agents, carries a communicative force, which – besides delivering legal outcomes concerning the guilt or innocence of the defendant – forms a system of narration. In the expressivist view, the trial's framework is significantly suited to facilitating the presentation of diverse and often conflicting storytelling.[106] The performative and communicative value of the narrative is strengthened by taking the form of judicial process, which is governed by the fair trial principles and the rules of evidence that guarantee impartiality, reliability, and authority to the whole process.[107] Such narrative is shaped by courtroom interaction of a whole range of actors in the justice process, such as Judges, Prosecutors, Defence lawyers, and victims, who create a narrative based on its own perception of the events.[108] To properly appreciate the nature of the narrative in the context of different perspectives on the events surrounding mass atrocities, Damaška envisages the trial as 'theatre for the clash of ideas'.[109] Similarly, Houge asserts that the international criminal trial 'becomes a public

100 Julie Stone Peters, 'Legal Performance Good and Bad Law' (2008) 4 Culture and the Humanities 179, 185.
101 Stahn (n 30) 254.
102 ibid 268.
103 See section 5.3.
104 See sections 5.4. and 5.5.
105 Thomas Mathiesen, *Prison on Trial* (Waterside Press 2006) 67.
106 Glasius and Meijers, 'Expression of Justice or Political Trial?' (n 16) 725–726; Mohamed (n 44) 1670; Drumbl (n 38) 17, 173–175; Antonio Cassese, 'On the Current Trends Towards Criminal Prosecution and Punishment of Breaches of International Humanitarian Law' (1998) 9 European Journal of International Law 2, 10.
107 Drumbl (n 38) 17.
108 Osiel (n 82) 3.
109 Mirjan Damaška, 'What Is the Point of International Criminal Justice?' (2008) 83 Chicago-Kent Law Review 329, 346.

theatre of different and contesting ideas – a place to test and rename, pronounce and project, and also, establish history about mass harms'.[110]

4.8 The expressivist functions of the trial

The intrinsic performative and communicative nature of the international criminal trial turns expressivism into a structural feature of international criminal justice. Expressivism, rather than being merely a theoretical justification, becomes a way for international criminal justice to define itself by means of 'different expressive acts and communicative relationships'.[111] International criminal trials do not simply or even principally lead to outcomes resulting from verdicts, such as retribution and deterrence, trials are rather about a process, intended, in Durkheimian terms, to be society-constituting and to reinforce fundamental norms that the society considers central. In doing so, international criminal justice takes a turn towards the functionalist.[112] The ways in which expressivism manifests itself through the international criminal proceedings and the messages that are shaped through such proceedings may be labelled as expressivist functions of international criminal justice. They entail different phenomena, namely the crafting of historical records and the didactic function, which illustrate the heterogeneity of communicative acts and their interconnections.

4.8.1 Crafting a historical record and truth-telling

International crimes create historical discontinuity because they often occur in situations of civil conflict, where large-scale violence often targets communities on ethnic, political, religious, ideological, or economic grounds, in order to destabilise and eventually cause the disintegration of the community not simply physically, but also in terms of its identity.[113] In the expressivist view, the goal of the trial is the expression of messages, not only about the guilt of a defendant, but also about the historical understanding of episodes of mass violence.[114] Trials create archives of information through documents and testimonies, to the extent that they can help to settle historical controversies after mass violence and prevent the past from being denied by revisionists.[115] In his study of the Eichmann and

110 Anette Bringedal Houge, 'Narrative Expressivism: A Criminological Approach to the Expressive Function of International Criminal Justice' (2018) 19 Criminology & Criminal Justice 277, 282.

111 Stahn (n 30) 68.

112 Frédéric Mégret, 'In Defense of Hybridity: Towards a Representational Theory of International Criminal Justice' (2005) 38 Cornell International Law Journal 725, 743.

113 Mina Rauschenbach and Damien Scalia, 'Victims and International Criminal Justice: A Vexed Question?' (2008) 90 International Review of the Red Cross 441, 450.

114 Mohamed (n 44) 1670; Damaška (n 109) 339; Cassese (n 106) 10.

115 Ruti G Teitel, *Transitional Justice* (Oxford University Press 2000) 72.

Demjanjuk trials, Douglas illustrated that history and law are intertwined because trials adjudicating mass atrocities are intended to mark a tribute to history and memory.[116] While acknowledging that historical methods of research differ from the methodology of the judicial process, Douglas makes the powerful argument that what happens during the trial, namely evidence, testimonies, and judgments, may contribute to historical clarification and, most importantly, to the formation of a collective memory that might otherwise be lost.[117]

The relevant question to address is thus not whether the international criminal trial can frame a historical discourse, but 'how it can do so responsibly'.[118] Trials involve a social production of reality, since the process of adjudication, by 'hearing, translating, weighing, and applying evidence to legal questions',[119] translates social facts into the form and language of the law and creates new categories regarding the nature of the crime, the conduct of individuals, and their nexus to the crime.[120] Trials perform a significant role in facilitating 'narrative pluralism',[121] since the construction of historical records of the events is shaped by courtroom interactions. Actors in the justice process create a narrative based on their own perception of the story, often presenting diverse and often conflicting historical narratives. The particular value of the trial lies in the fact that 'the pursuit of historical truth is embedded in a framework of accountability and in the pursuit of justice'.[122] Through the constraints of the criminal procedure, the rule of evidence, investigative process, and judicial customs, each party structures 'how the accounts of what happened unfold and are given meaning'.[123] The defendants and the Prosecutors confront each other in a process directed at the determination of the criminal conduct, constructing their stories around the rule of evidence; while witnesses give their testimony under a solemn oath.[124] At the end of the trial, the Judges, by identifying those who committed a crime, trace the historical context of the events and persuade others that they happened beyond reasonable doubt.[125] These multiple stories, emerging from a high degree

116 Douglas (n 98) 41.

117 Lawrence Douglas, 'The Didactic Trial: Filtering History and Memory into the Courtroom' (2006) 14 European Review 513, 515; Rachel López, 'The (Re) Collection of Memory After Mass Atrocity and the Dilemma for Transitional Justice' (2015) 47 New York University Journal of International Law & Politics 799, 841.

118 Douglas (n 117) 515.

119 Doris Buss, 'Knowing Women: Translating Patriarchy in International Criminal Law' (2014) 23 Social & Legal Studies 73, 75.

120 Stahn (n 30) 265.

121 See Barrie Sander, 'History on Trial: Historical Narrative Pluralism Within and Beyond International Criminal Courts' (2018) 67 International and Comparative Law Quarterly 547.

122 Teitel (n 115) 72.

123 Buss (n 119) 75.

124 Diane Marie Amann, 'Assessing International Criminal Adjudication of Human Rights Atrocities' (2000a) 16 Third World Legal Studies 169, 178.

125 Glasius and Meijers, 'Expression of Justice or Political Trial?' (n 16) 746.

of procedural story-telling, form a broader 'truthful narrative for the historical records',[126] which is the product of an assessment informed by correspondence to reality, plausibility and verification.[127]

The high degree of selectivity of the prosecution that operates in the context of international criminal justice can undermine its ability to achieve the expressivist potential of establishing historical truths.[128] In the case of mass violence, the selectivity of the prosecution puts the historical truth-telling goal in jeopardy because the Prosecutor focuses on proving the responsibility of a single perpetrator or of a small group of them, while one of the main characteristics of international crimes is the large-scale organised participation of perpetrators.[129] Therefore, since 'the trial achieves only a partial truth, it might not properly fulfil the expressivist potential'.[130] Moreover, by investigating, trying, and punishing only a few perpetrators, the international criminal justice system risks sending an unintended message to both the victims and the defendants. Victims may consider the lack of the prosecution of crimes which affected them as a defeat because those conducts are not taken seriously, while, for defendants, the fact that only members of a specific group in the conflict are on trial can be perceived as a bias.[131] First of all, we must acknowledge the limits of international criminal justice. It is a partial justice because it will not be feasible to successfully try all perpetrators or indeed all those people who were necessary for the atrocities to come about.[132] Thus, there will always be an inevitable tension between criminal procedure and historical truth-telling in the case of mass violence.[133] Nevertheless, the strength of the international criminal trial lies in its intrinsic nature of being a site for storytelling where contestations and conflicting narrative can legitimately coexist. Given the nature of international crimes and the context of political and social turmoil in which they occur, the international criminal trial should cultivate a shared and long-standing discourse on the examination of episodes of mass violence.

126 Shannon Fyfe, 'Truth, Testimony and Epistemic Injustice in International Criminal Law' in Morten Bergsmo and Emiliano J Buis (eds), *Philosophical Foundations of International Criminal Law: Foundational Concepts* (Torkel Opsahl Academic EPublisher 2019) 299.
127 Stahn (n 30) 266.
128 Drumbl (n 13) 593; Miriam J Aukerman, 'Extraordinary Evil, Ordinary Crime: A Framework for Understanding Transitional Justice' (2002) 15 Harvard Human Rights Journal 39, 88–89.
129 See sections 3.3., 3.4., and 5.5.2.
130 Marlies Glasius and Tim Meijers, 'Constructions of Legitimacy: The Charles Taylor Trial' (2012) 6 International Journal of Transitional Justice 229, 251.
131 Marlies Glasius and Tim Meijers, 'Trials as Messages of Justice: What Should Be Expected of International Criminal Courts?' (2016) 30 Ethics & International Affairs 429, 441.
132 Groenhuijsenme and Pemberton (n 1) 33.
133 Glasius and Meijers, 'Constructions of Legitimacy' (n 130) 251.

4.8.2 Didactic function

The didactic function of the trial is strictly linked to historical clarification and truth-telling because expressivists contend that the trial can be a forum for the creation of authoritative historical records and 'their pedagogical dissemination to the public'.[134] Some have opposed the idea that the trial can fulfil didactic purposes because of the absence of any discernible educational effects of their decisions.[135] Arendt maintained that the sole 'purpose of a trial is to render justice, and nothing else'[136] and warned that using the trial for didactic ends would turn it into a legal farce. Damaška rebutted those pessimistic conclusions, holding that the lack of these effects in the short term does not exclude them from occurring in a time horizon of longer range. Communities torn apart by conflicts and mass atrocities take time to recover.[137]

The key question to answer is what the desirable scope of the didactic function of the trials should be. While among expressivists there is a general consensus that all trials explicitly embrace a didactic purpose, expressivist theories do not give any guidance on which norms are the most appropriate to convey a didactic message. Expressivism states that a harmful message in itself causes harm and a good message causes good, but it does not determine what is good or bad.[138] In other words, expressivism suggests that the international criminal justice system should pay attention to the didactic message sent by its operation, but it does not provide a metric to establish a set of priorities. The debate on the scope of the didactic function of the trial has shown that there are two main strands of thought: the first argues that the didactic function operates 'primarily in negative space';[139] conversely, the second strand focuses on the 'positive side'[140] of the trial's didactic function.

According to the first strand, international criminal trials communicate what conduct should not be undertaken. Antonio Cassese writes that the purpose of establishing a system of international criminal justice was the stigmatisation of certain conduct.[141] Cryer affirmed that international criminal trials have the capacity to communicate the serious nature of the wrong done and educate society about the unacceptability of those conducts.[142] Similarly, Luban sees trials as 'expressive acts broadcasting the news that mass atrocities are, in fact, heinous crimes and not merely politics by other means'.[143] The general message of the

134 Drumbl (n 38) 173.
135 See Jack Snyder and Leslie Vinjamuri, 'Trials and Errors: Principle and Pragmatism in Strategies of International Justice' (2004) 28 International Security 5.
136 Arendt (n 94) 254.
137 Damaška (n 109) 346.
138 Anderson and Pildes (n 3) 1527–31, 1535–37, 1543–45, 1547–50.
139 Mohamed (n 44) 1670.
140 ibid 1671.
141 Cassese (n 106) 10.
142 Cryer et al. (n 44) 29.
143 Luban (n 80) 8.

trial about the veracity of a certain crime, provided that the evidence presented by the Prosecutor demonstrates that some specific criminal conducts occurred, encompasses disavowal of the crime. Once the truthfulness of the events has been proved, even in the case the defendant cannot be proven guilty beyond reasonable doubt, the fact that these conducts have happened remains true.[144] Thus, the simple fact that a trial takes place by appealing to the law, even if it does not end in conviction of the defendant, strongly demonstrates that the crime and laws are taken seriously.[145] Cryer and Luban further emphasise that the trial should communicate outrage and demonstrate society's intolerance of those criminal acts. By declaring that certain kinds of behaviour are violations of human rights in the context of a public process,[146] the trial conveys the message that international crimes are the most serious crimes concerning the international community.[147] Damaška argues that international criminal tribunals perform a socio-pedagogical role, since they place greater emphasis on suasion. The denunciatory aspect of the trial should aim at the exposure of extreme forms of violence amounting to international crimes and, thus, strengthening the public sense of accountability and inflicting shame and stigma on the perpetrators of mass violence.[148] Drumbl's account is even harsher because he specifies that the trial may educate the public through the performance of its closing act, which inflicts shame, sanction, and stigma upon those convicted.[149]

The second strand, by calling attention to the positive side of the didactic function, highlights that the stigmatisation of the offender who transgressed the law through the denunciatory and condemnatory aspects of the trial is not the only task of international criminal justice. The trial should not be conceived merely as 'a forum for enunciating societal condemnation of atrocities',[150] it should also serve to voice a positive message about 'how we should think about good (...), normal (...) [and] legitimate'.[151] As Amann observes, the trial should reflect both what a society abhors and what it esteems.[152] Deeply fractured societies, like those in which international crimes are committed, are in special need of a message of disavowal and non-acquiescence to the crimes. But there is more at stake. When Duff notes that '[t]o remain silent in the face of crime would be to betray the values

144 Glasius and Meijers, 'Trials as Messages of Justice' (n 131) 435.
145 ibid.
146 William A Schabas, 'Sentencing by International Tribunals: A Human Rights Approach' (1997) 7 Duke Journal of Comparative & International Law 461, 516.
147 Solange Mouthaan, 'Victim Participation at the ICC for Victims of Gender-Based Crimes: A Conflict of Interest' (2012) 21 Cardozo Journal of International and Comparative Law 619, 648–649.
148 Damaška (n 109) 345.
149 Drumbl (n 38) 175.
150 Amann, 'Assessing International Criminal Adjudication of Human Rights Atrocities' (n 124) 175.
151 See Garland, *Punishment and Modern Society: A Study in Social Theory* (n 37).
152 Amann, 'Group Mentality, Expressivism, and Genocide' (n 2) 118.

which the law expresses, and to which we are committed',[153] he implies that a trial should send a message, not only about the guilt of a defendant, but also about the value of the rule of law. Similarly, Amann remarks that the establishment of the truth and expressions of disapproval and stigmatisation contribute to strengthening the rule of law by invoking it.[154] According to van der Wilt[155] and Mohamed,[156] the essence of the didactic function is to contribute to imbuing the general public with core values and faith in the rule of law. International criminal trials, by narrating history and thereby expressing shared understandings of the origins, particulars, and effects of mass violence, enhance their educative value in asserting the importance of law and human rights principles.[157]

Damaška cautioned against this 'positive side' of the trial's didactic function. If there's not a general consensus on moral fundamentals or agreements on basic protection, human rights law and its penal branch are 'no more than an ethnic custom of the West'.[158] This claim is overstated because the didactic function is not simply a feature of the process of upholding largely uncontested social norms. Due to the nature of the crimes adjudicated, trials are charged with the task of making visible the efficacy of the law as a tool of their inquiry into episodes of mass atrocity.[159] The very heart of the didactic effectiveness of such trials serves a positive function in actively redefining and re-imposing a minimum of human rights principles into spaces where they have been either radically evacuated or perverted. Thus, the scope of the didactic function should be restricted to looking at affirming a common commitment to international human rights standards and the authority of the rule of law, which are the key tools for re-establishing a well-functioning society.[160]

The didactic function can be used as an argument to respond to the drawbacks of the selectivity of the prosecution. The expressivist emphasis on enunciating societal condemnation of atrocities and reaffirming the importance of the rule of law puts the limitations of prosecution and punishment in international criminal justice into perspective because it 'would make sense of an institution created to "end impunity" with the resources to prosecute but a few cases'.[161] Through the representation of both the nature of the crimes adjudicated and the constituencies affected by them, the value of investigation and prosecution, and the distribution of burden and shame, international criminal trials send 'a strong signal that a norm has been offended that is properly considered international

153 Antony Duff, *Trials and Punishments* (Cambridge University Press 1986) 236.
154 Amann, 'Assessing International Criminal Adjudication of Human Rights Atrocities' (n 124) 175.
155 van der Wilt (n 66) 55.
156 Mohamed (n 46) 1670–1671.
157 Glasius and Meijers, 'Trials as Messages of Justice' (n 131) 436.
158 Damaška (n 109) 347.
159 Douglas (n 117) 514. 4
160 Glasius and Meijers, 'Trials as Messages of Justice' (n 131) 437–438; Sloane (n 44) 93.
161 deGuzman (n 12) 320.

and in some peculiar way offends the dignity of mankind'.[162] This 'representational function'[163] allows international criminal justice to operate in an exemplary and selective manner because, even with a limited number of illustrative prosecutions, the trial successfully reinforces the fundamental status of certain norms that the international community considers central.[164] The sentencing given by the international criminal justice system can 'influence the practice and policy of states by acting as an engine of jurisprudential and normative development where it matters the most, within nation-states'.[165] In other words, an expressivist trial can manage selectivity because its focus on the exemplification of widespread crimes can potentially represent a wider class which, because of the gravity of the offence, is worthy and actually in need of expression of condemnation.[166]

Feminist scholarship has highlighted some of the benefits of the representative potential of the didactic function, such as its ability to serve as a normative foundation to justify the prioritisation of charges of sexual and gender-based violence in the selectivity practice. The framing of this type of charges is a process with a deeply expressive function, since it contains messages about disregard and stereotypes of sexual and gender-based violence and, at the same time, it makes those crimes more visible, highlighting the specific kind of harms caused and the need for a greater prosecution of such conducts.[167] Prosecuting and convicting individuals of the crime of sexual and gender-based violence send the message that rape and other forms of sexual harm are '*harms,* they are prosecuted *as crimes*, and they result in punishment through years of incarceration for those found guilty'.[168] The choice of prosecuting sexual and gender-based crimes contributes to advancing a substantial scholarly knowledge about the gendered effects of mass atrocities as well as 'gendered understandings of international legal order and disorder'.[169]

4.9 Conclusion

Expressivism has only recently gained acceptance as a theoretical foundation of international criminal justice. Indeed, specific features of expressivism, like the performative and communicative dimensions of the trial, can be traced back to the origins of international criminal justice. For instance, Osiel has shown in his

162 Mégret (n 112) 743.
163 ibid.
164 ibid; deGuzman (n 12) 316; Amann, 'Group Mentality, Expressivism, and Genocide' (n 2) 95; Glasius and Meijers, 'Trials as Messages of Justice' (n 131) 441.
165 Sloane (n 44) 93.
166 Glasius and Meijers, 'Trials as Messages of Justice' (n 131) 441.
167 deGuzman (n 62) 526.
168 Doris Buss, 'Performing Legal Order: Some Feminist Thoughts on International Criminal Law' (2011) 11 International Criminal Law Review 409, 414, emphasis in original.
169 ibid 414, 423.

work on the national post-conflict trials that criminal adjudication can operate as a performative and communicative institution, fostering a dialogue about the meaning of mass violence. That said, a more comprehensive understanding of expressivism emerged only through contemporary studies of the multiple forms and functions of international criminal justice. The normative claim underlying expressivism, according to which, by expressing valuable social messages, criminal law operates as a mechanism for altering social norms, can hold a greater importance within international criminal justice. Expressivism imposes a change in perspective: it advances a distinctive role for international criminal proceedings, continuous with, but not reducible to, the purposes of punishment. In particular, as opposed to punishing simply because the perpetrators deserve it or because potential perpetrators will be deterred, the expressivist potential lies in the didactic function of the trial and its capacity to create historical narratives as representations of truth and their pedagogical dissemination. These functions of the trial must be approached with modesty, in light of international criminal justice's retributive orientation, whose main focus is on individual responsibility and punishment as perpetrators' just deserts. There is a tension between the reality of the selectivity of the prosecution and the expressivist aims of establishing and disseminating historical truths, attaching stigma to perpetrators, and strengthening faith in the rule of law. However, even though expressivism is not able to completely overcome those limitations, it responds to those structural obstacles in a more effective way than other classical criminal justice frameworks analysed in the previous chapter. The communicative and performative features of the trial are as important as its outcomes or substantive findings, as they advance the idea of the proceedings as an attempt to craft historical records and create communal meaning. In this context, the trial becomes a forum for dialogue and open possibilities, rather than a forum to provide closure, providing a new way of thinking about atrocities amounting to international crimes and stimulating processes of historical memory building and internalisation of values.

References

Books and journals

Aiken NT, *Identity, Reconciliation and Transitional Justice: Overcoming Intractability in Divided Societies* (Routledge 2014)

Allen J, 'Theater of International Justice' (2012) 3 Creighton International & Comparative Law Journal 121

Allo AK, 'The 'Show' in the Show Trials: Contextualizing the Politicization of the Courtroom' (2010) 15 Barry Law Review 41

Aloisi R and Meernik J, *Judgment Day: Judicial Decision Making at the International Criminal Tribunals* (Cambridge University Press 2017)

Amann DM, 'Assessing International Criminal Adjudication of Human Rights Atrocities' (2000a) 16 Third World Legal Studies 169

Amann DM, 'Message as Medium in Sierra Leone' (2000b) 7 ILSA Journal of International and Comparative Law 237
Amann DM, 'Group Mentality, Expressivism, and Genocide' (2002) 2 International Criminal Law Review 93
Ambos K, *Treatise on International Criminal Law: Vol. I: Foundations and General Part* (Oxford University Press 2013)
Anderson ES and Pildes RH, 'Expressive Theories of Law: A General Restatement' (2000) 148 University of Pennsylvania Law Review 1503
Arendt H, *Eichmann in Jerusalem: A Report on the Banality of Evil* (Penguin 1977)
Aukerman MJ, 'Extraordinary Evil, Ordinary Crime: A Framework for Understanding Transitional Justice' (2002) 15 Harvard Human Rights Journal 39
Buss D, 'Performing Legal Order: Some Feminist Thoughts on International Criminal Law' (2011) 11 International Criminal Law Review 409
Buss D, 'Knowing Women: Translating Patriarchy in International Criminal Law' (2014) 23 Social & Legal Studies 73
Cassese A, 'On the Current Trends Towards Criminal Prosecution and Punishment of Breaches of International Humanitarian Law' (1998) 9 European Journal of International Law 2
Crocker DA, 'Democracy and Punishment: Punishment, Reconciliation, and Democratic Deliberation' (2002) 5 Buffalo Criminal Law Review 509
Cryer R et al., *An Introduction to International Criminal Law and Procedure* (Cambridge University Press 2014)
Damaška M, 'What Is the Point of International Criminal Justice?' (2008) 83 Chicago-Kent Law Review 329
D'Ascoli S, *Sentencing in International Criminal Law: The UN Ad Hoc Tribunals and Future Perspectives for the ICC* (Bloomsbury Publishing 2011)
De Greiff P, 'Deliberative Democracy and Punishment' (2002) 5 Buffalo Criminal Law Review 373
deGuzman M, 'Giving Priority to Sex Crime Prosecutions: The Philosophical Foundations of a Feminist Agenda' (2011) 11 International Criminal Law Review 515
deGuzman M, 'Choosing to Prosecute: Expressive Selection at the International Criminal Court' (2012) 33 Michigan Journal of International Law 265
Demko D, 'An Expressive Theory of International Punishment for International Crimes' in Florian Jessberger and Julia Geneuss (eds), *Why Punish Perpetrators of Mass Atrocities?* (Cambridge University Press 2020)
Douglas L, *The Memory of Judgment: Making Law and History in the Trials of the Holocaust* (Yale University Press 2001)
Douglas L, 'The Didactic Trial: Filtering History and Memory into the Courtroom' (2006) 14 European Review 513
Drumbl MA, 'Collective Violence and Individual Punishment: The Criminality of Mass Atrocity' (2005) 99 Northwestern University Law Review 539
Drumbl MA, *Atrocity, Punishment, and International Law* (Cambridge University Press 2007a)
Drumbl MA, 'The Expressive Value of Prosecuting and Punishing Terrorists: Hamdan, the Geneva Conventions, and International Criminal Law' (2007b) 75 The George Washington Law Review 1165
Duff A, *Trials and Punishments* (Cambridge University Press 1986)

Duff A, 'Penance, Punishment and the Limits of Community' (2003) 5 Punishment & Society 295

Duff A, *Punishment, Communication, and Community* (Oxford University Press 2011)

Durkheim É, *The Division of Labour in Society* (Macmillan 1984)

Edwards MA, 'Legal Expressivism: A Primer' (2009) Social Science Research Network <https://ssrn.com/abstract=1361101> accessed 19 June 2021

Feinberg J, *Doing and Deserving: Essays in the Theory of Responsibility* (Princeton University Press 1970)

Fisher KJ, *Moral Accountability and International Criminal Law: Holding Agents of Atrocity Accountable to the World* (Routledge 2013)

Fyfe S, 'Truth, Testimony and Epistemic Injustice in International Criminal Law' in Morten Bergsmo and Emiliano J Buis (eds), *Philosophical Foundations of International Criminal Law: Foundational Concepts* (Torkel Opsahl Academic EPublisher 2019)

Garland D, *Punishment and Modern Society: A Study in Social Theory* (University of Chicago Press 1990)

Garland D, 'Sociological Perspectives on Punishment' (1991) 14 Crime and Justice 115

Garland D, 'Punishment and Social Solidarity' in Jonathon Simon and Richard Sparks (eds), *The SAGE Handbook of Punishment and Society* (Sage Publishers 2013)

Glasius M and Meijers T, 'Constructions of Legitimacy: The Charles Taylor Trial' (2012) 6 International Journal of Transitional Justice 229

Glasius M and Meijers T, 'Expression of Justice or Political Trial? Discursive Battles in the Karadžić Case' (2013) 35 Human Rights Quarterly 720

Glasius M and Meijers T, 'Trials as Messages of Justice: What Should Be Expected of International Criminal Courts?' (2016) 30 Ethics & International Affairs 429

Golash D, 'The Justification of Punishment in the International Context' in Larry May and Zachary Hoskins (eds), *International Criminal Law and Philosophy* (Cambridge University Press 2010)

Groenhuijsenme MS and Pemberton A, 'Genocide, Crimes against Humanity and War Crimes' in Rianne Letschert et al. (eds), *Victimological Approaches to International Crimes: Africa* (Intersentia 2011)

Günther K, 'Criminal Law, Crime and Punishment as Communication' <https://d-nb.info/1054399557/34> accessed 20 June 2021

Hegel GF, *Elements of the Philosophy of Right* (Allen W Wood ed, Hugh Barr Nisbet tr, Cambridge University Press 1991)

Houge AB, 'Narrative Expressivism: A Criminological Approach to the Expressive Function of International Criminal Justice' (2018) 19 Criminology & Criminal Justice 277

Kahan DM, 'What Do Alternative Sanctions Mean?' (1996) 63 The University of Chicago Law Review 591

Kahan DM, 'The Secret Ambition of Deterrence' (1999) 113 Harvard Law Review 413

Leebaw B, 'Justice and the Faithless: The Demand for Disobedience in International Criminal Law' (2018) 24 European Journal of International Relations 344

López R, 'The (Re)Collection of Memory After Mass Atrocity and the Dilemma for Transitional Justice' (2015) 47 New York University Journal of International Law & Politics 799

Luban DJ, 'Fairness to Rightness: Jurisdiction, Legality, and the Legitimacy of International Criminal Law' (2008) Georgetown Public Law Research Paper No. 1154117 1Mathiesen T, Prison on Trial (Waterside Press 2006)
May L and Fyfe S, *International Criminal Tribunals: A Normative Defense* (Cambridge University Press 2017)
McAdams RH, 'A Focal Point Theory of Expressive Law' (2000) 86 Virginia Law Review 1649
Mégret F, 'In Defense of Hybridity: Towards a Representational Theory of International Criminal Justice' (2005) 38 Cornell International Law Journal 725
Mégret F, 'Practices of Stigmatization' (2013) 76 Law and Contemporary Problems 287
Mohamed S, 'Deviance, Aspiration, and the Stories We Tell: Reconciling Mass Atrocity and the Criminal Law' (2015) 124 Yale Law Journal 1628
Mouthaan S, 'Victim Participation at the ICC for Victims of Gender-Based Crimes: A Conflict of Interest' (2012) 21 Cardozo Journal of International and Comparative Law 619
Nozick R, *Philosophical Explanations* (Harvard University Press 1981)
O'Regan F, 'Prosecutor vs. Jean-Pierre Bemba Gombo: The Cumulative Charging Principle, Gender-Based Violence, and Expressivism' (2011) 43 Georgetown Journal of International Law 1323
Osiel M, *Mass Atrocity, Collective Memory and the Law* (Transaction Publishers 1997)
Peters JS, 'Legal Performance Good and Bad Law' (2008) 4 Culture and the Humanities 179
Primoratz I, 'Punishment as Language' (1989) 64 Philosophy 187
Rauschenbach M and Scalia D, 'Victims and International Criminal Justice: A Vexed Question?' (2008) 90 International Review of the Red Cross 441
Sander B, 'History on Trial: Historical Narrative Pluralism Within and Beyond International Criminal Courts' (2018) 67 International and Comparative Law Quarterly 547
Sander B, 'Justifying International Criminal Punishment: A Critical Perspective' in Morten Bergsmo and Emiliano J Buis (eds), *Philosophical Foundations of International Criminal Law: Foundational Concepts* (Torkel Opsahl Academic EPublisher 2019)
Schabas WA, 'Sentencing by International Tribunals: A Human Rights Approach' (1997) 7 Duke Journal of Comparative & International Law 461
Sloane RD, 'The Expressive Capacity of International Punishment: The Limits of the National Law Analogy and the Potential of International Criminal Law' (2007) 43 Stanford Journal of International Law 39
Snyder J and Vinjamuri L, 'Trials and Errors: Principle and Pragmatism in Strategies of International Justice' (2004) 28 International Security 5
Stahn C, *Justice as Message: Expressivist Foundations of International Criminal Justice* (1st edn, Oxford University Press 2020)
Strudler A, 'The Power of Expressive Theories of Law' (2001) 3 Maryland Law Review 60 492
Sunstein CR, 'On the Expressive Function of Law' (1996) 144 University of Pennsylvania Law Review 2021
Teitel RG, *Transitional Justice* (Oxford University Press 2000)

van der Wilt H, 'Why International Criminal Lawyers Should Read Mirjan Damaška', in Carsten Stahn and Larissa van den Herik (eds), *Future Perspectives on International Criminal Justice* (TMC Asser Press 2010)
Van Hoecke M, *Law as Communication* (Bloomsbury Publishing 2002)
Wise EM, 'The International Criminal Court: A Budget of Paradoxes' (2000) 8 Tulane Journal of International and Comparative Law 261

Legislation

Rome Statute of the International Criminal Court 1998 (2187 UNTS 90)

5 The expressivist dimension of victims' participation in international criminal proceedings

Harmonising the adversarial and inquisitorial systems

5.1 Introduction

The expressivist model of international criminal justice, which highlights the performative and communicative dimensions of the trial, puts forward a cutting-edge understanding of what the structure of the criminal process should be and what type of performance and message the individuals involved in the criminal process should convey. This is particularly relevant because one of the greatest challenges international criminal justice faces is the problem arising from the ideological and structural differences between the adversarial and inquisitorial procedural approaches, which almost exclusively inform international criminal procedure. The adversarial and inquisitorial models, which originate respectively in the common law and civil law systems, have different perceptions of the trial process and the methods adopted in reaching their primary goals. As this chapter will illustrate, while both systems share as primary goals pursuing the truth and establishing the guilt of an accused, their methods to achieve those goals are quite divergent. The adversarial approach is grounded in the belief that the best way to uncover the truth is framing the trial process as a contest between two opposing parties, who present their case; whereas, in the inquisitorial approach, the trial process is structured as an official inquiry through which the judicial authorities seek to obtain the truth. The divide between these two legal traditions is reflected in the antithetical features of the roles and rights conferred on actors in the criminal proceedings (Judges, Prosecutors, and the Defence) and, specifically, on victims, whose participatory role differs significantly between the civil law and the common law systems. The latter does not confer on victims the broad right to participate with an autonomous standing in the criminal process, while the former provides victims with procedural rights under the civil party model.

This chapter suggests that the adoption of the expressivist model by international criminal justice has important implications for the structure of proceedings, making a unique contribution to the academic debate on the need to harmonise the different legal traditions coexisting in the international criminal procedure. This chapter proposes that expressivism can be a mechanism able to bridge the gaps between the civil law and common law systems of criminal justice. As such, this chapter aims to establish a common grammar through the

DOI: 10.4324/9781003215448-5

adoption of the expressivist model, which combines and fuses the adversarial and inquisitorial procedural systems in a fair manner. Key elements of expressivism, such as the performative and communicative features of the trial, have a big impact on the articulation of the functions and procedural role of the different actors in the proceedings. The expressivist assumption that international criminal trials provide a platform for framing the narrative of gross human rights violations allows victims to express their independent voice and add another dimension to the proceedings. Expressivism, thus, becomes a vehicle for effectively tailoring victims' participation, which should be informed by the idea that victims act as 'participants' in criminal proceedings, whose voices are not tied to that of the parties. Against this background, this chapter also considers the change in perspective on the role and rights of all actors involved in the criminal process, as victims' rights are intertwined with the roles and rights of the Prosecutor, Judges, and defendants.

5.2 The civil law and the common law traditions

The adversarial and inquisitorial systems of criminal procedure originated respectively in the Anglo-American common law and the European or Continental civil law traditions.[1] The civil law or Romano-Germanic law is the most ancient legal tradition, as it can be traced back to the Roman law. In 451–450 BC, the *Leges Duodecim Tabularum* (the Laws of the Twelve Tables)[2] established what conducts affecting the individual's interest amount to crimes and provided Roman citizens with legal instruments to seek justice against the offender.[3] Civil law is the prevailing and most influential legal tradition worldwide, which is the basis of law systems in Europe, South America, some parts of North America, like Louisiana and Québec, some African and Asian countries.[4] Common law tradition originated in England in the late 11th century, following the Norman

1 Kai Ambos, 'International Criminal Procedure: "Adversarial", "Inquisitorial" or Mixed?' (2003) 3 International Criminal Law Review 1, 1–5; Mirjan Damaška, *The Faces of Justice and State Authority: A Comparative Approach to the Legal Process* (Yale University Press 1986) 16–17; Brianne McGonigle Leyh, 'Bridging the Divides in International Criminal Proceedings: An Examination into the Victim Participation Endeavor of the International Criminal Court' (2009) 21 Florida Journal of International Law 93, 97; Mugambi Jouet, 'Reconciling the Conflicting Rights of Victims and Defendants at the International Criminal Court' 26 Saint Louis University Public Law Review 249, 253.

2 The *Leges Duodecim Tabularum*, which were drafted by a commission of Ten Men (the *Decemviri*) and posted on 12 tablets of bronze in the Roman Forum, represent the first code of Roman law and formed the core of the *mos maiorum*, the customs of the ancestors. See Bernardo Santalucia, *Diritto e Processo Penale nell'Antica Roma* (Giuffrè Editore 1989).

3 Vincenzo Giuffré, *La Repressione Criminale nell'Esperienza Romana. Profili* (Jovene 1991) 43.

4 John Henry Merryman and Rogelio Pérez-Perdomo, *The Civil Law Tradition: An Introduction to the Legal System of Western Europe and Latin America* (Stanford University Press 1969) 2–3.

Conquest (1066).[5] As the monarchs and lords consolidated their power, they became increasingly involved in the administration of justice. Criminal conducts became acts breaching the King's Peace, under the exclusive jurisdiction of the King's Court.[6] Common law is the prevalent tradition in countries like the UK, the USA, Canada, Australia, New Zealand and former British colonies in Africa and Asia.[7]

The civil law and common law criminal procedures have framed the roles and rights of Judges, Prosecutors, the Defence, and victims in very different ways. Such divergence can be understood in light of the underlying beliefs and values of criminal law held by the common law and the civil law systems. As Damaška clarifies, each legal tradition has developed a procedural model that accords best with the objectives that have been set by its own social and political background. The common law tradition sees justice as a means of conflict resolution and, consequently, the proceedings are conceived as a contest between prosecution and Defence, aiming to ascertain the innocence or guilt of the defendant.[8] The adversarial procedure is informed by the belief that the best manner to uncover the truth is allowing opposing parties (Prosecutor and Defence) to present their case in a public trial, which is characterised by orality.[9] Conversely, within the civil law tradition, the inquisitorial model of procedure is focused on the notion of trial as an inquiry, seeking to obtain the truth, and develops around the concept of justice as a means for implementing policy within an activist State dedicated to the 'material and moral betterment of its citizens'.[10]

It is important to note that the use of the term 'civil law' does not mean that European jurisdictions are the same. Equally, the criminal procedures of countries of common law tradition present differences from one another. This makes it more difficult to classify a national system as inquisitorial or adversarial as 'criteria remain uncertain for the inclusion of specific features into the adversarial and the inquisitorial types'.[11] Moreover, no country has ever adopted a purely inquisitorial or adversarial system.[12] For instance, in 1989, Italy adopted a new Code of Criminal Procedure, which incorporated adversarial features in a

5 ibid 4.

6 Jonathan Doak, *Victims' Rights, Human Rights and Criminal Justice. Reconceiving the Role of the Third Parties* (Hart Publishing 2008) 2.

7 Brianne McGonigle Leyh, *Procedural Justice? Victim Participation in International Criminal Proceedings* (Intersentia 2011) 70.

8 Damaška, *The Faces of Justice and State Authority: A Comparative Approach to the Legal Process* (n 1) 73.

9 McGonigle Leyh (n 7) 71.

10 Damaška, *The Faces of Justice and State Authority: A Comparative Approach to the Legal Process* (n 1) 80.

11 ibid 3.

12 Alphons Orie, 'Accusatorial v. Inquisitorial Approach in International Criminal Proceedings Prior to the Establishment of the ICC and in the Proceedings Before the ICC' in Antonio Cassese, Paola Gaeta and John RWD Jones (eds), *The Rome Statute of the International Criminal Court: A Commentary, (Vol. 2)* (Oxford University Press 2002) 1441.

system that traditionally was associated with the inquisitorial family.[13] Therefore, references to either an adversarial or inquisitorial system must be understood as a way of helping to emphasise the philosophical divides between these two traditions and the predominant features they adopt.

5.2.1 The adversarial procedural system

The adversarial type of criminal proceedings is a party-driven dispute, since 'it unfolds as an engagement of two adversaries before a relatively passive decision maker whose principal duty is to reach a verdict'.[14] Thus, in the adversarial process, the two competing parties, Prosecutor and accused, Present Their Respective Cases during the trial in public hearings aiming to persuade the Judge/jury to take a favourable decision for their party. By virtue of the central role assigned to the parties in the adversarial system, Prosecutor and Defence undertake intensive fact-finding activities during the pre-trial stage, by conducting investigations and bearing the burden of evidence collection.[15] Since parties conduct their own investigations, disclosure is a vital aspect of the adversarial procedural model. The Prosecutor's obligation of disclosure of material and information is particularly important to provide the defendants with a fair opportunity to prepare their case. The extent to which the defendants are obliged to disclose their material varies; however, an obligation to disclose the very general lines of their Defence's strategy has begun to gain acceptance.[16]

The adversarial procedural approach, which conceives the criminal process as a contest between sides, properly unfolds at the trial stage, when the parties present their respective case and introduce evidence separately. The entire trial depends on the parties, who define the issues, present evidence, and call witnesses. Defendants can defend themselves in court and present their case by testifying as witnesses, meaning that they must take the oath and undergo the Prosecutor's cross-examination.[17]

The role of the Judge is complementary to the role of the parties, since the active parties find their complement in a relatively passive Judge, who acts as a 'referee' who decides mainly on issues of a procedural character raised by the parties. In particular, the Judge decides on the admissibility of the evidence

13 See e.g., Lawrence J Fassler, 'The Italian Penal Procedure Code: An Adversarial System of Criminal Procedure in Continental Europe' (1991) 29 Columbia Journal of Transnational Law 245; Enzo Zappalà, 'Le procés pénal italien entre système inquisitoire et système accusatoire' (1997) 68 Revue Internationale de Droit Pénal 111; Antoinette Perrodet, 'The Italian System' in Mireille Delmas-Marty and John Spencer (eds), *European Criminal Procedures* (Cambridge University Press 2002).

14 Damaška, *The Faces of Justice and State Authority: A Comparative Approach to the Legal Process* (n 1) 3.

15 Orie (n 12) 1445.

16 ibid 1450.

17 ibid 1445.

presented by the parties and how they can examine witnesses and experts.[18] The Judge's decision to admit or exclude evidentiary material, which depends on several factors such as the content of the evidence, how the information or the object was obtained, the need to protect the information contained in it, and how the evidence is presented in court, is aimed at keeping the parties on the right track when presenting evidence.[19] For instance, the examination of a witness can be interrupted by the parties' objections based on those grounds. Moreover, in a jury trial, the Judge plays a fundamental role as he/she is tasked with summing up and drawing the jury's attention to the relevant aspect of the case, including the law and the facts on which the jury has to decide.

Under the adversarial tradition, built on the premise of a contest between the prosecution and the defendant, victims are not formal parties and, consequently, do not have any right to participate in the proceedings.[20] Accordingly, victims can play the role of witnesses, when they are summoned by the parties to take the stand at trial. However, even if victims are not civil parties or participants, they can play a role at the sentencing stage, at which point they can explain the harm they suffered because of the criminal conduct, demand punishment, financial damages, and other forms of compensation.[21] Despite these improvements, victims are still largely excluded from the process because, under the adversarial contest model of a State v defendant, they are generally conceived as mere 'evidentiary cannon fodder'[22] and, thus, 'conscripted' into an operational role and treated as servants of the criminal justice system.[23] More generally, the possibility of conferring a proactive and meaningful role on victims challenges the nature of the contest between two parties since victims can 'cause immense structural and normative problems within any adversarial system'.[24]

5.2.2 *The inquisitorial procedural system*

In the civil law model, the trial is structured as an inquiry.[25] The inquisitorial-type system is characterised by a judicial-authorities-driven process, as Judges have the duty to initiate *ex officio* the procedure, control the investigation, gather evidence and, more generally, shape the trial. To safeguard the rights of the accused, the

18 ibid 1443.
19 ibid 1452.
20 Marion Eleonora Ingeborg Brienen and Ernestine Henriëtte Hoegen, *Victims of Crime in 22 European Criminal Justice Systems* (Wolf Legal Productions 2000) 245.
21 ibid 267–268, 481.
22 John Braithwaite and Kathleen Daly, 'Masculinities, Violence and Communitarian Control' in Susan Miller (ed), *Crime Control and Women: Feminist Implications of Criminal Justice Policy* (Sage 1998) 151, 154.
23 Doak (n 6) 35.
24 Jonathan Doak, 'Victims' Rights in Criminal Trials: Prospects for Participation' (2005) 32 Journal of Law and Society 294, 297.
25 Damaška, *The Faces of Justice and State Authority: A Comparative Approach to the Legal Process* (n 1) 80.

inquisitorial criminal process sets various levels of judicial control, since there is a clear distinction between the role played by the judicial authority responsible for the criminal investigation and those responsible for the trial. Moreover, at the various stages of a criminal process the different authorities ought to investigate both exculpatory and inculpatory evidence in the pursuit of truth.[26]

The pre-trial phase is central to the inquisitorial procedural model. It focuses on the preparation of the comprehensive official dossier, containing the results of the investigations that serve the Judge in the preparation or the conduct of the trial.[27] The pre-trial investigations are usually conducted in secret by the Prosecutor or the pre-trial Judge, assisted by the police.[28] The investigating magistrate, like the Spanish *Juez Instructor*, or the French *Juge d'Instruction*, plays a central role in gathering evidence, examining witnesses and experts, recording their statements and including them in the dossier. The parties are granted full access to the dossier and rely on it, rather that conducting their own investigations. However, the victim or the defendant can file an application requesting the investigation authority to undertake additional investigations. In particular, defendants can request a witness to be interviewed in order to defend themselves from the charges and offer counter evidence against that gathered by the investigation authority.[29] In this stage of the proceedings, the defendant can be questioned by the police, the Prosecutor, or the investigating Judge to provide him/her with the opportunity to provide his/her version of events.[30] In the pre-trial hearing, the Prosecutor's role is to recommend a trial only if he/ she is sure that there is sufficient evidence of guilt, whereas the task of determining whether the evidentiary material contained in the official dossier is enough to carry on with the trial or dismissing the case lies with the investigating Judge.[31]

The trial stage is conducted in public hearings and takes a one case approach. There is no distinction between the evidence introduced by the Prosecutor and the Defence since all evidence is part of the dossier, which is the object of discussion during the trial from a legal and factual viewpoint. The Judges normally have the dossier at hand, limiting the presentation of evidence to a reference to the dossier.[32] Nonetheless, sometimes the content of the dossier needs to be verified through the examination of the original sources, for instance a recorded statement

26 Christian Dadomo and Susan Farran, *The French Legal System* (Sweet & Maxwell 1996) 160.

27 Orie (n 12) 1451.

28 Stewart Field, 'Fair Trials and Procedural Tradition in Europe' (2009) 29 Oxford Journal of Legal Studies 365, 367.

29 John Jackson, 'Transnational Faces of Justice: Two Attempts to Build Common Standards beyond National Boundaries' in John Jackson, Máximo Langer and Peter Tillers (eds), *Crime, Procedure and Evidence in Comparative and International Context: Essays in Honour of Professor Mirjan Damaška* (Hart Publishing 2008) 231.

30 Richard Vogler, 'France' in Richard Vogler and Barbara Huber (eds), *Criminal Procedure in Europe* (Duncker & Humblot 2008) 239.

31 Orie (n 12) 1444.

32 McGonigle Leyh (n 7) 72.

of a witness is corroborated by testimony. Therefore, the Judges shape the trial proceedings, by deciding which witnesses they wish to summon. Moreover, the Judges can, *proprio motu* or on the request of the parties, order the presentation and examination of additional evidence. The defendant is not under an obligation to take an oath if he/she wants to speak in his/her Defence or in the case is questioned by the Judge, the Prosecutor, or the Defence counsel and, thus, he/she cannot be sanctioned for giving false statements.[33]

A defining feature of the inquisitorial model is the emphasis on narrative testimony. When questioning witnesses, the Judge asks them 'to explain fully and completely what happened. In short, the witness is invited to tell all she or he knows about the crime and its surrounding circumstances in a narrative fashion'.[34] Such an approach is believed to greatly help the Judge to make a reasoned decision on the facts because the content of the testimony is presented in an unrehearsed and unmanipulated way.[35] When witnesses have concluded their story-telling, the Judges can conduct question them, followed by the parties.[36] This narrative approach to testimony can potentially result in hearsay, opinions, or irrelevant statements that can be prejudicial to the Defence; nevertheless, the Judge's evaluation of what was presented at trial is guided by normative instruments, such as the rules of evidence. Under the rules of evidence of the inquisitorial systems, Judges assess whether and to what extent the dossier and the additional evidence presented at trial serve to reach a verdict on the guilt or innocence of the defendant. Judges are obliged to explain the reasonings underpinning their evaluation of the dossier and the additional evidence, meaning that, in their deliberations, they can conclude that they consider a certain statement of a witness is improper or pointless in respect to the determination of the guilt and they simply ignore it.

In civil law systems, the framework of the proceedings as 'an official inquiry'[37] provides a framework for 'allowing the victim to have a voice in the criminal process'.[38] The postulate of the inquisitorial model that places a larger duty on the Judges, rather than the parties, to investigate facts and seek the truth, promotes victims' participation in criminal proceedings to help the judicial authorities to reach a more accurate judgement.[39] Consistent with the judge-driven nature of the inquisitorial criminal proceedings, the accused and the Prosecutor do not

33 Orie (n 12) 1448–1449.

34 William T Pizzi and Walter Perron, 'Crime Victims in German Courtrooms: A Comparative Perspective on American Problems' (1996) 32 Stanford Journal of International Law 37, 42.

35 McGonigle Leyh (n 7) 73.

36 Jacqueline Hodgson, 'Conceptions of the Trial in Inquisitorial and Adversarial Procedure' in Antony Duff et al. (eds), *The Trial on Trial: Volume 2. Judgment and Calling to Account* (Calling to Account and Judgment, Hart Publishing 2006) 223–226.

37 Damaška, *The Faces of Justice and State Authority: A Comparative Approach to the Legal Process* (n 1) 3.

38 Brienen and Hoegen (n 20) 1169.

39 Pizzi and Perron (n 34) 51.

engage in an adversarial contest and victims can participate as a third party, without jeopardising the interests and rights of the accused.[40]

The view that victims' engagement in criminal proceedings is strictly intertwined with the judge's role in finding the truth affords victims broad participatory rights. Victims can serve not only as witnesses, they can also have an autonomous standing as individuals who suffered harm and have the right to be heard. Specifically, civil law systems provide victims with broad participatory rights under the concept of *partie civile*, which allows them to attach their civil claim for compensation to the criminal proceedings.[41] Victims acting as 'a full-fledged party'[42] in the criminal proceedings have the right to: request investigations; challenge the prosecutorial discretion not to prosecute; bring the name of potential witnesses to the investigating Judge or the Prosecutor; call witnesses; ask questions; make closing arguments; and claim reparations.[43] Additionally, the narrative character of the testimony allows victims to speak in a more natural and narrative manner, unlike their limited participation as cross-examined witnesses in the adversarial procedure. Thus, the inquisitorial procedural system can be considered to be more appropriate to enhance victims' active engagement in criminal proceedings.

5.3 Expressivism as the key to a common grammar between adversarial and inquisitorial systems

The previous section has extensively illustrated that the adversarial and inquisitorial procedures conceive the criminal proceedings in diametrically opposed ways. In light of this, the interaction between international and the different domestic criminal law systems is a critical issue for the procedural law of the international criminal tribunals. Article 21 of the RS, requiring the ICC to apply principles and rules of international law and, in the event of imprecision or a gap in international law, 'general principles of law derived by the Court from national laws of legal systems of the world',[44] raises practical problems in respect of the 'methodology when attempting to deduce general principles from laws representing "the legal systems of the world" and to verify their compatibility with international law

40 Gideon Boas et al., 'The Role and Status of Victims in International Criminal Procedure', *International Criminal Law Practitioner Library: International Criminal Procedure* (Cambridge University Press 2011) 307.

41 Brienen and Hoegen (n 20) 129, 203, 320.

42 Damaška, *The Faces of Justice and State Authority: A Comparative Approach to the Legal Process* (n 1) 200, 212–213.

43 Mirjan Damaška, 'The Uncertain Fate of Evidentiary Transplants: Anglo-American and Continental Experiments' (2007) 45 American Journal of Comparative Law 839, 841; Richard Frase, 'Comparative Criminal Justice as a Guide to American Law Reform: How Do the French Do It, How Can We Find Out, and Why Should We Care?' (1990) 78 California Law Review 539, 545, 671–672.

44 Article 21(c) Rome Statute of the International Criminal Court 1998 (2187 UNTS 90).

as a whole'.[45] Judges hold strong beliefs on the nature of the procedural law that are indissolubly linked to their own domestic system. Thus, lacking an interpretative tool, Judges from different legal traditions will maintain different understandings of the criminal process as well as of the role of actors involved in it, giving precedence to their personal knowledge.[46] It is, thus, important for justice purposes, fairness, and equality to adopt a consistent method that 'goes beyond simple juxtaposition, requiring genuine, creative re-composition through the search for a synthesis of, or equilibrium between, diverse elements or diverse systems'.[47] It is important in this method that a common grammar is adopted to harmonise the 'accusatory grammar' and the 'inquisitory grammar', based respectively on a party-driven fact-finding process and judge-driven fact-finding process. The idea of a more harmonised international procedural system is not a novelty in the academic debate. However, the concept of a common grammar is more advanced and radical. It does not entail a simple unilateral transplantation of common law and civil law elements within international criminal proceedings, since a mere transposition of those procedural elements cannot guarantee the efficiency and, eventually, the legitimacy of international criminal justice.

The concept of a common grammar makes it necessary to put an end to the 'obstinate adherence' to differing legal traditions in the operation of a vital international criminal tribunal.[48] What needs to be addressed 'is not to determine which legal system is superior, but rather to develop a functional international criminal justice process based on international human rights'.[49] In *Erdemović*, an early case before the ICTY, Judge Antonio Cassese put forward a type of interaction between inquisitorial and adversarial systems characterised by a progressive process of 'cross-fertilisation'.[50] He remarked that, even though international criminal procedure does not originate from a uniform body of law, it should combine and fuse in a fair manner the adversarial system with the inquisitorial approach. International criminal procedure should avoid upholding the philosophy behind one of the two legal systems to the exclusion of the other, since combining these legal systems does not mean mechanically incorporating

45 Mireille Delmas-Marty, 'The Contribution of Comparative Law to a Pluralist Conception of International Criminal Law' (2003) 1 Journal of International Criminal Justice 13, 18.
46 McGonigle Leyh (n 7) 11.
47 Delmas-Marty (n 45) 18.
48 Christoph Safferling, 'The Role of the Victim in the Criminal Process – A Paradigm Shift in National German and International Law?' (2011) 11 International Criminal Law Review 183, 212.
49 ibid. See also Rod Dixon, 'Developing International Rules of Evidence for the Yugoslav and Rwanda Tribunals' (1997) 7 Transnational Law & Contemporary Problems 81, 98; Richard May and Marieke Wierda, 'Trends in International Criminal Evidence: Nuremberg, Tokyo, The Hague, and Arusha' (1998) 37 Columbia Journal of Transnational Law 725, 735, 764; Patrick L Robinson, 'Ensuring Fair and Expeditious Trials at the International Criminal Tribunal for the Former Yugoslavia' (2000) 11 European Journal of International Law 569, 735, 764; Ambos (n 1) 34–35.
50 Delmas-Marty (n 45) 18.

into international criminal proceedings ideas, legal constructs, or concepts which only belong to common law or civil law traditions.[51] According to Cassese, the mechanical importation of notions from national systems has the ability to alter or distort the specificity of international criminal proceedings and ultimately generate great confusion and misapprehension. Such specificity of the international criminal procedure results from several features that differentiate it from national criminal proceedings, such as the Inter-State context of international criminal justice, which is marked by the absence of means at its disposal to enforce its orders, summonses, and other decisions.[52] Therefore, the logic underpinning national systems, where the fundamental law-making, adjudication, and law enforcement functions are carried out by a State's organs over individuals, cannot be simply transposed to the international level.[53] Notions and terms originating in national criminal law, once transposed to the international level, acquire a new lease of life, absolutely independent of their original meaning.[54] Thus, Judge Cassese concluded that international criminal procedure should result from the 'gradual decanting' of two different legal systems – common law and civil law – into the 'international receptacle'.[55]

The development of a true common grammar, distinct from simple transplant, should generate a logic 'that is qualitatively different from that of each of the two national criminal systems' and that gradually becomes 'autonomous from its national parents'.[56] Therefore, an international criminal proceedings shaped by a common grammar must be built and systematised with reference not only to common technical rules, but it should also entail 'the guiding and meta principles that structure the system'[57] of international criminal justice. Comparing international criminal law specialists to 'mariners on the ocean without compass, star or landmark',[58] Damaška, called for an innovation of the international criminal proceedings in order to give full effect to the pedagogical function of the trial, which is more appropriate for international criminal justice.

Expressivism challenges the adversarial nature of the proceedings, suggesting the need to adopt a flexible procedural system. A pure adversarial system is not suited to serve the didactic and communicative purposes of international criminal proceedings. In this regard, Allo remarked that '[t]he "either–or" binary

51 *Prosecutor v Dražen Erdemović* (Separate and Dissenting Opinion of Judge Cassese) IT-96–22-T, Appeals Chamber (7 October 1997), para 4.
52 ibid, para 5.
53 ibid, para 5.
54 ibid, para 6.
55 ibid, para 4.
56 ibid, para 4.
57 Mireille Delmas-Marty, 'Reflections on the "Hybridisation" of Criminal Procedure' in John Jackson and Máximo Langer (eds), *Crime, Procedure and Evidence in a Comparative and International Context: Essays in Honour of Professor Mirjan Damaška* (Hart Publishers 2008) 258.
58 Mirjan Damaška, 'Negotiated Justice in International Criminal Courts' (2004) 2 Journal of International Criminal Justice 1018, 1018–1019.

communication at trial structurally removes the many possible explanations of a historical or political event'.[59] The normative value of the trial, which aims at providing a narrative and its pedagogical dissemination, seems to clash with the proceedings structured as a contest between two parties. In an ideal type of adversarial mode of procedure, where the parties dominate the evidence-gathering process, the litigants may not always be motivated or able to disclose the whole historical truth.[60] The adversarial procedural system, designed to maximise the goal of dispute-resolution between the defendant and the Prosecutor, does not necessarily aim to maximise accurate fact-finding because a skilful strategy of evidence disclosure can cast a shadow over the event under adjudication rather than shed a light on what has actually happened.[61] Defendants have the right to have a Defence (which represents an essential feature of the fair trial principle); however, they can use the trial to disseminate ideas alien to the culture of human rights, which can easily take root within the audience among many communities.[62] Mechanisms such as plea bargaining or negotiated sentences, which allow the parties to bargain outcomes without the need for oral presentation of evidence, can silence the voices of victims and communities affected by the crimes. As result, the charges bear little relation to the bargained reality.[63] Moreover, the adversarial mode of procedure, based on the notion of the proceedings as a contest between prosecution and Defence, excludes the interests of victims and of the community affected by international crimes.[64] Specifically, at trial stage, victims as witnesses are hampered from giving a full version of events by the constraints of examination and cross-examination.[65]

One of the procedural implications of the didactic function of the trial is the 'desirability of relaxing the bipolar pressures that arise from the proceedings organised as a contest of two partisan cases'.[66] The expressivist account of international criminal proceedings calls for a system of 'tempered adversariality',

59 Awol Kassim Allo, 'The "Show" in the "Show Trial": Contextualizing the Politicization of the Courtroom' (2010) 15 Barry Law Review 41, 67.

60 Damaška, *The Faces of Justice and State Authority: A Comparative Approach to the Legal Process* (n 1) 122; J Jackson, 'Finding the Best Epistemic Fit for International Criminal Tribunals: Beyond the Adversarial-Inquisitorial Dichotomy' (2009) 7 Journal of International Criminal Justice 17, 22.

61 Damaška, *The Faces of Justice and State Authority: A Comparative Approach to the Legal Process* (n 1) 122–123.

62 Marlies Glasius and Tim Meijers, 'Expression of Justice or Political Trial? Discursive Battles in the Karadžić Case' (2013) 35 Human Rights Quarterly 720, 726; Mirjan Damaška, 'What Is the Point of International Criminal Justice?' (2008) 83 Chicago-Kent Law Review 329, 357.

63 Jackson, 'Finding the Best Epistemic Fit for International Criminal Tribunals' (n 60) 22.

64 ibid.

65 William Pizzi, 'Overcoming Logistical and Structural Barriers to Fair Trials at International Tribunals' (2007) 4 International Commentary on Evidence 3 <https://www.degruyter.com/view/j/ice.2007.4.1/ice.2007.4.1.1051/ice.2007.4.1.1051.xml> accessed 4 February 2019.

66 Damaška, 'What Is the Point of International Criminal Justice?' (n 62) 357.

which allows 'two passionately committed parties to adduce all relevant facts before a neutral adjudicator while allowing the adjudicator to play a secondary, but active, role in bringing out the evidence'.[67] The performative and communicative features of the trial and, consequently, of the role of the actors to the proceedings, are not an end in themselves, but a means to an end, since the trial bridges the story of the parties and the story of the law.

5.4 Victims' participation through the lens of the expressivist justice model

Expressivism provides an important conceptual justification for victims' participation in international criminal proceedings. It enhances the 'legal subject-hood'[68] of victims, as it recognises that the status of the victim goes beyond the simple recognition of the harmful character of the crime suffered. Victims are no longer 'the outcome of hardship and adversity',[69] useful only to achieve a more favourable outcome of the criminal justice process; instead, they are active agents in proceedings.[70] They contribute to re-enacting the crime and constructing reality, by making sense of violence and 'transforming [social conflict] into the system of social representations, exchanges, surrogacies that make up the law'.[71] This active role produces an authoritative acknowledgement that the action victims were subjected to is a specific and extremely serious kind of wrong, strictly speaking, a crime under international law.[72] The expressivist view on the role of victims allows them to counter the claim of superiority made by the defendant through the commission of the crime as well as to regain self-respect, dignity, and their status as rights holders and political subjects.[73]

Victims' participation in proceedings is key to pursuing fundamental expressivist goals. First, victims' story-telling contributes to the goals of truth-telling and historical clarification. Victims' participation and narration can potentially enhance the quality of the narrative shaped during the proceedings and contribute to the establishment of the truth, ultimately putting an end to impunity. In the 'Report

67 Peter Carmichael Keen, 'Tempered Adversariality: The Judicial Role and Trial Theory in the International Criminal Tribunals' (2004) 17 Leiden Journal of International Law 767, 811.
68 Shoshana Felman, 'Theaters of Justice: Arendt in Jerusalem, the Eichmann Trial, and the Redefinition of Legal Meaning in the Wake of the Holocaust' (2001b) 27 Critical Inquiry 201, 228, 233.
69 Conor McCarthy, 'Victim Redress and International Criminal Justice: Competing Paradigms, or Compatible Forms of Justice?' (2012) 10 Journal of International Criminal Justice 351, 366.
70 Carsten Stahn, *Justice as Message: Expressivist Foundations of International Criminal Justice* (1st edn, Oxford University Press 2020) 301.
71 Julie Stone Peters, 'Legal Performance Good and Bad Law' (2008) 4 Culture and the Humanities 179, 185.
72 Stahn (n 70) 301.
73 Colleen Murphy, *The Conceptual Foundations of Transitional Justice* (Cambridge University Press 2017) 176.

of the Bureau on the Impact of the Rome Statute System on Victims and Affected Communities', one of the panellists emphasised 'that victims' participation was significant for the historical record and legacy of the Court, as well as for the international criminal justice system, in general'.[74] Similarly, the more recent 'Court's Revised Strategy in Relation to Victims' affirms that

> victims' participation empowers them, recognises their suffering and enables them to contribute to the establishment of the historical record, the truth as it were of what occurred. Victims play an important role as active participants in the quest for justice and should be valued in that way by the justice process. Moreover, their participation in the justice process contributes to closing the impunity gap.[75]

The goals of framing a historical record and truth-finding involve a social production as 'most of the facts we seek to establish in adjudication are "social" facts rather than phenomena intrinsic to nature'.[76] In this process of knowledge production, victims to the proceedings have different approaches to the events and contribute to structuring 'how the accounts of what happened unfold and are given meaning'.[77] Paolina Massidda, Principal Counsel of the Office of the Public Counsel for Victims at the ICC, explained that 'victims are independent actors in the proceedings before this Court (…) [whose] position is to contribute to the establishment of the truth'.[78] This quote exemplifies that including history-telling by the victims contributes 'shedding light on what actually happened, to fill the gap that could take place between procedural establishment of facts and the truth itself'.[79] Victims can meaningfully impact the way proceedings are conducted and their outcomes because they provide the ICC with a 'privileged' access to the truth, giving the Judges a clearer picture of what actually happened to them and the suffering they endured.[80] In other words, victims carry an essential role in the establishment of facts, since the inputs they provide in proceedings are twofold: first, they present their knowledge about what happened and 'their vision and

74 Assembly of States Parties, 'Report of the Bureau on the Impact of the Rome Statute System on Victims and Affected Communities' (2010) ICC-ASP/9/25 17, para 15 <legal-tools.org/doc/343f96/pdf> accessed 24 October 2021.

75 Assembly of States Parties, 'Court's Revised Strategy in Relation to Victims' (2012) ICC-ASP/11/38 <https://asp.icc-cpi.int/iccdocs/asp_docs/ASP11/ICC-ASP-11-38-ENG.pdf> accessed 24 October 2021, para 10.

76 Mirjan Damaška, 'Truth in Adjudication' (1998) 49 Hastings Law Journal 289, 291.

77 Doris Buss, 'Knowing Women: Translating Patriarchy in International Criminal Law' (2014b) 23 Social & Legal Studies 73, 75.

78 *Prosecutor v Thomas Lubanga Dyilo* (Opening Statement by Victim Representative) ICC-01/04–01/06 (26 January 2009) 41.

79 ibid.

80 *Prosecutor v William Samoei Ruto and Joshua Arap Sang* (Opening Statement by Victim Representative) ICC-01/09–01/11, Trial Chamber V(A) (10 September 2013) 42–43.

an understanding of those who are responsible for what happened to them'.[81] Second, victim story-telling offers primary and unique information, as victims before the Court share their experiences of suffering, which is crucial for the establishment of the events.[82] Such historical clarification by victims is critical to providing an understanding of the general context of the atrocities under adjudication and establishing the contextual elements of crimes.

The exposure of the previously unheard and unknown accounts of victims finds a proper significant place in the juridified truth of the international criminal proceedings because it is articulated by the procedural constraints of the trial and combines the different interests and concerns, including the rights of the Defence and the interests of a fair trial in the course of the decision-making process. Therefore, having their voice heard in the proceedings confers on victims a 'historical and semantic authority over themselves and over others'.[83]

Secondly, victims' participation in proceedings reaffirms the importance of safeguarding basic standards of human rights. From an expressivist perspective, international criminal justice seeks not only to 'do justice', but also to 'make justice seen'.[84] This is reflected in the principle of 'open justice', which calls for public accessibility and visibility.[85] In a more specific sense, victims' participation in proceedings entails messages about access to justice to those who are being affected by crime and who should be given a voice in the criminal process.[86] The active role played by victims in proceedings conveys a message about the standards of fairness, which, to be assessed, requires a balancing of interests, including not only the rights of the accused, fairness and expeditiousness of proceedings and due process, but also the rights of victims. There is an inherent connection between fairness to victims and procedural justice, since preventing victims' views and concerns from being effectively heard reduces the right to a fair trial to a talk in the abstract. The concept of fairness cannot exist 'without the concept of justice and there can be no criminal trial without victims of the crimes charged'.[87] The articulation of victims' narratives as living, historical and legal records of the events is, therefore, in itself an unprecedented act of justice for victims.[88]

81 *Prosecutor v Germain Katanga and Mathieu Ngudjolo Chui* (Closing Statement by Victim Representative) ICC-01/04-01/07, Trial Chamber II (16 May 2012) 57.
82 Sofia Stolk, 'The Victim, the International Criminal Court and the Search for Truth: On the Interdependence and Incompatibility of Truths about Mass Atrocity' (2015) 13 Journal of International Criminal Justice 973, 984.
83 Felman (n 68) 233.
84 Shoshana Felman, 'A Ghosts in the House of Justice: Death and the Language of the Law' (2001a) 13 Yale Journal of Law & the Humanities 241, 277–278.
85 See Linda Mulcahy, *Legal Architecture: Justice, Due Process and the Place of Law* (GlassHouse 2011); Jason Bosland, 'The Principle of Open Justice and the Judicial Duty to Give Public Reasons' (2014) 38 Melbourne University Law Review 482; Denise Meyerson, 'Why Should Justice Be Seen to Be Done?' (2015) 34 Criminal Justice Ethics 64.
86 Stahn (n 70) 260.
87 *Prosecutor v William Samoei Ruto and Joshua Arap Sang* (n 80) 43.
88 Felman (n 68) 213.

Third, victims' participation in proceedings fulfils a didactic purpose, sending out the message that impunity will not be tolerated anymore. For expressivism, such a message can be sent not only through punishment, but also through victims' participation in proceedings. Victims can play an important role in communicating the denunciation and the disavowal of heinous conducts with greater clarity. Their voices and experiences heard in the courtroom communicate that the crime causes serious harm to concrete persons and expose the consequences of a campaign of violence or mass atrocity which affects hundreds, often thousands, of individuals.[89] These denunciatory and condemnatory aspects of victims' participation at trials, thus, strengthen the sense of accountability and inflict shame and stigma on perpetrators of mass violence.[90] It is around the victims' experience that a 'collective memory'[91] of the events is formed and kept alive.[92] The denunciatory expression by victims contributes to the potential of international criminal trials to send a didactic message to the international community about the importance of solidarity, the value of law, the prominence of human rights, and, eventually, educate the public about the respect of those rights.[93]

5.5 The role of the other actors in the proceedings

The expressivist features of the international criminal proceedings are shaped by the courtroom interactions of a whole range of actors in the justice process, namely Judges, Prosecutor, and defendants, who are assigned a specific role and serve different functions.

5.5.1 Judges

Tailoring the structure of the legal process in a way that reflects the norm-expression function of the trial calls for loosening the adversarial model and its nature of a contest between parties. One of the main elements of the common grammar is, therefore, the adoption of a more active role for the Judges. They play

89 McCarthy (n 69) 367.

90 Damaška, 'What Is the Point of International Criminal Justice?' (n 62) 345.

91 Lawrence Douglas, *The Memory of Judgment: Making Law and History in the Trials of the Holocaust* (Yale University Press 2001) 2; Mark Osiel, *Mass Atrocity, Collective Memory and the Law* (Transaction Publishers 1997) 2.

92 Doris Buss, 'Expert Witnesses and International War Crimes Trials: Making Sense of Large-Scale Violence in Rwanda' in Marlies Glasius and Dubravka Žarkov (eds), *Narratives of Justice In and Out of the Courtroom: Former Yugoslavia and Beyond* (Springer 2014a) 35.

93 Damaška, 'What Is the Point of International Criminal Justice?' (n 62) 339; Maria Elander, 'The Victim's Address: Expressivism and the Victim at the Extraordinary Chambers in the Courts of Cambodia' (2013) 7 International Journal of Transitional Justice 95, 100.

an important role in enacting the performative and communicative dimensions[94] of the trial: Judges operate as active fact finders to determine the truth and as interpreters that give meaning to the narratives expressed by the parties in the application of the law.

In essence, the fact-finding process represents the nucleus of the criminal justice process, given that the case at hand is adjudicated upon a scrutinised evaluation and analysis of the evidentiary material gathered in the course of the proceedings. As, undoubtedly, the ultimate objective of criminal proceedings is the establishment of the truth, it becomes evident that the key role of the parties in the fact-finding procedure does not, as a matter of principle, exempt the judicial authority from its core task of ascertaining the truth. The Judges' active involvement in the fact-finding process, the objective of which is the search for and the determination of the truth, takes place in proceedings before the ICC. An example in this regard is provided by Article 69(3) of the RS, which envisions the Chamber's general right – independent of the cooperation or the consent of the parties – to request the presentation of all evidence necessary for the determination of the truth.[95] While the said article does not explicitly impose upon the Chamber the *duty* of establishing the truth, the judicial authority to request the submission of all evidence conducive to the ascertainment of the truth is very close to an obligation to search for the truth.[96] To elucidate the facts and circumstances under examination, the Judges can question witnesses independently of the parties, hear directly from victims as participants, or call witnesses they consider relevant. In particular, allowing victims to present their views, casting a sort of 'third perspective', might be necessary for the Judges because parties are driven by partisan interests, which do not always coincide with the goal of establishing the truth.[97]

Judges' active engagement in establishing the truth might pose a challenge to the fairness of the adjudication process. From the epistemic perspective, a judge-driven fact-finding process may lead them to form some premature hypotheses about the events, making Judges more receptive to information more consistent with their tentative theories than to information which departs from them.[98] Potentially it may be difficult for the Judges to prevent the – either conscious or

94 See section 4.7.

95 See section 8.8.

96 Robert Heinsch, 'How to Achieve Fair and Expeditious Trial Proceedings before the ICC: Is It Time for a More Judge-Dominated Approach?' in Carsten Stahn and Göran Sluiter (eds), *The Emerging Practice of the ICC* (Martinus Nijhoff 2009) 486.

97 Sergey Vasiliev, 'Victim Participation Revisited: What the ICC Is Learning About Itself' in Carsten Stahn, *The Law and Practice of the International Criminal Court* (Oxford University Press 2015) 1177.

98 Mirjan Damaška, 'Epistemology and Legal Regulation of Proof' (2003) 2 Law, Probability and Risk 117, 121; Damaška, *The Faces of Justice and State Authority: A Comparative Approach to the Legal Process* (n 1) 162.

subconscious – development of premature conclusions on the merits of a case.[99] Partisans of adversarial systems hold that the neutrality of Judges and the accuracy of their ruling are independent variables. A Judge may pronounce the right decision on the merit, but it is also possible he/she may have treated parties unequally, or else he/she may have treated litigants equally but made the wrong decision. The potential tension between these two values is solved by placing the impartiality of the process above the accuracy of the decision.[100] In other words, an adversarial system, by valuing fairness above justice, promotes the view that the passive attitude of a judge is the greatest guarantee of his/her impartiality and of a fair trial. However, in a justice system which embodies a synthesis between adversarial and inquisitorial traditions, the judicial activism in the pursuit of the truth, impartiality, and fairness cannot and should not be mutually exclusive. The impartiality of the Judges cannot correspond to passivity; it should rather be associated with absence of personal prejudice and bias.[101] An antidote to partiality of the Judges is their willingness to explain to the parties the reasons for their initiative and, more specifically, a reasoned judgement which obliges them to make their decisions clear and consistent and subject to close scrutiny in appeal.[102]

Judges do not act simply as ultimate adjudicators of the facts; they are called to interpret and apply the law in order to make sense of the competing narratives presented during the proceedings. From a semiotic viewpoint, interpretation enables the Judges 'to decode the messages and understand the explicit or implicit signs embedded in the legal discourse'.[103] To put it simply, while parties and participants represent the reality of the events under adjudication through the mediation of words, complex codes, and sometimes ambiguous legal language, Judges need to unlock the meaning of such representations, making a decision on their legal relevance.[104] Judgements are the means through which Judges are able to build their own 'meta-story'[105] and produce 'a legally authoritative reading of words, signs, and signals expressed in the procedures'.[106] They translate the conflicting narratives and interpretations of the trial into one authoritative account.

99 Bert Swart, 'Damaska and the Faces of International Criminal Justice' (2008) 6 Journal of International Criminal Justice 87, 112.
100 Damaška, *The Faces of Justice and State Authority: A Comparative Approach to the Legal Process* (n 1) 136.
101 ibid 114.
102 ibid 113.
103 Susan W Tiefenbrun, 'Legal Semiotics' (1986) 5 Cardozo Arts & Entertainment Law Journal 89, 98–99.
104 Susan W Tiefenbrun, *Decoding International Law: Semiotics and the Humanities* (Oxford University Press 2010) 24.
105 Damaška, 'Epistemology and Legal Regulation of Proof' (n 98) 121; Damaška, 'What Is the Point of International Criminal Justice?' (n 62) 357.
106 Stahn (n 70) 299.

5.5.2 The Prosecutor

The Prosecutor plays a crucial role in the enactment of the performative and communicative features of the proceedings, as he/she carries out a narrative and educative function. The charges presented by the Prosecutor entail narratives, which can be seen as a 'counter-performance to the crime',[107] sending the message that the trial serves to overcome the criminal acts. The Prosecutor does not only relate facts to law, but he/she is required to construct his/her story around the rules of evidence, representing a particular view of the defendant's actions and, more generally, of the events under adjudication.[108] As affirmed by the ICC Judge Christine Van den Wyngaert, the Prosecutor's action aims to demonstrate 'the existence of specific relations between different facts and construct a particular narrative on the basis of which, if true, would cover all the legal elements of the charges with which it corresponds'.[109]

The Prosecutor's narrative must not only be persuasive, it also needs to convince the Judges that there is not any other plausible reading of the evidence. Therefore, the narrative function of the charges needs to be complemented by relating the role of the defendant to the broader historical reading of the atrocities committed. As Wilson observed, Prosecutors present in the courtroom their 'theory of the case', which is an 'explanation of why the crimes occurred in the first instance, and this theory is often based upon circumstantial and historical factors'.[110] The defendant is portrayed as part of a bigger picture, where crimes are ideological or political projects rather than simply by-products of violence.[111] This view recognises that the Prosecutor relies on historical and political analysis and engages in readings or interpretations of history.

The Prosecutor's narrative is often strengthened by the accounts of the sufferings of the victims. The latter are invoked as a collective and abstract entity, whose harm, grief, and suffering are re-enacted at trial and communicated through the law.[112] Approaching victims through the lens of the discourse of harm and suffering provokes empathy, as they are associated with the stereotype, captured in Nils Christie's concept of the *ideal victim*, of a powerless helpless

107 ibid 276.

108 John D Jackson, 'Law, Fact and Narrative Coherence: A Deep Look at Court Adjudication' (1990) 7 International Journal for the Semiotics of Law 81, 93.

109 *Prosecutor v Germain Katanga* (Judgment Pursuant to Article 74 of the Statute, Minority Opinion of Judge Christine Van den Wyngaert) ICC-01/04–01/07, Trial Chamber II (7 March 2014), para 32.

110 Richard Wilson, 'Humanity's Histories: Evaluating the Historical Accounts of International Tribunals and Truth Commissions' (2007) 80 Politix 31, 43.

111 Marlies Glasius, 'Terror, Terrorizing, Terrorism: Instilling Fear as a Crime in the Cases of Radovan Karadzic and Charles Taylor' in Dubravka Žarkov and Marlies Glasius (eds), *Narratives of Justice In and Out of the Courtroom: Former Yugoslavia and Beyond* (Springer 2014) 59.

112 Elander (n 93) 96.

innocent, who suffers from catastrophic events but lacks agency him/herself.[113] Such a representation of victims is central to shoring up the legitimacy of the Prosecutor's actions.[114] From a rhetorical viewpoint, subordinating victims' sufferings to the function of support for the prosecution's case gives a strong moral justification to the proceedings, which are seen as humanitarian acts, aimed primarily at achieving justice for victims. However, this objectification of victims or, using Stahn's words, the 'commodification of suffering'[115] is problematic because it clashes with the above-discussed expressivist perspective on the victims' role, which treats them as active subjects of the proceedings.[116] The Prosecutor often takes control of the victim's narrative to impose a particular frame or stereotype to keep the perceived injustice of the victim's suffering at bay. This instrumentalisation of the victim's narrative imposes a normative demand upon victims, who are tasked to conform to this frame, causing difficulties for victims whose story does not conform in some respect to the stereotype of the ideal victim.[117] Relying on this simplified representation of victims does not adequately address the complexity of victimhood. Not all victims are *ideal*; quite the opposite, the 'lines between victim, perpetrator and bystander are in reality often blurry',[118] as victims can suffer harm but also be victimisers.[119]

The Prosecutor's role does not simply aim to present evidence and persuade the Judges in order to win the case, it also has an educative aspiration. Prosecutions are a means of teaching a lesson, which goes beyond the perpetrators and other actors involved in the proceedings. The Prosecutor's action seeks to educate the whole of society and the international community generally about the world's horrors and consolidate declared norms and shared beliefs about the way individuals ought to behave. The didactic function of the Prosecutor visibly unfolds in the

113 Nils Christie, 'The Ideal Victim' in Ezzat A Fattah (ed), *From Crime Policy to Victim Policy* (Palgrave Macmillan 1986) 25; Stolk (n 82) 984, 989. See also Elander (n 93) 110–112; Liesbeth Zegveld, 'Victims as a Third Party: Empowerment of Victims?' (2019) 19 International Criminal Law Review 321, 344.

114 Vasiliev (n 97) 1185. See e.g., Marie-Bénédicte Dembour and Emily Haslam, 'Silencing Hearings? Victim-Witnesses at War Crimes Trials' (2004) 15 European Journal of International Law 151, 151; Laurel E Fletcher, 'Refracted Justice: The Imagined Victim and the International Criminal Court' in Christian De Vos, Sara Kendall and Carsten Stahn (eds), *Contested Justice: The Politics and Practices of International Criminal Court Interventions* (Cambridge University Press 2015) 302; Christine Schwöbel-Patel, 'Spectacle in International Criminal Law: The Fundraising Image of Victimhood' (2016) 4 London Review of International Law 247, 247.

115 Stahn (n 70) 287.

116 See section 5.4.

117 Antony Pemberton, Pauline GM Aarten and Eva Mulder, 'Stories as Property: Narrative Ownership as a Key Concept in Victims' Experiences with Criminal Justice' (2019) 19 Criminology & Criminal Justice 404, 410.

118 Christine Schwöbel-Patel, 'The "Ideal" Victim of International Criminal Law' (2018) 29 European Journal of International Law 703, 724.

119 Mark A Drumbl, 'Victims Who Victimize' (2016) 4 London Review of International Law 217, 218.

prosecutorial discretionary powers, which focus on specific categories of crimes to draw attention to and educate the public on certain forms of atrocities that would otherwise go unnoticed. deGuzman[120] and Drumbl[121] advance the need for an expressivist approach to the selection of cases for prosecution before the ICC. Specifically, deGuzman argues that when deciding whether to investigate and prosecute situations and cases, the Prosecutor should aim primarily at maximising the didactic function through which social norms and values are expressed.[122] This 'thematic charging'[123] has the merit of highlighting the need to prosecute certain crimes and patterns of victimisation and condemning the fact that those crimes 'are not considered serious domestically and their victims are not heard, and therefore their voices have been silenced'.[124]

The choice to prioritise thematic charges has some drawbacks. It is problematic to balance the Prosecutor's thematic charging with the expressivist approach to victims, which conceives victims as active agents in the proceedings, whose views and interests should be incorporated in the prosecutorial strategy. The decision to concentrate on certain crimes while excluding others implies that the Prosecutor acknowledges some victims and rejects others on the base of his/her prosecutorial strategy.[125] Like the Prosecutor at the domestic level, the Prosecutor of international criminal tribunals is expected to exercise his/her discretionary powers in the public interest. Therefore, the discretionary powers of the Prosecutor should come with the responsibility correlated to the concerns of those who suffered gross violations of international human rights and humanitarian law. Even if the Prosecutor cannot be held responsible for rendering justice to every victim, he/she should acknowledge that victims represent one of the constituencies he/she has to serve. The Prosecutor should be sensitive to the victims' expectations of justice.[126]

5.5.3 *The defendant*

The defendant is the procedural counterpart of the Prosecutor, as the international criminal trial entails an antagonistic contest, where two opposing parties challenge

120 See Margaret deGuzman, 'Choosing to Prosecute: Expressive Selection at the International Criminal Court' (2012) 33 Michigan Journal of International Law 265.

121 See Mark A Drumbl, 'The Expressive Value of Prosecuting and Punishing Terrorists: Hamdan, the Geneva Conventions, and International Criminal Law' (2007) 75 The George Washington Law Review 1165.

122 deGuzman (n 120) 319. See also Diane Marie Amann, 'Group Mentality, Expressivism, and Genocide' (2002) 2 International Criminal Law Review 93.

123 Stahn (n 70) 287.

124 Mohammad Hadi Zakerhossein, 'The Al-Mahdi Case and Thematic Prosecution' (*Justice Hub*, 7 September 2016) <justicehub.org/article/the-al-mahdi-case-and-thematic-prosecution> accessed 24 October 2021.

125 Cécil Aptel, 'Prosecutorial Discretion at the ICC and Victims' Right to Remedy: Narrowing the Impunity Gap' (2012) 10 Journal of International Criminal Justice 1357, 1372.

126 ibid 1374.

each other's narrative by putting forward their own truth. In order to counteract the charges, contest evidence, and challenge the alleged role of the defendant in the commission of crimes, the Defence presents its counter-narrative, which is an alternative to the prosecution's version of the events under adjudication. The Defence's narrative attempts to construct an image of the defendant diametrically opposed to that of the Prosecutor, which portrays him/her as an outlaw, an enemy of humankind, evil, a monster, or an extraordinary perpetrator who deviates from ordinary standards of behaviour.[127] The Defence often tells the story 'as a tragedy',[128] in which the defendant is a victim of the coercive circumstances and inauspicious conditions, suggesting that anybody placed in the same situation might have been turned into a perpetrator. The narrative is framed to shift the defendant's responsibility, arguing that he/she conformed to a group's system of values and identity that denied personal responsibility, denied the injury of others, denied victims, and required loyalty to higher-ranked decision-makers.[129] The recoding of the group's morality invalidates general social norms and transforms the normally criminal behaviour into conformed conduct. As the criminal conduct is not perceived as wrong, members of the group are expected to behave in a specific way. It is often argued that high-ranking perpetrators formulate and spread a specific ideology and exercise pressure on the group's members to strengthen their own system of norms.[130]

The Defence's narrative, which *per se* is the highest expression of the imperative right to a fair trial of the defendants, in practice has used legal language to make political speeches, promote the defendant's persona, delegitimise international criminal courts and challenge their authority. For instance, Meijers and Glasius' analysis of the Defence discourse in the *Karadžić* case before the ICTY demonstrates that Mr Karadžić used speech as a means of maintaining a leadership role. He took advantage of the media attention and the existence of a receptive Serbian audience to tell a story about himself as the defender of the Serbs and a martyr for the collective cause of the nation.[131] Mégret and Samson identified a set of practices used by the Defence not only to turn the proceedings into a forum to express protest and portray the defendant as a martyr or a victim but

127 Saira Mohamed, 'Of Monsters and Men: Perpetrator Trauma and Mass Atrocity' 115 Columbia Law Review 1157, 1213; Anette Bringedal Houge, 'Re-Presentations of Defendant Perpetrators in Sexual War Violence Cases Before International and Military Criminal Courts' (2016) 56 British Journal of Criminology 419, 425.

128 Osiel (n 91) 3.

129 Alex Alvarez, 'Destructive Beliefs: Genocide and the Role of Ideology' in Alette Smeulers and Roelof Haveman (eds), *Supranational Criminology: Towards a Criminology of International Crimes* (Intersentia 2008) 216.

130 Oliver Diggelmann, 'International Criminal Tribunals and Reconciliation: Reflections on the Role of Remorse and Apology' (2016) 14 Journal of International Criminal Justice 1073, 1093.

131 Glasius and Meijers (n 62) 746.

also to obstruct the trial and seek political vindication.[132] These practices include: discourteous and disruptive behaviours towards the Court's staff and officers; an aggressive and disdainful attitude towards victims and witnesses; strong opposition to the use of legal language or alternatively the adoption of the defendant's own perspective on the law; continuous politicisation of the trial, which is portrayed as a mere tool of power politics external to the law; refusal to engage in any discussion on issues of fact and law concerning the crimes allegedly committed by the defendant; and the attempt to steer the discussion towards broader political and historical events, rather than discussing the defendant's individual case.[133]

These practices are a threat to the expressivist concept of the trial as a performance of justice and to the legitimacy of the trial itself. If the defendant succeeds in portraying international criminal proceedings and the punishment meted out by tribunals as a mere display of power of one over the other, the whole international criminal justice endeavour would represent in the opinion of some of the audiences the continuation of a conflict by using other means.[134] The delegitimisation of the international criminal tribunals can seriously compromise their authority as a platform for crafting a historical record and truth-telling, reaffirming core values and faith in the rule of law, and sending a message of disapproval of the offender who transgressed the law.

5.6 Conclusion

Expressivism has emerged not only as one of the key foundations for international criminal justice, but also as a vehicle for effectively tailoring a common grammar that is able to harmonise the different legal traditions coexisting in the international criminal procedure, namely the common law tradition, largely associated with the adversarial procedural approach, and the civil law tradition, largely associated with the inquisitorial procedural approach. The development of a common grammar is distinct from simple transplant. Establishing a common grammar does not only entail a systematisation of common technical rules of international criminal procedure, it also means structuring the international criminal proceedings around key elements of expressivism, namely the performative and communicative features of the trial through which the truth-telling and educative functions unfold.

The common gramma rooted in the expressivist account of international criminal proceedings leads to a change in the articulation of the goals and procedural role of individuals involved in the proceedings. It demonstrates

132 Frédéric Mégret and Marika Giles Samson, 'Defiance, Defence, Repentance and What Lies Between' (2019) 17 Journal of International Criminal Justice 151, 167.

133 ibid 155.

134 Marlies Glasius and Tim Meijers, 'Trials as Messages of Justice: What Should Be Expected of International Criminal Courts?' (2016) 30 Ethics & International Affairs 429, 437; Anthony J Skillen, 'How to Say Things with Walls' (1980) 55 Philosophy 509, 522.

that a fair criminal proceedings does not require a criminal process framed as a bipolar procedure between the Defence and the prosecution. Most importantly, by bridging the gap between civil law and common law, the common grammar contributes to developing a legal language and, perhaps in the future, a legal culture, which are essential for the articulation of victims' participatory rights in a consistent manner. The expressivist conceptualisation of victims as a crucial constituent of the trial, rather than passive objects, highlights their potential contribution to the norm-expression function of the international criminal trial, which entails conveying disavowal of the moral unacceptability of atrocity, crafting authoritative truths about the past atrocities, and reaffirming the importance of human rights. Victims' active involvement in the proceedings has the potential to lead international criminal justice institutions to embrace more effective modalities of participatory justice. This can be an asset *per se*, as it can provide a greater sense of justice to victims and, most importantly, offer a broader view of the prevailing ideas, standards, and trends of victims' related issues on a scale beyond the criminal justice horizon. The expressivist model of victims' participation sends a strong message about fairness to victims, which should represent a genuine standard to assess the quality of the international criminal procedure.

References

Books and journals

Allo AK, 'The 'Show' in the 'Show Trial': Contextualizing the Politicization of the Courtroom' (2010) 15 Barry Law Review 41

Alvarez A, 'Destructive Beliefs: Genocide and the Role of Ideology' in Alette Smeulers and Roelof Haveman (eds), *Supranational Criminology: Towards a Criminology of International Crimes* (Intersentia 2008)

Amann DM, 'Group Mentality, Expressivism, and Genocide' (2002) 2 International Criminal Law Review 93

Ambos K, 'International Criminal Procedure: 'Adversarial', 'Inquisitorial' or Mixed?' (2003) 3 International Criminal Law Review 1

Aptel C, 'Prosecutorial Discretion at the ICC and Victims' Right to Remedy: Narrowing the Impunity Gap' (2012) 10 Journal of International Criminal Justice 1357

Assembly of States Parties, 'Report of the Bureau on the Impact of the Rome Statute System on Victims and Affected Communities' (2010) ICC-ASP/9/25 <legal-tools.org/doc/343f96/pdf> accessed 24 October 2021

Assembly of States Parties, 'Court's Revised Strategy in Relation to Victims' (2012) ICC-ASP/11/38 <https://asp.icc-cpi.int/iccdocs/asp_docs/ASP11/ICC-ASP-11-38-ENG.pdf> accessed 24 October 2021

Boas G et al., 'The Role and Status of Victims in International Criminal Procedure', *International Criminal Law Practitioner Library: International Criminal Procedure* (Cambridge University Press 2011)

Bosland J, 'The Principle of Open Justice and the Judicial Duty to Give Public Reasons' (2014) 38 Melbourne University Law Review 482

Braithwaite J and Daly K, 'Masculinities, Violence and Communitarian Control' in Susan Miller (ed), *Crime Control and Women: Feminist Implications of Criminal Justice Policy* (Sage 1998)
Brienen MEI and Hoegen EH, *Victims of Crime in 22 European Criminal Justice Systems* (Wolf Legal Productions 2000)
Bringedal Houge A, 'Re-Presentations of Defendant Perpetrators in Sexual War Violence Cases Before International and Military Criminal Courts' (2016) 56 British Journal of Criminology 419
Buss D, 'Expert Witnesses and International War Crimes Trials: Making Sense of Large-Scale Violence in Rwanda' in Marlies Glasius and Dubravka Žarkov (eds), *Narratives of Justice In and Out of the Courtroom: Former Yugoslavia and Beyond* (Springer 2014a)
Buss D, 'Knowing Women: Translating Patriarchy in International Criminal Law' (2014b) 23 Social & Legal Studies 73
Christie N, 'The Ideal Victim' in Ezzat A Fattah (ed), *From Crime Policy to Victim Policy* (Palgrave Macmillan 1986)
Dadomo C and Farran S, *The French Legal System* (Sweet & Maxwell 1996)
Damaška M, *The Faces of Justice and State Authority: A Comparative Approach to the Legal Process* (Yale University Press 1986)
Damaška M, 'Truth in Adjudication' (1998) 49 Hastings Law Journal 289
Damaška M, 'Epistemology and Legal Regulation of Proof' (2003) 2 Law, Probability and Risk 117
Damaška M, 'Negotiated Justice in International Criminal Courts' (2004) 2 Journal of International Criminal Justice 1018
Damaška M, 'The Uncertain Fate of Evidentiary Transplants: Anglo-American and Continental Experiments' (2007) 45 American Journal of Comparative Law 839
Damaška M, 'What Is the Point of International Criminal Justice?' (2008) 83 Chicago-Kent Law Review 329
deGuzman M, 'Choosing to Prosecute: Expressive Selection at the International Criminal Court' (2012) 33 Michigan Journal of International Law 265
Delmas-Marty M, 'The Contribution of Comparative Law to a Pluralist Conception of International Criminal Law' (2003) 1 Journal of International Criminal Justice 13
Delmas-Marty M, 'Reflections on the 'Hybridisation' of Criminal Procedure' in John Jackson and Máximo Langer (eds), *Crime, Procedure and Evidence in a Comparative and International Context: Essays in Honour of Professor Mirjan Damaška* (Hart Publishers 2008)
Dembour M-B and Haslam E, 'Silencing Hearings? Victim-Witnesses at War Crimes Trials' (2004) 15 European Journal of International Law 151
Diggelmann O, 'International Criminal Tribunals and Reconciliation: Reflections on the Role of Remorse and Apology' (2016) 14 Journal of International Criminal Justice 1073
Dixon R, 'Developing International Rules of Evidence for the Yugoslav and Rwanda Tribunals' (1997) 7 Transnational Law & Contemporary Problems 81
Doak J, 'Victims' Rights in Criminal Trials: Prospects for Participation' (2005) 32 Journal of Law and Society 294
Doak J, *Victims' Rights, Human Rights and Criminal Justice. Reconceiving the Role of the Third Parties* (Hart Publishing 2008)
Douglas L, *The Memory of Judgment: Making Law and History in the Trials of the Holocaust* (Yale University Press 2001)

Drumbl MA, 'The Expressive Value of Prosecuting and Punishing Terrorists: Hamdan, the Geneva Conventions, and International Criminal Law' (2007) 75 The George Washington Law Review 1165

Drumbl MA, 'Victims Who Victimize' (2016) 4 London Review of International Law 217

Elander M, 'The Victim's Address: Expressivism and the Victim at the Extraordinary Chambers in the Courts of Cambodia' (2013) 7 International Journal of Transitional Justice 95

Fassler LJ, 'The Italian Penal Procedure Code: An Adversarial System of Criminal Procedure in Continental Europe' (1991) 29 Columbia Journal of Transnational Law 245

Felman S, 'A Ghosts in the House of Justice: Death and the Language of the Law' (2001a) 13 Yale Journal of Law & the Humanities 241

Felman S, 'Theaters of Justice: Arendt in Jerusalem, the Eichmann Trial, and the Redefinition of Legal Meaning in the Wake of the Holocaust' (2001b) 27 Critical Inquiry 201

Field S, 'Fair Trials and Procedural Tradition in Europe' (2009) 29 Oxford Journal of Legal Studies 365

Fletcher LE, 'Refracted Justice: The Imagined Victim and the International Criminal Court' in Christian De Vos, Sara Kendall and Carsten Stahn (eds), *Contested Justice: The Politics and Practices of International Criminal Court Interventions* (Cambridge University Press 2015)

Frase R, 'Comparative Criminal Justice as a Guide to American Law Reform: How Do the French Do It, How Can We Find Out, and Why Should We Care?' (1990) 78 California Law Review 539

Giuffré V, *La Repressione Criminale nell'Esperienza Romana. Profili* (Jovene 1991)

Glasius M, 'Terror, Terrorizing, Terrorism: Instilling Fear as a Crime in the Cases of Radovan Karadzic and Charles Taylor' in Dubravka Žarkov and Marlies Glasius (eds), *Narratives of Justice In and Out of the Courtroom: Former Yugoslavia and Beyond* (Springer 2014)

Glasius M and Meijers T, 'Expression of Justice or Political Trial? Discursive Battles in the Karadžić Case' (2013) 35 Human Rights Quarterly 720

Glasius M and Meijers T, 'Trials as Messages of Justice: What Should Be Expected of International Criminal Courts?' (2016) 30 Ethics & International Affairs 429

Heinsch R, 'How to Achieve Fair and Expeditious Trial Proceedings Before the ICC: Is It Time for a More Judge-Dominated Approach?' in Carsten Stahn and Göran Sluiter (eds), *The Emerging Practice of the ICC* (Martinus Nijhoff 2009)

Hodgson J, 'Conceptions of the Trial in Inquisitorial and Adversarial Procedure' in Antony Duff et al. (eds), *The Trial on Trial: Volume 2. Judgment and Calling to Account* (Calling to Account and Judgment, Hart Publishing 2006)

Jackson J, 'Transnational Faces of Justice: Two Attempts to Build Common Standards beyond National Boundaries' in John Jackson, Máximo Langer and Peter Tillers (eds), *Crime, Procedure and Evidence in Comparative and International Context: Essays in Honour of Professor Mirjan Damaška* (Hart Publishing 2008)

Jackson J, 'Finding the Best Epistemic Fit for International Criminal Tribunals: Beyond the Adversarial-Inquisitorial Dichotomy' (2009) 7 Journal of International Criminal Justice 17

Jackson JD, 'Law, Fact and Narrative Coherence: A Deep Look at Court Adjudication' (1990) 7 International Journal for the Semiotics of Law 81

Jouet M, 'Reconciling the Conflicting Rights of Victims and Defendants at the International Criminal Court' 26 Saint Louis University Public Law Review 249

Keen PC, 'Tempered Adversariality: The Judicial Role and Trial Theory in the International Criminal Tribunals' (2004) 17 Leiden Journal of International Law 767

May R and Wierda M, 'Trends in International Criminal Evidence: Nuremberg, Tokyo, The Hague, and Arusha' (1998) 37 Columbia Journal of Transnational Law 725

McCarthy C, 'Victim Redress and International Criminal Justice: Competing Paradigms, or Compatible Forms of Justice?' (2012) 10 Journal of International Criminal Justice 351

McGonigle Leyh B, 'Bridging the Divides in International Criminal Proceedings: An Examination into the Victim Participation Endeavor of the International Criminal Court' (2009) 21 Florida Journal of International Law 93

McGonigle Leyh B, *Procedural Justice? Victim Participation in International Criminal Proceedings* (Intersentia 2011)

Mégret F and Samson MG, 'Defiance, Defence, Repentance and What Lies Between' (2019) 17 Journal of International Criminal Justice 151

Merryman JH and Pérez-Perdomo R, *The Civil Law Tradition: An Introduction to the Legal System of Western Europe and Latin America* (Stanford University Press 1969)

Meyerson D, 'Why Should Justice Be Seen to Be Done?' (2015) 34 Criminal Justice Ethics 64

Mohamed S, 'Of Monsters and Men: Perpetrator Trauma and Mass Atrocity' 115 Columbia Law Review 1157

Mulcahy L, *Legal Architecture: Justice, Due Process and the Place of Law* (GlassHouse 2011)

Murphy C, *The Conceptual Foundations of Transitional Justice* (Cambridge University Press 2017)

Orie A, 'Accusatorial v. Inquisitorial Approach in International Criminal Proceedings Prior to the Establishment of the ICC and in the Proceedings Before the ICC' in Antonio Cassese, Paola Gaeta and John RWD Jones (eds), *The Rome Statute of the International Criminal Court: A Commentary' (Vol. 2)* (Oxford University Press 2002)

Osiel M, *Mass Atrocity, Collective Memory and the Law* (Transaction Publishers 1997)

Pemberton A, Aarten PG and Mulder E, 'Stories as Property: Narrative Ownership as a Key Concept in Victims' Experiences with Criminal Justice' (2019) 19 Criminology & Criminal Justice 404

Perrodet A, 'The Italian System' in Mireille Delmas-Marty and John Spencer (eds), *European Criminal Procedures* (Cambridge University Press 2002)

Peters JS, 'Legal Performance Good and Bad Law' (2008) 4 Culture and the Humanities 179

Pizzi WT, 'Overcoming Logistical and Structural Barriers to Fair Trials at International Tribunals' (2007) 4 International Commentary on Evidence <https://www.degruyter.com/view/j/ice.2007.4.1/ice.2007.4.1.1051/ice.2007.4.1.1051.xml> accessed 4 February 2019

Pizzi WT and Perron W, 'Crime Victims in German Courtrooms: A Comparative Perspective on American Problems' (1996) 32 Stanford Journal of International Law 37

Robinson PL, 'Ensuring Fair and Expeditious Trials at the International Criminal Tribunal for the Former Yugoslavia' (2000) 11 European Journal of International Law 569

Safferling C, 'The Role of the Victim in the Criminal Process – A Paradigm Shift in National German and International Law?' (2011) 11 International Criminal Law Review 183

Santalucia B, *Diritto e Processo Penale nell'Antica Roma* (Giuffrè Editore 1989)

Schwöbel-Patel C, 'Spectacle in International Criminal Law: The Fundraising Image of Victimhood' (2016) 4 London Review of International Law 247

Schwöbel-Patel C, 'The 'Ideal' Victim of International Criminal Law' (2018) 29 European Journal of International Law 703

Skillen AJ, 'How to Say Things with Walls' (1980) 55 Philosophy 509

Stahn C, *Justice as Message: Expressivist Foundations of International Criminal Justice* (1st edn, Oxford University Press 2020)

Stolk S, 'The Victim, the International Criminal Court and the Search for Truth: On the Interdependence and Incompatibility of Truths about Mass Atrocity' (2015) 13 Journal of International Criminal Justice 973

Swart B, 'Damaska and the Faces of International Criminal Justice' (2008) 6 Journal of International Criminal Justice 87

Tiefenbrun SW, 'Legal Semiotics' (1986) 5 Cardozo Arts & Entertainment Law Journal 89

Tiefenbrun SW, *Decoding International Law: Semiotics and the Humanities* (Oxford University Press 2010)

Vasiliev S, 'Victim Participation Revisited: What the ICC Is Learning About Itself' in Carsten Stahn, The Law and Practice of the International Criminal Court (Oxford University Press 2015)

Vogler R, 'France' in Richard Vogler and Barbara Huber (eds), *Criminal Procedure in Europe* (Duncker & Humblot 2008)

Wilson R, 'Humanity's Histories: Evaluating the Historical Accounts of International Tribunals and Truth Commissions' (2007) 80 Politix 31

Zakerhossein MH, 'The Al-Mahdi Case and Thematic Prosecution' (*Justice Hub*, 7 September 2016) <justicehub.org/article/the-al-mahdi-case-and-thematic-prosecution> accessed 24 October 2021

Zappalà E, 'Le procés pénal italien entre système inquisitoire et système accusatoire' (1997) 68 Revue Internationale de Droit Pénal 111

Zegveld L, 'Victims as a Third Party: Empowerment of Victims?' (2019) 19 International Criminal Law Review 321

Cases

Prosecutor v Dražen Erdemović (Separate and Dissenting Opinion of Judge Cassese) IT-96–22-T, Appeals Chamber (7 October 1997)

Prosecutor v Germain Katanga (Judgement Pursuant to Article 74 of the Statute, Minority Opinion of Judge Christine Van den Wyngaert) ICC-01/04–01/07, Trial Chamber II (7 March 2014)

Prosecutor v Germain Katanga and Mathieu Ngudjolo Chui (Closing Statement by Victim Representative) ICC-01/04-01/07, Trial Chamber II (16 May 2012)
Prosecutor v Thomas Lubanga Dyilo (Opening Statement by Victim Representative) ICC-01/04–01/06 (26 January 2009)
Prosecutor v William Samoei Ruto and Joshua Arap Sang (Opening Statement by Victim Representative) ICC-01/09–01/11, Trial Chamber V(A) (10 September 2013)

Legislation

Rome Statute of the International Criminal Court 1998 (2187 UNTS 90)

6 A lesson from the regional human rights courts

An expressivist underpinning for victims' right to participate in criminal proceedings

6.1 Introduction

Developments at the level of the main regional human rights treaties, namely the European Convention on the Protection of Human Rights and Fundamental Freedoms (ECHR) and the American Convention of Human Rights (ACHR), have greatly contributed to enhancing victims' status in criminal proceedings. In particular, the case law of their oversight monitoring bodies, respectively the European Court of Human Rights (ECtHR) and the Inter-American Court of Human Rights (IACtHR), has been central to the elaboration of victims' right to participate in criminal proceedings. Although the ECHR and the ACHR do not explicitly provide victims with rights to specific involvement in criminal proceedings, the IACtHR and the ECtHR have progressively interpreted violations of the right to life and the prohibition against torture and ill-treatment in conjunction with the right to an effective remedy, the right of access to justice, the right to truth, the right to a fair trial, and the right to be heard as a way of enhancing victims' status as participants in criminal proceedings for serious human rights violations such as torture, arbitrary/extrajudicial execution, and enforced disappearance of persons. Although the IACtHR and the ECtHR have adopted two distinct approaches, they have, nevertheless, moved towards the same result: a call upon States to provide victims with greater access to the criminal process and participatory rights in order to enforce the obligations of States to effectively investigate and prosecute serious violations of human rights.

The first goal of this chapter is to review the case law of the IACtHR and the ECtHR to identify the rights and principles, which form the core of victims' participation in criminal proceedings for serious human rights violations. The analysis focuses on two basic issues: victims' right to access to justice to obtain an investigation, prosecution, and punishment of those responsible by a competent, impartial, and independent authority; and the right of victims to participate in criminal proceedings. The second goal is to illustrate that the IACtHR and the ECtHR have developed a case law that conveys a system of values that responds to the expressivist dimension of the criminal justice system, with a particular emphasis on the expressivist value of victims' right to participate in criminal proceedings. The case law of these two regional human rights bodies suggests

DOI: 10.4324/9781003215448-6

ways of effectively implementing the rights of victims in international criminal proceedings.

However, the reason for relying on the suggested experiences must be established. First of all, we need to be aware of two conceptual differences between regional human rights mechanisms and international criminal justice. While the former is based on the State responsibility framework and, by addressing gross violations of human rights, especially in the case of isolated violations, entails the recognition of fundamental human rights, the latter is based on individual responsibility and the prosecution of international crimes results in the criminalisation of particularly heinous conducts. Nevertheless, both bodies are underpinned by common principles. International criminal tribunals show the close relationship between international criminal law, international human rights, and international humanitarian law. Conducts that international criminal law recognises as international crimes also embody violations of human rights sanctioned under international human rights treaties.[1] Several international crimes have been established to guarantee the fundamental rights of civilians in time of both peace and conflict. For instance, conduct amounting to crimes against humanity is essentially premised on violation of international human rights law.[2] The elaboration of the right to life, the right to be free from torture and other inhuman or degrading treatment, the right to equality and, thus, to be free from discrimination and prosecution based on political, racial, or religious reasons contributes to the clarification of the scope of crimes against humanity.[3] Similarly, the case law on international crimes throws a light on the way fundamental human rights should be protected in times of conflict or exceptional circumstances.[4] More importantly, at a general level, Article 38 of the International Court of Justice Statute and, at a more specific level, Article 21 of the RS contemplate the interplay between international criminal law and international/regional human rights law. By requiring international criminal courts to apply as secondary sources treaties, principles, and rules of international law, whose 'application and interpretation (…) must be consistent with internationally recognized human rights'[5], these articles, which are generally regarded as a statement of the sources of international law, are open to the international criminal justice's reliance on

1 REDRESS, 'Victim Participation in Criminal Law Proceedings: Survey of Domestic Practice for Application to International Crimes Prosecutions' (2015) 7 <http://www.redress.org/downloads/1508victim-rights-report.pdf.> accessed 1 July 2021.

2 Antonio Cassese, Guido Acquaviva and Alex Whiting, *International Criminal Law: Cases and Commentary* (Oxford University Press 2011) 41.

3 ibid 42. See *Prosecutor v Kupreškić et al.* (Judgment) ICTY-IT-95–16-T, Trial Chamber (14 January 2000) paras 562–566. In this case, in order to determine the scope of crimes against humanity and, specifically the various categories of conducts that amount to such crimes, the Trial Chamber established the meaning of 'other inhumane acts' by referring to human rights provisions.

4 Cassese, Acquaviva and Whiting (n 2) 42.

5 Rome Statute of the International Criminal Court 1998 (2187 UNTS 90) Article 21.

the case law of the ECtHR and the IACtHR as a source of principles and rules that can be applied for purposes relating to the participation of victims.

6.2 The State's obligation to investigate, prosecute, and punish human rights violations as norm expression

The historical records of civil disorders and repressive governments in Central and South America were brought before the IACtHR, which dealt with cases involving States' commission of, or at least acquiescence to, acts of torture, extra-judicial executions, massacres, and forced disappearances, for which the perpetrators were very often left unpunished.[6] The IACtHR clearly showed its commitment to fight against impunity and prosecute those responsible for human rights violations. In the first 'trilogy' of cases involving systematic forced disappearances which occurred in Honduras during the 1980s, the IACtHR interpreted Article 1(1) of the ACHR, which imposes a general obligation on States to respect and ensure the full exercise of the rights and freedoms recognised herein, as having a criminal law feature. In *Velásquez-Rodríguez v Honduras*, the IACtHR found that forced disappearance of human beings is a violation of Article 7 (right to personal liberty) of the ACHR[7] and recognised that Article 1(1) entails the legal duty of States to carry out a serious investigation of the violations committed within their jurisdiction, to identify those responsible, and to impose the appropriate punishment.[8] If States leave unpunished those serious breaches of human rights, they fail to comply with their duty to ensure the free and full exercise of those rights to the persons within their jurisdiction.[9] The IACtHR further clarified that, while States' obligation to investigate is not breached merely because the outcome is not satisfactory, investigations must be undertaken in a serious manner and not as a mere formality preordained to be ineffective.[10] In *Godínez Cruz v Honduras* and *Fairén Garbi and Solís Corrales v Honduras*, which complete the trilogy of cases involving systematic forced disappearances occurred in Honduras, the IACtHR confirmed the orientation expressed in the *Velásquez-Rodríguez* case. The obligation to prevent, investigate, and punish any violation of human rights can be imputed to a State as a consequence of the general duty to respect and ensure the free and full exercise of rights and freedoms recognised by the ACHR.[11]

6 Raquel Aldana-Pindell, 'An Emerging Universality of Justiciable Victims' Rights in the Criminal Process to Curtail Impunity for State-Sponsored Crimes' (2004) 26 Human Rights Quarterly 605, 623.
7 *Velásquez-Rodríguez v Honduras* (Judgment) IACtHR Series C No 4, (29 July 1988) para 155.
8 ibid para 174.
9 ibid para 176.
10 ibid para 177.
11 *Godínez Cruz v Honduras* (Judgment, Merits) IACtHR Series C No. 5, (20 January 1989) paras 174–175; *Fairén Garbi and Solís Corrales v Honduras* (Judgment, Merits) IACtHR Series C No. 6, (15 March 1989) para 152. See also Aldana-Pindell (n 6) 623; Juan Car-

In a similar way, the ECtHR interpreted the ECHR as requiring States Parties to prosecute violations of Article 2 (right to life) and Article 3 (prohibition of torture and inhumane treatment). Specifically, in the case *McCann and Others v the United Kingdom*, from the joint reading of Article 2 along with the general obligation of Article 1 imposing on States the duty to respect and secure the rights and freedoms of the ECHR, the ECtHR concluded that States have an imperative mandate to undertake an effective investigation in order to prosecute and punish perpetrators.[12] Likewise, in the case *Assenov and Others v Bulgaria*, the ECtHR interpreted Article 3, in conjunction with Article 1, as requiring that, where an individual raises an arguable claim that he/she has been seriously ill-treated by the police or other agents of the State, there should be an effective official investigation.[13]

The emphasis of the IACtHR and ECtHR on the State's obligation to investigate and prosecute violation of human rights can be read as consistent with the expressivist norm-expression and truth-telling functions of the trial.[14] First, the official and public nature of the criminal proceedings, which allows the State to carry out an independent and effective investigation and to identify, prosecute, and punish those responsible for the crimes, plays a critical role in revealing the truth and publicly acknowledging the events that occurred. Secondly, the IACtHR and the ECtHR have taken the view that the criminal proceedings aim to reaffirm the importance that society places on those serious infringements and renewing the vital importance of the rule of law. Violations of human rights protected by the ECHR and ACHR involve breaches of rights that have a special status, as they cannot be derogated or limited by law. For example, in the case *Aksoy v Turkey*, the ECtHR held that States have the obligation to undertake effective investigations into allegations of ill-treatment because of the fundamental importance of the nature of the right to be safeguarded under Article 3.[15] The same *ratio* was used to derive States' procedural obligation in criminal proceedings in cases concerning alleged violations to the right to life. In *Kaya v Turkey*, the ECtHR emphasised the special nature of this right enshrined in Article 2, which is 'one of the most fundamental in the scheme of the Convention'.[16] When dealing with gender-based crimes, such as rape, the ECtHR held that the recourse to criminal procedure is requested because of the fundamental values and essential

los Ochoa Sanchez, *The Rights of Victims in Criminal Justice Proceedings for Serious Human Rights Violations* (Martinus Nijhoff Publishers 2013) 112; Mahmoud Cherif Bassiouni, 'International Recognition of Victims' Rights' (2006) 6 Human Rights Law Review 203, 226.

12 *McCann and Others v the United Kingdom* App No 18984/91 (ECtHR 5 September 1995) para 161. See also Aldana-Pindell (n 6) 634.

13 *Assenov and Others v Bulgaria* App No 24760/94 (ECtHR 28 October 1998) para 102.

14 See Chapter 4.

15 *Aksoy v Turkey* App No 21987/93 (ECtHR 18 December 1996) para 98.

16 *Kaya v Turkey* App No 22729/93 (ECtHR 19 February 1998) para 107.

aspects of private life that are at stake.[17] The IACtHR has also emphasised the special status of infringements of rights protected by the ACHR, which affect society as well as the fundamental rights of the individual. In *La Cantuta v Peru*, the IACtHR affirmed that the duty to investigate and eventually conduct trials in case of crimes against humanity and forced disappearance 'becomes particularly compelling and important in view of the seriousness of the crimes committed and the nature of the rights wronged (...)'.[18] The IACtHR stated that the right to effective recourse to a competent court is one of the fundamental pillars not only of the American Convention, but of the very rule of law in a democratic society.[19] On the same page, the ECtHR held the great importance of the expression 'rule of law', given that preventing the denial of justice ranks as one of the universally recognised fundamental principles of law.[20]

These remarks illustrate that the position of the IACtHR and ECtHR is that the goal of criminal proceedings is not simply to identify and punish the perpetrator. The criminal proceedings, therefore, becomes the mechanism to express disavowal and condemnation of those conducts violating human rights to reaffirm the importance of human rights and the rule of law, and educate the public to respect those rights. With this in mind, the next sections will analyse the relevant case law of the IACtHR and ECtHR on the rights of victims in the criminal proceedings, focusing on two broad issues: victims' right to recourse to the administration of justice to obtain an investigation, prosecution, and punishment of those responsible for the violation of human rights by a competent, impartial, and independent authority; and victims' right to participate in criminal proceedings.

6.3 The IACtHR

In its jurisprudence establishing the right of victims to access to justice and to participate in the criminal proceedings, the IACtHR has found that the State's failure to carry out a prompt, thorough, effective, impartial, and independent investigation into allegations of serious violation of human rights violates: victims' right to an effective remedy (Article 25), victims' right to a fair trial (Article 8), and victims' right to the truth.

6.3.1 Victims' right to access to justice to obtain an investigation, prosecution, and punishment

Over the years, the evolving jurisprudence of the IACtHR rooted victims' right to access to justice in the combined reading of the general State's duty under

17 *X and Y v The Netherlands* App No 8978/80 (ECtHR 26 March 1985) para 27. See also *MC v Bulgaria* App No 39272/98 (ECtHR 4 December 2003) para 150.

18 *La Cantuta v Peru* (Judgment, Merits, Reparations and Costs) IACtHR Series C No. 162, (29 November 2006) para 157.

19 *Castillo Páez v Peru* (Judgment, Merits) IACtHR Series C No. 34, (3 November 1997) para 82.

20 *Golder v the United Kingdom* App No 4451/70 (ECtHR 21 February 1975) paras 34–35.

Article 1(1), together with Article 25, Article 8(1), and victims' right to the truth. In *Loayza Tamayo v Peru*, the IACtHR's interpretation of the right to judicial protection (Article 25) along with Article 1(1) obliged the State to guarantee every individual access to the administration of justice, and, in particular, with simple and prompt recourse, so that those responsible for human rights violations may be prosecuted.[21] In *Castillo Páez v Peru*, the IACtHR read Article 25 in conjunction also with Article 8(1) and upheld the right of every person to a hearing within a reasonable time and with the due guarantees before a competent, independent, and impartial tribunal for the determination of his/her rights of any nature.[22] This interpretation of Article 25 charged States with the obligation to guarantee the right of all persons under their jurisdiction to an effective judicial remedy against violations of their fundamental rights.

In several decisions, the IACtHR insistently stated that the mere availability of judicial remedies is not enough[23] and took a deeper look into the concept of the effectiveness of a judicial remedy. To be effective, a judicial remedy ought to be 'suitable to fight the violation, its application by the competent authority must be effective',[24] and it should give 'a person a real opportunity to pursue a simple and prompt recourse which, if applicable, will secure the judicial protection sought from the competent authority'.[25] To guarantee victims' right to access to justice in accordance with Article 25, the judicial mechanism has to take every necessary step to ensure, within a reasonable time, the right of the alleged victims or their next of kin to learn the truth about what happened and to punish those who may be responsible.[26] In *Castillo Páez*, the IACtHR affirmed that 'only a criminal trial

21 *Loayza Tamayo v Peru* (Judgment, Reparations and Costs) IACtHR Series C No. 42, (27 November 1998) para 169.

22 *Castillo Páez v Peru* (Judgment Reparations and Costs) IACtHR Series C No. 34, (27 November 1998) para 106.

23 *Baldeón García v Peru* (Judgment, Merits, Reparations and Costs) IACtHR Series C No. 147, (6 April 2006) para 144. See also *Claude Reyes et al. v Chile* (Judgment, Merits, Reparations and Costs), IACtHR Series C No. 151, (19 September 2006) para 131; *Ximenes Lopes v Brazil* (Judgment, Merits, Reparations and Costs) IACtHR Series C No. 149, (4 July 2006) para 192; *Acevedo-Jaramillo et al. v Peru* (Preliminary Objections, Merits, Reparations and Costs) IACtHR Series C No. 144, (7 February 2006) para 213.

24 *López Álvarez v Honduras* (Judgment, Merits, Reparations and Costs) IACtHR Series C No. 141, (1 February 2006) para 139.

25 *Palamara Iribarne v Chile* (Judgment, Merits, Reparations and Costs) IACtHR Series C No. 135, (22 November 2005) para 184.

26 *The "Mapiripán Massacre" v Colombia* (Judgment, Merits, Reparations and Costs) IACtHR Series C No. 134, (15 September 2005) para 216. See also *Myrna Mack Chang v Guatemala* (Judgment, Merits, Reparations and Costs) IACtHR Series C No. 101, (25 November 2003) para 209; *19 Merchants v Colombia* (Judgment, Merits, Reparations and Costs) IACtHR Series C No. 109, (5 July 2004) 1 para 188; *Serrano Cruz Sisters v El Salvador* (Judgment, Merits, Reparations and Costs) IACtHR Series C No. 120, (1 March 2005) para 66; *La Cantuta v Peru* (n 18) para 149; *Bulacio v Argentina* (Judgment, Merits, Reparations and Costs) IACtHR Series C No. 100, (18 September 2003) para 114; *Hilaire, Constantine and Benjamin et al. v Trinidad and Tobago* (Judgment, Merits, Reparations and Costs)

could guarantee [the victims] the appropriate remedy; namely, the punishment of the perpetrators'.[27] However, the right of victims to access to justice does not imply that the prosecution becomes a purely private victim's right. The duty of States to investigate, prosecute, and punish is independent of the right of the victim to access to justice.[28]

In addition to the right of victims to the State's investigation, prosecution, and punishment of those responsible for gross violation of human rights as way of resorting to an effective remedy, the IACtHR recognised that victims' access to justice should be conducted with due process guarantees.[29] In particular, in *Genie Lacayo v Nicaragua*, the IACtHR further developed the principle of a fair hearing, contained in Article 8(1), to include the right of victims and their relatives to a fair hearing, with due guarantees and within a reasonable time, by a competent, independent, and impartial tribunal. The IACtHR argued that the victims and their next of kin enjoy the right to a fair hearing, since a violation of their right to have identified those responsible for the death of Genie-Lacayo amounts to a breach of Article 8(1).[30] In *Blake v Guatemala*, the IACtHR maintained this broad interpretation of Article 8(1) based on its letter and spirit, read in accordance with Article 29(c) of the ACHR, whereby none of the Convention's provisions should be interpreted as precluding other rights or guarantees that are inherent in the human personality or derived from a representative democratic form of government.[31] The IACtHR acknowledged that the right to a fair trial includes the right to access to justice and judicial guarantees for victims and their relatives because any act of forced disappearance places the victim outside the protection of the law and causes grave suffering to him/her and to his/her family.[32] The IACtHR found that Article 8(1) recognised the rights of Blake's relative to have his disappearance and death effectively investigated by

---

IACtH Series C No. 94, (21 June 2002) paras 142–144;*Suárez Rosero v Ecuador* (Judgment Merits) IACtHR Series C No. 35, (12 November 1997) paras 71–72.

27 *Castillo Páez v Peru* (n 22) para 105–107.

28 *Trujillo Oroza v Bolivia* (Judgment Reparations and Costs) IACtHR Series C No. 92, (27 February 2002) para 99. See also *Caracazo v Venezuela* (Judgment, Reparations and Costs) IACtHR Series C No. 95, (29 August 2002) para 115; *Heliodoro-Portugal v Panama* (Preliminary Objections, Merits, Reparations and Costs) IACtHR Series C No. 186, (12 August 2008) para 146; *García Prieto et al. v El Salvador* (Preliminary Objections, Merits, Reparations and Costs) IACtHR Series C No. 168, (20 November 2007) para 103;*Cantoral Benavides v Peru* (Judgment, Reparations and Costs) IACtHR Series C No. 88, (3 December 2001) para 69.

29 *Bámaca-Velásquez v Guatemala* (Judgment, Merits) IACtHR Series C No. 70, (25 November 2000) paras 182–196; *Durand and Ugarte v Peru* (Judgment, Merits) IACtHR Series C No. 68, (16 August 2000) paras 111–130.

30 *Genie Lacayo v Nicaragua* (Judgment, Merits, Reparations and Costs) IACtHR Series C No. 30, (29 January 1997) paras 74–75.

31 *Blake v Guatemala* (Judgment, Merits), IACtHR Series C No. 36, (24 January 1998) para 96.

32 ibid para 97.

the Guatemalan authorities, to have those responsible prosecuted and, where appropriate, punished.[33]

The IACtHR sustained that the dynamic interpretation of Articles 1(1), 8 and 25 of the ACHR subsumed victims' right to know the truth.[34] The IACtHR has systematically held that the State has 'the duty to reach the truth through judicial proceedings'[35] and that there is a link between the denial of the State to provide victims with access to criminal justice mechanisms – specifically to criminal trials – and victims' right to learn the truth.[36] Following this interpretation, the right to the truth included the right of victims or their next of kin to obtain clarification of the facts relating to the violations and the corresponding responsibilities from the competent State organs, through the investigation, prosecution, and punishment of those responsible.[37]

6.3.2 The right of victims to participate in criminal proceedings

The IACtHR's case law has systematically upheld that Articles 8(1) and 25, which determined victims' rights to access to justice, to the truth, and to be heard, entail victims' right to participation in criminal proceedings.[38] In the case *Villagrán-Morales et al. v Guatemala*, better known as the *Street Children* case, the IACtHR confirmed the extensive interpretation of Article 8(1), according to which the right to a hearing should provide victims of human rights violations or their next of kin with substantial possibilities of being heard and acting in the respective proceedings, in order to clarify the facts and punish those responsible.[39] This orientation is based on the interpretation of the wording and spirit of Article 8(1), which require the observation of the right to a fair hearing for the determination of everyone's 'rights and obligations of a civil, labour, fiscal, *or any other nature* (emphasis added)'. Specifically, the caveat 'or any other nature' leaves room to

33 ibid para 97. See also *Paniagua Morales et al. v Guatemala (the case of the 'White Van')* (Judgment, Merits) IACtHR Series C No. 37, (8 March 1998) paras 155–156; *Durand and Ugarte v Peru* (n 29) para 130.

34 *Bámaca-Velásquez v Guatemala* (n 29) para 201.

35 *Almonacid-Arellano et al. v Chile* (Preliminary Objections, Merits, Reparations and Costs) IACtHR Series C No. 154, (26 September 2006) para 150; *Gómez Palomino v Peru* (Judgment, Merits, Reparations and Costs) IACtHR Series C No. 136, (2 November 2005) paras 78–79.

36 Aldana-Pindell (n 6) 627.

37 *Bámaca-Velásquez v Guatemala* (n 29) para 201. See also *Castillo Páez v Peru* (n 22) paras 105–106; *Trujillo Oroza v Bolivia* (n 28) paras 110, 112–116; *Barrios Altos v Peru* (Judgment, Merits) IACtHR Series C No. 75, (14 March 2001) para 48; *Bulacio v Argentina* (n 26) para 114; *Hilaire, Constantine and Benjamin et al. v Trinidad and Tobago* (n 26) paras 142–144; *Suárez Rosero v Ecuador* (n 26) paras 71–72.

38 Ochoa Sanchez (n 11) 117–118.

39 *Villagrán-Morales et al. v Guatemala* (Judgment, Merits) IACtHR Series C No. 63, (19 November 1999) para 227.See also *Durand and Ugarte v Peru* (n 29) para 129; *Las Palmeras v Colombia* (Judgment, Merits) IACtHR Series C No. 90, (6 December 2001) para 59.

include in the scope of the right to a fair hearing the right of victims to participate in the criminal proceedings.[40]

Interrelated with Art 8(1), the IACtHR's case law on Article 25 broadened the notion of judicial remedy for victims to provide a rather comprehensive array of victims' rights in criminal proceedings. The IACtHR relied on the wording of Article 25, which not only covers those remedies that are simple, prompt, and effective, but it also set forth 'any other effective recourse' in order to protect the fundamental rights recognised by the State concerned or by the ACHR. The IACtHR recognised that Article 25 established the recourse of a writ (simple and prompt), as well as a second type of recourse that, though not simple or prompt, is effective.[41] This interpretation of Article 25 finds support in the *travaux préparatoires* of the ACHR, which showed that the expression 'any other effective recourse' is very far from being meaningless and accidental. In the original version of Article 25 the part 'any other effective recourse' was not intended. After the representatives from the Dominican Republic observed that, in some cases, the judicial protection could be effective, without being simple and prompt, the effectiveness became the only mandatory requirement of a legitimate recourse.[42] In light of this broad notion of judicial remedy for victims, in *Caracazo v Venezuela* the IACtHR affirmed that

> [t]he next of kin of the victims and the surviving victims must have full access and the capacity to act during all stages and levels of said investigations, pursuant to domestic law and to the provisions of the American Convention.[43]

The reference to both the domestic law and the ACHR as legal sources seems to suggest that right of victims to participate in criminal proceedings is directly based, besides the local law, on the dispositions of the ACHR and its relative interpretation. Moreover, it is significant that through the expression 'must have full access and the capacity to act' the IACtHR explicitly acknowledged that the right to judicial protection incorporates victims' entitlement to take part in all stages and levels of the investigations on infringements of the rights

40 Ochoa Sanchez (n 11) 121.

41 *Salvador Chiriboga v Ecuador* (Partially Dissenting Opinion of Judge Medina Quiroga) IACtHR Series C No. 179, (6 May 2008) para 3.

42 Organización de los Estados Americanos, 'Conferencia Especializada Interamericana sobre Derechos Humanos, San José, Costa Rica, 7-22 de noviembre de 1969', *Actas y documentos*, doc. OEA/Ser.K/xvi/1.2 (1969) p. 66.

43 *Caracazo v Venezuela* (n 28) para 118. See also *Juan Humberto Sánchez v Honduras* (Preliminary Objection, Merits, Reparations and Costs) IACtHR Series C No. 99, (7 June 2003) 1 para 186;*Montero Aranguren et al. (Detention Center of Catia) v Venezuela* (Preliminary Objection, Merits, Reparations and Costs) IACtHR Series C No. 150, (5 July 2006) para 139; *Blanco Romero et al. v Venezuela* (Judgment, Merits, Reparations and Costs) IACtHR Series C No. 138, (28 November 2005) para 97; *Vargas Areco v Paraguay* (Judgment, Merits, Reparations and Costs) IACtHR Series C No. 155, (26 September 2006) para 155.

protected by the ACHR.[44] While the *Caracazo* case refers to all stages and levels of investigations, in *Baldeón García v Peru*, the IACtHR further expanded the degree of participation for victims, affirming that

> [t]he next of kin of the victim or his representatives shall have full access to and participate in *all stages and instances of the domestic criminal proceedings* (emphasis added) initiated in relation to the instant case, in accordance with domestic laws and the American Convention.[45]

In this way, the IACtHR fully recognised the right of victims to actively participate in the criminal proceedings, requiring States to grant them 'substantial possibilities of being heard and acting in the respective proceedings, both in order to clarify the facts and punish those responsible, and to seek due reparation'.[46]

6.4 The ECtHR

While assessing States' compliance with their obligations to investigate and prosecute violations of the right to life (Article 2 ECHR) and prohibition of inhumane treatment (Article 3 ECHR), the jurisprudence of the ECtHR acknowledged victim's right of access to and participation in criminal proceedings as a remedy for such violations. In particular, based on the right to an effective remedy (Article 13 ECHR), the Court granted victims the right to be informed regarding how the proceedings are progressing and about the decisions made therein; the right to be heard, and the right to have access to the case files.

6.4.1 The right of victims to have access to and participate in the criminal proceedings

The ECtHR has examined Article 2 (right to life), together with Article 3 (prohibition against torture and inhuman and degrading treatment), Article 13 (right to a remedy), and Article 6 (right to a fair trial) to find that a State's violation of its duties may also violate the rights of victims. The case law of the ECtHR acts as a base to confer on victims the right to be informed regarding how the proceedings are evolving and about the decisions made therein; the right to be heard, and the right to have access to the case files. This orientation was strongly sustained by the ECtHR while dealing with situations characterised by the unwillingness of States to investigate, prosecute, and punish those responsible for serious human rights violations that occurred in Southeast Turkey and the UK (more precisely Northern Ireland) in the late 1990s and early 2000s.[47]

44 Ochoa Sanchez (n 11) 118.
45 *Baldeón García v Peru* (n 23) para 199.
46 *Villagrán-Morales et al. v Guatemala* (n 39) para 227.
47 Ochoa Sanchez (n 11) 120.

6.4.1.1 Complaints against Turkey

The majority of complaints against Turkey dealt with alleged extrajudicial executions, forced disappearances, inhumane treatments and tortures committed by the Turkish forces against persons, who were allegedly involved with the Kurdish Worker's Party (PKK). The common feature of these cases was that alleged victims of gross violations of human rights appealed to the ECtHR claiming that Turkey was not complying with its duty to conduct an effective investigation, leaving unpunished those responsible.[48] The ECtHR argued that, given the relevance of Articles 2 and 3, the right of victims to an effective remedy required States to grant effective access to the investigation into such violations for victims and their next of kin.

In *Kaya v Turkey*, the ECtHR found an infringement of Article 2, read in conjunction with the State's general duty under Article 1 to 'secure to everyone within [its] jurisdiction the rights and freedoms defined in [the] Convention', because Turkey did not comply with the obligation to effectively involve victims in the investigation, pursuant to the right to an effective remedy. Accordingly, the notion of an effective remedy, for the purposes of Article 13, entails a thorough and effective investigation capable of leading to the identification and punishment of those responsible. In the view of the ECtHR, effective remedy also includes effective access for the relatives to the investigatory procedure.[49] In following cases, the ECtHR has interpreted Article 2 as providing victims and their next of kin with the right to be informed regarding measures taken by the State after notice of violation. In *Güleç v Turkey*, the ECtHR acknowledged a violation of Article 2 on two accounts: the lack of effective investigations capable of leading to the identification and punishment of those responsible for the events in question, and the impossibility for the victim's close relatives to access the case file.[50]

In *Oğur v Turkey*, the ECtHR viewed the right of victims to information as essential and found a violation of Article 2 because the Turkish authorities did not notify the applicant's lawyer of the decision on the case by the Turkish judicial body, with the result that the applicant was deprived of the possibility of lodging an appeal.[51] Once an investigation has commenced, the right to be informed requires the investigating authorities to allow victims access to the investigation and court documents. In particular, the ECtHR held that Turkey

48 Aldana-Pindell (n 6) 634.

49 *Kaya v Turkey* (n 16) para 107. See also *Ergi v Turkey* App No 23818/94 (ECtHR 28 July 1998) para 98; *Yaşa v Turkey* App No 22495/93 (ECtHR 2 September 1998) para 114; *Salman v Turkey* App No 21986/93 (ECtHR 27 June 2000) para 121; *Tumurtas v Turkey* App No 23531/94 (ECtHR 13 June 2000) para 11; *Orhan v Turkey* App No 25656/94 (ECtHR 18 June 2002) paras 383–385.

50 *Güleç v Turkey* App No 21593/93 (ECtHR 27 July 1998) paras 82–83, 93.

51 *Oğur v Turkey* App No 21594/93 (ECtHR 20 May 1999) para 92.

violated Article 2 because it failed to inform victims or close relatives of the State's decision not to prosecute. This lack of information was particularly problematic because it deprived the next of kin of the possibility of appealing the decision not to prosecute to a higher authority.[52] The *Oğur v Turkey* case is particularly relevant because the ECtHR required the State not only to provide victims' next of kin with access to the investigation files, but also to allow them to introduce evidence to substantiate the record.[53] The mere fact that the decision of the relevant national tribunal was based solely on the record of the State prosecution amounts to a violation of victims' right of access to the proceedings because victims' relatives were not given the possibility to introduce evidence.[54] In *Gül v Turkey*, the ECtHR reiterated this orientation since it recognised a violation of Article 2 when victims and their family members not only were not informed of the proceedings, but also were not given the opportunity to tell the court their different version of events.[55] The ECtHR concluded that, on the basis of the lack of involvement of victims and/or their next of kin in the investigatory procedure, Articles13 and 2 had been violated.[56]

In a similar way, in relation to the prohibition of inhumane treatment, set in Article 3 of the ECHR, the ECtHR upheld that the State has the duty to investigate violations of the said article, grounding its argumentation on the right of victims to remedy. In *Aydin v Turkey*, the ECtHR maintained that, because of the nature of the right safeguarded under Article 3 and the vulnerable position of victims of torture, Article 13 imposes on States an obligation to carry out a thorough and effective investigation of such tortures.[57] The ECtHR consolidated the concept of effective remedy, as formulated in its case law on the violation of the Article 2, to entail a thorough and effective investigation in order to identify and punish those responsible as well as effective access for the complainant to the investigatory procedure.[58]

6.4.1.2 Complaints against the UK

More recently, the ECtHR dealt with numerous cases against the UK, which, like the Turkish cases, involved disproportionate use of force and inhuman treatment of alleged criminals or terrorists committed in Northern Ireland by State agents.[59]

52 ibid para 92.
53 ibid para 92.
54 ibid para 92.
55 *Gül v Turkey* App No 22676/93 (ECtHR 14 December 2000) para 93.
56 Ochoa Sanchez (n 11) 122. See also *Orhan v Turkey* (n 49) para 384.
57 *Aydin v Turkey* App No 23178/94 (ECtHR 25 September 1997) para 103.
58 ibid para 103. See also *Aksoy v Turkey* (n 15) para 98; *Menteş and Others v Turkey* App No 23186/94 (ECtHR 28 November 1997) para 98; *Selçuk and Asker v Turkey* App No 23184/94 and 23185/94 (ECtHR 24 April 1998) para 96; *Tekin v Turkey* App No 22496/93 (ECtHR 9 June 1998) para 66.
59 Aldana-Pindell (n 6) 666.

This case law is particularly relevant because the ECtHR interpreted the right to an effective remedy for violations of Articles 2 and 3 as entailing States' obligations to carry out effective official investigations that can lead to the identification and possible punishment of those responsible. In *Hugh Jordan v the United Kingdom*, the ECtHR found that Article 2 requires 'a sufficient element of public scrutiny of the investigation or its results to secure accountability in practice as well as in theory'[60] because, in cases where authorities investigate a use of lethal force, it is essential 'in maintaining public confidence in their adherence to the rule of law and in preventing any appearance of collusion in or tolerance of unlawful acts'.[61] To this end, the ECtHR maintained that, even though the degree of public scrutiny can vary from case to case, 'the next-of-kin of the victim must be involved in the procedure to the extent necessary to safeguard his or her legitimate interests'.[62] In *Paul and Audrey Edwards v the United Kingdom*, the ECtHR specified that victims' involvement in the investigation and subsequent prosecution is necessary to safeguard their interests in the procedure in light of 'their close and personal concern with the subject matter of the inquiry (...)'.[63] Therefore, the right of victims and their next of kin to take part to the investigatory proceedings is a necessary requirement of the State duty to protect the rights and freedoms of the ECHR (Article 1) and its failure to conduct effective investigations and prosecutions amounts to violations of Articles 1 and 13.[64]

The ECtHR regarded its express acknowledgement of the right of victims and their next of kin to take part in the investigatory proceedings for alleged violation of the right to life, based on their legitimate interests, as conferring to victims certain participatory rights in criminal proceedings. Specifically, the ECtHR has explored to what extent victims can exercise their rights within the investigations and subsequent criminal proceedings. In *Kelly and Others v the United Kingdom*, the ECtHR criticised the British criminal justice system for not requiring the Prosecutor to justify the decision not to prosecute and for not subjecting such decisions to judicial review. The ECtHR established that the lack of reasons for the decision not to prosecute cannot be compatible with the requirements of Article 2 because it denies the family of the victim access to information about a matter of crucial importance to them and prevents any legal challenge of the decision.[65]

60 *Hugh Jordan v the United Kingdom* App No 24746/94 (ECtHR 4 May 2001) para 109.
61 ibid para 108.
62 ibid para 109. See also *Kelly and Others v the United Kingdom* App No 30054/96 (ECtHR 4 May 2001) para 98; *McKerr v the United Kingdom* App No 28883/95 (ECtHR 4 May 2001) para 115; *Shanaghan v the United Kingdom* App No 37715/97 (ECtHR 4 May 2001) para 92.
63 *Paul and Audrey Edwards v the United Kingdom* App No 46477/99 (ECtHR 14 March 2002) para 84.
64 *McCann and Others v the United Kingdom* (n 12) para 161; *Assenov and Others v Bulgaria* (n 13) para 102 (relating to Article 3).
65 *McKerr v the United Kingdom* (n 62) paras 117–118.

With regard to the disclosure of investigatory material and, specifically, witnesses' statements, the ECtHR affirmed that the non-disclosure of such statements places the victims and their family at a disadvantage. The impossibility to have access to the witnesses' statements prejudiced the ability of the applicants to participate in the inquest and contributed to long adjournments in the proceedings.[66] The ECtHR specifically considered that the families' lack of access to witness statements before the appearance of the witness placed them at a disadvantage in terms of preparation and ability to participate in questioning.[67] In *McKerr v the United Kingdom*, the ECtHR held that the invocation of 'public interest immunity' to prevent the posing of certain questions or the disclosure of certain documents that were material to the investigation also hindered an effective investigation.[68]

6.4.2 Victims' right to a fair hearing in criminal proceedings

In addition to the findings concerning the violations of Articles 2 and 3 of the ECHR, the ECtHR granted victims participatory rights in criminal proceedings on the basis of its interpretation of the right to a fair trial, which had previously been interpreted as protecting defendants' rights exclusively. Relying on the wording of Article 6(1), which provides that 'in the determination of his civil rights and obligations or of any criminal charge against him, everyone is entitled to a fair and public hearing', the ECtHR held that the fair trial right applies to victims only when victims had attached their civil reparation claims to the criminal proceedings, which, therefore, turn to be determining for the compensation for damages victims suffered as result of the crime.[69] The scope of the fair hearing right for victims encompasses almost exclusively those rights characterised by a private nature and, more specifically, by a pecuniary content, since Article 6(1) did not apply when the civil party did not claim for compensation.[70] In *Perez v France*, the ECtHR confirmed that Article 6(1) applies to victims participating in criminal trials as civil party; however, unlike the earlier cases, it is irrelevant that the victim did not lodge a formal claim for compensation.[71] For the ECtHR 'it is conceivable that Article 6 may be applicable even in the absence of a claim for financial reparation'[72] because, by acquiring the status of civil parties, victims

66 ibid paras 128–136.

67 ibid para 128. See also *Hugh Jordan v the United Kingdom* (n 60) para 300.

68 *McKerr v the United Kingdom* (n 62) para 151.

69 *Antunes Rocha v Portugal* App No 64330/01 (ECtHR 31 May 2005) para 43.

70 *Editions Périscope v France* App No 11760/85 (ECtHR 26 March 1992) paras 33–44; *Benthem v The Netherlands* App No 8848/80 (ECtHR 23 October 1985) para 36. See also Ochoa Sanchez (n 11) 156.

71 *Perez v France* App No 47287/99 (ECtHR 12 February 2004) para 64.

72 ibid para 65.

demonstrate the importance not only of securing financial reparation, but also of contributing to the criminal conviction of the offender.[73]

The ECtHR remarked that 'the right to a fair trial holds so prominent a place in a democratic society that there can be no justification for interpreting Article 6 § 1 restrictively'[74] and, therefore, it should include a civil party complaint because

> from the moment when the applicant is joined as a civil party until the conclusion of those criminal proceedings, the civil component remains closely connected with the criminal component (...) in other words whether the criminal proceedings affect the civil component.[75]

This holding essentially means that the ECtHR restricted the right of victims who can claim a violation under Article 6(1) to participate in domestic criminal proceedings, only if the civil component is directly related to the criminal one. Article 6(1) is applicable to a civil-party complaint in criminal proceedings, except in the case of a civil action brought purely to obtain private vengeance or for punitive purposes,[76] as the ECHR does not confer any right, as such, to have an alleged perpetrator prosecuted or sentenced for a criminal offence. To fall within the scope of Article 6(1), the prosecution and punishment of the perpetrator must be indissociable from the victim's exercise of the right to a civil-party complaint in criminal proceedings, even if only to secure symbolic reparation or to protect a civil right such as the right to a 'good reputation'.[77] Therefore, Article 6(1) applies to proceedings involving civil-party complaints from the moment the victims-complainants have joined as a civil party, unless they have waived the right to reparation in an unequivocal manner.[78] In the view of the ECtHR, this approach is coherent 'with the need to safeguard victims' rights and their proper place in criminal proceedings'.[79] The fact that the ECHR does not contain detailed provisions similar to those of Article 6, which involve criminal trials, for disputes about civil rights and obligations 'does not mean that the Court can ignore the plight

73 ibid para 64.
74 ibid para 64.
75 ibid para 67. See also *Kraska v Switzerland* App No 13942/88 (ECtHR 19 April 1993) para 30; *Van de Hurk v the Netherlands* App No 16034/90 (ECtHR 19 April 1994) para 59.
76 *Perez v France* (n 71) paras 70–71; *Sigalas v Greece* App No 19754/02 (ECtHR 22 September 2005) para 29.
77 *Perez v France* (n 71) para 70. Regarding a symbolic award see *Gorou v Greece (no 2)* App No 12686/03 (ECtHR 20 March 2009) para 24; *Helmers v Sweden* Series A no 212-A (ECtHR 29 October 1991) para 27; *Tolstoy Miloslavsky v the United Kingdom* Series A no 316-B (ECtHR 13 July 1995) para 58.
78 *Perez v France* (n 71) para 70; *Colozza and Rubinat v Italy* App No 9024/80 (ECtHR 12 February 1985) para 28; *Meftah and Others v France* App Nos 32911/96, 35237/97 and 34595/97 (ECtHR 26 July 2002) para 46.
79 *Perez v France* (n 71) para 72.

of victims and downgrade their rights'.[80] In more than one decision, the ECtHR stated that Article 6(1) aims at forbidding the denial of justice and, consequently, the right to a fair hearing ranks as one of the universally recognised fundamental principles of the rule of law.[81]

6.5 A lesson for international criminal justice

The development of the rights of victims in criminal justice processes at the level of regional human rights courts emphasises that the evolution of the role of victims has been part of a larger, more profound transformation of the nature of criminal justice. International criminal justice can draw relevant lessons from the case law of the IACtHR and the ECtHR. To begin with, the case law elaborated by the IACtHR and ECtHR can represent a valid contribution to the enhancement of an expressivist justice model and provide a sound foundation for victims' participatory rights within the criminal process. Secondly, the developments by the IACtHR and the ECtHR can encourage the call for greater advancement of the rights for victims in international criminal proceedings.

6.5.1 The expressivist value of the right of victims to participate in criminal proceedings

Due to the fact that the history of South-American States has often been turbulent with many instances of civil unrest, many of the cases adjudicated by the IACtHR dealt with torture, murder, and forced disappearances, often committed, condoned, or acquiesced by governments. Against this background, the evolution of the jurisprudence of the IACtHR on the victim's right to access to and participation in criminal proceedings has been clearly marked by the Court's battle against impunity. The analysis of the case law of the IACtHR provides values that can be interpreted as responding to the expressivist dimension of the criminal justice system, going, therefore, beyond the traditional retributive and deterrent criminal justice models. The IACtHR acknowledged that, due to the serious nature of the violation of human rights suffered by the victims, the criminal proceedings should contribute to the ascertainment of the truth, by providing a narrative of the events and conveying a message of denunciation and repudiation of those heinous infringements. The joint reading of the legal justifications for victims' right to access to and participation in criminal proceedings indicates that the IACtHR considered victims fundamental to achieve these goals. In fact, rooting victims' right to access to and participation in criminal proceedings in victims' right to truth, to

80 ibid para 72.
81 *Golder v the United Kingdom* (n 20) paras 34–35.

remedy, and to a fair hearing reflects the view that victims' voices contribute to enhancing the quality of the narrative, carrying on an effective prosecution of perpetrators and putting an end to impunity.

Differently from the context in which the IACtHR operates, the deep-rooted culture of human rights in most of Europe limited the ECtHR caseload relating to the category of cases of gross human rights violations (Turkey and the United Kingdom being the main sources). Compared to the jurisprudence of the IACtHR, the case law of the ECtHR represents a much less developed body of jurisprudence on the rights of victims of serious violations of human rights. Although the idea of an ends-focused process of justice aimed to fight impunity and effectively provide an impartial history in judgements is marginally developed by the ECtHR, some key elements of the expressivist paradigm can be traced in the ECtHR's elaboration of the rights of victims of serious violations of human rights.

According to the ECtHR, because of the serious nature of the violations of the right to life and prohibition of inhumane treatment, the criminal process should express rejection of any appearance of collusion in or tolerance of those criminal conducts. In this regard, the ECtHR has held that victims' rights in the criminal process have been violated when their participation in the criminal process, aimed at ensuring public accountability, has been curtailed. The public scrutiny that victims would bring to the criminal process could decrease the likelihood the States would wilfully or through omission taint the prosecution in favour of the accused. This point is particularly important because the Court acknowledged that victims have legitimate interests in the criminal proceedings. In this orientation of the ECtHR, it is possible to recognise features corresponding to the expressivist model of criminal justice, since the rationale for victims' involvement in criminal investigation and subsequent criminal proceedings is based on their close and personal concern with the violation at stake. Victims have a personal interest in participating in criminal trials, as they can express the condemnatory message when States' institutions of justice are unable or unwilling to prosecute. Therefore, given the importance of the rights to life and humane treatment, the ECtHR read the right of victims to an effective remedy as requiring States not only to undertake investigation and prosecution, but also to grant victims effective access to the process.

The decisions of the IACtHR and the ECtHR have evolved to consider effective prosecutions an essential part of the effective remedy States must guarantee victims for violations of the right to life or humane treatment. States not only have a duty to the public but also to the victims to prosecute grave human rights abuses. Victims' participation can improve the public's identification with the plight of victims because the more societies accept the justificatory story for the atrocities, the less likely it is there will be prosecutions. The IACtHR and the ECtHR have begun to require States to grant victims meaningful participation, since they espouse the idea that only the effective prosecution of human rights violations will yield the goals of truth and justice and prevent future violence and further victimisation.

6.5.2 *The influence of the case law of the IACtHR and ECtHR on the international criminal process*

The case law developed by the IACtHR and ECtHR has had an impact on the scope of victims' rights in international criminal proceedings because over the past two decades this case law 'has developed to create norms that respond to many of the concerns expressed by surviving human rights victims about their exclusion from the criminal proceedings, especially when states rampantly refuse to comply with their duty to prosecute'.[82] The case law of the IACtHR and the ECtHR specifically supports two propositions: the State's duty to prosecute serious crimes is also a right that is owed to victims; and their participation is necessary to enforce such a right. The IACtHR and the ECtHR assert the right of individuals, whose basic entitlement to life and to bodily integrity have been violated, to participate in related criminal proceedings to articulate their concerns and to learn the truth about the criminal events.

The emerging principle that victims should have greater access to the criminal process to ensure that criminal prosecutions are effective and that States are accountable to victims is particularly relevant because it can influence how international criminal justice can enhance victims' rights. The IACtHR and the ECtHR have articulated with clarity certain participatory rights of victims and why they should have access to proceedings. In particular, emphasis was placed on victims' participation in the investigation stage of the preceding as a fundamental part of ensuring the effectiveness of the process and countering impunity. This position is justified on the ground that the participation of victims as independent parties can provide oversight of the prosecutorial discretion in the selection of perpetrators and charges and identify those responsible more accurately. The role of victims in this stage is necessary to safeguard their interests, to provide public scrutiny and accountability, and to ensure individuals have a right to review decisions.

A closer look at the jurisprudence of the IACtHR shows that the provisions of the ACHR have been interpreted to accommodate several key entitlements of victims: the affirmation of a victim's right to an effective prosecution; victims' right to participate in proceedings; victims' right of standing to monitor the State's actions and to advance their interests; and the right to truth related to the State's duty to investigate. The IACtHR has determined that victims in an investigation should have 'substantial possibilities of being heard and acting in the respective proceedings, both in order to clarify the facts and punish those responsible, and to seek due reparation'.[83] The jurisprudence of the IACtHR not only reinforces the stand represented by the international criminal courts that certain serious human rights violations – those that amount to international

82 Raquel Aldana-Pindell, 'In Vindication of Justiciable Victims' Rights to Truth and Justice for State- Sponsored Crimes' (2002) 35 Vanderbilt Journal of Transnational Law 1399, 1413.

83 *Villagrán-Morales et al. v Guatemala* (n 39) para 227.

crimes – must attract criminal sanction, but also holds that victims' participation would serve an accountability function.

In a similar way, the ECtHR has acknowledged that investigations play a significant role in the determination of truth and justice, since the selection of charges and perpetrators to prosecute takes place at this stage of the proceedings. According to the jurisprudence of the ECtHR, the duty to conduct an effective investigation has a bearing on victims' rights to participate, attaching procedural rights to fundamental rights, such as the right to life.

To ensure meaningful participation, victims' right to obtain information regarding measures taken by the State after notice of violation should include the right to be informed of a decision not to prosecute, the right to request information about the investigation or trial, and the right to have access to the investigation and case file, including witness statements. Issues relating to the right to be informed are some of the most difficult in the practice of international criminal tribunals, where the Prosecutor is likely to plead confidentiality and the integrity of investigations among other reasons to prevent victims from having access to the files. If the international criminal proceedings are to have the greatest potential to give publicity to the international crimes victims have suffered, they should strive to ensure the best procedural practices, including a transparent investigation where victims can participate as independent parties. In particular, the ICC found persuasive the trend in cases from the IACtHR and the ECtHR to grant victims the right to participate in proceedings during the investigation stage.[84] In *Lubanga*, Pre-Trial Chamber I noted that the ICC had been created as a result of 'a debate that took place in the context of a growing emphasis placed on the role of victims by the international body of human rights law and by international humanitarian law'.[85] Pre-Trial Chamber I relied on rulings from the IACtHR and the ECtHR in making its central determination of conferring victims a general right to participate in an ICC investigation, as it acknowledged that the goal pursued by those regional human rights courts was to grant victims an independent voice and role.[86] In light of this, the ICC's Judges recognised that victims are important at the investigation stage 'to clarify the facts and to punish the perpetrators of crimes',[87] and that their participation is not inconsistent or prejudicial to the 'integrity and objective of the investigation' nor to 'efficiency and security'.[88]

While the IACtHR and the ECtHR held that victims have the right to articulate their personal interests at trial stage, victims' participatory rights are dictated in

84 For a discussion on the case law of the ICC on victims' right to participate in the investigations see Chapter 8.

85 *Prosecutor v Thomas Lubanga Dyilo* (Decision on the Applications for participation in the proceedings of VPRS 1, VPRS 2, VPRS 3, VPRS 4, VPRS 5 and VPRS 6 (Public Redacted Version)) ICC-01/04-01/06, Pre-Trial Chamber I (19 January 2006) para 50.

86 ibid paras 50–54.

87 ibid paras 57–58.

88 ibid paras 58–59.

a broad way, by setting minima standards for the State to comply with. It can be argued that this holding back to prescribe models of participation for victims at trial stage should be considered to be indicative of the deference of the IACtHR and the ECtHR to national systems.[89] The IACtHR and the ECtHR preferred to grant victims' participation during the early phases of the criminal proceedings, as a way of ensuring that States are adequately investigating and prosecuting alleged violations. Nevertheless, the participation of victims at trial stage, seen as an opportunity to have their interests considered by the relevant tribunal, to be heard, to clarify the facts, and to determine the responsibility of the accused, is an international law hallmark for enhancing victims' status in international criminal proceedings. In particular, this is consistent with the type of standing victims have at the ICC, where they can exercise the right to present their views and concerns at certain stages of the criminal proceedings.[90] The case law of the IACtHR and the ECtHR, by including the right to obtain an investigation, prosecution, and punishment, the right to effective access to justice, the right to be heard, the right to information, and the right to truth, has the potential to trigger a process of enhancement of victims' status as participants in international criminal proceedings.

6.6 Conclusion

Regional human rights courts are central to the elaboration of victims' rights to participation in criminal proceedings. The relevant developments on victims' status at the ECtHR and IACtHR illustrates that, despite the fact that no explicit right of victims is provided in the ECHR and ACHR, victims are entitled to exercise an assortment of rights, arising from corresponding obligations for States. The case law of the IACtHR and ECtHR has been articulated around two basic issues: the right of victims to have access to justice, to obtain an investigation, prosecution, and punishment; and victims' right to participate in criminal proceedings. In regard to the first issue, both the ECtHR and IACtHR held the right of victims, whose basic rights to life and of prohibition to inhuman treatment are violated, and of their relatives to be involved at the investigation stage is a fundamental element of victims' right to an effective remedy. Victims have the right to complain and resort to the administration of justice to obtain impartial independent investigations by the State's authorities within a reasonable time, to actively participate in the investigations, to be informed of their development, to be heard, and to learn the truth about events.

The second issue, namely the case law on the right of victims to participate in criminal proceedings, has been more controversial. The IACtHR broadly acknowledges the right of victims to take part in the criminal proceedings and bases it on the fair hearing principle, the right to judicial protection and victims'

89 Aldana-Pindell (n 6) 668.
90 Article 68(3), Rome Statute of the International Criminal Court 1998 (2187 UNTS 90).

right to the truth. Although this case law guarantees victims participation in criminal proceedings on the ground of a systematic interpretation of the right to an effective remedy, to a fair hearing, and to the truth, the IACtHR does not prescribe what 'form' or 'modes' such participation must take. Conversely, the ECtHR advanced that the right to an effective remedy should include the right to submit a complaint to the competent authorities; the right to have an effective and impartial investigation carried out; the right to be informed about the conduct of the procedures and of major decisions taken in this procedure; the right to be present at the trial and to be heard at the key stages of the procedure; and the right to offer and examine evidence and to challenge its admissibility or relevance. On this account, the jurisprudence of the ECtHR seems more helpful in the elaboration of the broad and multifaceted right of victims to participate in international criminal proceedings.

The system of legal bases advanced by the ECtHR and the IACtHR to justify the role of victims can be interpreted as consistent with the framework of the expressivist function of the trial. The ECtHR and the IACtHR acknowledged that, because of values that their respective Conventions protect, human rights violations involve breaches of rights that have a special status. The criminal proceedings, thus, become a mechanism to reaffirm the importance that society places on those serious infringements and the importance of educating societies in the respect of those rights. The systematic interpretation of the provision of the ECHR and the ACHR granting victims the right to have access to and participate in criminal proceedings reflects the view that the victim's voice contributes to expressing disavowal and condemnation of those conducts violating human rights, enhancing the quality of the narrative, carrying out an effective prosecution of perpetrators, and putting an end to impunity.

References

Books and journals

Aldana-Pindell R, 'In Vindication of Justiciable Victims' Rights to Truth and Justice for State- Sponsored Crimes' (2002) 35 Vanderbilt Journal of Transnational Law 1399

Aldana-Pindell R, 'An Emerging Universality of Justiciable Victims' Rights in the Criminal Process to Curtail Impunity for State-Sponsored Crimes' (2004) 26 Human Rights Quarterly 605

Bassiouni MC, 'International Recognition of Victims' Rights' (2006) 6 Human Rights Law Review 203

Cassese A, Acquaviva G and Whiting A, *International Criminal Law: Cases and Commentary* (Oxford University Press 2011)

Ochoa Sanchez JC, *The Rights of Victims in Criminal Justice Proceedings for Serious Human Rights Violations* (Martinus Nijhoff Publishers 2013)

Organización de los Estados Americanos, 'Conferencia Especializada Interamericana sobre Derechos Humanos, San José, Costa Rica, 7–22 de noviembre de 1969', Actas y documentos doc. OEA/Ser.K/xvi/1.2 (1969)

REDRESS, 'Victim Participation in Criminal Law Proceedings: Survey of Domestic Practice for Application to International Crimes Prosecutions' (2015) <http://www.redress.org/downloads/1508victim-rights-report.pdf> accessed 1 July 2021

Cases

Acevedo-Jaramillo et al. v Peru (Preliminary Objections, Merits, Reparations and Costs) IACtHR Series C No. 144, (7 February 2006)

Aksoy v Turkey App No. 21987/93 (ECtHR 18 December 1996)

Almonacid-Arellano et al. v Chile (Preliminary Objections, Merits, Reparations and Costs) IACtHR Series C No. 154, (26 September 2006)

Antunes Rocha v Portugal App No. 64330/01 (ECtHR 31 May 2005)

Assenov and Others v Bulgaria App No. 24760/94 (ECtHR 28 October 1998)

Aydin v Turkey App No. 23178/94 (ECtHR 25 September 1997)

Baldeón García v Peru (Judgment, Merits, Reparations and Costs) IACtHR Series C No. 147, (6 April 2006)

Bámaca-Velásquez v Guatemala (Judgment, Merits) IACtHR Series C No. 70, (25 November 2000)

Barrios Altos v Peru (Judgment, Merits) IACtHR Series C No. 75, (14 March 2001)

Benthem v The Netherlands App 8848/80 (ECtHR 23 October 1985)

Blake v Guatemala (Judgment, Merits), IACtHR Series C No. 36, (24 January 1998)

Blanco Romero et al. v Venezuela (Judgment, Merits, Reparations and Costs) IACtHR Series C No. 138, (28 November 2005)

Bulacio v Argentina (Judgment, Merits, Reparations and Costs) IACtHR Series C No. 100, (18 September 2003)

Cantoral Benavides v Peru (Judgment, Reparations and Costs) IACtHR Series C No. 88, (3 December 2001)

Caracazo v Venezuela (Judgment, Reparations and Costs) IACtHR Series C No. 95, (29 August 2002)

Castillo Páez v Peru (Judgment, Merits) IACtHR Series C No. 34, (3 November 1997)

Castillo Páez v Peru (Judgment Reparations and Costs) IACtHR Series C No. 34, (27 November 1998)

Claude Reyes et al. v Chile (Judgment, Merits, Reparations and Costs), IACtHR Series C No. 151, (19 September 2006)

Colozza and Rubinat v Italy App 9024/80 (ECtHR 12 February 1985)

Durand and Ugarte v Peru (Judgment, Merits) IACtHR Series C No. 68, (16 August 2000)

Editions Périscope v France App No. 11760/85 (ECtHR 26 March 1992)

Ergi v Turkey App No. 23818/94 (ECtHR 28 July 1998)

Fairén Garbi and Solís Corrales v Honduras (Judgment, Merits) IACtHR Series C No. 6, (15 March 1989)

García Prieto et al. v El Salvador (Preliminary Objections, Merits, Reparations and Costs) IACtHR Series C No. 168, (20 November 2007)

Genie Lacayo v Nicaragua (Judgment, Merits, Reparations and Costs) IACtHR Series C No. 30, (29 January 1997)

Godínez Cruz v Honduras (Judgment, Merits) IACtHR Series C No. 5, (20 January 1989)

Golder v the United Kingdom App 4451/70 (ECtHR 21 February 1975)

Gómez Palomino v Peru (Judgment, Merits, Reparations and Costs) IACtHR Series C No. 136, (2 November 2005)
Gorou v Greece (No. 2) App No. 12686/03 (ECtHR 20 March 2009)
Gül v Turkey App No. 22676/93 (ECtHR 14 December 2000)
Güleç v Turkey App No. 21593/93 (ECtHR 27 July 1998)
Heliodoro-Portugal v Panama (Preliminary Objections, Merits, Reparations and Costs) IACtHR Series C No. 186, (12 August 2008)
Helmers v Sweden Series A no 212-A (ECtHR 29 October 1991)
Hilaire, Constantine and Benjamin et al. v Trinidad and Tobago (Judgment, Merits, Reparations and Costs) IACtH Series C No. 94, (21 June 2002)
Hugh Jordan v the United Kingdom App No. 24746/94 (ECtHR 4 May 2001)
Juan Humberto Sánchez v Honduras (Preliminary Objection, Merits, Reparations and Costs) IACtHR Series C No. 99, (7 June 2003) 1
Kaya v Turkey App No. 22729/93 (ECtHR 19 February 1998)
Kelly and Others v *the United Kingdom* App No 30054/96 (ECtHR 4 May 2001)
Kraska v Switzerland App No. 13942/88 (ECtHR 19 April 1993)
La Cantuta v Peru (Judgment, Merits, Reparations and Costs) IACtHR Series C No. 162, (29 November 2006)
Las Palmeras v Colombia (Judgment, Merits) IACtHR Series C No. 90, (6 December 2001)
Loayza Tamayo v Peru (Judgment, Reparations and Costs) IACtHR Series C No. 42, (27 November 1998)
López Álvarez v Honduras (Judgment, Merits, Reparations and Costs) IACtHR Series C No. 141, (1 February 2006)
MC v Bulgaria App No. 39272/98 (ECtHR 4 December 2003)
McCann and Others v *the United Kingdom* App No 18984/91 (ECtHR 5 September 1995)
McKerr v the United Kingdom App No. 28883/95 (ECtHR 4 May 2001)
Meftah and Others v France App Nos 32911/96, 35237/97 and 34595/97 (ECtHR 26 July 2002)
Menteş and Others v Turkey App No. 23186/94 (ECtHR 28 November 1997)
Montero Aranguren et al. (Detention Center of Catia) v Venezuela (Preliminary Objection, Merits, Reparations and Costs) IACtHR Series C No. 150, (5 July 2006)
Myrna Mack Chang v Guatemala (Judgment, Merits, Reparations and Costs) IACtHR Series C No. 101, (25 November 2003)
Oğur v Turkey App No. 21594/93 (ECtHR 20 May 1999)
Orhan v Turkey App No. 25656/94 (ECtHR 18 June 2002)
Palamara Iribarne v Chile (Judgment, Merits, Reparations and Costs) IACtHR Series C No. 135, (22 November 2005)
Paniagua Morales et al. v Guatemala (*the case of the 'White Van'*) (Judgment, Merits) IACtHR Series C No. 37, (8 March 1998)
Paul and Audrey Edwards v the United Kingdom App No. 46477/99 (ECtHR 14 March 2002)
Perez v France App No. 47287/99 (EctHR 12 February 2004)
Prosecutor v Kupreškić et al. (Judgment) ICTY-IT-95–16-T, Trial Chamber (14 January 2000)
Prosecutor v Thomas Lubanga Dyilo (Decision on the Applications for participation in the proceedings of VPRS 1, VPRS 2, VPRS 3, VPRS 4, VPRS 5 and VPRS 6

(Public Redacted Version)) ICC-01/04-01/06, Pre-Trial Chamber I (19 January 2006)
Salman v Turkey App No. 21986/93 (ECtHR 27 June 2000)
Salvador Chiriboga v Ecuador (Partially Dissenting Opinion of Judge Medina Quiroga) IACtHR Series C No. 179, (6 May 2008)
Selçuk and Asker v Turkey App No 23184/94 and 23185/94 (ECtHR 24 April 1998)
Serrano Cruz Sisters v El Salvador (Judgment, Merits, Reparations and Costs) IACtHR Series C No. 120, (1 March 2005)
Shanaghan v the United Kingdom App No. 37715/97 (ECtHR 4 May 2001)
Sigalas v Greece App No. 19754/02 (ECtHR 22 September 2005)
Suárez Rosero v Ecuador (Judgment Merits) IACtHR Series C No. 35, (12 November 1997)
Tekin v Turkey App No. 22496/93 (ECtHR 9 June 1998)
The "Mapiripán Massacre" v Colombia (Judgment, Merits, Reparations and Costs) IACtHR Series C No. 134, (15 September 2005)
Tolstoy Miloslavsky v the United Kingdom Series A no 316-B (ECtHR 13 July 1995)
Trujillo Oroza v *Bolivia* (Judgment Reparations and Costs) IACtHR Series C No. 92, (27 February 2002)
Tumurtas v Turkey App No. 23531/94 (ECtHR 13 June 2000)
Van de Hurk v the Netherlands App No. 16034/90 (ECtHR 19 April 1994)
Vargas Areco v Paraguay (Judgment, Merits, Reparations and Costs) IACtHR Series C No. 155, (26 September 2006)
Velásquez-Rodríguez v Honduras (Judgment) IACtHR Series C No 4, (29 July 1988)
Villagrán-Morales et al. v Guatemala (Judgment, Merits) IACtHR Series C No. 63, (19 November 1999)
X and Y v The Netherlands App 8978/80 (ECtHR 26 March 1985)
Ximenes Lopes v Brazil (Judgment, Merits, Reparations and Costs) IACtHR Series C No. 149, (4 July 2006)
Yaşa v Turkey App No. 22495/93 (ECtHR 2 September 1998)
19 Merchants v Colombia (Judgment, Merits, Reparations and Costs) IACtHR Series C No. 109, (5 July 2004)

Legislation

Rome Statute of the International Criminal Court 1998 (2187 UNTS 90)

7 Victims before the Nuremberg IMT, the ICTY, and the ICTR

An expressivist deficit

7.1 Introduction

The analysis of the expressivist foundation of international criminal justice discussed in Chapter 4 is extended to the proceedings before the post-Second World War Nuremberg IMT, the ICTY, and the ICTR. This chapter aims to identify the expressivist nature of these tribunals and explore the limitations on the development of the role of victims in these early international criminal trials. Expressivism is an important factor in the institutional foundation and operation of international criminal justice institutions. Specifically, the expressivist value of the Nuremberg IMT, the ICTY, and the ICTR can be traced in the multiple goals underpinning their creation, such as promoting the national and international rule of law; ending impunity for those who violate human rights; providing a mechanism for the transformation of social norms in developing democracies; conveying expressions of shame and apology; safeguarding basic standards of human rights; and communicating the denunciation and disavowal of heinous conducts.

However, while these international criminal tribunals were vested with an expressivist value, there was a corresponding expressivist 'deficit' with regard to the way the procedural role of victims was framed in the founding legal instruments and implemented in the practices of the Nuremberg IMT, the ICTY, and the ICTR. Due to the predominance of the adversarial procedural model, victims played the somewhat marginal role of witnesses in the proceedings, which proved to be inadequate to meet the need of victims to secure justice through international criminal justice tribunals. Actors in the criminal justice process, such as Prosecutors and Judges, took control of victims' narratives and imposed a particular frame or stereotype to the point of taking any prospect of agency away from victims, who were tasked to conform to this frame, and excluding victims whose story did not conform to the stereotype in one way or another. This chapter seeks to illustrate that victims' procedural role before the Nuremberg IMT, the ICTY, and the ICTR re-silences victims, negating their potential to shaping the expressivist message of the international criminal trials. The practices of these tribunals undermined the capacity of victims' narrative expressed during the trials to present their perspective on events and to bring about a potential

DOI: 10.4324/9781003215448-7

qualitative change in the message the trial conveys. *De facto*, victims' role was cast in the 'harm and suffering' vernacular, void of choice and action on the part of the victim.

7.2 Expressivist dimension of international criminal justice institutions

The making and dynamics of institutions of international criminal justice have usually been approached from the point of view of their functions, namely, retribution, deterrence, redress for victims, and maintenance of peace. The focus on the legal nature of international criminal justice institutions has undermined their socio-pedagogical function, which entails the crafting of historical records and didactic purposes.[1] Expressivism is an important element in the establishment and functioning of international criminal justice institutions. Durkheim's idea that a particular conduct is criminal because it shocks the common conscience, rather than 'an action shocks the common conscience because it is criminal',[2] is at the heart of this radical perspective on the functions of laws and institutions. The construction of criminal law as societal reaction to crime provides an added dimension to the functionalist explanations of criminal justice institutions, arguing that the adoption of organisational structures possesses and creates symbolic meaning through acts of representation and rituals.[3] The symbolic dimension of justice institutions becomes 'an act reaffirming networks of community existing beyond nations, rather than mere legal creations'.[4] More recently, echoing Durkheimian thinking, Stahn observed that '[i]nstitutions are symbolic and behavioural systems that define social and legal meanings. They shape behaviour, choices, and perceptions'.[5]

This vision provides a broader and more articulated foundation for the adoption of international criminal justice institutions, which cannot be conceived simply as technocratic and administrative structures, tasked with the prosecution and punishment of individuals. The creation of a new international criminal body carries symbolic and normative functions in itself. It represents a communicative act aimed at encouraging the protection of certain norms and principles. According to this logic, international criminal justice institutions become the 'medium' to convey different messages, namely promoting the national and international rule of law; ending the impunity of those who violate human rights; providing a mechanism for the transformation of social norms in developing

1 See section 4.8.

2 Émile Durkheim, *The Division of Labour in Society* (Macmillan 1984) 81.

3 Joachim J Savelsberg and Ryan D King, 'Law and Collective Memory' (2007) 3 Annual Review Law Social Science 189, 202.

4 Carsten Stahn, *Justice as Message: Expressivist Foundations of International Criminal Justice* (Oxford University Press 2020) 168.

5 ibid 165.

democracies; conveying expressions of shame and apology; safeguarding basic standards of human rights; and communicating the denunciation and disavowal of heinous conducts.

If the establishment of these institutions is relevant 'not for what they *do* but for what they *signify*',[6] the form of institutional reaction to crimes matters, as it sends a message about the *raison d'être* of the institution and the nature of the reaction to crimes. It makes a difference whether the entity in whose name a court acts is national or international. First, it 'marks a transition between the conception of a society of states and a community of mankind'.[7] Second, prosecution by international criminal institutions brands 'crimes themselves as forms of reprehensible deviancy'[8] and, consequently, perpetrators are 'designated as one of the gravest international criminals'.[9] Third, the choice of international institution not only reflects the expression of outrage and the international gravity of the offences, it also designates and acknowledges the communities that have been affected by the violations.[10]

7.3 The Nuremberg IMT

The Nuremberg IMT, which was to try Nazi statesmen, military leaders, administrators, bankers, industrialists, propagandists, and educators, was the result of a path that began after the outbreak of the hostilities of the Second World War. As reports of the mass murder of Jews, deportation of civilian populations to slave labour, destruction of cities, and extermination of their inhabitants were received,[11] the three principal powers, United Kingdom, the United States, and the Soviet Union, signed the Moscow Declaration on Atrocities (November 1943), which laid down the foundation for the post-war trials, as they solemnly committed themselves to the punishment of those responsible for war crimes.[12] Justice Robert Jackson, the American representative and Chief Prosecutor of the Nuremberg IMT, negotiated with the delegates from the Allied Powers the norms establishing the Nuremberg IMT, which, in fact, were mainly based on

6 Jelena Subotić, *Hijacked Justice: Dealing with the Past in the Balkans* (Cornell University Press 2016) 24.
7 Salif Nimage, 'An International Conscience Collective? A Durkheimian Analysis of International Criminal Law' (2007) 7 International Criminal Law Review 561, 607.
8 Frédéric Mégret, 'Practices of Stigmatization' (2013) 76 Law and Contemporary Problems 287, 305.
9 Frédéric Mégret, 'What Sort of Global Justice Is "International Criminal Justice"?' (2015) 13 Journal of International Criminal Justice 77, 82.
10 Frédéric Mégret, 'In Defense of Hybridity: Towards a Representational Theory of International Criminal Justice' (2005) 38 Cornell International Law Journal 725, 743.
11 John Alan Appleman, *Military Tribunals and the International Crimes* (Greenwood Press Publishers 1954) vii.
12 William A Schabas, *An Introduction to the International Criminal Court* (3rd edn, Cambridge University Press 2007) 5.

the American proposal.[13] The American view called for a display of due process principle, as Jackson was aware that the legitimacy of the IMT proceedings would have been irremediably compromised if the right of the defendants to a fair trial was not respected.[14] It is undeniable that the Nuremberg trial represented an instance of 'victor's justice', but in Jackson's vision the trial was not a facade to impose a punishment.[15] His main concern was not to breach the juridical principle that there cannot be punishment without the criminal conduct of the defendants having been proved.[16] Jackson's activities culminated in the London Agreement, signed by the leaders of the four allies (the United States, the United Kingdom, the Soviet Union, and France) in August 1945, which established the Charter of the Nuremberg IMT to prosecute the leaders of the European Axis and their principal agents.[17]

Since its inception, the Nuremberg IMT has proved to be vested with expressivist functions. The significance of its creation lies in its ability to recreate core values and faith in the rule of law as well as renew community relations. This tribunal was established at a historical moment when most nations were experiencing a great collective shock, following the atrocities committed by Germans prior to the outbreak of and during the Second World War, which resulted in millions of victims losing their life and an equally numerous number of victims surviving but physically and psychologically affected. The Nuremberg IMT marked a moment of transformation of social and normative structures, as it can be conceived as a 'colossal event in international politics that aimed at carrying out a dramatic change from war to peace'.[18] This is reflected in the focus in the trial on crimes against peace and crimes against humanity, as set respectively in Articles 6(a) and 6(b) of the Nuremberg IMT Charter.

The Tribunal construed crimes against peace, which included 'planning, preparation, initiation or waging of a war of aggression, or a war in violation of international treaties', as rooted in the larger principle of justice, in circumstances where treaties are defined and States are attacked without warning.[19] This provision

13 Leo Gross, 'The Punishment of War Criminals: The Nuremberg Trial (First Part)' (1955) 2 Netherlands International Law Review 356, 360.

14 Robert H Jackson, 'Report to the President from Justice Robert Jackson, Chief of Counsel for the United States in the Prosecution of the Axis War Criminal' (1945) 39 American Journal of International Law 178, 182; Gary Jonathan Bass, *Stay the Hand of Vengeance: The Politics of War Crimes Tribunals*, vol 142 (Princeton University Press 2014) 151.

15 Sonali Chakravarti, 'More than "Cheap Sentimentally": Victim Testimony at Nuremberg, the Eichmann Trail, and Truth Commissions' (2008) 15 Constellations 223, 224.

16 Jeffrey D Hockett, 'Justice Robert H. Jackson, the Supreme Court, and the Nuremberg Trial' (1990) The Supreme Court Review 257, 260.

17 Bradley F Smith, *Reaching Judgment at Nuremberg* (Andre Deutsch 1977) 58.

18 Yuki Takatori, 'Remembering the War Crimes Trial: The Tokyo Trial View of History' in Sven Saaler and Wolfgang Schwentker (eds), *The Power of Memory in Modern Japan* (Global Oriental 2008) 92.

19 Lawrence D Egbert (ed), 'International Military Tribunal (Nuremberg), Judgment and Sentences, October 1 1946' (1947) 41 American Journal of International Law 172, 219.

was an attempt to 'juridify the logic of war'[20] and prove the point that the war was illegal, and, consequently, an aggressive war and any recourse to force as a means of national policy were to be condemned because they were also illegal.[21] The objective of the invocation of crimes against peace was to promote the ethical and political vision of the Allies, according to which the determination that aggressive war is a crime under international law, requiring the prosecution of those most responsible, would serve peace worldwide.[22] Ultimately, the Nuremberg Tribunal sought to clearly mark the divide between the Allies' vision and the conduct and ideology of the defeated Nazi powers. The prosecution and punishment of the German rulers as well as the exposure of their cruelty and folly 'would educate the people, causing them to reject all that the men who had led them represented and leaving an indelible impression on the consciousness of the defeated nations'.[23]

Crimes against humanity,[24] an innovative offence in the language of international law,[25] represented the first attempt to realise a system of international justice, which could potentially address the needs of communities who had experienced the tragic events of the Second World War. Despite the fact that many conducts amounting to crimes against humanity were committed on German territory in conformity with domestic law by the German government against its own citizens, belonging to a specific political, racial, or religious group, or being political opponents to the Nazi regime,[26] the legal status of these charges transcended the principle of State sovereignty.[27] This kind of crime represented an offence to humanity based on the law of nations, natural law, and the concept of humanity itself and, consequently, perpetrators were conceived as enemies of humankind under international law, subject to universal jurisdiction.[28] The concept of crimes against humanity symbolised a deep change in the normative structure of State powers and sovereignty because the Nuremberg IMT acknowledged that 'individuals have international duties which transcend the national obligations of obedience imposed by the individual State'.[29] Justice Jackson stated that the Nuremberg Tribunal had incontrovertibly and unambiguously established for the first time that

20 Lawrence Douglas, 'From IMT to NMT: The Emergence of a Jurisprudence of Atrocity' in Kim C Priemel and Alexa Stiller (eds), *Reassessing the Nuremberg Military Tribunals: Transitional Justice, Trial Narratives, and Historiography* (Berghahn Books 2012) 280.

21 Robert K Woetzel, *The Nuremberg Trials in International Law: With a Postlude on the Eichmann Case* (Stevens & Sons Limited 1962) 145–146.

22 Bass (n 14) 75.

23 Takatori (n 18) 92.

24 Article 6(c), Charter of the International Military Tribunal – Annex to the Agreement for the prosecution and punishment of the major war criminals of the European Axis 1945.

25 Francis Biddle, 'The Nuremberg Trial' (1947) 91 Proceedings of the American Philosophical Society 294, 301.

26 Woetzel (n 21) 177.

27 Diane Orentlicher, 'Settling Accounts' (1991) 100 Yale Law Journal 2537, 2556.

28 ibid 2556–2557.

29 Egbert (n 19) 221.

> to persecute, oppress, or do violence to individuals or minorities on political, racial, or religious grounds in connection with such a war, or to exterminate, enslave, or deport civilian populations, is an international crime, and that for the commission of such crimes individuals are responsible.[30]

The aspiration of the provision of crimes against humanity was to build a more comprehensive concept of international justice by creating a connection between the claims of justice for the mass atrocities committed during the war, their impact on society, and the experience of the victims.[31] This new concept of justice, which went beyond the accountability and punishment of perpetrators, sought to give room to the experiences of suffering of the victims, conceived as a legacy to society. The experiences of war victims were fundamental to having a thorough understanding of the impact of war on politics and society and, consequently, to reflecting on ethical and political concerns, the values and practices that were necessary to rebuild society after Second World War.[32]

The Nuremberg IMT also served to convey a formal and public message of censure, educating society about the unacceptable nature of the actions condemned and demonstrating societal intolerance and stigmatisation of certain conducts. Drumbl observed that the prosecution envisioned that the trial would expose to all the value of law and the depth of the defendants' culpability.[33] Similarly, Amann remarked that '[c]ondemnation, the process of compiling a record of evil and expressing repulsion, received as much attention as punishment', as perpetrators had become cast 'as symbols of an evil that had befallen Europe and that must never recur'.[34] In his opening statement, Justice Robert Jackson argued that the defendants

> represent influences that will lurk in the world long after their bodies have turned to dust. We will show them to be living symbols of racial hatreds, of terrorism and violence, and of the arrogance and cruelty of power. They are symbols of fierce nationalism and of militarism, of intrigue and war-making which have embroiled Europeans generation after generation, crushing its manhood, destroying its homes, and impoverishing its life.[35]

30 Robert H Jackson, 'Final Report to the President Concerning the Nuremberg War Crimes Trial' (1946) 20 Temple Law Quarterly 338, 342.

31 Chakravarti (n 15) 223–224.

32 ibid 233.

33 Mark A Drumbl, *Atrocity, Punishment, and International Law* (Cambridge University Press 2007) 3.

34 Diane Marie Amann, 'Group Mentality, Expressivism, and Genocide' (2002) 2 International Criminal Law Review 93, 121.

35 Opening Statement of Supreme Court Justice, Robert H. Jackson, Chief Prosecutor for the International Military Tribunal (21 November 1945) in *Trial of the Major War Criminals before the International Military Tribunal*, vol 2 (1948) 99.

Couched in these terms, the denunciatory and condemnatory functions of the trial have a specific expressivist value because they hold guilty only the effective perpetrator, namely the Nazi authorities, rather than the German nation as a whole. Such individuation of criminals, by removing guilt from others, was aimed at promoting the reconstruction of the social fabric.[36]

While enunciating societal condemnation of atrocities, reaffirming the importance of human rights, and educating the public, the Nuremberg trial also provided historical records of mass atrocities to prevent the past from being denied by revisionists. In his final report on the Nuremberg War Crimes Trial, Justice Robert Jackson stated that one of the primary purposes of the trial was to use German sources to document in detail the atrocities, prosecutions, and aggressions committed by the Nazis in order to prevent the denial of these crimes in the future and the arousal of a tradition of martyrdom of the Nazi leaders.[37] The prosecution of acts of aggressive war and crimes against humanity reconstructed the course of events with a view to providing a 'post mortem examination of a totalitarian regime'[38] and its evils and, at the same time, magnifying the strength of democracies.[39] Robert Jackson concluded his report affirming that the Nuremberg Trial exposed the methods used by the Nazi regime to subvert people's liberties and establish its dictatorship.[40]

The narrative structure of the trial based on the 'good v evil dichotomy' was seen as the most effective way of presenting to the public an accurate historical record in a credible and transparent manner.[41]

7.4 Victims before the Nuremberg IMT

Victims were often evoked in the rhetoric of the Prosecutors. For instance, Sir Hartley Shawcross, the Chief Prosecutor for the United Kingdom, urged the Tribunal to convict the defendants so that 'justice may be done to these individuals as to their countless victims'.[42] In a similar way, the Soviet Prosecutor Rudenko declared that the Judges 'have no right to leave unpunished those who organized and were guilty of monstrous crimes (...) [i]n sacred memory of millions of innocent victims of the fascist terror (...) May justice be done!'.[43]

36 Diane Marie Amann, 'Assessing International Criminal Adjudication of Human Rights Atrocities' (2000) 16 Third World Legal Studies 169, 178.
37 Jackson (n 30) 342.
38 ibid.
39 Göran Sluiter et al. (eds), *International Criminal Procedure: Principles and Rules* (Oxford University Press 2013) 46.
40 Jackson (n 30) 342–343.
41 Sluiter et al. (n 39) 46.
42 Sir Hartley Shawcross' Opening Statement, Chief Prosecutor for the United Kingdom (26 July 1946) in *Trial of the Major War Criminals Before the International Military Tribunal*, vol 7 (1948) 434.
43 General Rudenko's Opening Statement (2 August 1946) ibid 193.

However, the idea of obtaining justice for victims was mainly used to justify the punishment of the defendants.[44] Despite the sincere and great shock over the large-scale atrocities committed, in the trial before the Nuremberg IMT little attention was paid to the role and rights of the victims of international crimes.[45] The role of victims was overlooked for four main reasons. First of all, under international law, the concept of victim was pretty much unknown at that time. The general position was that, when an individual suffers harm as a consequence of a violation of rules of international law, the injuries resulting are not those of the harmed person, but those of the State.[46] Second, the procedural framework of the Tribunal was shaped following the common law adversarial procedural model, which prevents victims from participating with an autonomous standing.[47] The fundamental notion underlying the criminal process was based on the dialectic structure of the adversarial contest, since the prosecution presented its version of facts and the Defence was allowed to rebut it by pointing out any contradictions or inaccuracies.[48] Each of the four Chief Prosecutors undertook, individually or in collaboration with one another, the investigation, collection, and production of all necessary evidence, the preparation of the indictment, the preliminary examination of all necessary witnesses and of the defendants, and any other matter necessary for preparation and conduct of the trial.[49] The oral character of the evidence-testing process, the public character of the hearings, and the phases in which the trial unfolded, namely opening statements, prosecution case first (including examination and cross-examination of prosecution witnesses) and then the Defence case, are strongly influenced by the adversarial mode of organising the criminal process.[50] The adversarial process was not conducive to the better protection of the rights of victims. In the Nuremberg Charter, which established the constitution, jurisdiction, and functions of the Nuremberg Tribunal, the word 'victim' is completely absent. The drafters did not grant victims any procedural right, protection, or support during the trial.[51]

44 Luke Moffett, 'The Role of Victims in the International Criminal Tribunals of the Second World War' (2012) 12 International Criminal Law Review 245, 248–249.
45 Michael Bachrach, 'The Protection and Rights of Victims under International Criminal Law' (2000) 34 The International Lawyer 7, 12.
46 Conor McCarthy, 'Victim Redress and International Criminal Justice: Competing Paradigms, or Compatible Forms of Justice?' (2012) 10 Journal of International Criminal Justice 351, 354.
47 Moffett (n 44) 247.
48 Sluiter et al. (n 39) 46. For the analysis of the features of the adversarial procedural system see section 5.2.1.
49 Article 15, the International Military Tribunal – Annex to the Agreement for the prosecution and punishment of the major war criminals of the European Axis.
50 Sluiter et al. (n 39) 47.
51 Sam Garkawe, 'The Role of Victims at the Nuremberg International Military Tribunal' in Herbert R Reginbogin and Christoph Safferling (eds), *The Nuremberg Trials: International Criminal Law Since 1945: 60th Anniversary International Conference* (De Gruyter Saur 2006) 86.

Third, while victims were implicitly acknowledged by the charges for crimes against humanity, a caveat contained in Article 6(c) of the Nuremberg IMT Charter strongly limited this crime to the context of war or aggression towards other States. The said caveat, which stated that crimes against humanity should have been committed 'in execution of or in connection with any crime within the jurisdiction of the Tribunal', conferred on crimes against humanity a subsidiarity nature, as they were ancillary to crimes against peace and war crimes. In practical terms, a wide range of criminal conducts, like murder, extermination, enslavement, deportation, and other inhumane acts, committed against any civilian population prior to the war have been left outside the jurisdiction of the Nuremberg IMT and, consequently, those responsible have never been prosecuted or convicted. This was reflected in the prosecution's strategy, which principally decided to focus on proving that, behind the crimes against humanity, crimes against peace, and war crimes, there was a conspiracy or common plan to commit aggression. Proving this link became more relevant than dealing with the myriad of crimes.[52] In his opening statement, the American Chief Prosecutor, Justice Jackson, affirmed that his purpose was

> to deal with the Common Plan or Conspiracy to achieve ends possible only by resort to Crimes against Peace, War Crimes, and Crimes against Humanity. My emphasis will not be on individual barbarities and perversions which may have occurred independently of any central plan.[53]

To prove that Germans were planning aggressive war, the prosecution needed only the kind of witnesses who could provide evidence of any war crimes that implied conspiracy and planning a war.[54] The prosecution's ideal witness was an 'insider', an individual who, because of his/her political or military role, knew the hierarchical structure of the Nazi regime and the decision-making procedure and had eye-witnessed the meetings between political and military leaders, where the main decisions regarding planning an aggressive war were taken. It was unlikely for the victims to have copies of the documentation that provided specific information about the orders the defendants gave. The horrors that survivors endured were mostly linked to perpetrators, who were so much lower in the chain of the Nazi hierarchy that they were not even indicted before the Tribunal.[55]

Fourth, in order to provide an impartial method for international justice, the prosecution strategy was to focus on the individual responsibility of the defendants and to provide incontrovertible evidence upon which the Judges could base their

52 Moffett (n 44) 250.
53 Robert H Jackson United States Chief Prosecutor, Opening speech at the Nuremberg Trail (21 November 1945) in *Trial of the Major War Criminals Before the International Military Tribunal*, vol 1 (1948) 103.
54 Smith (n 17) 88.
55 Garkawe (n 51) 90.

decision. For this reason, Justice Jackson's approach was to anchor the cases in the detailed material evidence, like documents, communications, and photographs gathered from the Nazis. Documents provided a sounder foundation to the case, as victims and survivors, despite their potential substantial public impact, under the pressure to perform before the Tribunal at a public hearing could retract their confessions.[56] The American Prosecutor was influenced by the assumption, largely widespread in the immediate aftermath of the Second War World, that because of the horrible events they had experienced victims were psychologically unable to testify. Victims were considered counterproductive for the case of the prosecution because they were perceived to be too emotional and, thus, not able to provide objective evidence.[57] The prosecution feared that victims' credibility could be subject to criticism and that witnesses could be charged of perjury because, paradoxically, there was a general disbelief of the whole range of atrocities committed by Nazis. Thus, presenting the case through the Nazis' materials reinforced the idea that the trial was based on objective and impartial evidence.[58]

The case of the Jews who survived the Holocaust is a symbolic example of the minimal involvement of victims of crimes at the Nuremberg IMT, which kept the trial within narrow limits. In his opening statement, Justice Jackson clearly captured the breadth of the Holocaust and the victimisation of European Jewry, as it affirmed that

> of the 9,600,000 who lived in Nazi dominated Europe, 60% are authoritatively estimated to have perished. 5,700,000 Jews are missing from their countries in which they formerly lived, and over 4,500,000 cannot be accounted for by the normal death rate nor by immigration; nor are they included among displaced persons.[59]

Nevertheless, only three Jews, who survived the Holocaust, testified before the Tribunal. The prosecution recognised that the exposure of the Nazi policy against the Jews was relevant evidence to prove the conspiracy to wage aggressive war, but the Holocaust was seen as one of the numerous pieces of evidence of the Germans' criminal plans.[60] This does not imply that the representation by the Tribunal of the Nazi genocide of European Jews was not accurate. The prosecution provided documentary and graphic evidence of the Jewish mass

56 Donald Bloxham, *Genocide on Trial: War Crimes Trials and the Formation of Holocaust History and Memory* (Oxford University Press 2001) 61.

57 Garkawe (n 51) 90.

58 Chakravarti (n 15) 225.

59 Robert H Jackson United States Chief Prosecutor, Opening speech at the Nuremberg Trail (21 November 1945) in *Trial of the Major War Criminals Before the International Military Tribunal*, vol 1 (n 53) 119.

60 Laura Jockusch, 'Justice at Nuremberg? Jewish Responses to Nazi War-Crime Trials in Allied-Occupied Germany' (2012) 19 Jewish Social Studies 107, 133.

extermination, but it is undeniable that the trial focused on the murdered victims, rather than on the Holocaust survivors.[61]

The representatives of Jewish organisations (e.g., the World Jewish Congress) asked the prosecution for a more active participatory role for the victims of the Holocaust, but the American Chief Prosecutor partially rejected such requests. The prosecution had no intention of turning the Nuremberg trial into a Holocaust trial and, to minimise the issues raised by Jewish associations, reassured them that the mass extermination of the Jews would be treated in the trial through the new crime category of crimes against humanity.[62] The reality was that Jackson was afraid that allowing the Jewish victims to present their case before the Tribunal could turn the trial into a vengeance trial and provoke racial tension. Moreover, while evidence of the crimes provided by the documents collected from the Nazis was lauded for its 'indisputable character', victims were seen as lacking in objectivity, given that they had a strong bias against the Hitler regime.[63] Jackson also feared that there was a possibility that other groups of victims, following the Jewish precedent, would ask for more representation in the trial, which would have made it more difficult to keep the focus on the responsibilities of the Nazi leaders.[64]

The decision of the prosecution to present the Nazi crimes through a long list of bureaucratic documents and statistics generated a general disinterest in the trial in the press and public opinion. The main issues discussed during the hearings mostly concerned the admission and relevance of the evidence. Despite the promises beforehand, rather than being perceived as a memorable event, the Nuremberg trial was quite tedious most of the time.[65] For this reason, Prosecutor Jackson decided to present a few witnesses to 'try out the defence' and to 'introduce a little drama into the case'.[66] Of the 33 witnesses for the prosecution who testified before the IMT, three were actually Jews who had survived the war.[67] The few Jewish victims admitted as witnesses had in common that, because of their position, they could provide detailed and objective evidence of the responsibility of the key figures of the Nazi regime, instead of providing representations of vexations, suffering, and the genocide of Jews in Europe. The prosecution feared that tales of the dramatic fate of Jews and human tragedies could do more harm than good because they could represent a distraction.[68]

The role of the prosecution's witnesses was that of 'corroborating evidence' of the documentation on the criminal plans of the German leaders, without

61 ibid 109–110.
62 Lawrence Douglas, *The Memory of Judgment: Making Law and History in the Trials of the Holocaust* (Yale University Press 2001) 6.
63 Bloxham (n 56) 61.
64 Jockusch (n 60) 115.
65 Garkawe (n 51) 88–89.
66 Smith (n 17) 87.
67 Jockusch (n 60) 108; Appleman (n 11) viii.
68 Jockusch (n 60) 122.

having the chance to provide their own narrative.[69] For instance, the first Jewish witness was Abram Gerzevitch Suzkever who was called by Soviet Prosecutor Smirnov to testify before the Court to support the charge of crimes against humanity committed in Vilna.[70] Suzkever's testimony matched the evidence needs of the prosecution. First, he revealed the names of those responsible for the mass extermination of the Jewish people in Vilna;[71] secondly, he provided a clear picture of the wide scale of the atrocities committed during the German occupation of Vilna.[72] The second Jewish witness was Samuel Rajzman, who was deported to Treblinka extermination camp (Poland).[73] Rajzman's task was to load the clothes of the murdered persons on the trains[74] and, because of his position, he was well-acquainted with the rules regulating the treatment of the people in this camp and he was able to provide a detailed description of the conduct of Nazis towards Jewish prisoners.[75] He confirmed that, under the control of the camp commander, Kurt Franz, '[o]n an average, I believe they killed in Treblinka from ten to twelve thousand persons daily'.[76]

However, when the victim-witnesses tried to provide their own narratives, by expressing their experiences and sufferings, the Judges often interrupted them, considering that information irrelevant to the case. For instance, when Severina Shmaglevskaya, a Jew who survived the Auschwitz concentration camp, began to describe the conditions of the camp and the violence she suffered in her testimony she was interrupted by a Judge:

> Severina Shmaglevskaya: What I want to say is that in some cases the kitchen utensils and pots contained remains of food, and in others there was human excrement (...) These kitchen utensils, which were sometimes very badly washed, were given to people who had just arrived at the concentration camp. From these pots and pans they had to eat, so that often they caught dysentery and other diseases from the first day.
>
> The President: Colonel Smirnov, I don't think the Tribunal wants quite so much of the detail with reference of these domestic matters.[77]

The small number of Jewish witnesses who spoke before the Tribunal and the peripheral role they played represented a lost occasion for the Nuremberg IMT

69 Ann Tusa and John Tusa, *The Nuremberg Trial* (Macmillan 1983) 171.

70 Abram Gerzevitch Suzkever testimony (27 February 1946) in *Trial of the Major War Criminals Before the International Military Tribunal*, vol 8 (1948) 300–301.

71 ibid 303.

72 ibid 306.

73 Jockusch (n 60) 120.

74 Samuel Rajzman testimony (27 February 1946) in *Trial of the Major War Criminals Before the International Military Tribunal*, vol 8 (n 70) 327.

75 ibid 324.

76 ibid 327.

77 Testimony of Severina Shmaglevskaya (27 February 1946) in *Trial of the Major War Criminals Before the International Military Tribunal*, vol 8 (n 71) 321.

to provide a sense of justice for the millions of victims of the Nazis.[78] Although the story-telling of the victims did not seem to fit within the juridical and political context of the Nuremberg trial, nonetheless, they were part of the events the Tribunal had the jurisdiction to try. There were several reasons why victims should have been given a greater role in the proceedings. Including the voice of victims would have represented a way of coping with ethical and political concerns and of highlighting the values that were necessary to rebuild society after the Second World War.[79] Hearing the victims' narratives would have led the Tribunal to trace a broader historical account of the crimes against Jews, Roma, Slavs, homosexuals, disabled persons, religious minorities, and people of colour, which were a fundamental element of the Second World War. Victims' involvement would have counterweighted the focus of the prosecution on the conspiring to wage and waging of aggressive war. Evidence from victims would have personalised the crimes committed by the Nazis and given a more dramatic dimension to the trial, thus enhancing the pedagogical message of the IMT in front of the worldwide community.[80] Most importantly, the practice of the Nuremberg Tribunal, which underestimated the value of the role of victims,, influenced the pattern of the following 60 years of international criminal justice, which was mainly focused on punishing the perpetrators.[81]

7.5 The ICTY and the ICTR

Following the conflicts in the former Yugoslavia and Rwanda, the UN Security Council pursuant to its powers under Chapter VII of the United Nations Charter, i.e., to maintain or restore international peace and security, decided to establish the ICTY and the ICTR in 1993 and 1994, respectively.[82] There were a number of reasons for turning to these two international criminal justice institutions half a century after the Nuremberg IMT. On the one hand, the ICTY and the ICTR represented 'powerful symbols that convey moral, social, as well as legal approbation of the guilty and the political objectives that drove them to commit their misdeeds',[83] but, on the other hand, they marked an attempt to respond to the failures of the international community, by creating 'relations of global

78 Garkawe (n 51) 86.
79 Chakravarti (n 15) 233.
80 Garkawe (n 51) 88–89.
81 Moffett (n 44) 248–249.
82 UN Security Council, 'Security Council Resolution 827 (1993) on Establishment of the International Tribunal for Prosecution of Persons Responsible for Serious Violations of International Humanitarian Law Committed in the Territory of the Former Yugoslavia since 1991' (25 May 1993) UN Doc S/RES/827; UN Security Council, 'Security Council Resolution 955 (1994) on Establishment of an International Tribunal for Rwanda and Adoption of the Statute of the Tribunal' (8 November 1994) UN Doc S/RES/955.
83 Laurel Fletcher, 'From Indifference to Engagement: Bystanders and International Criminal Justice' (2005) 26 Michigan Journal of International Law 1013, 1028–1029.

responsibility for the suffering of others'.[84] Despite the numerous reports made by the United States to the Security Council in early 1993, which substantiated the spectre of 'ethnic cleansing' in Bosnia and Croatia, involving the forced removal of populations, brutality, and inhumane acts against civilians, it took a year for the Council to unanimously adopt Resolution 808, which established a criminal tribunal to address identified crimes in the former Yugoslavia.[85] The statement by Madeleine Albright in support of the establishment of the ICTY reflected a sense of blame and apology. In addressing the Security Council, she affirmed that

> [t]here is an echo in this chamber today. The Nuremburg principles have been reaffirmed. We have preserved the long-neglected compact made by the community of civilised nations 48 years ago in San Francisco to create the United Nations and enforce the Nuremburg principles. (…) By its action today, with Resolution 808 (1993), the Security Council has shown that the will of this Organization can be exercised, even if it has taken nearly half of a century for the wisdom of our earliest principles to take hold.[86]

The failure to prevent the heinous events in Srebrenica, described as 'scenes from hell, written on the darkest pages of human history',[87] which took place between 11 and18 July 1995, when the ICTY was already operational, exacerbated the international community's feelings of guilt and shame. While acknowledging that 'the international community as a whole must accept its share of responsibility for allowing this tragic course of events', the UN Secretary-General pointed at the 'architects and implementers of the attempted genocide in Bosnia' as those primarily and most directly responsible.[88] In the view of the UN Secretary-General, the Serb campaign of mass murder made it untenable to dismiss the issue of the exercise of individual criminal responsibility by the ICTY, which inevitably became a remedy to make up for the collective failure to help save the people of Srebrenica.[89] In light of this, criminal prosecution symbolised the need to address 'the scope of the evil confronting us',[90] since those charged with this

84 Mahmoud Cherif Bassiouni *et al.*, 'War Crimes Tribunals: The Record and the Prospects. Conference Convocation' (1998) 13 American University International Law Review 1383, 1407; Nesam McMillan, 'Imagining the International: The Constitution of the International as a Site of Crime, Justice and Community' (2016) 25 Social & Legal Studies 163, 170.

85 David Scheffer, *All the Missing Souls: A Personal History of the War Crimes Tribunals* (Princeton University Press 2012) 22; David P Forsythe, 'International Criminal Courts: A Political View' (1997) 15 Netherlands Quarterly of Human Rights 5, 8.

86 Security Council, 'Provisional Verbatim Record of the 3175th Meeting' (1993) UN Doc S/PV.3175 11.

87 UN Secretary-General, 'Report of the Secretary-General Pursuant to General Assembly Resolution 53/35: The Fall of Srebrenica' (1999) UN Doc A/54/549, para 2.

88 ibid 501.

89 ibid 503.

90 UN Secretary-General, 'Report of the Secretary-General Pursuant to General Assembly Resolution 53/35: The Fall of Srebrenica' (n 87), para 503.

crime 'reminded the world and, in particular, the United Nations, that evil exists in the world'.[91]

The establishment of the ICTR occurred under similar circumstance, reflecting a message of solidarity with victims, but also expressing shame and apology for the failure of the international community to address frictions that were shaped by colonial practices.[92] During the meeting to establish the ICTR, Rwanda's representatives stressed that the international community became cognisant of the unprecedented nature of the massacres before the wake of the tragedy of April 1994, when a murderous rampage by Rwandan extremists attempted to expel the Tutsi people from Rwanda. The Special Rapporteur of the United Nations Commission on Human Rights, René Degni-Ségui, had already reported that genocide had occurred in Rwanda in 1993.[93] Rwanda's representatives also blamed the international community for its non-intervention, noting that its troops, which were already in Rwanda, 'could have saved hundreds of thousands of human lives by, for example, establishing humanitarian safe zones'.[94] However, when the genocide began, those troops had been withdrawn, abandoning 'the victims to their butchers'.[95] A later independent inquiry into the action of the UN during the Rwanda genocide highlighted that the creation of the ICTR was prompted by the West's guilt over having turned its back on those atrocities.[96]

Despite their troubled inception and the operational issues in their early years, the ICTY and ICTR secured the convictions of high-level perpetrators and provided a mechanism for the enforcement of international humanitarian law and the development of a body of jurisprudence to transform social norms within torn societies.[97] Although the ICTY and the ICTR mainly relied on the retributivist and deterrent criminal justice models,[98] they seemed to endorse the expressivist value of criminal punishment.[99] Diane Marie Amann argued that, in some decisions by the *ad hoc* tribunals, it is possible to identify values having an 'expressivist flavour'.[100] In *Erdemović*, the ICTY held that one of the essential functions of punishment is 'public reprobation and stigmatisation by the international

91 ibid, para 506.
92 Stahn (n 4) 183–184.
93 Security Council, '3453rd Meeting: The Situation Concerning Rwanda' (1994) UN Doc S/PV.3453 15.
94 ibid 14.
95 ibid.
96 UN Commission of Inquiry on Rwanda, 'Report of the Independent Inquiry into the Actions of the United Nations during the 1994 Genocide in Rwanda' (1999) UN Doc S/1999/1257 51.
97 José E Alvarez, 'Crimes of States/Crimes of Hate: Lessons from Rwanda' (1999) 24 Yale Journal of International Law 365, 372; Ruti Teitel, 'Transitional Jurisprudence: The Role of the Law in Political Transformation' (1997) 106 Yale Law Journal 2009, 2036–2037.
98 See sections 3.3., 3.4., and 3.5.
99 Margaret deGuzman, 'Choosing to Prosecute: Expressive Selection at the International Criminal Court' (2012) 33 Michigan Journal of International Law 265, 314.
100 Amann (n 34) 123.

community, which would thereby express its indignation over heinous crimes and denounce the perpetrators'.[101] The understanding of retribution by both the ICTY and the ICTR is not only conceived as achieving 'just deserts' for the perpetrator, but also as expressing the outrage of the international community for international crimes. In *Kambanda*, the ICTR affirmed that penalties imposed on accused persons found guilty by the Tribunal should make plain the condemnation of the international community of the behaviour in question and show that 'the international community was not ready to tolerate the serious violations of international humanitarian law and human rights'.[102] In *Kordić and Čerkez*, the Appeal Chamber explicitly refers to the educational function of a sentence, which aims

> at conveying the message that rules of humanitarian international law have to be obeyed under all circumstances. In doing so, the sentence seeks to internalise these rules and the moral demands they are based on in the minds of the public.[103]

The didactic function of the trial was emphasised by Judge Antonio Cassese, who affirmed that, through the Tribunal proceedings, 'a fully reliable record is established of atrocities so that future generations can remember and be made fully cognisant of what happened'.[104] Similarly, in *Furundžija*, the Trial Chamber stated that the *ius cogens* nature of the prohibition of torture is one of the most fundamental standards of human rights and, therefore, its prohibition 'signals to all members of the international community and the individuals over whom they wield authority, that the prohibition of torture is an absolute value from which nobody must deviate'.[105]

The ICTY and the ICTR also contributed to developing and expanding the normative content of international criminal law in the area of war crimes and

101 *Prosecutor v Dražen Erdemović* (Sentencing Judgment) IT-96–22-T, Trial Chamber (29 November 1996), para 65.

102 *Prosecutor v Jean Kambanda* (Judgement and Sentence) ICTR-97–23-S, Trial Chamber I (4 September 1998), para 28. See also *Prosecutor v Zlatko Aleksovski* (Judgement) IT-95–14/1-A, Appeals Chamber (24 March 2000), para 185; *Prosecutor v Zejnil Delalić et al.* (Trial Judgement) IT-96–21-T, Trial Chamber (16 November 1998), para 1234; *Prosecutor v Georges Rutaganda* (Judgement and Sentence) ICTR-96–3-T, Trial Chamber I (6 December 1999), para 456; *Prosecutor v Alfred Musema* (Judgement and Sentence) ICTR-96–13-A, Trial Chamber I (27 January 2000), para 986; *Prosecutor v Jean Paul Akayesu* (Sentence) ICTR-96–4-T, Trial Chamber I (2 October 1998), para 19; *Prosecutor v Omar Serushago* (Sentence) ICTR-98–39-S, Trial Chamber I (5 February 1999), paras 40–41.

103 *Prosecutor v Dario Kordić and Mario Čerkez* (Appeal Judgement) IT-95–14/2-A, Appeals Chamber (7 December 2004), paras 1080–1081.

104 Antonio Cassese, 'Reflections on International Criminal Justice' (1998) 61 The Modern Law Review 1, 6.

105 *Prosecutor v Anto Furundžija* (Judgement) IT-95–17/1-T, Trial Chamber (10 December 1998), para 154.

sexual violence. With regard to war crimes, in *Tadić*, the ICTY addressed the sovereignty-oriented dichotomy between internal and international armed conflicts, which regarded the former 'as rebellion, mutiny and treason coming within the purview of national criminal law' and, therefore, left outside the realm of international legal provisions regulating war crimes. The ICTY held that it had jurisdiction over the acts amounting to war crimes, 'regardless of whether they occurred within an internal or an international armed conflict'. War crimes included the 'protection of civilians from hostilities (...) as well as prohibition of means of warfare proscribed in international armed conflicts and ban of certain methods of conducting hostilities' breaking out in the territory of a sovereign State.[106]

Similarly, the judgment in the *Akayesu* case was extremely innovative since the ICTR formulated a definition of rape within international law, on which subsequent international criminal tribunals grounded their reflections on how rape can be categorised. Copelon has argued that where rape is mentioned in the Geneva Convention (1949) it is conceptualised as an 'attack against honour', rather than depicted as a crime of violence, marginalising, therefore, the seriousness and the violent nature of rape under international humanitarian law.[107] In the silence of regional and UN human rights instruments, which neither point to an overarching definition of rape nor designate it on its own as an enumerated international crime, *Akayesu* established that rape could be tried as a component of genocide if committed 'with the specific intent to destroy, in whole or in part, a particular group targeted as such'.[108] Mirroring the way in which the Genocide Convention (1948) was formulated, the Trial Chamber argued that sexual violence and rape represented 'one of the worst ways of inflicting harm on the victim as he or she suffers both bodily and mental harm'.[109]

In its findings, the Trial Chamber stated that 'rape is a form of aggression and that the central elements of the crime of rape cannot be captured in a mechanical description of objects and body parts'[110] and defined it as 'a physical invasion of a sexual nature, committed on a person under circumstances which are coercive'.[111] In *Kunarac et al.*, the ICTY determined that rape could be understood as 'a serious violation of sexual autonomy'.[112] In its overview of several common and civil law jurisdictions in relation to definitions of rape, the Trial Chamber concluded

106 *Prosecutor v Duškö Tadić* (Decision on the Defence Motion for Interlocutory Appeal on Jurisdiction) ICTY-94–1-A, Trial Chamber (2 October 1995), paras 97–137.

107 Rhonda Copelon, 'Surfacing Gender: Reengraving the Crimes against Women in Humanitarian Law' in Nicole A Dombrowski (ed), *Women and War in the Twentieth Century: Enlisted with or without Consent* (Routledge 1999) 337.

108 *Prosecutor v Jean-Paul Akayesu* (Judgement) ICTR-96–4-T, Trial Chamber I (2 September 1998), para 731.

109 ibid, para 731.

110 ibid, para 597.

111 ibid, para 598.

112 *Prosecutor v Dragoljub Kunarac et al.* (Trial Judgement) IT-96–23-T& IT-96–23/1-T, Trial Chamber (22 February 2000), para 457.

that, despite force, threat of force, and coercion are relevant elements of rape, 'the true common denominator which unifies the various systems may be a wider or more basic principle of penalising violations of sexual autonomy'.[113] The basic principle underlying the crime of rape is that 'sexual autonomy is violated wherever the person subjected to the act has not freely agreed to it or is otherwise not a voluntary participant'.[114] In *Delalić et al.*, the ICTY held that rape can constitute torture whenever rape and other forms of sexual violence meet the criteria of torture.[115] The Trial Chamber considers that, like torture, rape 'strikes at the very core of human dignity (...) [and] causes severe pain and suffering, both physical and psychological', that can be particularly acute and long lasting.[116] Also, similar to torture, when rape is inflicted 'by, or at the instigation of a public official, or with the consent or acquiescence of an official, it could be considered as occurring for a purpose that (...) involves punishment, coercion, discrimination or intimidation'.[117]

7.6 The limited role of victims

Bearing in mind that the procedural model of the Nuremberg Tribunal did not include the word 'victim', some steps forward have been made since the Statutes and RPE of the ICTY and ICTR introduced a number of innovative measures to assist and protect victim-witnesses, who, because of their testimonies, could be subjected to intimidation and retaliation.[118] However, in the normative framework of the ICTY and the ICTR, victims do not have any independent standing in the criminal proceedings as their role is limited to that of serving as witnesses. There are four main reasons behind this narrow notion of the role of victims. First, the founding instruments of the ICTY and the ICTR were strongly influenced by the approach to justice adopted at Nuremberg, characterised by the focus on the punishment of perpetrators. The UN Security Council resolutions setting up the *ad hoc* international criminal tribunals affirmed that they had been established 'for the sole purpose of prosecuting persons responsible for serious violations of humanitarian law'.[119] Second, the criminal procedure of both the ICTY and the ICTR was, to a very large extent, predominantly based on the adversarial approach, according to which victims are not formal parties and, consequently,

113 ibid, para 440.
114 ibid, para 457.
115 *Prosecutor v Zdravko Mucić et al.* (Judgement) IT-96–21-T, Trial Chamber (16 November 1998), para 496.
116 ibid, para 495.
117 ibid, para 495.
118 See e.g., Articles 20 and 22 of both ICTY and ICTR Statutes; rule 34 of the RPE of the ICTY and ICTR establishing the Victims and Witnesses Unit.
119 UNSC, Res 827 (25 May 1993) UN Doc S/RES/827; UNSC, Res 955 (8 November 1994) UN Doc S/RES/955.

can only play the role of witnesses when they are summoned by the parties.[120] The prevalence of the adversarial system can be explained by factors such as the common law background of the draftsmen, the perception of the adversarial system as better equipped to guarantee the accused's rights, and the Nuremberg IMT as antecedent.[121] Third, considering that the Prosecutor is entrusted to protect the interests of the international community, it was assumed that his/her interest coincides in its entirety with that of the victims at every stage of the proceeding.[122] Fourth, victims' role as participants was considered to jeopardise the defendant's right to a fair trial and, specifically, to the equality of arms, as well as to interfere in the Prosecutor's case and lead to a delay in the proceeding.[123]

Despite victims lacking the official status of participants, the ICTY and the ICTR developed some forms of victim participation in the proceedings other than the role of witnesses, namely the *amicus curiae* briefs, writing a letter to the Prosecutor and the victim impact statement for sentencing purposes. However, it must be observed that letters to the Prosecutor and *amicus curiae* briefs have mainly been filed by human rights NGOs because victims do not usually have the necessary expertise, resources, and information to advocate their interests.

7.6.1 Writing a letter to the Prosecutor

Contacting The Prosecutor via letter became a way of bringing victims' interests to the attention of the ICTY and ICTR at the pre-trial stage of the proceedings. For example, in *Milošević*, the NGO Coalition for Women's Human Rights in Conflict Situations (hereafter the Coalition) sent a letter to Prosecutor Carla Del Ponte, asking her to include charges of sexual violence in the indictment against Slobodan Milosevic at the ICTY.[124] Over 30 international women's groups and individuals signed the letter and, in October 2001, Prosecutor Del Ponte

120 See section 5.2.1.

121 Antonio Cassese, *International Criminal Law* (2nd edn, Oxford University Press 2008) 369.

122 Jérôme De Hemptinne and Claude Jorda, 'The Status and Role of the Victim' in Antonio Cassese, Paola Gaeta and John R Jones (eds), *The Rome Statute of the International Criminal Court: A Commentary*, vol 2 (Oxford University Press 2002) 1394–1395.

123 Brianne McGonigle Leyh, 'Victim-Oriented Measures at International Criminal Institutions: Participation and Its Pitfalls' (2012) 12 International Criminal Law Review 375, 375; Christine H Chung, 'Victims' Participation at the International Criminal Court: Are Concessions of the Court Clouding the Promise?' (2008) 6 Northwestern Journal of Human Rights 459, 461; Salvatore Zappalà, 'The Rights of Victims v. the Rights of the Accused' (2010) 8 Journal of International Criminal Justice 137, 150; Virginia Morris and Michael Scharf, *An Insider's Guide to the International Criminal Tribunal for the Former Yugoslavia*, vol I (Transnational Publishers 1995) 167.

124 Coalition for Women's Human Rights in Conflict Situations, 'Letter to Carla Del Ponte, Prosecutor, Regarding the Urgent Need to Include Charges of Sexual Violence in the Indictment against Milošević' (14 August 2001), referred to by Anne-Marie de Brouwer, *Supranational Criminal Prosecution of Sexual Violence: The ICC and the Practice of the ICTY and the ICTR*, vol 20 (Intersentia 2005) 299.

included the charges of sexual violence in the Croatia, Kosovo, and Bosnia indictment.[125] In *Muvunyi*, the Coalition sent a letter to Prosecutor Hassan Jallow, asking him to reconsider his decision to drop rape charges and support sexual violence investigations.[126] In this case, the Prosecutor did not respond positively to the Coalition's call. Nevertheless, Trial Chamber II rejected the Prosecutor's motion to remove rape from the indictment, stating that 'once an indictment has been confirmed the Prosecutor cannot obtain an amendment without providing the Chamber with a convincing legal justification'.[127] Directly contacting the Office of the Prosecutor proved to be a way, although an extremely marginal one, for victims to indirectly participate in the pre-trial stage.

7.6.2 Amicus curiae *briefs*

Similar to the letters to the Prosecutor, the *amicus curiae* briefs, to some extent, provided indirect venues for victims to express their views and concerns.[128] This was because Rule 74 ('Amicus Curiae'), common to the RPE of the ICTY and ICTR, provides broad discretion to a Chamber to permit any individual or group, including, therefore, victims and their representatives, to appear as *amici* under either invitation or spontaneous application.[129] In *Furundžija*, the Coalition submitted an *amicus curiae* to challenge the Trial Chamber decision to make a rape victim 'available for cross-examination on any medical, psychological or psychiatric treatment or counselling received' and, for this purpose, 'disclose any documents in its possession relating to the material and relevant to the issue of any medical, psychological or psychiatric treatment or counselling received' by

125 *Prosecutor v Slobodan Milošević* (Initial Indictment 'Croatia') IT-01–50-I (27 September 2001); *Prosecutor v Slobodan Milošević, Milan Milutinović, Nikola Šainović, Dragoljub Ojdanić and Vlajko Stojiljković* (Second Amended Indictment 'Kosovo') IT-99–37-PT (16 October 2001); *Prosecutor v Slobodan Milošević* (Initial Indictment 'Bosnia and Herzegovina') IT-01–51-I (22 November 2001); *Prosecutor v Slobodan Milošević* (Amended Indictment 'Bosnia and Herzegovina') IT-02–54-T (22 November 2002).

126 Coalition for Women's Human Rights in Conflict Situations, 'Letter to Prosecutor Hassan Jallow' (8 February 2005) referred to by Anne-Marie de Brouwer, *Supranational Criminal Prosecution of Sexual Violence: The ICC and the Practice of the ICTY and the ICTR*, vol 20 (Intersentia 2005) 299.

127 *Prosecutor v Tharcisse Muvunyi* (Decision on the Prosecutor's Motion for Leave to File an Amended Indictment) ICTR-00–55, Trial Chamber II (23 February 2005), paras 28, 30–34.

128 Mikaela Heikkilä, *International Criminal Tribunals and Victims of Crime: A Study of the Status of Victims before International Criminal Tribunals and of Factors Affecting This Status* (Institute for Human Rights Åbo Akademi University 2004) 155; Anne-Marie de Brouwer, *Supranational Criminal Prosecution of Sexual Violence: The ICC and the Practice of the ICTY and the ICTR*, vol 20 (Intersentia 2005) 291.

129 Sarah Williams and Hannah Woolaver, 'The Role of the Amicus Curiae before International Criminal Tribunals' (2006) 6 International Criminal Law Review 151, 155.

the victim.[130] While the *amicus curiae* brief was admitted, the Trial Chamber did not take into account its merits, failing to engage in balancing the rights of the defendant and the rights to equality, privacy, security, and the protection of victims of sexual violence.[131] Nonetheless this *amicus curiae* brief produced the intended effects, as the Prosecutor filed a request to protect the rights of the witness in question.[132]

At the ICTR, the Coalition filed two *amicus curiae* briefs to back up a similar matter concerning the rights of victims of sexual violence in *Akayesu* and *Ntagerura et al.*, but the outcomes were diametrically opposed. In *Ntagerura et al.*, the Prosecutor opposed application to submit the *amicus curiae* brief[133] and his arguments convinced the Trial Chamber, which held that granting the *amicus curiae* would equate 'to transgressing upon the independence of the Prosecutor and impugning the integrity of the Tribunal as an arbiter of international law'.[134] Conversely, in *Akayesu*, the Trial Chamber acknowledged that the *amicus curiae* brief importantly influenced its decision on the need to conduct subsequent investigations into sexual violence.[135] Because of this new investigation, the Prosecutor found additional evidence of sexual violence linked to the defendant and, consequently, the indictment was amended to include charges of sexual crimes.[136]

Considering that victims' participation does not exist in the ICTY and ICTR, the *amicus curiae* briefs have been used to submit victims' views and concerns indirectly. Nevertheless, this modality of introducing victims' voices has been highly constrained by Chamber's discretion to invite or admit the briefs or the Chamber's consideration whether those submissions could be useful for its judicial functions. More importantly, it was not individual victims who submitted the *amicus curiae,* but NGOs or law schools who usually used this modality.

130 *Prosecutor v Anto Furundžija* (Amicus Curiae Brief Respecting the Decision and Order of the Tribunal of 16 July 1998 Requesting that the Tribunal Reconsider its Decision Having Regard to the Rights of Witness 'A' to Equality, Privacy and Security of the Person and to Representation by Counsel) IT-95–17/1-T, Coalition for Women's Human Rights in Conflict Situations (5 November 1998), para 1.

131 *Prosecutor v Anto Furundžija* (Order Granting Leave to File Amicus Curiae Brief) IT-95–17/1-T, Trial Chamber (10 November 1998); *Prosecutor v Anto Furundžija* (Corrigendum to Order Granting Leave to File Amicus Curiae Brief) IT-95–17/1-T, Trial Chamber (11 November 1998).

132 *Prosecutor v Anto Furundžija* (n 105), para 37.

133 *Prosecutor v André Ntagerura, Emmanuel Bagambiki, and Samuel Imanishimwe* (Prosecutor's Response to Application for Leave to File an Amicus Brief) ICTR-99–46 (8 May 2001).

134 *Prosecutor v André Ntagerura, Emmanuel Bagambiki, and Samuel Imanishimwe* (Decision on the Application to File an Amicus Curiae Brief According to Rule 74 of the Rules of Procedure and Evidence Filed on Behalf of the NGO Coalition for Women's Human Rights in Conflict Situations) ICTR-99–46-T, Trial Chamber (24 May 2001), para 22.

135 de Brouwer (n 128) 295.

136 *Prosecutor v Jean-Paul Akayesu* (n 108), para 417.

7.6.3 Victims' impact statements

Rule 92 *bis* of the RPE of both the ICTY and the ICTR provides that evidence on the impact of crimes upon victims may be presented, as it reads as follows

> A Trial Chamber may admit, in whole or in part, the evidence of a witness in the form of a written statement in lieu of oral testimony (…) Factors in favour of admitting evidence in the form of a written statement include, but are not limited to, circumstances in which the evidence in question: (…) concerns the impact of crimes upon victims.

That said, victims do not have a right to provide impact statements and the ICTY and ICTR are not required to accept such statements. However, in their proceedings, both the ICTY and the ICTR have allowed the Prosecutor's submission of victims' impact statements for the purposes of the sentencing.[137]

These statements, which depict the extent of suffering and harm inflicted on victims, have proved to have an impact on the sentence, as they have been considered by Trial Chambers when assessing aggravating and mitigating factors. In *Krstić*, the Trial Chamber held that assessing the seriousness of the crimes requires taking 'into account quantitatively the number of victims and qualitatively the suffering inflicted on the victims'.[138] The Chamber went on to state that the circumstances concerning the defencelessness of the victims, the physical and psychological suffering inflicted upon them, the indiscriminate, disproportionate, terrifying, and heinous means and methods used to commit the crimes, are all relevant in assessing the gravity of the crimes. Accordingly, the '[a]ppropriate consideration of those circumstances gives "a voice" to the suffering of the victims'.[139]

In *Delalić et al.* and *Bralo*, the Trial Chamber has explicitly acknowledged the value of victims' impact statements. With regard to the first case, the Trial Chamber considered that 'Ms. Antic testified as to the effect these crimes had on her, including feelings of misery, constant crying and the feeling that she had

137 *Prosecutor v Zejnil Delalić, Zdravko Mucić, Hazim Delić and Esad Landžo* (Judgement) IT-96-21-T, Trial Chamber (16 November 1998), para 1263; *Prosecutor v Miroslav Bralo* (Sentencing Judgement) IT-95-17-S, Trial Chamber (7 December 2005), para 25, 36; *Prosecutor v Duško Tadić* (Sentencing Judgement) IT-94-1, Trial Chamber II (11 November 1999), para 4; *Prosecutor v Stevan Todorović* (Sentencing Judgement) IT-95-9/1-S, Trial Chamber (31 July 2001), para 53.

138 *Prosecutor v Radislav Krstić* (Judgement) IT-98-33-T, Trial Chamber (2 August 2001), para 701. See also *Prosecutor v Zejnil Delalić, Zdravko Mucić, Hazim Delić and Esad Landžo* (n 137), para 1226; *Prosecutor v Dražen Erdemović* (Judgement) IT-96-22-A, Appeals Chamber (7 October 1997), para 15; *Prosecutor v Jean Kambanda* (n 102), para 42.

139 *Prosecutor v Radislav Krstić* (n 138), para 703; See also *Prosecutor v Zejnil Delalić, Zdravko Mucić, Hazim Delić and Esad Landžo* (n 137), paras 1226, 1260, 1273; *Prosecutor v Anto Furundžija* (n 105) para 281.

gone crazy'.[140] The Chamber also cited a statement from the victim's impact statement submitted by the prosecution in which the victim affirmed that '[t]he wounds that I carry from the rapes in Čelebići will never go away'.[141] In *Bralo*, the Chamber made it clear that '[i]n addition to examining the manner in which Bralo committed the crimes of which he has been convicted, the Trial Chamber takes into consideration the submissions of the Prosecution on the impact of these crimes on his victims'.[142]

After having examined the statements from the victims submitted by the Prosecutor,[143] in its determination of the sentence the Tribunal explicitly acknowledged that '[t]hese statements paint a picture of shattered lives and livelihoods, and of tremendous ongoing pain and trauma'[144] and remarked that 'the consequences of the persecution, murders, rape, and other crimes committed by Bralo are profound and long-lasting' .[145]

In addition to victims' impact statements, when the Prosecutor called victim-witnesses to give testimony, he/she raised the issue of the impact of the crime on the victim during examination, or the victim-witnesses brought it up themselves while answering the questions posed by the Prosecutor.[146] For instance in *Nikolić*, the prosecution called three witnesses to testify, intending to 'describe the closer circumstances and the environment in which the crimes were committed and the impact these crimes had on surviving victims and their relatives'.[147] In *Nyiramasuhuko et al.*, the Prosecutor asked the witness about any physical effect, problem, or pain experienced and medical treatments needed as result of the events under adjudication.[148] Similarly, in *Gacumbitsi*, the Prosecutor questioned a witness-victim of sexual violence about the impact of rape on her life:

Q.: Witness TAP, are you able to tell this Court what it means to be a single Rwandan woman who was raped before she is married?
A.: Yes, I can.
Q.: Please go ahead. Just take your time, Witness.
A.: I would use myself as an example, from the time of those events. I suffer a great deal as a consequence of those events. I have many side-effects.

140 *Prosecutor v Zejnil Delalić, Zdravko Mucić, Hazim Delić and Esad Landžo* (n 137), para 1263.
141 ibid, para 1263.
142 *Prosecutor v Miroslav Bralo* (n 137), para 36.
143 ibid, para 37.
144 ibid, para 40.
145 ibid, para 40.
146 Anne-Marie de Brouwer and Mikaela Heikkilä, 'Victim Issues: Participation, Protection, Reparation, and Assistance' in Göran Sluiter et al. (eds), *International Criminal Procedure: Principles and Rules* (Oxford University Press 2013) 1328.
147 *Prosecutor v Dragan Nikolić* (Sentencing Judgement) IT-94-2-S, Trial Chamber (18 December 2003), para 41.
148 *Prosecutor v Pauline Nyiramasuhuko et al.* (transcript) ICTR-98-42, Trial Chamber (29 October 2001) 109–111.

In the judgement of *Musema*, the Chamber implicitly understood the negative effect of crimes on victim-witnesses. The Trial Chamber recognised that many witnesses had seen or experienced terrible atrocities and noted 'that recounting and revisiting such painful experiences is likely to be a source of great pain to the witness'.[149]

7.6.4 Victims serving as witnesses

The possibility of the victim being able to tell his/her story at trial-stage relied on either one of the parties summoning him/her to support their case and the Chamber approving the summoning,[150] or the Chamber *proprio motu* calling him/her to testify to complete the evidence produced by the parties.[151] In practice, since victims were solely allowed to serve as witnesses, their participation was ruled by the general legal regime applicable to any witness's testimony.[152] Victims, as witnesses of the Prosecutor or the Defence, cannot refuse to give evidence; cannot be assisted by a lawyer while testifying; can speak only during the examination and cross-examination conducted by the parties,[153] and, before testifying, have to take the oath.[154] Further, the witness cannot be present in the courtroom while other witnesses are testifying and cannot have access to the evidence produced by the Prosecutor and the Defence.[155] Additionally, under Rule 89 of the RPE of both the ICTY and the ICTR, the 'Chamber may admit any relevant evidence which it deems to have probative value',[156] meaning that only those victims whose testimony can contribute to the determination of the case were allowed to testify. The said rule of the ICTY RPE further states that the 'Chamber may exclude evidence if its probative value is substantially outweighed by the need to ensure a fair trial'[157] and that it 'may receive the evidence of a witness orally or, where the interests of justice allow, in written form'.[158]

The role of victim-witnesses has been important because their testimonies contributed to the determination of the case and the ascertainment of the truth.[159]

149 *Prosecutor v Alfred Musema* (n 102), para 100; *Prosecutor v Jean-Paul Akayesu* (n 108) paras 142–144.
150 Rule 85, ICTY RPE
151 Rule 98 RPE of both the ICTY and ICTR.
152 Heikkilä (n 128) 74.
153 ICTY RPE, rule 85; ICTR rule 85;
154 ICTY RPE, rule 90 (A); ICTR RPE, rule 90 (A);
155 Emily Haslam, 'Victim Participation at the International Criminal Court: A Triumph of Hope Over Experience?' in Dominic McGoldrick, Peter Rowe and Eric Donnelly, *The Permanent International Criminal Court: Legal and Policy Issues* (Hart Publishing 2004) 320.
156 Rule 89(c) RPE of both the ICTY and ICTR.
157 Rule 89(d), ICTY RPE
158 Rule 89(f), ICTY RPE
159 Brianne McGonigle Leyh, *Procedural Justice? Victim Participation in International Criminal Proceedings* (Intersentia 2011) 140.

Carla Del Ponte, the ICTY Chief Prosecutor, expressly acknowledged the significant contribution of the courtroom testimonies of eyewitnesses, which

> tell us about the horrifying conditions of the detention camps, ethnic cleansing campaigns, torture, rape and sexual slavery, mass executions, destruction of property and religious institutions, plunder and looting. Most importantly they tell us about human suffering. They must be told and listened to. (…) Those willing to listen will understand that the testimonies of the very modest, not sophisticated people, very ordinary people can bring to understanding the core issues.[160]

However, the experience of the ICTY and ICTR showed that the storytelling of the victim-witnesses was constrained and their testimonies were shaped according to the evidentiary needs of the prosecution and the Defence.[161] Many victim-witnesses were deprived of the opportunity to tell their stories in a narrative form because of the adversarial construct of the trial process and subjected to repetitive and, often, aggressive and degrading questioning.[162]

The *Krstić* case represents a clear example where victim-witnesses' narratives were interrupted by the Prosecutor and Judges when their statements deviated from the purpose of determining the case. Specifically, the analysis of the transcripts of the victims' testimonies illustrated that the Prosecutor, instead of giving victims the opportunity to tell their story, interrupted victims' testimonies on several occasions when their accounts became irrelevant so as to assess the responsibility of the defendant.[163] In the testimony of witness J, the Prosecutor seemed to manifest frustration and impatience, as he wanted to finish the witness examination:

Q.: Witness, I realise that the trip that you made to Zepa was very difficult and very frightening, but I would just like you to simply confirm a number of points to the Judges by simply answering yes or no. Otherwise, I think we're going to be here a very long time, and I know you want to go home to Bosnia tomorrow. So simply answer yes or no. Do you understand?
A.: Why should I say yes or no to your questions?
Q.: Did you arrive in Zepa on the 26th of July?

160 Carla Del Ponte, 'Address by Prosecutor Del Ponte on Importance of War Crimes Trials for Truth-Telling Process' (Conference on 'Establishing the Truth about War Crimes and Conflicts', Zagreb, Croatia, 8 February 2007) <https://www.icty.org/fr/press/address-prosecutor-del-ponte-importance-war-crimes-trials-truth-telling-process> accessed 29 May 2022.

161 Haslam (n 156) 318; Marie-Benedicte Dembour and Emily Haslam, 'Silencing Hearings? Victim-Witnesses at War Crimes Trials' (2004) 15 European Journal of International Law 151, 154.

162 Martien Schotsmans and François-Xavier Nsanzuwera, 'Victims in the Balance: Challenges Ahead for the International Criminal Tribunal for Rwanda' (International Federation for Human Rights 2002) 329/2.

163 Dembour and Haslam (n 162) 158.

A.: On the 26th of July, I arrived in Zepa, about 3.00 in the afternoon.
Q.: And then I think, on the 29th of July, Zepa fell, you --
A.: On the 29th, Zepa fell.
Q.: You left Zepa and you spent a long time -- Witness, listen to my question and simply answer yes or no to the question. I think you left Zepa on the 29th of July and you spent over 40 days wandering in Bosnian Serb territory, and then you eventually made your way to the free territory on the 17th of September of 1995. Is that right? Just yes or no.
A.: Yes. Yes. Yes.
Q.: Thank you, Witness.
MR. CAYLEY: Mr. President, I have no further questions for the witness.[164]

Victim-witnesses' continually referring to members of family, friends and neighbours they lost because of the mass killings clashed with the Tribunal's efforts to render their testimony relevant and concise. When victim-witnesses sought to narrate their pain and their suffering, the Chamber and the Prosecutor proved not to be interested in details about the lives of the murdered victims. In her testimony, witness DD tried to tell her story about her child, but the Prosecutor considered this part of the testimony irrelevant,[165]

A.: I was going to tell you the whole story from Tuesday to Thursday. Can I do it?
Q.: Witness, the Judges have already heard quite a lot of evidence in this case about the events in Pocari, so for the purposes of my examination, I'm not going to ask you questions about those days.[166]

The *Krstić* case showed to what extent the procedure of fact-finding constrained the manner in which victims conveyed their tragic experience. Victims as witnesses were objectified by the Prosecutor, who tended to examine them 'to dissect facts in a perpetrator-driven narrative according to the basic rules of evidence', devaluing anything said by the witnesses not required to prove the legal issue.[167] This Prosecutor's approach to the examination of witnesses-victims at a trial alienates and disembodies them, to the point that a victim is not relevant as her/his agent, but only as her/his actions demonstrate what the perpetrator did or did not.

At the ICTR, the *Nyiramasuhuko et al.* case raised further concerns about the method by which victims were questioned while testifying. Emblematic is the testimony of witness TA, a rape victim, to whom the Defence counsel purposefully

164 *Prosecutor v Radislav Krstić* (transcript of the witness J testimony) IT-98-33-T, Trial Chamber (10 April 2000), para 2474-2475.
165 Dembour and Haslam (n 162) 159.
166 *Prosecutor v Radislav Krstić* (transcript of the witness DD testimony) IT-98–33-T, Trial Chamber (26 July 2000), para 5752.
167 Stephanie K Wood, 'A Woman Scorned for the Least Condemned War Crime: Precedent and Problems with Prosecuting Rape as a Serious War Crime in the International Criminal Tribunal for Rwanda' (2004) 13 Columbia Journal of Gender and the Law 274, 286, 311.

addressed questions seeking unnecessary and excessive details of the rape in order to stun or incapacitate the victim on the stand, making her appear unreliable or contradictory. During the witness cross-examination, a Defence lawyer asked many times whether TA had not taken a bath before she was raped, insinuating that she could not have been raped because she smelled.[168] Additionally, reports circulated in the international press alleging that the presiding trial Judges 'burst out laughing' after this line of questioning.[169] Because the so-called 'laughing Judges' incident received much press following, the excruciating detail and extraordinary length of TA's cross-examination went almost unnoticed. As specified by the tribunal records, TA was on the witness stand from 24 October until 8 November 2001. The Defence questioned her in detail about the times she was raped. For instance, a Defence lawyer ineptly and insensitively questioned the witness:

Q.: Was she injured in the process of that bad exercise of being raped by the nine men?
A.: If you were to put yourself in my position, Counsel, if you are raped by nine people you cannot still be in order.[170]

On day 14 of witness TA's testimony, a Defence attorney asked:

Q.: Now, Madam, you were sexually attacked, according to your testimony, on the first time (…) behind the buildings of the prefecture and then subsequently by eight other persons (…) that first time, is that correct?
A.: Counsel, I would like you to be told on my behalf that since I have been here, this matter has been put to me more than a hundred times. I don't want to answer as if I have come here to sing some kind of chorus before the Tribunal.[171]

Judges at the ICTR showed a reluctance to limit or restrain excessive and gratuitously repetitive cross-examination of rape victims. Victim-witnesses had to

168 *Prosecutor v Pauline Nyiramasuhuko et al.* (transcript) ICTR-98–42, Trial Chamber (31 October 2001), p 60 lines 5–6, p 62 lines 21–22, p 63 lines 24–25, p 64 line 1, p 89 lines 13–16.

169 Hirondelle News Agency, 'Rwanda: Government "Concerned" About Alleged Mistreatment of ICTR Rape Witness' (4 December 2001); *International Justice Tribune*, 'Unprotected Witness' (*International Justice Tribune*, 1 November 2001 <rnw.nl/international-justice/article/unprotected-witness> accessed 25 January 2022. President Pillay addressed the so-called "laughing judges" incident in Press Release, Navanethem Pillay, 'Statement of Judge Pillay, President of the Tribunal' (*United Nations International Residual Mechanism for Criminal Tribunals*, 14 December 2001) <unictr.irmct.org/en/news/statement-judge-pillay-president-tribunal> accessed 25 January 2022.

170 *Prosecutor v Pauline Nyiramasuhuko et al.* (n 167) p 77 lines 13–14, 24–25, p. 78 line 1.

171 *Prosecutor v Pauline Nyiramasuhuko et al.* (transcript) ICTR-98–42, Trial Chamber (6 November 2001) 45–46.

endure days of repeated, detailed and often offensive questioning by Defence lawyers about the intimate details of the rapes they endured without intervention by the prosecution or the Judges. As victims were being used by the Prosecutor and the Defence as a means of proving the guilt or innocence of the offender, they had little control over their narrative.[172]

7.7 Conclusion

Expressivism proved to be a key element of the development of international criminal justice institutions. The action of creating these institutions is not only grounded in the need to prosecute those believed to be responsible for the most serious crimes, it also is highly symbolic in itself. The decision to establish an 'international' criminal tribunal, instead of a national one, sends multiple messages, such as expressions of shame and apology, the importance of safeguarding basic standards of human rights, and communicating the denunciation and disavowal of heinous conducts with greater clarity. The institutional history and practices of the Nuremberg IMT, the ICTY, and the ICTR illustrated that they reflected these types of messages, which, nevertheless, took on different priorities and nuances. The post-Second World War Nuremberg IMT symbolised a dramatic change in the normative structures as it caused the first cracks in the otherwise impenetrable edifice of national jurisdiction over war crimes. The introduction of offences such as crimes against humanity and crimes against peace, which transcended State sovereignty, sent a powerful message about a new concept of international justice, which shaped the international community's common identity. After 50 years, the action of the ICTY and the ICTR carried on the endeavour of the Nuremberg IMT, by refining the contours of the normative content of international criminal law. The establishment of the *ad hoc* tribunals also conveyed feelings of shame and apology because of the 'failure of states to muster the collective political will to prevent or forestall systematic human rights atrocities' in the former Yugoslavia and Rwanda.[173]

While the institutional action of the Nuremberg IMT, the ICTY, and the ICTR conveyed messages about types of criminality, victimization, crimes and their context, as well as responsibility for them, their procedural regimes undermined the interests and role of the victims in the trials. In the adversarial system adopted by these tribunals, victims serving as witnesses were treated as 'weapons' to be used against the other party. While expressivism envisages them as active agents in proceedings, whose storytelling is fundamental to pursuing expressivist goals, in the proceedings before these international criminal tribunals, victims were systematically denied the chance to tell their narratives. Judges and

172 Dembour and Haslam (n 162) 164.

173 Robert D Sloane, 'The Expressive Capacity of International Punishment: The Limits of the National Law Analogy and the Potential of International Criminal Law' (2007) 43 Stanford Journal of International Law 39, 47.

prosecution appropriated victims' suffering to shore up the legitimacy of their actions. The parties' examination and cross-examination of victim-witnesses constantly sought to take control of their story-telling to elicit only those facts considered relevant to the case. This form of control over victim-witnesses and, more generally, the party-driven contest feature of the adversarial trial did not promote the participation of individual victims.[174] The potential of victims to play a fundamental role in the construction of messages and narratives has been underappreciated since the Nuremberg IMT, the ICTY and the ICTR have relied on simplified representations of victimhood. They have conceived the victim mainly as an object of grief, as he/she is associated with the image of a powerless, helpless innocent, who suffers from catastrophic events but lacks agency him/herself. Consequently, victims, who should be constitutive parts of the Defence and prosecution's discursive battles about how mass violence is best understood, explained, and responded to, are only an instrumentally important means to achieve a more favourable outcome from the criminal justice process. This limited role re-silences victims, negating their potential to shape the expressivist message of the international criminal trials. The drafters of the ICC looked at the work and failures of these first international criminal justice institutions in order to learn from them. The next chapter discusses to what extent the expressivist assumption that victims' stories and perspectives can make criminal proceedings more meaningful is consistent with the role granted to victims at the ICC, which recognises them as 'participants' in criminal proceedings who are entitled to present their own 'views and concerns' in proceedings, independently of the story of the prosecution or the Defence.

References

Books and journals

Alvarez JE, 'Crimes of States/Crimes of Hate: Lessons from Rwanda' (1999) 24 Yale Journal of International Law 365

Amann DM, 'Assessing International Criminal Adjudication of Human Rights Atrocities' (2000) 16 Third World Legal Studies 169

Amann DM, 'Group Mentality, Expressivism, and Genocide' (2002) 2 International Criminal Law Review 93

Appleman JA, *Military Tribunals and the International Crimes* (Greenwood Press Publishers 1954)

Bachrach M, 'The Protection and Rights of Victims under International Criminal Law' (2000) 34 The International Lawyer 7

Bass GJ, *Stay the Hand of Vengeance: The Politics of War Crimes Tribunals*, vol 142 (Princeton University Press 2014)

Bassiouni MC et al., 'War Crimes Tribunals: The Record and the Prospects. Conference Convocation' (1998) 13 American University International Law Review 1383

174 Jonathan Doak, 'Victims' Rights in Criminal Trials: Prospects for Participation' (2005) 32 Journal of Law and Society 294, 298.

Biddle F, 'The Nuremberg Trial' (1947) 91 Proceedings of the American Philosophical Society 294

Bloxham D, *Genocide on Trial: War Crimes Trials and the Formation of Holocaust History and Memory* (Oxford University Press 2001)

Cassese A, 'Reflections on International Criminal Justice' (1998) 61 The Modern Law Review 1

Cassese A, *International Criminal Law* (2nd edn, Oxford University Press 2008)

Chakravarti S, 'More than 'Cheap Sentimentally': Victim Testimony at Nuremberg, the Eichmann Trail, and Truth Commissions' (2008) 15 Constellations 223

Chung CH, 'Victims' Participation at the International Criminal Court: Are Concessions of the Court Clouding the Promise?' (2008) 6 Northwestern Journal of Human Rights 459

Coalition for Women's Human Rights in Conflict Situations, 'Letter to Carla Del Ponte, Prosecutor, Regarding the Urgent Need to Include Charges of Sexual Violence in the Indictment against Milošević' (14 August 2001) referred to by Anne-Marie de Brouwer, *Supranational Criminal Prosecution of Sexual Violence: The ICC and the Practice of the ICTY and the ICTR*, vol 20 (Intersentia 2005) 299

Coalition for Women's Human Rights in Conflict Situations, 'Letter to Prosecutor Hassan Jallow' (8 February 2005) referred to by Anne-Marie de Brouwer, *Supranational Criminal Prosecution of Sexual Violence: The ICC and the Practice of the ICTY and the ICTR*, vol 20 (Intersentia 2005) 299

Copelon R, 'Surfacing Gender: Reengraving the Crimes against Women in Humanitarian Law' in Nicole A Dombrowski (ed), *Women and War in the Twentieth Century: Enlisted with or without Consent* (Routledge 1999)

de Brouwer A-M, *Supranational Criminal Prosecution of Sexual Violence: The ICC and the Practice of the ICTY and the ICTR*, vol 20 (Intersentia 2005)

de Brouwer A-M and Heikkilä M, 'Victim Issues: Participation, Protection, Reparation, and Assistance' in Göran Sluiter et al. (eds), *International Criminal Procedure: Principles and Rules* (1st edn, Oxford University Press 2013)

deGuzman M, 'Choosing to Prosecute: Expressive Selection at the International Criminal Court' (2012) 33 Michigan Journal of International Law 265

De Hemptinne J and Jorda C, 'The Status and Role of the Victim' in Antonio Cassese, Paola Gaeta and John R Jones (eds), *The Rome Statute of the International Criminal Court: A Commentary*, vol 2 (Oxford University Press 2002)

Del Ponte C, 'Address by Prosecutor Del Ponte on Importance of War Crimes Trials for Truth-Telling Process' (Conference on 'Establishing the Truth about War Crimes and Conflicts', Zagreb, Croatia, 8 February 2007) <https://www.icty.org/fr/press/address-prosecutor-del-ponte-importance-war-crimes-trials-truth-telling-process> accessed 29 May 2022

Dembour M-B and Haslam E, 'Silencing Hearings? Victim-Witnesses at War Crimes Trials' (2004) 15 European Journal of International Law 151

Doak J, 'Victims' Rights in Criminal Trials: Prospects for Participation' (2005) 32 Journal of Law and Society 294

Douglas L, *The Memory of Judgment: Making Law and History in the Trials of the Holocaust* (Yale University Press 2001)

Douglas L, 'From IMT to NMT: The Emergence of a Jurisprudence of Atrocity' in Kim C Priemel and Alexa Stiller (eds), *Reassessing the Nuremberg Military Tribunals: Transitional Justice, Trial Narratives, and Historiography* (Berghahn Books 2012)

Drumbl MA, *Atrocity, Punishment, and International Law* (Cambridge University Press 2007)

Durkheim É, *The Division of Labour in Society* (Macmillan 1984)

Egbert LD (ed), 'International Military Tribunal (Nuremberg), Judgment and Sentences, October 1 1946' (1947) 41 American Journal of International Law 172, 219

Fletcher L, 'From Indifference to Engagement: Bystanders and International Criminal Justice' (2005) 26 Michigan Journal of International Law 1013

Forsythe DP, 'International Criminal Courts: A Political View' (1997) 15 Netherlands Quarterly of Human Rights 5

Garkawe S, 'The Role of Victims at the Nuremberg International Military Tribunal' in Herbert R Reginbogin and Christoph Safferling (eds), *The Nuremberg Trials: International Criminal Law Since 1945*: 60th Anniversary International Conference (De Gruyter Saur 2006)

Gross L, 'The Punishment of War Criminals: The Nuremberg Trial (First Part)' (1955) 2 Netherlands International Law Review 356

Haslam E, 'Victim Participation at the International Criminal Court: A Triumph of Hope over Experience?' in Dominic McGoldrick, Peter Rowe and Eric Donnelly, *The Permanent International Criminal Court: Legal and Policy Issues* (Hart Publishing 2004)

Heikkilä M, *International Criminal Tribunals and Victims of Crime: A Study of the Status of Victims before International Criminal Tribunals and of Factors Affecting This Status* (Institute for Human Rights Åbo Akademi University 2004)

Hirondelle News Agency, 'Rwanda: Government 'Concerned' About Alleged Mistreatment of ICTR Rape Witness' (4 December 2001)

Hockett JD, 'Justice Robert H. Jackson, the Supreme Court, and the Nuremberg Trial' (1990) The Supreme Court Review 257

International Justice Tribune, 'Unprotected Witness' (*International Justice Tribune*, 1 November 2001) <rnw.nl/international-justice/article/unprotected-witness> accessed 25 January 2022

International Military Tribunal, *Trial of the Major War Criminals before the International Military Tribunal*, vol 1 (1948)

International Military Tribunal, *Trial of the Major War Criminals before the International Military Tribunal*, vol 2 (1948)

International Military Tribunal, *Trial of the Major War Criminals before the International Military Tribunal*, vol 7 (1948)

International Military Tribunal, *Trial of the Major War Criminals before the International Military Tribunal*, vol 8 (1948)

Jackson RH, 'Report to the President from Justice Robert Jackson, Chief of Counsel for the United States in the Prosecution of the Axis War Criminal' (1945) 39 American Journal of International Law 178

Jackson RH, 'Final Report to the President Concerning the Nuremberg War Crimes Trial' (1946) 20 Temple Law Quarterly 338

Jockusch L, 'Justice at Nuremberg? Jewish Responses to Nazi War-Crime Trials in Allied-Occupied Germany' (2012) 19 Jewish Social Studies 107

McCarthy C, 'Victim Redress and International Criminal Justice: Competing Paradigms, or Compatible Forms of Justice?' (2012) 10 Journal of International Criminal Justice 351

McGonigle Leyh B, *Procedural Justice? Victim Participation in International Criminal Proceedings* (Intersentia 2011)

McGonigle Leyh B, 'Victim-Oriented Measures at International Criminal Institutions: Participation and Its Pitfalls' (2012) 12 International Criminal Law Review 375

McMillan N, 'Imagining the International: The Constitution of the International as a Site of Crime, Justice and Community' (2016) 25 Social & Legal Studies 163

Mégret F, 'In Defense of Hybridity: Towards a Representational Theory of International Criminal Justice' (2005) 38 Cornell International Law Journal 725

Mégret F, 'Practices of Stigmatization' (2013) 76 Law and Contemporary Problems 287

Mégret F, 'What Sort of Global Justice Is 'International Criminal Justice'?' (2015) 13 Journal of International Criminal Justice 77

Moffett L, 'The Role of Victims in the International Criminal Tribunals of the Second World War' (2012) 12 International Criminal Law Review 245

Morris V and Scharf M, *An Insider's Guide to the International Criminal Tribunal for the Former Yugoslavia*, vol I (Transnational Publishers 1995)

Nimage S, 'An International Conscience Collective? A Durkheimian Analysis of International Criminal Law' (2007) 7 International Criminal Law Review 561

Orentlicher D, 'Settling Accounts' (1991) 100 Yale Law Journal 2537

Pillay N, 'Statement of Judge Pillay, President of the Tribunal' (*United Nations International Residual Mechanism for Criminal Tribunals*, 14 December 2001) <unictr.irmct.org/en/news/statement-judge-pillay-president-tribunal> accessed 25 January 2022

Savelsberg JJ and King RD, 'Law and Collective Memory' (2007) 3 Annual Review Law Social Science 189

Schabas WA, *An Introduction to the International Criminal Court* (3rd edn, Cambridge University Press 2007)

Scheffer D, *All the Missing Souls: A Personal History of the War Crimes Tribunals* (Princeton University Press 2012)

Schotsmans M and Nsanzuwera F-X, 'Victims in the Balance: Challenges Ahead for the International Criminal Tribunal for Rwanda' (International Federation for Human Rights 2002) 329/2

Security Council, 'Provisional Verbatim Record of the 3175th Meeting' (1993) UN Doc S/PV.3175

Security Council, '3453rd Meeting: The Situation Concerning Rwanda' (1994) UN Doc S/PV.3453

Sloane RD, 'The Expressive Capacity of International Punishment: The Limits of the National Law Analogy and the Potential of International Criminal Law' (2007) 43 Stanford Journal of International Law 39

Sluiter G et al. (eds), *International Criminal Procedure: Principles and Rules* (1st edn, Oxford University Press 2013)

Smith BF, *Reaching Judgment at Nuremberg* (Andre Deutsch 1977)

Stahn C, *Justice as Message: Expressivist Foundations of International Criminal Justice* (1st edn, Oxford University Press 2020)

Subotić J, *Hijacked Justice: Dealing with the Past in the Balkans* (Cornell University Press 2016)

Takatori Y, 'Remembering the War Crimes Trial: The Tokyo Trial View of History' in Sven Saaler and Wolfgang Schwentker (eds), *The Power of Memory in Modern Japan* (Global Oriental 2008)

Teitel R, 'Transitional Jurisprudence: The Role of the Law in Political Transformation' (1997) 106 Yale Law Journal 2009

Tusa A and Tusa J, *The Nuremberg Trial* (Macmillan 1983)

Williams S and Woolaver H, 'The Role of the Amicus Curiae before International Criminal Tribunals' (2006) 6 International Criminal Law Review 151

UN Commission of Inquiry on Rwanda, 'Report of the Independent Inquiry into the Actions of the United Nations during the 1994 Genocide in Rwanda' (1999) UN Doc S/1999/1257

UN Secretary-General, 'Report of the Secretary-General Pursuant to General Assembly Resolution 53/35: The Fall of Srebrenica' (1999) UN Doc A/54/549

Woetzel RK, *The Nuremberg Trials in International Law: With a Postlude on the Eichmann Case* (Stevens & Sons Limited 1962)

Wood SK, 'A Woman Scorned for the Least Condemned War Crime: Precedent and Problems with Prosecuting Rape as a Serious War Crime in the International Criminal Tribunal for Rwanda' (2004) 13 Columbia Journal of Gender and the Law 274

Zappalà S, 'The Rights of Victims v. the Rights of the Accused' (2010) 8 Journal of International Criminal Justice 137

Cases

Prosecutor v Alfred Musema (Judgment and Sentence) ICTR-96–13-A, Trial Chamber I (27 January 2000)

Prosecutor v André Ntagerura, Emmanuel Bagambiki, and Samuel Imanishimwe (Prosecutor's Response to Application for Leave to File an Amicus Brief) ICTR-99–46 (8 May 2001)

Prosecutor v André Ntagerura, Emmanuel Bagambiki, and Samuel Imanishimwe (Decision on the Application to File an Amicus Curiae Brief According to Rule 74 of the Rules of Procedure and Evidence Filed on Behalf of the NGO Coalition for Women's Human Rights in Conflict Situations) ICTR-99–46-T, Trial Chamber (24 May 2001)

Prosecutor v Anto Furundžija (Judgement) IT-95–17/1-T, Trial Chamber (10 December 1998)

Prosecutor v Anto Furundžija (Amicus Curiae Brief Respecting the Decision and Order of the Tribunal of 16 July 1998 Requesting that the Tribunal Reconsider its Decision Having Regard to the Rights of Witness 'A' to Equality, Privacy and Security of the Person and to Representation by Counsel) IT-95–17/1-T, Coalition for Women's Human Rights in Conflict Situations (5 November 1998)

Prosecutor v Anto Furundžija (Order Granting Leave to File Amicus Curiae Brief) IT-95–17/1-T, Trial Chamber (10 November 1998)

Prosecutor v Anto Furundžija (Corrigendum to Order Granting Leave to File Amicus Curiae Brief) IT-95–17/1-T, Trial Chamber (11 November 1998)

Prosecutor v Dario Kordić and Mario Čerkez (Appeal Judgement) IT-95–14/2-A, Appeals Chamber (7 December 2004)

Prosecutor v Dragan Nikolić (Sentencing Judgement) IT-94–2-S, Trial Chamber (18 December 2003)

Prosecutor v Dragoljub Kunarac et al. (Trial Judgement) IT-96–23-T& IT-96–23/1-T, Trial Chamber (22 February 2000)

Prosecutor v Dražen Erdemović (Sentencing Judgement) IT-96–22-T, Trial Chamber (29 November 1996)

Prosecutor v Dražen Erdemović (Judgement) IT-96–22-A, Appeals Chamber (7 October 1997)

Prosecutor v Duško Tadić (Decision on the Defence Motion for Interlocutory Appeal on Jurisdiction) ICTY-94–1-A, Trial Chamber (2 October 1995)

Prosecutor v Duško Tadić (Sentencing Judgement) IT-94–1, Trial Chamber II (11 November 1999)

Prosecutor v Georges Rutaganda (Judgement and Sentence) ICTR-96–3-T, Trial Chamber I (6 December 1999)

Prosecutor v Jean Kambanda (Judgement and Sentence) ICTR-97–23-S, Trial Chamber I (4 September 1998)

Prosecutor v Jean Paul Akayesu (Sentence) ICTR-96–4-T, Trial Chamber I (2 October 1998)

Prosecutor v Jean-Paul Akayesu (Judgement) ICTR-96–4-T, Trial Chamber I (2 September 1998)

Prosecutor v Miroslav Bralo (Sentencing Judgement) IT-95–17-S, Trial Chamber (7 December 2005)

Prosecutor v Omar Serushago (Sentence) ICTR-98–39-S, Trial Chamber I (5 February 1999)

Prosecutor v Pauline Nyiramasuhuko et al. (transcript) ICTR-98–42, Trial Chamber (29 October 2001)

Prosecutor v Pauline Nyiramasuhuko et al. (transcript) ICTR-98–42, Trial Chamber (31 October 2001)

Prosecutor v Pauline Nyiramasuhuko et al. (transcript) ICTR-98–42, Trial Chamber (6 November 2001)

Prosecutor v Radislav Krstić (Judgement) IT-98–33-T, Trial Chamber (2 August 2001)

Prosecutor v Radislav Krstić (transcript of the witness J testimony) IT-98–33-T, Trial Chamber (10 April 2000)

Prosecutor v Radislav Krstić (transcript of the witness DD testimony) IT-98–33-T, Trial Chamber (26 July 2000)

Prosecutor v Slobodan Milošević (Initial Indictment 'Croatia') IT-01–50-I (27 September 2001)

Prosecutor v Slobodan Milošević (Initial Indictment 'Bosnia and Herzegovina') IT-01–51-I (22 November 2001)

Prosecutor v Slobodan Milošević (Amended Indictment 'Bosnia and Herzegovina') IT-02–54-T (22 November 2002)

Prosecutor v Slobodan Milošević, Milan Milutinović, Nikola Šainović, Dragoljub Ojdanić and Vlajko Stojiljković (Second Amended Indictment 'Kosovo') IT-99–37-PT (16 October 2001)

Prosecutor v Stevan Todorović (Sentencing Judgment) IT-95–9/1-S, Trial Chamber (31 July 2001)

Prosecutor v Sylvestre (transcript) ICTR-01–64, Trial Chamber (6 August 2003)

Prosecutor v Tharcisse Muvunyi (Decision on the Prosecutor's Motion for Leave to File an Amended Indictment) ICTR-00–55, Trial Chamber II (23 February 2005)

Prosecutor v Zdravko Mucić et al (Judgement) IT-96–21-T, Trial Chamber (16 November 1998)

Prosecutor v Zejnil Delalić et al. (Trial Judgement) IT-96–21-T, Trial Chamber (16 November 1998)

Prosecutor v Zejnil Delalić, Zdravko Mucić, Hazim Delić and Esad Landžo (Judgement) IT-96–21-T, Trial Chamber (16 November 1998)
Prosecutor v Zlatko Aleksovski (Judgement) IT-95–14/1-A, Appeals Chamber (24 March 2000)

Legislation

Charter of the International Military Tribunal – Annex to the Agreement for the Prosecution and punishment of the major war criminals of the European Axis 1945
UN Security Council, 'Security Council Resolution 827 (1993) on Establishment of the International Tribunal for Prosecution of Persons Responsible for Serious Violations of International Humanitarian Law Committed in the Territory of the Former Yugoslavia since 1991' (1993) UN Doc S/RES/827
UN Security Council, 'Security Council Resolution 955 (1994) on Establishment of an International Tribunal for Rwanda and Adoption of the Statute of the Tribunal' (1994) UN Doc S/RES/955

8 Expressivism and the participatory rights of victims before the International Criminal Court

8.1 Introduction

It was only with the establishment of the International Criminal Court (hereafter ICC or the Court) in 1998 that victims of gross violations of human rights were conferred the status of participants in proceedings with an autonomous standing. This is an absolute novelty because, for the first time in international criminal proceedings, the provisions of the RS and the RPE of the ICC set up a scheme of victims' participatory rights. This chapter begins by reflecting on the *sui generis* nature of the procedural law of the ICC, which seems to depart from the strict divide between the civil law and the common law traditions; then it looks at the case law on victims' participation in the proceedings with the objective of establishing whether and to what extent it is possible to identify elements that can be interpreted as envisaging the expressivist framework.

The analysis of the case law of the ICC looks at the participatory rights of victims at the investigation, pre-trial, and trial stages to understand whether and how the arguments advanced by the Court successfully envisage a model of participation informed by the expressivist conceptualisation of victims as fundamental actors in the trial. The chapter discusses whether the rationale put forward by the Judges to justify victims' participation in proceedings are consistent with the expressivist conception of the role of victims, recognising their contribution to pursuing fundamental expressivist goals, namely, truth-telling and historical clarification; reaffirming the importance of safeguarding basic standards of human rights and communicating the denunciation and the disavowal of heinous conducts with greater clarity.

Among the practices relating to victims' participation, this chapter pays particular attention to the possibility of victim-participants being involved in the stage where the processing of evidence unfolds. The role of victims in the evidence-gathering process presents a multifaceted issue as victims can contribute to the collection of evidentiary material in either a passive or a more proactive way. On the one hand, the procedural phenomenon of the duality of victim-witness status envisages a scenario where victims take the witness stand at the

DOI: 10.4324/9781003215448-8

initiative of the parties[1] or at the discretion of the relevant Chamber acting *proprio motu*.[2] On the other hand, a different scenario in which victims play a more pro-active role in the processing of evidence has emerged with a body of case law giving rise to the possibility of victims intervening and, eventually, having an impact on the ICC's evidence-gathering process. What is under investigation is the willingness of the ICC's Judges to provide a model which, by allowing victims to present evidence, enhances the victims' ability to contribute to the didactic function of the trial, as envisaged by expressivism, with due regard for the accused's right to a fair trial.

Finally, the chapter will consider the challenges that the ICC faces to make it possible for a larger number of victims to participate in the proceedings. To solve this issue, the ICC developed a unique modality of participation: victims' common legal representation. The discussion about this modality is extremely useful in illustrating how the Chambers deal with the need to guarantee participator rights to a large number of victims and safeguard the expeditiousness of the trial. The analysis of the case law investigates whether victims' common legal representation, as developed by the Chambers, is able to fulfil the expressivist goals of the trial and offer a valid set of participatory rights to a wide range of victims.

8.2 The *sui generis* approach to the procedural law of the ICC

The ICC Statute is a treaty and, thus, the fruit of negotiations conducted between State parties that represent different legal systems. Participants in the negotiations characterised the discussions on the procedural model of the ICC as a 'clash of cultures between the civil law and the common law'.[3] This is due to the fact that each legal tradition has developed a procedural model that accords with the objectives that have been set by its own social and political background.[4] During the drafting of the procedural rules of the ICC '[d]elegations were often tempted to push discussions in a certain direction in order to obtain [...] an interpretation of the Statute that would alter the balance in favour of a particular view or particular legal system',[5] nonetheless, huge efforts were made to find solutions that were acceptable to the different legal traditions.[6] The extensive debates on

1 Article 69(3), Rome Statute of the International Criminal Court 1998 (2187 UNTS 90).

2 Article 69(3) read in conjunction with Article 64(6)(d) ibid.

3 Peter Lewis, 'Trial Procedure' in Roy S Lee (ed), *The International Criminal Court: Elements of Crimes and Rules of Procedure and Evidence* (Transnational Publishers 2001) 547–550.

4 See sections 5.2. and 5.3.

5 Silvia A de Gurmendi Fernández, 'Elaboration of the Rules and Procedure of Evidence' in Roy S Lee (ed), *The International Criminal Court: Elements of Crimes and Rules of Procedure and Evidence* (Transnational Publishers 2001) 235.

6 On the ICC negotiations see e.g., Silvia A de Gurmendi Fernández, 'International Criminal Law Procedures: The Process of Negotiations' in Roy S Lee (ed), *The International Criminal Court: The Making of the Rome Statute: Issues, Negotiations and Results* (Martinus Nijhoff Publishers 1999) 217–227; Silvia A de Gurmendi Fernández and Håkan Friman, 'The Rules

the procedural rules of the ICC suggested that the Statute, while reflecting a basically adversarial approach associated with common law jurisdictions, incorporates some significant civil law features, including a greater system of victim participation.[7] Thus, the procedural law is based neither on a pure adversarial model nor on a pure inquisitorial model. Instead, it is based on what Kress describes as a 'fundamental compromise formula', where the Judges have to determine a balance between competing adversarial and inquisitorial elements.[8]

Several commentators argue that the ICC has a unique procedural system which is *sui generis* in the sense that it departs from the dominant adversarial and inquisitorial systems of justice. Although, inevitably, the ICC has elements from the two major legal traditions.[9] Triffterer describes the *sui generis* nature of the procedure of the ICC as 'the "melting pot" of the most adequate and fortunate tendencies of criminal procedures stemming from all families of legal systems, forming thus a "highest common denominator" attainable by all legal models'.[10] In this respect, a cursory examination of the terminology of the RS already shows that the aspirations of the drafters to devise a procedure that best assists the Court in accomplishing its tasks as an international judicial body far outweighed the desire to strictly follow either an accusatorial or inquisitorial judicial approach. Legal terms like '*juge d'instruction*' (investigating Judge), or 'cross-examination' have been replaced by neutral terms, such as, respectively, 'Pre-Trial Chamber' and the right of the defendant 'to have examined the witnesses against him or her',[11] in order to avoid the terminology language of one particular legal tradition having too much influence.

---

of Procedure and Evidence of the International Criminal Court' (2000) 3 Yearbook of International Humanitarian Law 289.

7 Mahmoud Cherif Bassiouni, 'Negotiating the Treaty of Rome on the Establishment of an International Criminal Court' (1999) 32 Cornell International Law Journal 443, 464; Antonio Cassese, 'The Statute of the International Criminal Court: Some Preliminary Reflections' (1999) 10 European Journal of International Law 144, 168; Salvatore Zappalà, *Human Rights in International Criminal Proceedings* (Oxford University Press 2003) 24; Robert Cryer et al., *An Introduction to International Criminal Law and Procedure* (Cambridge University Press 2014) 428.

8 Claus Kress, 'The Procedural Law of the International Criminal Court in Outline: Anatomy of a Unique Compromise' (2003) 1 Journal of International Criminal Justice 603, 605.

9 Kai Ambos, 'International Criminal Procedure: "Adversarial", "Inquisitorial" or Mixed?' (2003) 3 International Criminal Law Review 1, 34–35; Gabrielle Kirk McDonald, 'Trial Procedures and Practice' in Gabrielle Kirk McDonald and Olivia Q Swaak-Goldman (eds), *Substantive and Procedural Aspects of International Criminal Law: The Experience of International and National Courts* (Kluwer 2000) 556; Gideon Boas, James L Bischoff and Natalie L Reid, *International Criminal Law Practitioner Library: Elements of Crimes in International Criminal Law*, vol II (Cambridge University Press 2008) 8; Cryer et al. (n 7) 425, 429.

10 Otto Triffterer (ed), *Commentary on the Rome Statute of the International Criminal Court: Observers' Notes, Article by Article* (2nd edn, Nomos Verlagsgesellschaft 2008) 904.

11 Article 67(e), Rome Statute of the International Criminal Court.

The ICC procedural law is a macrocosm, as the proceedings follow the sequence of investigation, confirmation hearing, trial, and, as the case may be, appeals and revision of proceedings. It would be beyond the scope of this work to engage with an analysis of the whole procedure; therefore, this section provides an analysis of those articles of the RS that are considered to best illustrate that the *sui generis* nature of the procedure of the ICC reflects the expressivist norm-expression function of the trial. Specifically, the discussion highlights those features of the RS that are consistent with the elements of the common grammar grounded in the expressivist justice model[12] and shape the role and functions of the Office of the Prosecutor[13] and Judges.[14]

At the pre-trial stage of the proceedings, the roles of the Prosecutor and the Pre-Trial Chamber and the interplay between them constitute a striking example of the expressivist model, which 'relaxes' the adversarial procedural model and its characteristic of contest between parties, envisaging an active role for the Judge as fact-finder as well as a narrative function for the Prosecutor. The first important procedural issue that requires interaction between the Prosecutor and the Pre-Trial Chamber is the review of the Prosecutor's *proprio motu* power to initiate investigations under Article 15(3), which requests the Pre-Trial Chamber to authorise the commencement of the investigation. Secondly, according to Article 18(2) of the RS, when a State that has jurisdiction over a crime requests the Prosecutor to defer to the State's investigation, the Pre-Trial Chamber is responsible, upon a request from the Prosecutor, for authorizing the ICC investigation. Similarly, in extraordinary circumstances, the Pre-Trial Chamber can authorize the Prosecutor to take steps to preserve evidence, in a case where the Prosecutor has deferred an investigation to a State.[15] Another remarkable procedural issue which exemplifies the interplay between the Prosecutor and the Pre-Trial Chamber is the Prosecutor's decision not to initiate an investigation. In that event, Article 53 confers to the Pre-Trial Chamber, at the request of the State making a referral[16] or *proprio motu*,[17] the authority to review the Prosecutor's decision and, potentially, may request the Prosecutor to reconsider that decision.

Turning to the role of the prosecution at the pre-trial stage, Article 54(1)(a) of the ICC Statute gives the Prosecutor a more explicit truth-finding duty, stating that

> the Prosecutor shall in order to establish the truth, extend the investigation to cover all facts and evidence relevant to an assessment of whether there is

12 See section 5.3.
13 See section 5.5.2.
14 See section 5.5.1.
15 Article 18(6), Rome Statute of the International Criminal Court.
16 Article 53(3)(a), ibid.
17 Article 53(3)(b), ibid.

criminal responsibility under the Statute and, in doing so, shall investigate incriminating and exonerating circumstances equally.

From the wording of the said article, it is evident the attempt to tilt the balance of prosecutorial powers towards a system where the Prosecutor acts not only as a party that presents the facts and evidence to prosecute and to obtain the defendant's conviction, but is also responsible for an impartial search for the truth. More generally, the above analysis illustrates that, at the pre-trial stage, the roles and functions of the Prosecutor and the Pre-Trial Chamber demonstrate features which introduce an expressivist account of the procedural framework of the ICC, in which the Pre-Trial Chamber is given greater control over the pre-trial proceedings, whereas the Prosecutor has more explicit truth-finding duties.

With regard to the trial stage, Article 64 of the RS, which governs the functions and powers of the Trial Chamber, confers great discretion on the Judges, as they can 'give directions for the conduct of proceedings, including to ensure that they are conducted in a fair and impartial manner'.[18] An example of the discretion of the Judges in tailoring the trial proceedings is Article 64(6), which states that the Trial Chamber can summon witnesses and admit documentary or material evidence *proprio motu*. Those powers of the Trial Chamber are fundamental to ascertaining the truth, as the Judges can intervene in a situation where finding the truth might not always be the main concern of parties who are litigating in an adversarial manner.[19] Article 64 is not the only article of the RS that confers upon the Judges the discretion to not only govern the presentation of the parties but also admit evidence *proprio motu*. Article 69(3) of the RS, which outlines the evidentiary procedures, bestows on the Trial Chamber a pro-active role with regard to evidence.[20] The Judges are allowed to ask the parties for additional evidence in order to achieve their truth-finding mandate. Indeed Article 69(3) goes beyond the pure adversarial model as the active determination of the truth is not left solely to the prosecution and the Defence. Nevertheless, it is important to highlight that although the trial Judges are not conceived as being passive arbiters anymore, the wording of Article 69(3) does not embody a purely inquisitorial model in which the trial Judges have the duty to determine the truth.[21] Article 69(3) is one of the features of the proceedings which best represents the expressivist dimension of the judicial process at the ICC, and it will be the object of special attention later in this chapter, as this article confers on the Trial Chamber the power to request victims to present evidence and to challenge the admissibility and relevance of the evidence submitted by the parties.[22]

18 Article 64(8)(b), ibid.
19 Stefan Kirsch, 'The Trial Proceedings before the ICC' (2006) 6 International Criminal Law Review 275, 286.
20 Cassese (n 7) 169.
21 Kress (n 8) 612.
22 See section 8.8.

Article 65 of the RS, governing the proceedings on an admission of guilt, is another example of the constructive approach towards a common grammar, which blends the common law 'plea of guilty' and the civil law 'admission of the facts'.[23] Where the accused makes an admission of guilt, the Trial Chamber is required to determine whether the three conditions set in Article 65 have been met. The first two conditions, that the admission must be both informed[24] and voluntary,[25] reflect the common law system whereby the court needs to satisfy itself that the accused understands the nature and consequences of the admission of guilt and that such admission is free and voluntary. The third condition requires the admission of guilt to be supported by facts contained in the charges and admitted by the accused; and in any material or evidence presented by the Prosecutor or the accused.[26] Such conditions require the Trial Chamber to carry out an active fact-checking function because the plea is not simply the result of consensus between the parties, but requires the Judges to consider the evidence.

This *tour de force* through some procedural features of the role of the Prosecutor and Judges highlights the fact that the RS does not simply replicate a particular legal model. The roles and functions of the Prosecutor and Judges, as defined by the RS, can be read as advancing key elements of expressivism, such as the didactic, truth-telling and communicative purposes of the criminal proceedings. In the same vein, the role assigned to victims in proceedings before the ICC is extremely innovative, as it is indicative of the acceptance of a fundamental feature of the inquisitorial approach within a procedure mainly grounded in the adversarial system. The following sections are entirely devoted to exploring the case law of the ICC on the participatory rights of victims at the investigation, pre-trial, and trial stages to understand whether and to what extent victims' participation can be interpreted as putting forward the expressivist framework.

8.3 Victims' participation framework

The drafters of both the Statute and the RPE of the ICC were fully aware of the incredible opportunity to provide victims with adequate procedural rights, filling the gaps left by the legal framework of the *ad hoc* tribunals.[27] The energetic work

23 Colin McLaughlin, 'The *Sui Generis* Trial Proceedings of the International Criminal Court' (2007) 6 The Law & Practice of International Courts and Tribunals 343, 348.
24 Article 65(1)(a), Rome Statute of the International Criminal Court.
25 Article 65(1)(b), ibid.
26 Article 65(1)(c), ibid.
27 David Donat-Cattin, 'Article 68: Protection of Victims and Witnesses and Their Participation in the Proceedings' in Otto Triffterer (ed), *Commentary on the Rome Statute of the International Criminal Court: Observers' Notes, Article by Article* (2nd edn, Nomos Verlagsgesellschaft 2008) 1277; Jérôme De Hemptinne and Claude Jorda, 'The Status and Role of the Victim' in Antonio Cassese, Paola Gaeta and John R Jones (eds), *The Rome Statute of the International Criminal Court: A Commentary*, vol 2 (Oxford University Press 2002) 1387–1388.

of several NGOs, such as Amnesty International[28] and Human Rights Watch,[29] was fundamental in terms of supporting the inclusion in the ICC Statute of dispositions on victims' procedural rights. Fiona McKay, as representative of the Victims' Rights Working Group, addressed the plenary of the UN Diplomatic Conference on the Establishment of the International Criminal Court and firmly stated that 'it is important that victims are involved in the judicial process as more than mere bystanders. Adequate provision must be made for their effective participation in the proceedings'.[30] Indeed, it must be acknowledged that the provisions of the ICC Statute and RPE on victims' participation have introduced a new dynamic to the international criminal procedure.

The victims' participatory rights scheme establishes a highly complex system, consisting of multiple legal regimes[31] developed around three main features. The first feature includes provisions aimed at protecting victims' wellbeing and safety. Whereas Article 43 of the RS set up a Victims and Witnesses Unit to provide protective measures and security arrangements and counselling,[32] Article 68(1)(2) empowers the Court to take appropriate measures to protect the safety, physical, and psychological wellbeing, dignity, and privacy of victims, paying particular attention to victims of crimes involving sexual or gender violence and violence against children. The second feature involves victims' right to receive reparations, as the Court is entitled, either upon request or on its own initiative in exceptional circumstances, to determine the scope and extent of any damage, loss, or injury to, or in respect of, victims.[33] The possibility to award reparations to victims was not a novelty, as Rule 106 of the RPE of both the ICTY and ICTR allowed victims to rely on judgements delivered by the *ad hoc* tribunals and to bring an action in a national court to obtain compensation. The RS marks a remarkable development because victims can seek reparations directly from the ICC.[34]

28 Amnesty International, *The International Criminal Court: Ensuring an Effective Role for Victims* (1999) <amnesty.org/en/documents/ior40/010/1999/en/> accessed 17 January 2022.

29 Human Rights Watch, 'Commentary to the Second Preparatory Commission on Rules of Procedure and Elements of Crimes–Section II: Victims in the ICC' (1999) <hrw.org/legacy/campaigns/icc/docs/prepcom-july99.htm> accessed 17 January 2022.

30 Fiona McKay, REDRESS on behalf of the Victims' Rights Working Group, 'Address to the Plenary' (1998) <legal-tools.org/doc/46e5ed/pdf> accessed 17 January 2022.

31 Sergey Vasiliev, 'Article 68 (3) and Personal Interests of Victims in the Emerging Practice of the ICC' in Carsten Stahn and Göran Sluiter (eds), *The Emerging Practice of the International Criminal Court*, vol 48 (Brill 2009) 638.

32 Article 43(6), Rome Statute of the International Criminal Court.

33 Article 75(1), ibid.

34 Charles Trumbull, 'The Victims of Victim Participation in International Criminal Proceedings' (2007) 29 Michigan Journal of International Law 777, 778.

The third feature represents a 'major structural achievement',[35] a 'significant step forward'[36] within the international criminal justice system, since, for the first time in the history of international criminal law, victims have an autonomous standing in proceedings before the ICC. The *lex generalis*[37] on victims' participation is Article 68(3) of the RS, which requires that:

> Where the personal interests of the victims are affected, the Court shall permit their views and concerns to be presented and considered at stages of the proceedings determined to be appropriate by the Court and in a manner which is not prejudicial to or inconsistent with the rights of the accused and a fair and impartial trial. Such views and concerns may be presented by the legal representatives of the victims where the Court considers it appropriate, in accordance with the Rules of Procedure and Evidence.[38]

This article has been portrayed in the literature as 'the most general authority'[39] on victims' participation before the ICC, since it sets out both the criteria for the admission of victims' participation and the modality of such participation. The article at hand confers on the Court great discretionary powers to authorise victims to participate in the proceedings. The Chambers have to evaluate whether three conditions, set out in Article 68(3), are satisfied: first, victims' personal interests must be affected; second, the participation is deemed appropriate with regard to the stage of the proceedings and, third, such participation would not be prejudicial to or inconsistent with the rights of the accused and a fair and impartial trial. Victims who fulfil these three requirements can exercise their procedural rights by expressing 'their views and concerns' through a legal representative.

In addition to Article 68(3), which has provided a generalised victims' participatory right, the ICC Statute contains Articles 15(3) and 19(3), which on account of their specific nature can be defined as *leges speciales* on victims' participation.[40] The participation regime under Article 15(3) enshrines victims' right to make representations to the Pre-Trial Chamber, in the case where the Prosecutor

35 Carsten Stahn, Héctor Olásolo and Kate Gibson, 'Participation of Victims in Pre-Trial Proceedings of the ICC' (2006) 4 Journal of International Criminal Justice 219, 219.

36 Adrian Di Giovanni, 'The Prospect of ICC Reparations in the Case Concerning Northern Uganda: On a Collision Course with Incoherence?' (2005) 2 Journal of International Law & International Relations 25, 25.

37 Yvonne McDermott, 'Some Are More Equal than Others: Victim Participation in the ICC' (2008) 5 Eyes on the ICC 27, 27; Mikaela Heikkilä, *International Criminal Tribunals and Victims of Crime: A Study of the Status of Victims before International Criminal Tribunals and of Factors Affecting This Status* (Institute for Human Rights Åbo Akademi University 2004) 148; Vasiliev (n 31) 639.

38 Article 68(3), Rome Statute of the International Criminal Court.

39 Stahn, Olásolo and Gibson (n 35) 235.

40 McDermott (n 37) 27; James L Bischoff, Gideon Boas and Natalie L Reid, *International Criminal Law Practitioner Library: International Criminal Procedure*, vol 3 (Cambridge University Press 2011) 312.

has submitted to the Pre-Trial Chamber a request for authorisation of an investigation. Article 19(3) of the RS enables victims to submit observations to the Court in proceedings regarding the jurisdiction of the Court or the admissibility of a case.

The RPE further implement the Articles of the RS on victims' participation, by specifying the circumstances in which victims may participate. Victims and their legal representatives have the right: to make opening and closing statements;[41] to attend and participate in the proceedings (hearings included) following the terms set by the Chamber, including the right to file written observations or submissions;[42] and the right to access to documents and notification;[43] to question a witness, an expert or the accused, subject to the Chamber's authorisation and subject to its control.[44] Under the new regime of RPE, victims' participation extends to issues on amendment of the charges,[45] conditional release or any condition amending liberty constriction,[46] disclosure of the record of all proceedings,[47] questioning the admissibility and relevancy of evidence[48] and other decisions of the Court on matters related to sentence and, if applicable, reparations.[49]

8.4 Problematic nature and scope of victims' participation

Victims' participation framework is heavily charged with implications with respect to the challenges as well as the potential of victims' active role in proceedings at the ICC. Although the specificity of the legal text and nature of Articles 15(3) and 19(3) have not given rise to controversy with regard to the modality and stage of the proceedings those articles apply to,[50] Article 68(3) raises multiple and complex legal issues, with substantive and procedural implications, since it only addresses the general principles of such participation.[51] Although the RPE provide more detailed procedural provisions, they do not clarify the general principles of victims' participation, as they fail to indisputably establish a clear scheme

41 Rule 89(1), Rules of Procedure and Evidence of the International Criminal Court 2002 (ICC-ASP/1/3).
42 Rule 91(2), ibid.
43 Rule 131(2), ibid.
44 Rule 91(3a), ibid.
45 Combined reading of Rules 93 and 128, ibid.
46 Rule 119(3), ibid.
47 Rule 121(10), ibid.
48 Rule 72, ibid.
49 Rules 143–145, ibid.
50 Articles 15(3) and 19(3) of the Rome Statute refer respectively to the investigation stage and the pre-trial stage of a case.
51 Emily Haslam, 'Victim Participation at the International Criminal Court: A Triumph of Hope Over Experience?' in Dominic McGoldrick, Peter Rowe and Eric Donnelly, *The Permanent International Criminal Court: Legal and Policy Issues* (Hart Publishing 2004) 315, 324; Elisabeth Baumgartner, 'Aspects of Victim Participation in the Proceedings of the International Criminal Court' (2008) 90 International Review of the Red Cross 409, 411.

of participatory rights for victims.[52] Article 68(3) enables victims to present 'their views and concerns', at 'stages of the proceedings determined to be appropriate' when their 'personal interests' are affected and 'in a manner' not prejudicial to the rights of the accused and a fair trial, but neither the RS nor the RPE provide a definition of any of these terms.[53]

The travaux préparatoires of the RS does not provide any further guidance as to the interpretation of Article 68(3). Actually, the drafting process of the RS showed to what extent the inclusion of Article 68(3) proved to be problematic because it was not an easy task to allow a third protagonist to play an active role in the proceedings. One of earliest drafts of Article 68(3) – dated 1995 – which was originally Article 43 of the ILC Draft Statute for an International Criminal Court, made provisions to protect victims, but it did not provide a mechanism to allow victims to participate in the proceedings.[54] At the Preparatory Committee meeting, which took place in August 1996, the French delegation put forward a draft of an Article 50 on 'The Rights of Victims',[55] while the Egyptian delegation suggested adding the following to Article 43: 'Legal representatives of victims of crimes have the right to participate in the proceedings with a view to presenting additional evidence needed to establish the basis of criminal responsibility as a foundation for their right to pursue civil compensation'.[56] The Preparatory Committee acknowledged that 'this article was of a very general nature and should be further elaborated and more precisely formulated'[57] and included the Egyptian suggestion in its Report.[58] However, at the session in August 1997,

52 Marianna Tonellato, 'The Victims' Participation at a Crossroads: How the International Criminal Court Could Devise a Meaningful Victims' Participation While Respecting the Rights of the Defendant' (2012) 20 European Journal of Crime, Criminal Law and Criminal Justice 315, 316.
53 Trumbull (n 34) 793–794.
54 Article 43, Committee of Experts on an International Criminal Court, 'Draft Statute for an International Criminal Court: Alternative to the ILC Draft (Siracusa-Draft)' (1995) <legal-tools.org/doc/39a534/pdf/> accessed 2 March 2022: 'The Court shall take necessary measures available to it to protect the accused, victims and witnesses and may to that end conduct closed proceedings or allow the presentation of evidence by electronic or other special means, provided that the measures are consistent with the rights of the accused'.
55 See Article 50, Preparatory Committee on the Establishment of an International Criminal Court, 'Draft Statute of The International Criminal Court – Working Paper Submitted by France' (1996a) A/AC.249/L.3 43 <legal-tools.org/doc/4d28ee/pdf/> accessed 2 March 2022.
56 See Preparatory Committee on the Establishment of an International Criminal Court, 'Proposal Submitted by Egypt for Article 43: Proposal Concerning the Protection and Rights of Witnesses and Victims (Article 43 of the ILC Draft Statute)' (1996b) A/AC.249/WP.11 <legal-tools.org/doc/41a017/pdf/> accessed 2 March 2022.
57 UN General Assembly, 'Report of the Preparatory Committee on the Establishment of an International Criminal Court – Volume I (Proceedings of the Preparatory Committee during March–April and August 1996)' (1996a) A/51/22 <legal-tools.org/doc/e75432/pdf/> accessed 2 March 2022, para 280.
58 UN General Assembly, 'Report of the Preparatory Committee on the Establishment of ICC – Vol II (Compilation of Proposals)' (1996b) A/51/22.

where the Preparatory Committee drafted the consolidated text of the convention for the ICC, the proposal by Egypt was not included in the final text of Article 43 of the ILC Draft Statute. It had been replaced by the proposal from the New Zealand delegation, which explicitly replicated the wording of Principle 6(b) of the 1985 UN Declaration of Basic Principles of Justice for Victims of Crime and Abuse of Power (hereafter Declaration for Victims of Crime).[59] Eventually, the New Zealand proposal was adopted in the consolidated text of Article 43, which, with minor modifications, became Article 68(3) of the ICC Statute.[60]

Indeed, Principle 6(b) served as a symbolic legal foundation for victims' right to participate in criminal proceedings; however, the copying and pasting – almost word for word – of this provision into Article 68(3) shows that the drafters preferred to avoid drawing on the model of civil law promoted by the Egyptian and French delegations. Unable to find an agreement on victims' participation between the systems of civil law and common law, the drafters decided to align Article 68(3) with the standards of the Declaration for Victims of Crime, which 'reflects the collective will of the international community to restore the balance between the fundamental rights of suspects and offenders, and the rights and interests of victims'.[61]

A closer look at Principle 6(b) sheds light on its modest contribution to the establishment of a well-defined model of victims' participation in international criminal proceedings. The drafters did not consider the important caveat contained in Principle 6(b), according to which victims should be allowed to present their views and concerns in a way 'consistent with the relevant national criminal justice system'. The subordination of Principle 6(b) to domestic criminal law means that it was not created to operate as a self-executing norm. The rights of victims enshrined in the Declaration for Victims of Crime are contingent on the domestic law of States, since the elaboration of a detailed victims' participation scheme is explicitly a prerogative of national legislators. Thus, this uncritical borrowing of Principle 6(b) demonstrated that 'drafters to all appearance did not intend anything specific in terms of exact rationales for the victim participation'.[62]

In absence of provisions that clearly indicate the nature and admissible manner of victims' participation, the challenging task of determining the procedural scheme is left to the Judges, by means of judicial determination. The Chambers are required to determine the several unknowns of this equation, advancing

59 'Proposal by New Zealand on Article 43' (1997b) Non-Paper/WG.4/No.19 <legal-tools.org/doc/658b45/pdf/> accessed 2 March 2022, para 3.

60 See Article 43(3), Preparatory Committee on the Establishment of an International Criminal Court, 'Decisions Taken by the Preparatory Committee at Its Session Held from 4 to 15 August 1997' (1997a) A/Ac.249/1997/L.8/Rev.1 <digitallibrary.un.org/record/243787?ln=en> accessed 2 March 2022.

61 UN Office for Drug Control and Crime Prevention, 'Guide for Policy Makers on the Implementation of the United Nations Declaration of Basic Principles of Justice for Victims of Crime and Abuse of Power' (1999) UNDCP/ODCCP(09)/V642 1.

62 Vasiliev (n 31) 651.

solutions to issues concerning the scope of victims' procedural rights, which has resulted in experimentalism and inconsistencies across different Chambers.[63] Besides the above-described modality of victims' participation explicitly provided in the RS and RPE, the different Chambers developed another category of victims' procedural rights, those detailed by the different Trial Chambers. This category of victims' procedural rights includes: the right to challenge admissibility or relevance of parties' evidence; the possibility for victims to introduce or produce evidence; the right to attend and participate in closed and *ex parte* hearings; witnesses may be called by the Chamber at victims' request; and the right to file *ex parte* or confidential written submissions. The following sections will examine in detail the modalities of victims' participation in the different stages of the proceedings, namely, the investigation, pre-trial, and trial stages. Special attention is given to how the practice of the ICC has expanded or restricted the scope of victims' procedural rights.

8.5 Victims' participation at the investigation stage of a situation

Article 42 of the RS manifestly recognises that the authority to initiate and conduct investigations lies with the Office of the Prosecutor (OTP). Despite the fact that victims do not have a right to make 'a formal report of a crime (…) which automatically triggers an investigation',[64] under Article 15 of the RS, they are allowed to submit a communication to the Prosecutor concerning potential situations and cases. Having closely followed a situation, if the Prosecutor concludes that there is a reasonable basis to proceed with an investigation, he/she needs to seeks authorisation from the Pre-Trial Chamber to exercise his/her *proprio motu* powers. In this eventuality, once the victims known to the Prosecutor or to the Victims and Witnesses Unit have been notified by the Prosecutor,[65] Article 15(3) of the RS explicitly confers on victims the statutory right to make a written representation to the Pre-Trial Chamber, which can discretionally request additional information from these victims and, if it considers it necessary, have a hearing in order to hear their views and concerns.[66] In the situation in the Republic of Kenya, which was the first investigation was initiated by the Prosecutor *proprio motu*, the Pre-Trial Chamber II considered the impact of the crimes on victims and the harm caused to them and their families to be an important factor when examining the gravity threshold. The Judges concluded that victims' representations had

63 Sergey Vasiliev, 'Victim Participation Revisited: What the ICC Is Learning About Itself' in Carsten Stahn, *The Law and Practice of the International Criminal Court* (Oxford University Press 2015) 1146.

64 Cryer et al. (n 7) 488.

65 Rules 50(1) and (4), 92(2), Rules of Procedure and Evidence of the International Criminal Court.

66 Rules 50(3) and (4), ibid.

backed up their findings to the extent that it broadened the temporal scope of investigation beyond the Prosecutor's original request.[67]

With regard to victims' participation under Article 68(3) of the RS in the investigation stage of a situation (before the Prosecutor identifies a defendant), the practice of the ICC has shown a heterogeneous approach. In the situation in the DRC, the Pre-Trial Chamber I had to face issues concerning victims' access to justice for the first time. On 26 May, 2005, the legal representative of six alleged victims submitted applications to allow the views and concerns of those victims to be presented and considered at the investigation stage, pursuant to Article 68(3) of the Statute. In its first decision on victims' participation, the Pre-Trial Chamber I was requested to answer three important questions: whether the RS and the RPE accord victims the right to participate at the investigation stage; whether the conditions of application of Article 68(3) are fulfilled during the investigation stage and, if so, what modalities such participation should take.

Concerning the first question, the Pre-Trial Chamber I, relying on terminological, contextual and teleological standpoints, concluded that at the investigation stage victims had 'a general right of access to the Court'.[68] From a terminological perspective, the Pre-Trial Chamber I provided a number of examples where the Statute's provisions include the stage of investigation within the meaning of the terms 'proceedings' and '*la procédure*'.[69] With regard to the contextual argument, the Pre-Trial Chamber observed that paragraph 1 of Article 68 – which imposes on the Court the obligation to take appropriate measures to protect victims and witnesses – refers to the investigation stage and that paragraph 3 of the same article does not contain any explicit exclusion of victims' participation from the investigation stage.[70] The teleological argument presented by the Pre-Trial Chamber I held that the application of Article 68(3) to the investigation stage is consistent with the object and purpose of the victims' participation regime, which ensued from the *dicta* of both the ECtHR and IACtHR. These international bodies of human rights have interpreted the respective provisions on the right to access to a judicial process as granting victims certain participatory rights at the investigation stage and prior to confirmation of the charges.[71]

67 *Situation in the Republic of Kenya* (Decision Pursuant to Article 15 of the Rome Statute on the Authorization of an Investigation into the Situation in the Republic of Kenya) ICC-01/09-19, Pre-Trial Chamber II (31 March 2010), paras 62, 196, 203–207. See also *Situation in the Republic of Côte d'Ivoire* (Decision Pursuant to Article 15 of the Rome Statute on the Authorisation of an Investigation into the Situation in the Republic of Côte d'Ivoire) ICC-02/11-14, Pre-Trial Chamber III (3 October 2011), para 8.

68 *Situation in the Democratic Republic of the Congo* (Decision on the Applications for participation in the proceedings of VPRS 1, VPRS 2, VPRS 3, VPRS 4, VPRS 5 and VPRS 6 (Public Redacted Version)) ICC-01/04, Pre-Trial Chamber I (19 January 2006), para 23.

69 ibid, paras 32–38.

70 ibid, para 45.

71 ibid, para 50–53.

In addressing the second issue, the Pre-Trial Chamber I gave leave to victims' participation during the stage of investigation because the two conditions for such participation, set in Article 68(3), are fulfilled. Victims' interests are affected in general at the investigation stage because, although at this stage the proceedings are not related to specific crimes, the participation of victims can serve to clarify the facts and to identify the perpetrators of crimes.[72] The participation of victims during the investigation stage is appropriate, since it does not *per se* jeopardise the integrity, objectivity, efficiency, and security of the investigation.[73] The Pre-Trial Chamber I answered the third question by interpreting Article 68(3) as imposing a twofold positive obligation on the Court vis-à-vis victims: to permit victims to concretely and effectively present their views and concerns and to examine them. Specifically, victims can address the Chamber in order to present their views and concerns, to file documents pertaining to the current investigation, to access public documents and request the Pre-Trial Chamber I to order specific measures.[74]

This first decision on victims' participation was particularly encouraging because it emphasised the important role that victims can play from the early stage in the proceedings. In deciding the situations in Uganda, the DRC, and Darfur, the Pre-Trial Chambers continued along the path laid out, conferring upon victims a general right to participate at the investigation stage.[75] They acknowledged that it is in this phase that the decisions that are most important to the victims are made. The decision to open a formal investigation, the choice of the defendants to be prosecuted, the events to be investigated, the confirmation of charges and the admissibility or not of a case all have major consequences for victims' participation in the proceedings.[76] By presenting their views and concerns and filing documents pertaining to the investigation, victims are able to make a meaningful contribution to shaping the narrative and identifying and punishing the perpetrators.

The Prosecutor appealed the first decision on victims' participation in the DRC situation and his grounds were upheld by the Appeals Chamber, which

72 ibid, paras 63, 72.

73 ibid, para 57.

74 ibid, para 71.

75 *Situation in the Democratic Republic of the Congo* (Corrigendum to the "Decision on the Applications for Participation Filed in Connection with the Investigation in the Democratic Republic of the Congo by a/0004/06 et al) ICC-01/04, Pre-Trial Chamber I (31 January 2008), paras 4–5; *Situation in Uganda* (Decision on victims' applications for participation a/0010/06 et al) ICC-02/04, Pre-Trial Chamber II (10 August 2007), paras 102–103; *Situation in Darfur, Sudan* (Corrigendum to Decision on the Applications for Participation in the Proceedings of Applicants a/0011/06 et al) ICC-02/05, Pre-Trial Chamber I (14 December 2007), paras 45–47.

76 Luc Walleyn, 'Victims' Participation in ICC Proceedings: Challenges Ahead' (2016) 16 International Criminal Law Review 995, 999; Luke Moffett, 'Meaningful and Effective? Considering Victims' Interests Through Participation at the International Criminal Court' (2015) 26 Criminal Law Forum 255, 270–271.

considered the arguments of the Pre-Trial Chamber I granting victims the general right to participate in the investigation stage ill-founded on several grounds.[77] First, the wording of Article 68(3), referring to victims' participation in 'proceedings', does not include the investigation stage, which is not a judicial proceeding, but an inquiry conducted by the Prosecutor into the commission of a crime.[78] Second, the Appeals Chamber rejected the broad concept of victims' personal interests, previously elaborated by the Pre-Trial Chamber I. Victims' personal interests are affected by a specific issue, legal or factual, arising at the stage in hand, rather than by the entire proceedings. Whether or not the personal interests of victims are affected in relation to particular proceedings will require an assessment on a case-by-case basis.[79] This means that victims can only be allowed to request authorisation to participate in those specific procedural activities that the Chamber identified as having a direct impact on their personal interests. Third, acknowledging that Article 68(3) grants victims the right to participate in any proceedings jeopardises the domain and powers of the Prosecutor, as outlined in Article 42 of the RS, which manifestly recognised that the authority to conduct investigations lies with the Prosecutor.[80] The approach of the Appeals Chamber represents a step back for victims' right to participate in the proceedings, as it considerably downsizes the role of victims, as although they still have an input at the investigation stage, their role is more to inform than to participate.

Following the decision by the Appeals Chamber, Pre-Trial Chambers in the DRC, Kenya, Libya, and Uganda situations established a new framework for victims participating in the investigation stage of a situation. These Pre-Trial Chambers implemented the casuistic approach adopted by the Appeals Chamber and determined in application of Article 68(3) that victims could participate at the investigation stage only within specific judicial proceedings.[81] According to the Pre-Trial Chambers, the RS and RPE envisage different judicial proceedings at the situation stage of an investigation, like those connected to the review by

77 *Situation in the Democratic Republic of the Congo* (Judgement on victim participation in the investigation stage of the proceedings in the appeal of the OPCD against the decision of Pre-Trial Chamber I of 7 December 2007 and in the appeals of the OPCD and the Prosecutor against the decision of Pre-Trial) ICC-01/04, Appeals Chamber (19 December 2008), para 3.

78 ibid, para 45.

79 ibid, para 28.

80 ibid, para 52.

81 *Situation in the Republic of Kenya* (Decision on Victims' Participation in Proceedings Related to the Situation in the Republic of Kenya) ICC-01/09–24, Pre-Trial Chamber II (3 November 2010), para 16; *Situation in the Democratic Republic of the Congo* (Decision on Victims' Participation in Proceedings Relating to the Situation in the Democratic Republic of Congo) ICC-02/04, Pre-Trial Chamber I (11 April 2011), para 9; *Situation in Libya* (Decision on Victim's Participation in Proceedings Related to the Situation in Libya) ICC-01/11, Pre-Trial Chamber I (24 January 2012) 3–4; *Situation in Uganda* (Decision on Victim's Participation in Proceedings Related to the Situation in Uganda) ICC-02/04, Pre-Trial Chamber II (9 March 2012), para 10.

the Pre-Trial Chamber of a decision by the Prosecutor not to proceed with an investigation or prosecution (Article 53); the preservation of evidence or the protection and privacy of victims and witnesses (Article 57(3)(c)); and the preservation of evidence in the context of a unique investigative opportunity (Article 56 (3)).[82] Consequently, victims are allowed to participate in these judicial proceedings once they have demonstrated that their interests are affected.[83] Moreover, under Rule 93, the Chamber can seek the views of victims on any issue and, as a result, victims can be entitled to participate in judicial proceedings by presenting their views at the investigation stage of a situation.[84]

8.5.1 Evaluation

The decisions that are examined above can be read as upholding an expressivist justice model. The Pre-Trial Chambers emphasised the important role that victims can play from the early stages of the proceedings, acknowledging that the decisions that are most important for the victims are made in this phase. The decision to open a formal investigation, the choice of the defendants to be prosecuted, the events to be investigated, the confirmation of charges, and the admissibility or not of a case all have major consequences for victims' participation in the proceedings. Victims' voices can influence whether there is a reasonable basis for investigation and a sufficient basis for prosecuting individual(s) for specific crimes. The Pre-Trial Chambers gave victims a general right to participate at the investigation stage, allowing them to present their views and concerns and file documents pertaining to the investigation, acknowledging their significant contribution to shaping the trial's narrative and identifying and punishing the perpetrators. This is in accordance with the expressivist justice paradigm which focuses on victims as crucial actors in the trial, who play a fundamental role in the crafting of authoritative truths about past atrocities and reaffirming the importance of human rights.

It important to observe that the approach of the Appeals Chamber considerably diminished the role of victims at this stage. Nevertheless, victims' input at the investigation stage can still enhance the legitimacy of international criminal justice. The position of the Appeals Chamber upholding the role of the prosecution as the sole organ to conduct investigation means that the Prosecutor should be independent, but, at the same time, he/she should be accountable when he/she exercises his/her discretionary powers. In this regard, Article 54(1)(c) of the RS, which requires the Prosecutor to 'fully respect the rights of persons arising

82 *Situation in the Democratic Republic of the Congo* (n 81), para 10; *Situation in the Republic of Kenya* (n 81), para 12; *Situation in Libya* (n 81) 3; *Situation in Uganda* (n 81), para 12.
83 *Situation in the Democratic Republic of the Congo* (n 81), para 10; *Situation in the Republic of Kenya* (n 81), para 12; *Situation in Libya* (n 81) 3; *Situation in Uganda* (n 81), para 12.
84 *Situation in the Democratic Republic of the Congo* (n 81), para 10; *Situation in the Republic of Kenya* (n 81), para 12; *Situation in Libya* (n 81) 3; *Situation in Uganda* (n 81), para 12.

under [the] Statute', would imply that the Prosecutor should balance the prosecutorial discretion with the respect and protection of the rights of victims and defendants. This seems to be consistent with the expressivist goals, as the Appeals Chamber acknowledged that victims' role at the investigation stage of a situation may have a very important impact on the core of the ICC's substantive operation.

8.6 Victims' participation at the pre-trial stage of a case

The pre-trial stage of a case begins when a suspect is singled out upon the expedition of an arrest warrant or a summons to appear.[85] At this stage, the focus of the proceedings is directed towards specific individuals and crimes allegedly committed and, therefore, victims should have an interest in expressing their views and concerns on matters like the scope of the indictments. However, in the situation in the Republic of Kenya, victims were excluded from participation in proceedings under Article 58 of the RS related to the issuance by the Pre-Trial Chamber III of a warrant of arrest because such 'proceedings that are to be conducted with the exclusive participation of one party (…) are, by definition, not "appropriate" for the purposes of victims' participation'.[86] With regard to the initial appearance of a suspect, in *Ruto et al.*, the Pre-Trial Chamber II held that the participation of victims would not have been appropriate because this would go beyond the scope and purpose of the initial appearance, which consists of informing the suspects of the charges and their rights under the ICC Statute.[87] Therefore, although victims can indirectly influence the charges of the arrest warrants by giving information to the Prosecutor, they have a very limited influence over the initial charges brought against a suspect. In a similar manner, victims' influence during the confirmation of the charges is constrained only by the crimes included in the charges brought against that suspect.

An example of the limited understanding of the potential of the role of victims as active participants in proceedings related to the issuance of a warrant of arrest is portrayed by the narrow approach to charges in *Lubanga*. The accused was charged with the offence of enlisting and conscripting children under the age of 15 years and using them to participate actively in both international and non-international hostilities.[88] Indeed, this showed the commitment of the ICC to condemn and put an end to this kind of heinous crime, but the prosecutor failed to take into consideration many offences that Mr Lubanga allegedly committed in the DRC. Victims expressed their indignation at the limited set of charges, which did not

85 Article 58, Rome Statute of the International Criminal Court.

86 *Situation in the Republic of Kenya* (Decision on a Request for Leave to Appeal) ICC-01/09, Pre-Trial Chamber III (11 February 2011), paras 9, 13.

87 *Prosecutor v William Samoei Ruto et al.* (Decision on the Motion by Legal Representative of Victim Applicants to Participate in Initial Appearance Proceedings) ICC-01/09–01/11, Pre-Trial Chamber II (30 March 2011), para 6.

88 *Prosecutor v Thomas Lubanga Dyilo* (Decision on the confirmation of charges) ICC-01/04–01/06, Pre-Trial Chamber I (29 January 2007), para 156.

mirror the events they experienced.[89] Despite the widespread documentation of gender-based crimes, including rape, sexual violence, and sexual slavery,[90] such crimes were not effectively investigated in the *Lubanga* case. On the grounds of prosecutorial discretion, the Prosecutor decided to focus on charges of recruitment and use of child soldiers, closing the door to the participation of victims of gender-based crimes. In a later decision, the Trial Chamber I seemed to broaden the narrow approach to the charges of the Prosecutor, since it affirmed that it would give greater consideration to the allegations of rape, sexual violence, and sexual slavery for the purposes of sentencing and reparations.[91] This may open up some recognition of the sufferings of victims of gender-based crimes, but it is hard to reconcile this opening of the Trial Chamber I with the concept of victims as an important actor in the international criminal proceedings.

With regard to the modalities of victims' participation during the pre-trial stage, Judge Sylvia Steiner, sitting as a Single Judge for the Pre-Trial Chamber I of *Katanga and Chui*, rejected the use of a casuistic approach to determine the procedural rights, which those who are granted the status of victim at the pre-trial stage can exercise.[92] This approach, which required a case-by-case analysis to evaluate the relationship between victims' personal interests and a particular procedural step or activity during the proceedings, caused significant delays in the proceedings, greatly limited the role of victims and, as result, contributed to the uncertainty over which participatory rights victims can exercise.[93] The Single Judge preferred to opt for a systematic approach, which consisted of two features. First, it entailed the development of the definition of victims' personal interests affected, pursuant to Article 68(3), and second, a clear determination of the set of procedural rights granted to victims at the pre-trial stage.[94]

89 ASF, Center for Justice and Reconciliation, DRC Coalition for the ICC, FIDH, HRW, REDRESS, and the Women's Initiative for Gender Justice, 'DR Congo: ICC Charges Raise Concern, Joint letter to the Chief Prosecutor of the International Criminal Court' (31 July 2006) https://www.hrw.org/news/2006/07/31/dr-congo-icc-charges-raise-concern accessed 3 June 2022.

90 Kofi A Annan, 'Letter Dated 16 July 2004 from the Secretary-General Addressed to the President of the Security Council' (July 2004) <un.org/en/ga/search/view_doc.asp?symbol=S/2004/573> accessed 24 January 2022, para 80; UN General Assembly, 'Report of the International Criminal Court' (2005) A/60/177, para 37; Assembly of States Parties, 'Report on the Activities of the Court' (2005) ICC-ASP/4/16, para 53; Amnesty International, 'Democratic Republic of Congo – Mass Rape: Time for Remedies' (2004) AFR 62/018/2004 <amnesty.org/en/documents/afr62/018/2004/en/> accessed 24 January 2022; Human Rights Watch, 'Seeking Justice: The Prosecution of Sexual Violence in the Congo War' (2005) <hrw.org/reports/2005/drc0305/drc0305.pdf>.

91 *Prosecutor v Thomas Lubanga Dyilo* (Judgement pursuant to Article 74 of the Statute) ICC-01/04-01/06, Trial Chamber I (14 March 2012), paras 630–631.

92 *Prosecutor v Germain Katanga and Mathieu Ngudjolo Chui* (Decision on the Set of Procedural Rights Attached to Procedural Status of Victim at the Pre-Trial Stage of the Case) ICC-01/04-01/07, Pre-Trial Chamber I (13 May 2008), para 49.

93 ibid, para 48.

94 ibid, para 49.

The concept of victims' interests elaborated by Judge Steiner is consistent with the key values of expressivism because it recognised that victims' central interests in the outcome of such proceedings, the clarification of the events that occurred and bridging the potential gaps between the factual findings resulting from the criminal proceedings and the actual truth are based on 'the well-established right to the truth for the victims of serious violations of human rights'.[95] Thus, the determination of the guilt or innocence of the defendant 'also affects the core interests of those granted the procedural status of victim in any case before the Court, because this issue is closely linked to the satisfaction of their right to justice'.[96] It follows that the interests of victims are affected under Article 68(3) by the stages of the proceedings, rather than by each specific procedural activity at a given stage of the proceedings, including the pre-trial stage. This specific stage of the proceedings aims to ascertain whether the evidence presented provided sufficient grounds to presume that the suspects are responsible for the charges brought against them.[97]

The most relevant contribution of the systematic approach embraced by Judge Steiner is the formulation of a set of victims' procedural rights, since it envisaged the pre-trial stage as a vehicle for norm expression, which contributes to the important goal of giving a voice to victims. In the first instance, Judge Steiner analysed the procedural rights of victims at the pre-trial stage in domestic systems of criminal justice of the Romano-Germanic tradition and their relationship to the rights of the accused and the fair and impartial trial principle. She concluded that the respect of the accused's rights and of the principle of a fair and impartial trial was not dependent on the adoption at a national level of a specific model of victims' participation in criminal proceedings, but on the existence of sufficient safeguards to ensure that the defendants' rights can be satisfied through the relevant national criminal proceedings.[98] Those safeguards required a criminal justice system to be based on a comprehensive investigation, where the Prosecutor investigates the incriminating and exculpatory evidence and the case file created by the investigative body is placed at the disposal of the Defence and of those granted the procedural status of victim, after the completion of the investigation.[99] Secondly, she drew heavily on the internationally recognised standards concerning the rights of victims of serious violations of human rights to truth and justice. She observed that the jurisprudence of the European and Inter-American Courts of Human Rights never found that procedural rights of victims in the pre-trial stage constitute *per se* a violation of internationally recognised standards of the rights of the accused and of the fair and impartial trial principle.[100] In light of

95 ibid, paras 32 and 34.
96 ibid, para 42.
97 ibid, para 45.
98 ibid, paras 73–75.
99 ibid, paras 62–63.
100 ibid, paras 52–75.

this, Judge Steiner identified six groups of specific procedural rights for victims pursuant to Article 68(3) of the RS.[101] The following paragraphs discuss these six groups as identified by the Pre-Trial Chamber I's decision in *Katanga and Ngudjolo Chui*, integrating the analysis with developments in later decisions.

The first group embraced the right to be notified and to have access, prior to and during the confirmation hearing, to the record of the case kept by the Registry, including to the evidence filed by the prosecution and the Defence and to all filings and decisions contained in the record of the case.[102] Although this right includes access to all filings and decisions in the case record regardless of their classification as public or confidential, as well as access to the transcripts of public and closed hearings, it does not include the access to *ex parte* filings, decisions and hearings' transcripts.[103] In a following decision, the Pre-Trial Chamber I clarified that only the legal representatives of the non-anonymous victims are granted access to the confidential part of the case record and, consequently, they cannot transmit to their clients copies of any document or evidence in the confidential part of the case record and closed session hearing transcripts.[104] That said, victims are entitled to be notified in the same manner as the prosecution and Defence of all decisions and documents which are filed in the record of the case and are not classified *ex parte*.[105] However, different Pre-Trial Chambers limited this first group of procedural rights. In *Bemba*, Pre-Trial Chamber III granted victims access to all public decisions, transcripts, documents and evidence in the case record, except those that were *ex parte* and confidential.[106] In *Ruto et al.*, the Pre-Trial Chamber II affirmed that victims' access to confidential decisions, filings, and evidence should be determined on a case-by-case basis.[107] Granting victims access to all confidential material would contravene the exceptional nature of a request to access confidential material. Hence, victims' requests to access confidential material pursuant to Article 68(3) should cover only the specific material the parties intend to rely on at confirmation of charges hearings.[108]

The second group of procedural rights conferred upon victims the right to submit observations concerning the admissibility and probative value of the evidence, which the prosecution and the Defence intend to present at the

101 ibid, paras 126–127.
102 ibid, para 127.
103 ibid, paras 127–128, 130.
104 *Prosecutor v Germain Katanga and Mathieu Ngudjolo Chui* (Decision on Limitations of Set of Procedural Rights for Non-Anonymous Victims) ICC-01/04–01/07, Pre-Trial Chamber I (30 May 2008), paras 22–26.
105 *Prosecutor v Germain Katanga and Mathieu Ngudjolo Chui* (n 92), para 129.
106 *Prosecutor v Jean-Pierre Bemba Gombo* (Fourth Decision on Victims' Participation) ICC-01/05–01/08, Pre-Trial Chamber III (12 December 2008), paras 103–105.
107 *Prosecutor v William Samoei Ruto et al.* (Second Decision on the 'Request by the Victims' Representative to Access to Confidential Materials') ICC-01/09–01/11, Pre-Trial Chamber II (23 September 2011), paras 9–17.
108 *Prosecutor v William Samoei Ruto et al.* (Decision on the 'Request by the Victims' Representative for Access to Confidential Materials') ICC-01/09–01/11, Pre-Trial Chamber II (21 September 2011), para 10.

confirmation hearing and, consequently, the right to examine such evidence.[109] The Single Judge remarked that the prosecution is the organ primarily in charge of conducting the investigation of the situations and of every case arising out of the situations under investigation[110] and, thus, 'granting investigative powers, independent from those of the Prosecution, to (…) victim[s] would not be consistent with the procedural system embraced by the Statute and the Rules'.[111] Accordingly, at the confirmation hearing, victims' participation should be limited to the submission of observations concerning the evidence the prosecution and the Defences rely on. Furthermore, because of the limited scope, object, and purpose of confirmation hearings, as defined by the RS, victims admitted to participate at this stage cannot introduce additional evidence not intended to be relied on by the parties.[112]

In *Bemba*, victims were able to make succinct submissions to specific issues of law and fact once they had proved that their interests were affected by the issue under examination and the Chamber had regarded their application as appropriate.[113] Moreover, in this decision, the Pre-Trial Chamber III did not distinguish between anonymous and non-anonymous victims, holding that anonymous victims have the right to make submissions on law and fact. The Single Judge stated that no differentiation should be made between anonymous and non-anonymous victims because this kind of divide can potentially be to the detriment of those victims applying for protective measures.[114] Similarly, in *Ruto et al.*, Pre-Trial Chamber II confirmed that the possibility for anonymous victims to make submissions on the evidential foundation of the parties does not *per se* prejudice the accused's right. A determination on this issue is made by the Chamber on a case-by-case basis taking into account victims' personal interests, the scope of the procedural right requested and the fairness and expeditiousness of the proceedings.[115]

The third group of procedural rights concerned the victim's right to examine the witnesses called by the Prosecutor or the Defence at the confirmation hearing.[116] The Pre-Trial Chamber specified that this right is applicable to non-anonymous victims only, in compliance with the principle of prohibiting anonymous accusations.[117] This orientation was followed in *Abu Garda*,[118] whereas in *Ruto et al.* the Pre-Trial Chamber II preferred to adopt a case-by-case determi-

109 *Prosecutor v Germain Katanga and Mathieu Ngudjolo Chui* (n 92), para 134.
110 ibid, para 82.
111 ibid, para 83.
112 ibid, paras 17, 101–102.
113 *Prosecutor v Jean-Pierre Bemba Gombo* (n 106), para 110.
114 ibid, para 99.
115 *Prosecutor v William Samoei Ruto et al.* (Decision on Victims' Participation at the Confirmation of Charges Hearing and in the Related Proceedings) ICC-01/09–01/11, Pre-Trial Chamber II (5 August 2011), para 126.
116 *Prosecutor v Germain Katanga and Mathieu Ngudjolo Chui* (n 92), paras 137–138.
117 ibid, paras 136–137.
118 *Prosecutor v Bahar Idriss Abu Gaiuda* (Decision on Victims' Modalities of Participation at the Pre-Trial Stage of the Case) ICC-02/05–02/09, Pre-Trial Chamber I (6 October 2009), paras 23–24.

nation, considering victims' personal interests, the scope of the procedural right requested, and the fairness and expeditiousness of the proceedings.[119]

The fourth group included the right to attend all public and closed hearings leading to and during the confirmation hearing, with the exception of those hearings held *ex parte.*[120] In *Bemba*, victims' participation was limited to the attendance at public hearings,[121] whereas in *Gbagbo*, the Pre-Trial Chamber I concluded that in the event that parts of the confirmation hearing are held in camera or *ex parte*, 'it retains the option to decide, on a case-by-case basis, whether to authorise, *proprio motu* or upon a motivated request, the Common Legal Representative to attend those sessions'.[122]

The fifth group includes the right to participate through oral motions, responses and submissions in all those hearings in which those granted the procedural status of victim have the right to attend concerning all matters, excluding those in which their intervention has been excluded by the Statute and the Rules.[123] Although the victims' right to participate at the confirmation hearing cannot be extended to the factual basis included in the prosecution's Charging Document,[124] victims can try to extend the legal characterisation of the facts.[125] In the view of the Single Judge, upon request of the Pre-Trial Chamber, the prosecution should consider amending the legal characterisation of the facts.[126] This is in line with what was decided in *Lubanga*, where the Pre-Trial Chamber I established that victims during the confirmation of charges hearing could, in their opening and closing statements, address any point of law,[127] but they were not able to add any point of fact.[128] In *Bemba*, the Single Judge recognised that victims should be entitled to make succinct oral submissions on issues of law and fact raised during the confirmation hearing. Such participatory right is granted based on a case-by-case approach, as the Single Judge pointed out that victims have to successfully demonstrate that their specific personal interests were affected by a specific issue of law or fact.[129]

119 *Prosecutor v William Samoei Ruto et al.* (n 115), para 126.

120 *Prosecutor v Germain Katanga and Mathieu Ngudjolo Chui* (n 92), para 140.

121 *Prosecutor v Jean-Pierre Bemba Gombo* (n 106), para 101.

122 *Prosecutor v Laurent Gbagbo* (Decision on Victims' Participation and Victims' Common Legal Representation at the Confirmation of Charges Hearing and in the Related Proceedings) ICC-02/11–01/11, Pre-Trial Chamber I (4 June 2012), para 50.

123 *Prosecutor v Germain Katanga and Mathieu Ngudjolo Chui* (n 92), para 141.

124 ibid, para 122.

125 ibid, para 123.

126 ibid, para 123.

127 *Prosecutor v Thomas Lubanga Dyilo* (Decision on the Schedule and Conduct of the Confirmation Hearing) ICC-01/04–01/06, Pre-Trial Chamber I (7 November 2006) 7.

128 *Prosecutor v Thomas Lubanga Dyilo* (Decision on the Arrangements for Participation of Victims a/0001/06, a/0002/06 and a/0003/06 at the Confirmation Hearing) ICC-01/04–01/06, Pre-Trial Chamber I (22 September 2006) 6–7.

129 *Prosecutor v Germain Katanga and Mathieu Ngudjolo Chui* (n 92), paras 108–110.

The last group of victims' participatory rights included the right to file written motions, responses, and replies concerning all matters other than those in which the victim's intervention has been excluded by the Statute and the Rules.[130] According to the Single Judge, the sixth group of rights includes the right to file written submissions to the Pre-Trial Chamber on evidentiary and legal issues to be discussed at the confirmation hearing and make observations or raise objections on issues concerning the proper conduct of the proceedings prior to the confirmation hearing, as set in Rule 122(3) of the RPE.[131]

8.6.1 Evaluation

The decisions of the Pre-Trial Chambers have the merit of emphasising the importance of victims' contribution to ascertaining the truth. From this point of view, these decisions can be read as enhancing the basic values of the expressivist framework of criminal justice, which orientates the interpretation of the provisions on victims' participation. As seen, victims' participation at the pre-trial stage of a case has transpired to be more active and significant than during the investigation stage of a situation. In *Katanga and Ngudjolo Chui*, the Pre-Trial Chamber I found victims to have a right to participate in the determination of issues affecting the guilt or innocence of an accused because they have an interest in the truth, which corresponds to the confirmation of charges. However, victims were not allowed to introduce evidence on the accused's guilt, since the Pre-Trial Chamber explicitly remarked that 'we cannot allow a second Prosecutor in this process'.[132]

The set of procedural rights for victims' participation at the pre-trial stage granted victims a meaningful role in criminal proceedings. The systematic approach to victims' participation has the great merit of establishing a core of participatory rights for victims, and, consequently, enhancing the guarantee of legal certainty to all parties and participants in the proceedings. It also ensures that those procedural rights are meaningful rather than purely symbolic and, at the same time, systematically consistent with the main features of the proceedings at the pre-trial stage.[133] However, the systematic approach represents an exception to the case-by-case approach, which has been largely adopted in early decisions of Pre-Trial Chambers I and III. The case-by-case approach has been an ineluctable path for the Court since the beginning of its operation and, to a certain extent, has contributed to the development of its case law.[134] It has been

130 ibid, para 142.

131 ibid, para 143.

132 *Prosecutor v Germain Katanga and Mathieu Ngudjolo Chui* (Transcripts) ICC-01/04-01/07 (15 July 2008) 70.

133 *Prosecutor v Germain Katanga and Mathieu Ngudjolo Chui* (n 92), para 51.

134 Brianne McGonigle Leyh, 'Victim-Oriented Measures at International Criminal Institutions: Participation and Its Pitfalls' (2012) 12 International Criminal Law Review 375, 404.

regarded as a rather flexible method, which effectively ensures the protection of the defendant's right to a fair trial.[135] Nevertheless, such an approach can be a double-edged sword. The lack of harmonisation changes the nature of victims' participatory rights, which seem to have become the characteristic of a privilege, as the conferral of rights depends on the specific factual circumstances of the case and upon judicial discretion in every proceeding. From the expressivist viewpoint, victims' participation reaffirms the importance of safeguarding basic standards of human rights and, specifically, granting victims a general right to fairness. When victims' views and concerns are not effectively heard because their participation relies essentially on the exercise of the Chamber's discretion, fairness to victims is no more than an abstract concept. *Mutatis mutandis* the case-by-case approach can have a prejudicial impact on the Defence as well. The lack of harmonisation jeopardises the defendant's right to legal certainty. When the rules are not sufficiently clear and precise, it is hard to maintain an acceptable degree of predictability of the possible outcome of decisions.[136]

8.7 Victims' participation at the trial stage

As previously observed, both the RS and the RPE left gaps with regard to the provisions for victims' participation, conferring upon the Judges wide discretion in shaping victims' procedural rights in practice. Judges were believed to be in the best position to provide greater clarification, but, in reality, they undoubtedly struggled to provide a harmonised approach to victims' participation. However, the following analysis of the Judges' interpretation of the provisions concerning the procedural rights of victims illustrates that it is possible to identify some elements consistent with the expressivist justice model.

8.7.1 The right to notification and access to documents

Under Rule 92, victims or their legal representatives participating in proceedings should be notified by the Registrar in a timely manner of the proceedings, requests, submissions, motions, and other documents. In *Lubanga*, with regard to the right to access documents, the Trial Chamber I held that, as a general rule, participating victims are entitled to consult the record of the proceedings and public filings, with the exception of confidential filings concerning sensitive information related to national security, protection of witnesses and victims, and the prosecution's investigations.[137] However, if the confidential filings are of

135 Anni Pues, 'A Victim's Right to a Fair Trial at the International Criminal Court?: Reflections on Article 68(3)' (2015) 13 Journal of International Criminal Justice 951, 963.

136 Salvatore Zappalà, 'The Rights of Victims v. the Rights of the Accused' (2010) 8 Journal of International Criminal Justice 137, 138.

137 *Prosecutor v Thomas Lubanga Dyilo* (Decision on victims' participation) ICC-01/04–01/06, Trial Chamber I (18 January 2008), para 105.

relevance to victims' personal interests, the Trial Chamber I will consider providing this information to the relevant victims, as long as this would not breach protective measures.[138] In a following decision, the Trial Chamber I set up a mechanism whereby victims' legal representatives could be provided with any material in the possession of the prosecution considered to affect victims' personal interests.[139] This mechanism was dealt with by victims' legal representatives and the Prosecutor *inter se*,[140] as the former have to identify the victims' personal interests and the nature of the information in the possession of the prosecution, while the latter has to identify whether the material in his/her possession is relevant.[141] A filing before the competent Chamber should therefore only be made in the event of a disagreement.[142] In *Katanga and Chui*, the Trial Chamber II turned down the request by victims' legal representatives to adopt the same mechanism of access to documents adopted in *Lubanga*, holding that it would assess on a case-by-case basis whether victims' access to documents and material in the possession of the Prosecutor was necessary to guarantee their effective participation according to Article 68(3) of the RS.[143] Moreover, the Trial Chamber II only allowed legal representatives to access confidential materials, excluding, *de facto*, victims.[144] In *Bemba*, the Trial Chamber III took a different approach, making it possible for victims to access confidential material subject to a case-by-case evaluation by the Chamber.[145]

8.7.2 Participation in public hearings

Under Rule 91(2), victims are entitled to attend and participate in public hearings. With regard to victims' participation in closed and *ex parte* hearings, the practice of the Trial Chambers provided a mixed picture. In *Lubanga*, the Trial Chamber I stated that, upon its discretion, victims' participation can encompass

138 ibid, para 106.

139 *Prosecutor v Thomas Lubanga Dyilo* (Decision on the legal representative's request for clarification of the Trial Chamber's 18 January 2008 'Decision on victims' participation') ICC-01/04–01/06, Trial Chamber I (2 June 2008), para 31.

140 ibid, para 34.

141 ibid, para 31.

142 ibid, para 34.

143 *Prosecutor v Germain Katanga and Mathieu Ngudjolo Chui* (Transcripts) ICC-01/04–01/07, (21 April 2011) p. 4, lines 16–25; p. 5, lines 1–11.

144 *Prosecutor v Germain Katanga and Mathieu Ngudjolo Chui* (Decision on the Modalities of Victim Participation at Trial) ICC-01/04–01/07, Trial Chamber II (22 January 2010), paras 121–123.

145 *Prosecutor v Jean-Pierre Bemba Gombo* (Corrigendum to Decision on the participation of victims in the trial and on 86 applications by victims to participate in the proceedings) ICC-01/05–01/08, Trial Chamber III (12 July 2010), para 47. See also *Prosecutor v William Samoei Ruto and Joshua Arap Sang* (Decision on victims' representation and participation) ICC-01/09–01/11, Trial Chamber V (3 October 2012), para 68; *Prosecutor v Francis Kirimi Muthaura and Uhuru Muigai Kenyatta* (Decision on victims' representation and participation) ICC-01/09–02/11, Trial Chamber V (3 October 2012), para 67.

closed session hearings and exceptionally hearings that are *ex parte*, depending on the circumstances and facts of the particular application. Conversely, in *Katanga and Chui*, the Trial Chamber II permitted victims to attend and participate in all closed session hearings, excluding those that were *ex parte*.[146] In *Ruto and Sang*, the Trial Chamber V established whether or not victims' legal representatives could participate in *ex parte* hearings through the Office of Public Counsel for Victims (OPCV) was determined on a case-by-case basis.[147]

8.7.3 Participation by way of oral and written submissions

In *Lubanga*, the Trial Chamber I considered that, in accordance with Rule 89(1), victims are expressly authorised to make statements. In light of this, at the request of some legal representatives of the victims, the Trial Chambers granted victims leave to make opening and closing statements at the trial.[148] Although victims' opening statements at trial are not evidence, they are still a relevant part of the trial and, in this regard, it is interesting to observe the different strategies adopted by victims' legal representatives seeking to point out victims' various interests and rights. Several legal representatives emphasised that the personal interest of victims in the proceedings coincided with their rights to the truth and justice, as their central concern is the establishment of the facts about events that occurred and the identification of those responsible.[149] Some talked about the violence suffered by victims, which caused them serious harm,[150] including repeated victimisation,[151] and also affected their dignity and security.[152] Others highlighted the importance of enacting protection and reparation measures to protect victims from intimidation and harassment and granting victims the right to an expeditious criminal process.[153] In their statements, legal representatives did not directly engage with the criminal responsibility of the defendants; however,

146 *Prosecutor v Germain Katanga and Mathieu Ngudjolo Chui* (n 144), para 71.

147 *Prosecutor v William Samoei Ruto and Joshua Arap Sang* (n 145), para 71; *Prosecutor v Francis Kirimi Muthaura and Uhuru Muigai Kenyatta* (n 145), para 70.

148 *Prosecutor v Thomas Lubanga Dyilo* (n 137), para 117. See also *Prosecutor v Jean-Pierre Bemba Gombo* (n 145), para 27; *Prosecutor v Germain Katanga and Mathieu Ngudjolo Chui* (n 144), para 68.

149 *Prosecutor v Thomas Lubanga Dyilo* (Opening Statement by Victim Representative) ICC-01/04–01/06 (26 January 2009) 37–41 and 47–48; *Prosecutor v Jean-Pierre Bemba Gombo* (Transcripts) ICC-01/05–01/08 (22 November 2010) 40–41.

150 *Prosecutor v Thomas Lubanga Dyilo* (n 149) 45, 47, 49 and 52–54; *Prosecutor v Germain Katanga and Mathieu Ngudjolo Chui* (Transcripts) ICC-01/04–01/07 (24 November 2009) 40; *Prosecutor v William Samoei Ruto and Joshua Arap Sang* (Opening Statement by Victim Representative) ICC-01/09–01/11, Trial Chamber V(A) (10 September 2013) 41 lines 13–20.

151 *Prosecutor v William Samoei Ruto and Joshua Arap Sang* (n 150) 38 lines 24–25.

152 Ibid, lines 2–10.

153 *Prosecutor v Thomas Lubanga Dyilo* (n 149) 59, 67; *Prosecutor v Germain Katanga and Mathieu Ngudjolo Chui* (n 150) 46; *Prosecutor v William Samoei Ruto and Joshua Arap Sang* (n 150) 39 lines 15–17.

a few of them made some comments in this regard. For instance, in *Bemba*, one legal representative, echoing the observations made by the Prosecutor, stated that the defendant should be held responsible for the crimes committed before the Court as well as before the populations of the Central African Republic in order to achieve real justice and peace.[154]

In addition to oral submissions, victims can also participate at trial by means of written observations or submissions.[155] According to the Trial Chamber I, this modality of participation entails the right to make submissions on matters of evidence and the opportunity to challenge the admissibility or relevance of evidence,[156] including *ex parte* filing.[157] More broadly, whenever an issue arises that affects their interests, victims are granted the right to initiate procedures, by filing applications and requests.[158]

8.7.4 Presenting views and concerns

In its *Decision on Victims' Participation*, the Trial Chamber I clarified that, pursuant to Article 68(3), when the Court considers it appropriate, victims have the right to participate directly in the proceedings to express their views and concerns.[159] At trial stage, a legal representative requested the Trial Chamber I to permit three participants to appear in person to present 'views and concerns' and to give testimony under oath.[160] When the three participating victims had completed their evidence, they would then be in the best position to decide whether they wished to express their views and concerns personally. The Chamber drew a critical distinction between presenting views and concerns and giving testimony. These represent two possible means of placing material before the Chamber; however, the former corresponds to the presentation of submissions, which assist the Chamber in its approach to the evidence, but are not evidence. Unlike testimony, views and concerns do not have a probative value for the purpose of the decision, since victims can only make suggestions as to how to orientate the fact-

154 *Prosecutor v Jean-Pierre Bemba Gombo* (n 149) 43 lines 19–21; *Prosecutor v Thomas Lubanga Dyilo* (n 149) 55.

155 Rule 91(2), Rules of Procedure and Evidence of the International Criminal Court.

156 *Prosecutor v Thomas Lubanga Dyilo* (n 137), para 109.

157 ibid, paras 114, 118; *Prosecutor v William Samoei Ruto and Joshua Arap Sang* (Decision on Common Legal Representative for Victims' Request to Participate in Hearings and Examine Witnesses) ICC-01/09–01/11, Trial Chamber V(A) (20 November 2013), para 18.

158 *Prosecutor v Germain Katanga and Mathieu Ngudjolo Chui* (n 144), para 58; *Prosecutor v Thomas Lubanga Dyilo* (n 137), para 118; *Prosecutor v William Samoei Ruto and Joshua Arap Sang* (n 145), para 72; *Prosecutor v Francis Kirimi Muthaura and Uhuru Muigai Kenyatta* (n 145), para 71.

159 *Prosecutor v Thomas Lubanga Dyilo* (n 137), para 115.

160 *Prosecutor v Thomas Lubanga Dyilo* (Decision on the request by victims a/0225/06, a/0229/06 and a/0270/07 to express their views and concerns in person and to present evidence during the trial) ICC-01/04–01/06, Trial Chamber I (26 June 2009), paras 1 and 4.

finding powers of the Judges. The choice of which modality of presenting views and concerns and giving testimony is appropriate is fact-specific and needs to take into account the circumstances of the trial as a whole.[161] The legal representatives have the crucial role to carefully and comprehensively advise victims as to the most appropriate form of participation.[162]

In *Bemba*, the Trial Chamber III showed its willingness to follow the path traced by *Lubanga*, however, because of the exponential increase in the number of victims applying to participate, which jeopardised the fair trial principle and the defendant's rights, it struggled to grant meaningful participation to a growing number of victims. The Trial Chamber III embraced the distinction between the process of victims 'expressing their views and concerns' and giving testimony, as delineated in *Lubanga*. The former is the equivalent of presenting submissions, which can assist the Chamber in its approach to the evidence in the case, but it does not form part of the trial evidence.[163] In essence, 'views and concerns' are conceived as an autonomous means of participation in the form of unsworn statements.[164] The Chamber further elaborated this distinction and the different requirements to allow these two modalities of victims' participation. It affirmed that the threshold victims need to meet to give evidence is significantly higher than the threshold applicable to submissions requesting to express views and concerns. Thus, even when victims are not authorised to give evidence, they might still be allowed to express their views and concerns in person.[165] The effort of Trial Chamber III to grant participation to a constantly growing number of victims, and, at the same time, to ensure that the proceedings are expeditious and that participation is not prejudicial to the accused's right to a fair trial, undermines the role of the victims to a certain extent. The imperative of granting the accused an expeditious trial requires that the determination of which victims can present their views and concerns relies on 'fact-specific decisions [...] taking into account the circumstances of the trial as a whole'.[166] For that purpose, the Trial Chamber III set two evaluating factors: 'whether the personal interests of the *individual* (emphasis added) victims are affected', and 'whether the accounts expected to be provided are representative of a larger number of victims'.[167] In other words, the Trial Chamber III emphasised that 'views and concerns' must be sufficiently reflective of the personal interests of broader classes of victims and

161 ibid, para 25.
162 ibid, para 27.
163 *Prosecutor v Jean-Pierre Bemba Gombo* (Decision on the supplemented applications by the legal representatives of victims to present evidence and the views and concerns of victims) ICC-01/05–01/08, Trial Chamber III (22 February 2012), para 19.
164 *Prosecutor v Jean-Pierre Bemba Gombo* (Order regarding applications by victims to present their views and concerns or to present evidence) ICC-01/05–01/08, Trial Chamber III (21 November 2011), para 3(c).
165 *Prosecutor v Jean-Pierre Bemba Gombo* (n 163), para 20.
166 ibid, para 22.
167 ibid, para 22.

make a contribution to the effective and efficient establishment of the truth.[168] This interpretation of the concept of victims' personal interests is contradictory because the Chambers are called to assess the personal interests of individual victims, but, at same time, such 'individual interest' has to represent a larger number of victims. As a result, victims seem to lose their individuality to an abstract concept of victimhood. This conception of victims does not find any validation in any dispositions of the RS or of the RPE. Broadly speaking, it is questionable to what extent an abstract victimhood can effectively contribute to the truth-finding mandate of the ICC.

A similar qualification of victims' personal interests was advanced in *Ruto and Sang*. The Trial Chamber V allowed victims willing to present their views individually to appear directly before the Chamber, in person or via video link.[169] In that event, common legal representatives must submit a request, where they explain the reason why the victims they represent are best placed to reflect *the interests of the victims.*[170] Victims, who have been selected by the Chambers, are authorised to personally present their views and concerns 'at critical junctures involving victims' interests',[171] notably during opening and closing statements by common legal representatives.[172] Importantly, this view by the Trial Chamber V can be read as an additional requirement to the conditions set out in Article 68(3). The expression of views and concerns by an individual victim should affect the 'personal interests' of the victim, as established in Article 68(3), but should also reflect the general interests of a broader group of victims or community. As in *Bemba*, the Trial Chamber V was concerned that 'the number of eligible victims is estimated to be in the thousands'[173] and decided to move from individualised participation in the direction of a more collectivised participation of victims. More thorough considerations on the concept of abstract victimhood will be addressed later in this chapter, when dealing with the common legal representation of victims.[174]

In *Katanga and Chui*, the Trial Chamber II rejected the distinction between the victims' expression of 'views and concerns' and giving testimony, as set in *Lubanga* and *Bemba*, showing a different understanding of the nature and scope of the participatory rights of victims at trial stage. Trial Chamber II considered that the requests by victims to submit incriminating or exculpatory evidence is a means of expressing their 'views and concerns' within the scope of Article 68(3) of the Statute. In *Lubanga*, victims' expressions of 'views and concerns' were treated like a self-standing procedural action, whereby victims can suggest to the

168 Vasiliev (n 63) 1175.
169 *Prosecutor v William Samoei Ruto and Joshua Arap Sang* (Decision on victims' representation and participation) ICC-01/09-01/11, Trial Chamber V (9 October 2012), para 56.
170 ibid, para 56.
171 ibid, para 71.
172 ibid, para 73.
173 ibid, para 30.
174 See section 8.9.

Judges how to orientate their fact-finding powers. In contrast, the Trial Chamber II appears to understand the expression of 'views and concerns' as a non-autonomous function, which merely serves as a tool for victims to request the submission of incriminating or exculpatory evidence.[175] Indeed, the possibility of victims presenting evidence is an important mechanism, which allows victims to craft the narrative of events. However, the Trial Chamber II seems to consider that 'views and concerns', as a mechanism without probative value with the objective of suggesting to the Judges how to orientate their fact-finding, can still achieve the same goal. This would suggest that the Trial Chamber II excluded the possibility that victims could monitor the accuracy of the work of the prosecution and the Judges through submissions of views, concerns, and opinions.

8.7.5 Evaluation

The practice of the Trial Chambers illustrates that the grounds for granting victims participatory rights is a corollary of the expressivist conceptualisation of victims as a critical actor in the trial. The broad modalities of participation as interpreted by the Trial Chambers are justified by invoking the right to know the truth about crimes of the surviving victims and their next of kin, consistent with what is recognised in international human rights law.[176] This case law is of cardinal importance to understanding the expressivist value of victims' contribution to the historical clarification of events.

The Court goes beyond the postulation of victims' narrative through the lens of 'harm and suffering' and rethinks the content and function of victims' storytelling. In line with the expressivist model, the ICC acknowledges victims' essential role in the crafting of historical records, since the input they provide in proceedings are twofold: first, they present their knowledge about what happened and 'their vision and an understanding of those who are responsible for what happened to them'.[177] Second, when expanding the modalities of participation to include those rights not explicitly contained under the ICC legal framework, the Trial Chambers have grounded their decision precisely on the assistance that victims can give the ICC in determining the truth. Given that victims have first-hand experience and knowledge of the specific circumstances of the case, a strengthened participation model can assist the Chamber by providing insiders' details and, thus, effectively contributing to the most important aim of the ICC, namely the fight against impunity in the context of the most serious international crimes.

Moreover, the acknowledgement of a broad scope of victims' participation, which aims to make victims active participants in the quest for justice, reflects the expressivist model of justice that advocates for fairness to victims in criminal

175 Vasiliev (n 63) 1167–1168.
176 See Chapter 6.
177 *Prosecutor v Germain Katanga and Mathieu Ngudjolo Chui* (Closing Statement by Victim Representative) ICC-01/04-01/07, Trial Chamber II (16 May 2012) 57.

proceedings. It is paramount to remark that the concept of fair access to justice for victims is conceptually and ideologically distinct from the right to a fair trial, which has been created for the benefit of the accused. Any violation of the fair trial principle shows the failure to guarantee the accused's right to be treated fairly, efficiently and effectively protected from abuse of power and arbitrariness, compromising the credibility of the whole criminal proceedings before the ICC.[178] Allowing victims to present views and concerns, unless they are prejudicial to or inconsistent with the rights of the accused to a fair and impartial trial, does not confer victims with any right to a fair trial. It would be paradoxical to hold that victims' participation is guaranteed by the fair trial right and simultaneously such participation can also jeopardise it. Nonetheless, victims are entitled to a general component of fairness within the criminal proceedings. As a result of the silence on the subject in the RS, which in Article 68(3) focuses on due process for the defendant to the detriment of fairness for victims, the scope and content of fairness can be understood in light of the case law of the IACtHR and the ECtHR, whose standards influence the operation of the ICC, pursuant to Article 21(3) of the RS. Neither the ACtHR nor the ECtHR explicitly refer to fairness to victims; however, they put forward the victims' right to obtain a remedy, which, as it entails the right to justice and access to it, the right to the truth, the right to be heard, shares the same goal as the right to fairness, that is to advance the rights of all victims to participate in criminal proceedings.[179] Together with the accused's right to a fair trial, the principle of fairness to victims represents the bedrock of the international criminal procedure, as it is a genuine standard to assess the quality of the criminal justice system.[180] The achievement of a fair balance between these two competing rights demands a move from the traditional mandate of exclusively ascribing individual criminal responsibility for international crimes to embrace a model of international criminal justice grounded on 'the principles underlying the framework of the human right regime, and the adherence of these rules [of international criminal procedure] to that regime'.[181]

8.8 The place of victims in the evidence-gathering process

The core provisions of the RS on the evidentiary procedure at the trial stage of the proceedings reflect both a party-driven and a judicially proactive approach.[182] According to the first sentence of Article 69(3), the parties – prosecution and

178 ibid. See also Miriam Cohen, 'Victims' Participation Rights within the International Criminal Court: A Critical Overview' (2009) 37 Denver Journal of International Law and Policy 351, 373–374.
179 See sections 6.3. and 6.4.
180 Zappalà (n 136) 143.
181 Bischoff, Boas and Reid (n 40) 12.
182 Brianne McGonigle Leyh, 'Bridging the Divides in International Criminal Proceedings: An Examination into the Victim Participation Endeavor of the International Criminal Court' (2009) 21 Florida Journal of International Law 93, 107.

Defence – may submit evidence relevant to the case. The second sentence of the same article confers on the Court the authority to request the submission of all evidence that it considers necessary for the determination of the truth. Under this legal text, the primary initiative for the processing of evidence 'belongs to and is a core right of the parties'[183] as the key stakeholders in the proceedings, while the Chambers can *proprio motu* order the production of all evidence necessary for the establishment of the truth, beyond the evidence adduced by the parties.

The ICC's legal framework makes no mention of whether victims may play an active part in the evidence-gathering process by way of placing material before the Chamber. Neither the wording of Article 68(3), nor any other provision of the RS explicitly grants victims the right to produce evidence at trial. Only Rule 91 of the ICC RPE introduces the conditional possibility of victims intervening in the examination of evidence through their legal representative(s).[184] However, the silence of the ICC's normative framework has not prevented the Court from allowing a piece(s) of evidence in the knowledge and/or possession of victims to be incorporated into the evidentiary material. This scenario reflects the reality that the participation of victims in proceedings through their views and concerns can bring to the attention of the Chamber and the parties material – neither requested by the parties nor ordered by the Chamber – which can prove necessary for the further clarification of facts and circumstances relevant to the case and, ultimately, for the determination of the truth.

8.8.1 The possibility for victims to submit evidence

The viewpoint that victims can 'whisper in the Court's ear about the need for, and perhaps even availability of, additional evidence'[185] beneficial to the ascertainment of the truth was espoused for the first time in *Lubanga*. The Trial Chamber I permitted victims participating in the proceedings to tender and examine evidence and to challenge evidence given by the parties, if this was necessary to assist the Court in its truth-finding task 'and if in this sense the Court has 'requested' the evidence'.[186] At the core of this modality of victims' participation was the interpretation of Article 69(3), which empowers the Court with a general right – independent of the cooperation or the consent of the parties – to request the presentation of all evidence necessary for the determination of the truth.[187]

This decision was appealed by both the Prosecutor and Defence on the ground that the burden of proof lies squarely with the Prosecutor and that the role of the Chamber should be exclusively to balance out the prosecution and the Defence

183 Håkan Friman, 'The International Criminal Court and Participation of Victims: A Third Party to the Proceedings?' (2009) 22 Leiden Journal of International Law 485, 494.

184 See section 8.8.3.

185 Friman (n 183) 494.

186 *Prosecutor v Thomas Lubanga Dyilo* (n 137), para 108.

187 ibid, paras 108–109.

and to guarantee a fair trial.[188] Indeed, the Trial Chamber I did not clarify how it can hold, on the one hand, that victims are not parties to the proceedings, yet find that they are entitled, under specific circumstances, to present evidence. This argument convinced Judge Pikis and Judge Kirsch, who, in their dissenting opinions, upheld that leading or challenging evidence is exclusively the right of the parties, and that victims are not parties. Both Judges agreed that allowing victims to lead evidence can considerably slow down the proceedings, causing inefficiency, and violate the principle of the equality of arms and, more generally, the overall right to a fair trial.[189] However, the majority of the Appeal Chamber rejected these objections. The majority's understanding was that the first sentence of Article 69(3) is categorical and makes clear that 'the right to lead evidence pertaining to the guilt or innocence of the accused (...) lies primarily with the parties'.[190] However, this entitlement is neither exclusive nor sufficient to dismiss the residual powers of the Court. The second sentence of Article 69(3) suggests that it is ultimately the responsibility of the Court to convince itself of the guilt of the accused beyond any reasonable doubt.[191] The two sentences comprising Article 69(3) should be treated 'as operating somewhat independently of each other'.[192] Moreover, the Appeals Chamber advanced that the second sentence of Article 69(3) should reflect the spirit and intention of Article 68(3) and, therefore, it must be interpreted as aiming to make victims' participation meaningful. The combined reading of these two articles, by allowing victims to introduce and challenge evidence, aims to prevent the potential ineffectiveness of victims' participation.[193] That said, the Appeals Chamber clarified its intention was not to create an independent and unfettered right for victims to lead and challenge the admissibility of evidence.[194]

188 *Prosecutor v Thomas Lubanga Dyilo* (Prosecution's Document in Support of Appeal against Trial Chamber I's 18 January 2008 Decision on Victims' Participation) ICC-01/04–01/06, Office of the Prosecutor (10 March 2008), paras 41–42, 45–46; *Prosecutor v Thomas Lubanga Dyilo* (Defence Appeal Against Trial Chamber I's 18 January 2008 Decision on Victims' Participation) ICC-01/04–01/06, Defence (10 March 2008), paras 48–50.

189 *Prosecutor v Thomas Lubanga Dyilo* (Partly Dissenting Opinion of Judge G M Pikis) ICC-01/04–01/06, Appeals Chamber (11 July 2008), para 13; *Prosecutor v Thomas Lubanga Dyilo* (Partly Dissenting Opinion of Judge Philippe Kirsch) ICC-01/04–01/06, Appeals Chamber (11 July 2008), para 30.

190 *Prosecutor v Thomas Lubanga Dyilo* (Judgement on the Appeals of the Prosecutor and the Defence against Trial Chamber I's Decision on Victims' Participation of 18 January 2008) ICC-01/04–01/06, Appeals Chamber (11 July 2008), para 93. See also *Prosecutor v Francis Kirimi Muthaura and Uhuru Muigai Kenyatta* (n 145), para 76; *Prosecutor v Jean-Pierre Bemba Gombo* (n 145), para 31.

191 *Prosecutor v Thomas Lubanga Dyilo* (n 137), para 95.

192 Adrian M Plevin, 'Beyond a "Victims' Right": Truth-Finding Power and Procedure at the ICC' (2014) 25 Criminal Law Forum 441, 444.

193 *Prosecutor v Thomas Lubanga Dyilo* (n 190) paras 97–98.

194 ibid, paras 5, 99, 101.

This decision of the Appeals Chamber has certainly given food for thought with regard to the controversial possibility for victims to present and challenge evidence. A misunderstanding surrounding this decision lies in the unfortunate lexical choice of the majority, which refers to the '*right* (emphasis added) for victims to lead or challenge evidence'.[195] This wording risks masking the true nature of Article 69(3), which has been clearly described in the Appeals Chamber's decision. When the Court is not satisfied by the evidence submitted by the parties for the purpose of unveiling the truth, it can exercise its residual power, which makes it possible for victims to be requested to submit evidence. Therefore, instead of saying victims have a right to present evidence, it would be correct to refer to the possibility of victims being requested to submit evidence, or *mutatis mutandis*, the Court's power to request victims to present all the evidence necessary for the determination of the truth.[196]

The opposing standpoints of the majority and the dissents in *Lubanga* have been reconciled to a certain extent in the subsequent decisions, which linked victims' role in truth-finding to the Chamber's power *ex officio* to request additional evidence. In *Katanga and Chui*, the Trial Chamber II clearly stated that presenting and challenging the admissibility of evidence 'is simply a *possibility* (emphasis added) afforded to the victims' by the Chambers to give full effect to the combined reading of the provisions of Articles 68(3) and 69(3) of the RS.[197] Similarly, in *Bemba* and *Ruto*, the Trials Chambers confirmed that victims' involvement in the evidence-gathering process under the mechanism of Article 69(3) reflects the reality that 'victims may possess evidence that may assist the Chamber in its determination of the truth'.[198] Accordingly, the Trial Chamber III has taken the view that the possibility for victims *to be requested* by the Chamber to submit evidence aims at assisting the Court in its implementation of Article 69(3), for which it is believed that the greatest accessibility to the evidence is necessary.[199]

8.8.2 Conditions to tender and examine evidence

In decisions granting victims the possibility to present evidence, the Court correctly stressed that '[v]ictims are not parties to the proceedings and are thus

195 ibid, para 99.

196 Plevin (n 192) 448.

197 *Prosecutor v Germain Katanga and Mathieu Ngudjolo Chui* (n 144), paras 47, 82–83.

198 *Prosecutor v Jean-Pierre Bemba Gombo* (n 145), paras 29–36; *Prosecutor v William Samoei Ruto and Joshua Arap Sang* (n 145), para 77.

199 *Prosecutor v Jean-Pierre Bemba Gombo* (n 145), paras 35–36. See also *Prosecutor v Germain Katanga and Mathieu Ngudjolo Chui* (n 144), paras 82, 86–101; *Prosecutor v Germain Katanga and Mathieu Ngudjolo Chui* (Decision on the implementation of regulation 55 of the Regulations of the Court and severing the charges against the accused person) ICC-01/04-01/07, Trial Chamber II (21 November 2012), para 8, footnote 21; *Prosecutor v William Samoei Ruto and Joshua Arap Sang* (n 145), para 77.

not vested with a self-standing right to present evidence'.[200] Consequently, the threshold to grant victims such a pro-active role 'is significantly higher than the threshold applicable to applications by victims to express their views and concerns in person'.[201] In addition to Article 69(3), victims' applications need to comply with some requirements developed in the case law of the ICC. Victims' ability to present evidence at trial is decided on a case-by-case basis, subject to the following conditions: (1) victims' discrete application; (2) notice to the parties; (3) demonstration of personal interests that are affected by the evidence; (4) compliance with disclosure obligations and protection orders; (5) determination of appropriateness; and (6) consistency with the rights of the accused and a fair trial.[202]

The requirement that victims have to demonstrate that their personal interests are affected has proved to be controversial. If victims fail to establish that their personal interests are affected, one could question whether the ICC can still require the presentation of any evidence it considers necessary to establish the truth. When confronted with this issue, the Trial Chamber III emphasised that victims' interests should not be limited to the physical commission of the alleged crimes under consideration, since victims have a general interest in the proceedings and their outcome.[203] Thus, any evidence relevant to the outcome of the case affects the personal interests of the victims. In a subsequent decision, the Trial Chamber III does not mention the criteria for 'victims' affected personal interests among the requirements that need to be satisfied by the victims to present evidence. The Trial Chamber III focused on whether the evidence was substantial new information, relevant to making a genuine contribution to the ascertainment of the truth and typical of a larger group of participating victims.[204]

8.8.3 Examination of evidence: questioning witnesses

After having discussed issues related to the modalities of victims' involvement in the submission of evidence, the next matter to address concerns the examination of evidence. The possibility for victims to engage in the evidence examination is envisaged in Rule 91(3) of the RPE of the ICC. This provision allows the victims'

200 *Prosecutor v Jean-Pierre Bemba Gombo* (n 163), paras 13–14; *Prosecutor v Germain Katanga and Mathieu Ngudjolo Chui* (Judgement on the Appeal of Mr Katanga Against the Decision of Trial Chamber II of 22 January 2010 Entitled 'Decision on the Modalities of Victim Participation at Trial') ICC-01/04–01/07, Appeals Chamber (16 July 2010), paras 39–48; *Prosecutor v William Samoei Ruto and Joshua Arap Sang* (n 145) paras 14, 77.

201 *Prosecutor v Jean-Pierre Bemba Gombo* (n 163), para 20.

202 *Prosecutor v Thomas Lubanga Dyilo* (n 137), para 4; *Prosecutor v Germain Katanga and Mathieu Ngudjolo Chui* (n 200), paras 44, 48, 112–114.

203 *Prosecutor v Jean-Pierre Bemba Gombo* (Decision (i) ruling on legal representatives' applications to question Witness 33 and (ii) setting a schedule for the filing of submissions in relation to future applications to question witnesses) ICC-01/05–01/08, Trial Chamber III (9 September 2011), para 15.

204 *Prosecutor v Jean-Pierre Bemba Gombo* (n 163) paras 23–24.

legal representative(s) to pose questions to witnesses, experts and the accused, subject to some conditions. Using the words of Judge Kirsch, Rule 91(3) 'regulates the limited manner in which victims may be permitted to put questions to a witness'.[205] The conditions set out in Rule 91(3) are in tune with the victims' non-party standing in proceedings before the ICC, as victims' legal representatives must be authorised to intervene in the examination of evidence by the Chamber on a case-by-case basis. Legal representatives must submit a discrete written application in advance, of which the Chamber and the Prosecutor are notified at least seven days before the appearance of the witness in court. Additionally, the list of proposed questions and how these are related to the victim participants' interests must be included in the application.[206] According to Rule 91(3)(b), the Court's decision whether to grant such a request has to consider the manifold interests at stake. The Chambers are entrusted with the responsibility of ensuring that the request by victims' legal representatives is appropriate at the respective stage of the proceedings and does not undermine the rights of the accused, the interests of witnesses, the need for a fair, impartial, and expeditious trial as well as the need to guarantee victims' participation according to Article 68(3).[207]

Concerning the extent of the examination of a witness, expert or accused, Rule 91(3) neither predetermines nor confines the scope and manner of the questioning conducted by the legal representative to a particular range of issues. Accordingly, the scope of the questions to be allowed and the way they will be put to the witness, expert or accused is determined at the discretion of the Chamber. As a general principle, questions by victims' legal representatives should aim at the ascertainment of the truth, given that their participation may be an important factor in helping the Chamber to better understand the contentious issues of the case in light of their local knowledge and socio-cultural background.[208] However, the practices of the Chambers have interpreted the interplay between the scope

205 *Prosecutor v Thomas Lubanga Dyilo* (n 137), para 31.

206 *Prosecutor v Jean-Pierre Bemba Gombo* (n 145), para 102 h; *Prosecutor v Jean-Pierre Bemba Gombo* (Decision on Directions for the Conduct of the Proceedings) ICC-01/05–01/08, Trial Chamber III (19 November 2010), para 18; *Prosecutor v Germain Katanga and Mathieu Ngudjolo Chui* (Directions for the conduct of the proceedings and testimony in accordance with rule 140) ICC-01/04–01/07, Trial Chamber II (20 November 2009), para 87.

207 *Prosecutor v Thomas Lubanga Dyilo* (Decision on the defence observations regarding the right of the legal representatives of victims to question defence witnesses and on the notion of personal interest -and- Decision on the defence application to exclude certain representatives of victims from the Chamber during the non-public evidence of various defence witnesses) ICC-01/04–01/06, Trial Chamber I (11 March 2010), para 35; *Prosecutor v Germain Katanga and Mathieu Ngudjolo Chui* (Corrigendum to Decision on the Conduct of the Proceedings and Testimony in Accordance with Rule 140) ICC-01/04–01/07, Trial Chamber II (1 December 2009), para 87.

208 *Prosecutor v Germain Katanga and Mathieu Ngudjolo Chui* (n 207), para 82; *Prosecutor v Thomas Lubanga Dyilo* (n 137), paras 95–98; *Prosecutor v Thomas Lubanga Dyilo* (Decision on the Manner of Questioning Witnesses by the Legal Representatives of Victims) ICC-01/04–01/06, Trial Chamber I (16 September 2009), para 27.

of the questioning by victims' legal representatives and the purpose of assisting the Court in its pursuit of the truth in different ways. In several decisions, the Court noted that questions by victims' legal representatives should be limited to questions about issues relevant to the interests of the victims in order to clarify the details of their evidence and to elicit additional facts.[209] Nonetheless, in *Katanga and Chui*, the Trial Chamber II allowed victims' legal representatives to ask questions concerning the facts that went beyond matters raised during examination-in-chief, provided that the questions (1) are not duplicative or repetitive and (2) are limited to matters that are in controversy between the parties and holding relevance for the victims' interests.[210]

The scope of questioning by victims' legal representatives has become quite controversial because, despite the fact that '[t]he onus is on the prosecutor to prove the guilt of the accused',[211] depending on the circumstances, the alleged guilt of the accused may be a subject that substantively affects the personal interests of the victims. This point is of crucial importance because it goes to the heart of the understanding of the expressivist foundation for this modality of victims' participation in light of the link between victims' evidence and the concept of assisting the Court in the determination of the truth. In *Lubanga* and *Bemba*, the Trial Chambers acknowledged a broad scope to the questioning by victims' legal representatives, since the latter may question witnesses on areas relevant to the interests of the victims in order to clarify the details of their evidence and to elicit additional facts, notwithstanding the relevance of their evidence to the guilt or innocence of the accused.[212] Despite the responsibility of proving the guilt of the accused being that of the prosecution, the Court does not exclude the possibility of victims leading evidence pertaining to the guilt of the accused, 'as it is the court that "must be convinced of the guilt of the accused beyond reasonable doubt" (Article 66(3) of the Statute)'.[213] The Chambers found support for this approach in the combined reading of the second sentence of Article 69(3), Article 68(3) and Rule 91(3) of the RPE, according to which, when the Chamber exercises its competent powers, it should consider the possibility of allowing victims to submit a request to present all the evidence that it believes necessary to ascertain the truth.[214]

209 *Prosecutor v Thomas Lubanga Dyilo* (n 208), para 26; *Prosecutor v Germain Katanga and Mathieu Ngudjolo Chui* (n 207), para 90; *Prosecutor v Jean-Pierre Bemba Gombo* (n 206), para 20.

210 *Prosecutor v Germain Katanga and Mathieu Ngudjolo Chui* (n 206), paras 82–91.

211 Article 66(2), Rome Statute of the International Criminal Court.

212 *Prosecutor v Thomas Lubanga Dyilo* (n 207), para 27; *Prosecutor v Jean-Pierre Bemba Gombo* (n 145), paras 38–40.

213 *Prosecutor v Thomas Lubanga Dyilo* (n 190), para 95, 102; *Prosecutor v Thomas Lubanga Dyilo* (n 207), para 25.

214 *Prosecutor v Thomas Lubanga Dyilo* (n 207), para 27; *Prosecutor v Thomas Lubanga Dyilo* (n 137), para 94; *Prosecutor v Jean-Pierre Bemba Gombo* (n 145), para 38.

Quite the opposite situation was found in *Katanga and Chui*, the Trial Chamber II took a narrow approach to the scope of victims' questioning. The link between victims' evidence and the notion of assisting the Court in the ascertainment of the truth did not include questions about the guilt of the accused, as 'victims are not parties to the trial and certainly have no role to support the case of the Prosecution'.[215] The Trial Chamber II often reminded the legal representatives that they neither reinforce nor supplement the Prosecutor and warned them not to pose questions that would provide some kind of assistance to the prosecution, directly or indirectly.[216] The Trial Chamber II explicitly affirmed that the legitimate interest that victims can invoke – when requesting to question a witness – should be exclusively that of contributing to the determination of the truth by helping the Chamber to establish the facts which are the subject of the proceedings.[217] Accordingly, questioning by the victims' legal representatives can provide the Court with their knowledge of the background to the case and draw the Judges' attention to relevant information of which they were not aware.[218]

8.8.4 Possibility for victims to testify as witnesses

Neither the RS nor the RPE establish whether a victim who participates in the proceedings as a victim-participant can also be a witness. However, the Trial Chambers granted legal representatives the opportunity to call one or more victims to participate in the proceedings by way of giving oral testimony in their own right and not as witnesses for either the prosecution or the Defence.[219] The possibility for victim-participants to give evidence cannot be totally excluded because a general ban of highly relevant and probative testimony of witnesses for the sole reason that they have also been authorised to participate in the proceedings as victims would be contrary to the aim and purpose of Article 68(3) and to the Chamber's obligation to establish the truth.[220]

The possibility for victims to give evidence under oath at trial is subject to the authorisation by the Chambers which have identified four important conditions, namely: (1) the presentation of evidence needs to be consistent with the accused's right to a fair and impartial trial, including the right to an expeditious

215 *Prosecutor v Germain Katanga and Mathieu Ngudjolo Chui* (n 206), para 82.

216 *Prosecutor v Germain Katanga and Mathieu Ngudjolo Chui* (Transcripts) ICC-01/04–01/07 (22 March 2010) 4; *Prosecutor v Germain Katanga and Mathieu Ngudjolo Chui* (Transcripts) ICC-01/04–01/07 (30 November 2009) 26, 33; *Prosecutor v Germain Katanga and Mathieu Ngudjolo Chui* (Transcripts) ICC-01/04–01/07 (23 June 2010) 20.

217 *Prosecutor v Germain Katanga and Mathieu Ngudjolo Chui* (n 144), para 60.

218 ibid, para 60; *Prosecutor v Germain Katanga and Mathieu Ngudjolo Chui* (n 199), para 82.

219 *Prosecutor v Thomas Lubanga Dyilo* (n 137), para 132; *Prosecutor v Thomas Lubanga Dyilo* (n 160), paras 26–27; *Prosecutor v Jean-Pierre Bemba Gombo* (n 163), para 23; *Prosecutor v Germain Katanga and Mathieu Ngudjolo Chui* (n 144), para 86.

220 *Prosecutor v Thomas Lubanga Dyilo* (n 137), para 133; *Prosecutor v Germain Katanga and Mathieu Ngudjolo Chui* (n 144), para 88.

trial, according to Article 67(1)(c), and the right to have adequate time and facilities to prepare his/her defence according to Article 67(1)(b);[221] (2) the Chamber will only permit victims' legal representatives to call the witnesses provided that they are not turned into auxiliary Prosecutors;[222] (3) victims' testimony needs to be considered to make a genuine contribution to the ascertainment of the truth;[223] and (4) victims are not allowed to testify anonymously.[224] Furthermore, in determining which victims are best placed to present evidence by personally appearing before the Court, the Trial Chambers identified the following factors: (1) whether the proposed testimony would be repetitive of the Prosecutor's case or of evidence already tendered by the parties; (2) whether the topics of the victims' proposed testimony are sufficiently closely related to the issues to be examined when the Chamber assesses the charges against the accused; (3) whether the proposed testimony is typical of a larger group of victim participants, who possess experiences similar to the victim who desires to testify, or whether the victim is uniquely apt to provide evidence on a particular matter; and (4) whether the testimony will probably bring new substantial information which is relevant to Chamber's examination on issues related to the charges.[225]

8.8.5 Disclosure rights and obligations

Another issue deserving to be addressed concerns the victims' disclosure regime, which can potentially conflict with the accused's right to a fair trial. As a general rule, the disclosure regime under Rules 77 and 78 of the RPE only concerns the prosecution and the Defence and, in principle, takes place before trial begins. Concerning the victims' disclosure right, in *Lubanga*, Trial Chamber I provided a mechanism whereby the victim-participants may be provided with any materials within the possession of the prosecution that are relevant to their personal interests.[226]

With regard to the disclosure to the Defence, the Trial Chamber I held that the disclosure regime under Article 67(2) of the Statute, Rule 77 or Rule 76 of the RPE is imposed on the prosecution alone, implying that victims do not

221 *Prosecutor v Germain Katanga and Mathieu Ngudjolo Chui* (n 206), para 22; *Prosecutor v Jean-Pierre Bemba Gombo* (n 163), para 23; *Prosecutor v Thomas Lubanga Dyilo* (n 137), para 134; *Prosecutor v Germain Katanga and Mathieu Ngudjolo Chui* (n 200), para 114.

222 *Prosecutor v Germain Katanga and Mathieu Ngudjolo Chui* (n 206), para 22.

223 *Prosecutor v Jean-Pierre Bemba Gombo* (n 163), para 23; *Prosecutor v Germain Katanga and Mathieu Ngudjolo Chui* (n 200), para 114; *Prosecutor v Germain Katanga and Mathieu Ngudjolo Chui* (n 206), para 20; *Prosecutor v Germain Katanga and Mathieu Ngudjolo Chui* (n 144), para 91.

224 *Prosecutor v Jean-Pierre Bemba Gombo* (n 163), para 23; *Prosecutor v Germain Katanga and Mathieu Ngudjolo Chui* (n 206), para 22; *Prosecutor v Germain Katanga and Mathieu Ngudjolo Chui* (n 144), para 92.

225 *Prosecutor v Germain Katanga and Mathieu Ngudjolo Chui* (n 206), para 30; *Prosecutor v Jean-Pierre Bemba Gombo* (n 163), para 24.

226 *Prosecutor v Thomas Lubanga Dyilo* (n 139), paras 30–31.

have any obligation to disclose exculpatory material to the Defence.[227] The Trial Chamber I acknowledged that this regime results in a critical tension between the right to appropriate protective measures of those holding the dual status of victim-participants and witnesses and the right of the accused to a fair trial, in particular with regard to the exculpatory material in the possession of the prosecution and Victims Participation and Reparations Section.[228] In its attempt to balance these conflicting interests, the Trial Chamber I maintained that the Prosecutor must disclose to the Defence the statements, including applications, of those who have the dual status of victims and witnesses.[229] However, prior to disclosure, the legal representatives of these particular witnesses who hold dual status can raise their objections, which should be brought to the attention of the Chamber immediately.[230]

In relation to the possibility of victim-participants leading evidence at trial, the Trial Chambers and Appeals Chamber have confirmed that neither the RS nor the RPE impose on victims and their legal representatives the obligation to disclose to the Defence any evidence in their possession, be it incriminating or exculpatory.[231] The rationale behind this decision is based on the acknowledgement that victims, rather than having the right to present evidence, can be requested by the Chamber to submit evidence and, therefore, they cannot be obliged 'to disclose to the parties any evidence in their possession, whether incriminating or exculpatory'.[232] In other words, if the Chamber authorises victims to present evidence, it is its responsibility to rule on the modalities for the proper disclosure of the said evidence and to decide on the necessary measure to safeguard both the right of the accused to a fair trial and the interests of the victims.[233]

This orientation might seem *prima facie* to breach the accused's right to a fair trial, in particular, in light of the fact that the evidence should be disclosed prior the beginning of the trial stage, but a closer look shows that it is consistent with the nature and purpose of the mechanism of truth-finding of Article 69(3). It is hard for the Trial Chamber to have a clear understanding of what evidence in the hands of victims is needed to determine the truth in advance of the proceedings. Article 64(6)(d), which states that '[i]n performing its functions (…) during the course of a trial, the Trial Chamber may, as necessary: (…) [o]rder the production of evidence in addition to that already (…) presented during the trial by the parties', supports the idea that the Chamber has the power to allow victims' presentation of evidence, even if the disclosure of such evidence has not occurred

227 *Prosecutor v Thomas Lubanga Dyilo* (Decision on the defence application for disclosure of victims applications) Trial Chamber I, ICC-01/04–01/06 (21 January 2009), para 10.

228 ibid, para 11.

229 ibid, para 12.

230 ibid, para 13.

231 *Prosecutor v Germain Katanga and Mathieu Ngudjolo Chui* (n 200), paras 71–72, 75; *Prosecutor v Thomas Lubanga Dyilo* (n 190), para 93.

232 *Prosecutor v Germain Katanga and Mathieu Ngudjolo Chui* (n 144), para 105.

233 ibid, para 107; *Prosecutor v Thomas Lubanga Dyilo* (n 190), para 100.

before the beginning of the trial.[234] Nevertheless, it is important to note that where victims' applications for participation indicate that they can possess potentially exculpatory information, the Prosecutor should extend the investigation to discover such information in the victims' possession, which would eventually be disclosed to the Defence pursuant to the framework of the RS and RPE.[235]

8.8.6 Evaluation

The case law of the ICC on victims' engagement in the evidence-gathering process has far-reaching implications for the active role of victims in proceedings at the ICC. This reading of Article 69(3) strengthens the expressivist dimension of the evidence-gathering process at the ICC, since it recognises the potential truth-finding contribution of victims seeking to present evidence to prove the events under adjudication. The ICC engagement with victims as 'third actors' in the fact-finding process is not simply aimed at determining the innocence or guilt of the accused, as it emerges from the action and initiatives of the parties, but also at making findings about the truth, based on an objective and substantive determination of all necessary evidence.[236] It is important to observe that there is a conceptual difference between the determination of the innocence or guilt of the defendant and the Court's task of establishing a substantive truth. The former requires assessments of fact and law, while the latter can be conceived as a purely fact-based assessment.[237] Those two aspects can overlap, but proceedings focused on proving or disproving the charges do not necessarily provide an accurate account of events because the adversarial procedural framework – directed at the determination of guilt beyond all reasonable doubt – places the parties' competing cases at the heart of the litigation process.[238] Allowing victims to present evidence, casting, therefore, a sort of 'third perspective', might be necessary for the Trial Chambers because parties calling evidence are driven by partisan interests, which do not always coincide with the goal of establishing the truth.[239] This truth-finding mechanism can potentially reduce the gap between traditional models of international criminal trials and a broader expressivist aspiration for the ICC in terms of crafting a robust and permanent record of history

234 Plevin (n 192) 460.
235 *Prosecutor v Germain Katanga and Mathieu Ngudjolo Chui* (n 200), para 81.
236 Volker Röben, 'The Procedure of the ICC: Status and Function of the Prosecutor' (2003) 7 Max Planck Yearbook of United Nations Law 513, 527.
237 Plevin (n 192) 450.
238 Declan Roche, 'Truth Commission Amnesties and the International Criminal Court' (2005) 45 British Journal of Criminology 565, 570; Darryl Robinson, 'Serving the Interests of Justice: Amnesties, Truth Commissions and the International Criminal Court' (2003) 14 European Journal of International Law 481, 481.
239 Vasiliev (n 63) 1176.

and creating a useful narrative for both post-conflict societies and the international community.[240]

Furthermore, in line with the aims of expressivism, victims' active role in the fact-finding process strengthens the denunciatory function of the trial. The evidence presented by victims sends a message, not only about the guilt of a defendant, but also about the value of the rule of law, as it can demonstrate that some specific criminal conduct occurred. Even in the case that the defendant cannot be proven guilty beyond reasonable doubt, the fact that this conduct happened remains true. The simple fact that a trial takes place by appealing to the law, even if it does not end in the conviction of the defendant, strongly demonstrates that the crime and laws are taken seriously.[241] In the context of a public process, victims' involvement in the evidence-gathering process communicates that certain kinds of behaviour are violations of human rights amounting to international crimes, which are the most serious crimes concerning the international community.[242] The victim's message of disavowal of crimes urges a commitment to the respect of international human rights standards and the rule of law, which, in deeply fractured communities like those in which international crimes are committed, are the key tools for re-establishing a well-functioning society.[243]

8.9 Victims' common legal representation

Article 68(3) of the RS and Rule 90(1) RPE, which respectively state that victims' views and concerns may be presented by legal representatives and victims are 'free to choose a legal representative', imply that victims do not need to be represented by a legal counsel. Although in *Kony et al*, the Pre-Trial Chamber II argued that victims have a right to self-representation,[244] due to the complexity of international criminal substantive and procedural law, it seems probable that the exercise of this right is a rarity. Moreover, victims acting on their own are precluded from attending and participating in hearings and, subject to the Chamber's decision, from questioning a witness, an expert or the accused. In the view of the

240 Cryer et al. (n 7) 31.

241 Marlies Glasius and Tim Meijers, 'Trials as Messages of Justice: What Should Be Expected of International Criminal Courts?' (2016) 30 Ethics & International Affairs 429, 435–436.

242 Solange Mouthaan, 'Victim Participation at the ICC for Victims of Gender-Based Crimes: A Conflict of Interest' (2012) 21 Cardozo Journal of International and Comparative Law 619, 648–649; William A Schabas, 'Sentencing by International Tribunals: A Human Rights Approach' (1997) 7 Duke Journal of Comparative & International Law 461, 516.

243 Glasius and Meijers (n 241) 437–438; Robert D Sloane, 'The Expressive Capacity of International Punishment: The Limits of the National Law Analogy and the Potential of International Criminal Law' (2007) 43 Stanford Journal of International Law 39, 93.

244 *Prosecutor v Joseph Kony et al* (Decision on legal representation, appointment of counsel for the defence, protective measures and time-limit for submission of observations on applications for participation a/0010/06, a/0064/06 to a/0070/06, a/0081/06 to a/0104/06 and a/0111/06 to a/012) ICC-02/04-01/05, Pre-Trial Chamber II (1 February 2007), para 4.

Pre-Trial Chamber II, victims have the right to participate in proceedings; however, 'enhanced' rights of participation are vested exclusively in victims acting via legal representatives.[245] When the number of prospective participants is large, Rule 90(2) empowers the Chamber to request victims to choose a common legal representative, but in the event that victims are unable to choose a representative, or fail to do so, according to Rule 90(3), the Chamber may request the Registrar to make such choice. Additionally, Rule 90(4) establishes that the Chamber and the Registry take 'all reasonable steps to ensure that the distinct interests of the victims, particularly as provided in Article 68, paragraph 1, are represented', and that 'any conflict of interest is avoided'.

This legal framework has been implemented by the Trial Chambers in such a way that the factor that significantly influenced the determination of the need and number of legal representatives permitted in court was the efficiency of the proceedings, rather than the victims' needs for shared representation. In *Lubanga*, the Judges were fully aware that the large number of victims could affect the defendant's right to an expeditious and fair trial. The Trial Chamber I, therefore, reserves the right to decide either *proprio motu*, or at the request of a party or participant, whether or not victims' views and concerns should be presented through a joint presentation of views and concerns by joint legal representatives.[246] The Trial Chamber I divided over 120 victims into two groups represented by two teams of external counsel, while the Office of Public Counsel for Victims represented four victims holding the dual status of participant-witnesses.[247] In *Katanga and Chui*, the Trial Chamber held that the common legal representation is closely related to issues of the fair trial right, such as efficiency, appropriate expeditiousness of the proceedings, and, therefore, the Chamber must seek to avoid repetition or multiplication of similar arguments and submissions.[248] Given these factors, the Chamber considered it appropriate to divide victims (more than 300) into only two groups: the first consisting of child soldiers, while the second was made up of other victims. These victim groupings were based on the harm inflicted, as the group of child soldier victims was identified by Trial Chamber II as giving rise to a potential conflict of interest with the other victims who did not participate in the attacks but only suffered harm from them.[249]

In *Bemba*, the Trial Chamber III emphasised that the common legal representation was a central procedural mechanism aimed at reconciling the defendants' right to a fair and expeditious trial with the entitlement to meaningful

245 ibid, para 7.
246 *Prosecutor v Thomas Lubanga Dyilo* (n 137), para 116.
247 *Prosecutor v Thomas Lubanga Dyilo* (n 91), para 20.
248 *Prosecutor v Germain Katanga and Mathieu Ngudjolo Chui* (Order on the organisation of common legal representation of victims) ICC-01/04–01/07, Trial Chamber II (22 July 2009), paras 10–11.
249 ibid, paras 12–13.

participation of potentially thousands of victims as far as practically possible.[250] Relying heavily on the criteria of the geographical location of the crimes, the Trial Chamber III divided the 1,335 victim-participants into two groups represented by only two common legal representatives.[251] The adoption of geographical criteria carried significant administrative benefits and savings for the operation of the Court, but, at the same time, it has been argued that the focus on such criteria did 'not serve the victims' interests in relation to the high number of victims of sexual violence expected to participate in the *Bemba* case'.[252]

In *Banda and Jerbo*, the appointment of the common legal representative has been a particularly debated issue. The Trial Chamber IV approved the Registry proposal to represent all 89 victims by one legal team.[253] The Chamber was not persuaded that there was a conflict of interest between the Darfuri victims and the non-Darfuri victims, which would justify a different grouping. Although the Chamber acknowledged that the Darfuri victims had particularities that distinguished them from other victims, namely they spoke Arabic and were nationals of a non-party state, it 'does not *per se* imply that the two victims have distinct interests that would warrant separate representation'.[254] Moreover, the interest of the Darfuri victims to broaden the factual circumstances of the case did not justify distinct legal representation.[255] From the Registry viewpoint, the 'existence among a subset of victims of an ***additional*** interest or viewpoint, which is not shared but also not disputed by other participating victims, would not necessarily justify separate representation'.[256] The Registry further clarified that as far as the interests of victims can be mainly identified with the desire to achieve justice and obtain reparations, 'these interests may substantially coincide'.[257] As observed by Haslam and Edmunds, this orientation 'seems to rest on a problematic assumption

250 *Prosecutor v Jean-Pierre Bemba Gombo* (Decision on common legal representation of victims for the purpose of trial) ICC-01/05–01/08, Trial Chamber III (11 November 2010), para 15; *Prosecutor v Jean-Pierre Bemba Gombo* (n 145), para 27.

251 *Prosecutor v Jean-Pierre Bemba Gombo* (n 250), para 34.

252 Women's Initiatives for Gender Justice, 'Statement by the Women's Initiatives for Gender Justice on the Opening of the ICC Trial of Jean-Pierre Bemba Gombo' (2010) <www.iccwomen.org/documents/Bemba_Opening_Statement.pdf.pdf> accessed 17 January 2022.

253 *Prosecutor v Abdallah Banda Abakaer Nourain and Saleh Mohammed Jerbo Jamus*, (Order inviting the Registrar to appoint a common legal representative) ICC-02/05–03/09, Trial Chamber IV (6 September 2011).

254 *Prosecutor v Abdallah Banda Abakaer Nourain and Saleh Mohammed Jerbo Jamus* (Decision on common legal representation) ICC-02/05–03/09, Trial Chamber IV (25 May 2012), para 34.

255 ibid, para 32.

256 *Prosecutor v Abdallah Banda Abakaer Nourain and Saleh Mohammed Jerbo Jamus* (Proposal for the Common Legal Representation of Victims) ICC-02/05–03/09, Registrar (25 August 2011), Annex 2 para 5.

257 ibid, Annex 2 para 7.

that victims share largely homogenous interests in participation'.[258] The central concern was the promotion of efficiency, glossing over the range of potential interests that victims might have as well as the different ways those interests (such as justice and reparations) were be understood. The emphasis on minimising the number of groups undermines the effectiveness of collective participation that, from a victim's perspective, is likely to depend on the extent to which he/she is allocated to a group which reflects and expresses his/her interests.[259]

This 'broad-brush approach to victim interests'[260] proved to be problematic in ensuring effective participation, as it clashes with the requirement, under Article 68(3) RS, that victims must demonstrate their individual personal interest in participation is affected. More specifically, the ICC held that the evaluation of a victim's personal interest is necessarily fact-dependent as it must relate to specific evidence and issues that the Chamber will consider on a case-by-case basis. Thus, in order to participate in different stages of the proceedings, victims are requested to demonstrate that their specific personal interests are affected in that part of the proceedings.[261] Based on this view, it is helpful to question whether it is even possible for the CLR to demonstrate what victims' specific personal interests are affected in a specific part of the proceedings, when operating on behalf of hundreds or thousands of victims. For instance, in *Bemba*, when the Trial Chamber III addressed the requests for anonymity by a victim who had applied to participate, the Judges adopted a more restrictive approach to participation to avoid anonymous accusations.[262] Distinguishing between the personal interests of anonymous and identified victims is extremely relevant because anonymous victims have been granted more limited participatory rights than identified victims.[263] However, where anonymous and non-anonymous victims are grouped and represented by one CLR, the latter is the unique voice, through which victims can speak, nullifying, therefore, the concept of a victim's personal interest.

It can be said that the CLR has the task of condensing victims' personal interests into 'generalizable interests'.[264] The consolidation of the practice of victims' participation through a CLR 'produces the "oracle effect" of representation identified by Bourdieu: When appearing on behalf of absent constituents – the victims

258 Emily Haslam and Rod Edmunds, 'Common Legal Representation at the International Criminal Court: More Symbolic than Real?' (2012) 12 International Criminal Law Review 871, 888.

259 REDRESS, 'Ensuring the Effective Participation of Victims Before the International Criminal Court Comments and Recommendations Regarding Legal Representation for Victims' (2005) 3.

260 Haslam and Edmunds (n 258) 888.

261 *Prosecutor v Thomas Lubanga Dyilo* (n 137), para 96; *Prosecutor v Jean-Pierre Bemba Gombo* (n 145), paras 27–28.

262 *Prosecutor v Jean-Pierre Bemba Gombo* (n 145), paras 70–71.

263 *Prosecutor v Thomas Lubanga Dyilo* (n 137), para 131.

264 Sara Kendall and Sarah Nouwen, 'Representational Practices at the International Criminal Court: The Gap between Juridified and Abstract Victimhood' (2013) 76 Law and Contemporary Problems 235, 250.

of a particular case – the representative "gives voice" to an abstract collectivity'.[265] In practice, the CLR enjoys considerable discretion because in drawing the victims' 'generalizable interests' the representative filters, weighs and selects the diverging personal interests of the victims. This evaluation risks damaging some of the interests of individual victims because of the diversity of interests that CLRs represent, which paradoxically may sometimes be in conflict with each other. Bruno Latour referred to a CLR as a 'mediator', rather than an 'intermediary'. The difference is that, while 'intermediaries' merely channel views, 'mediators' 'transform, translate, distort, and modify that meaning of the elements they are supposed to carry'.[266] The CLR dramatically changes the nature of the role of victims in the proceedings before the ICC because it contributes to developing the idea of an 'abstract collectivity' or, better, an abstract concept of victimhood. The participation through the CLR, which merges the interests and views of the individual victim within thousands of views of a broad number of victims, does not enhance effective victim participation.[267] The modality through which the CLR is carried out conflicts with the emerging victims' right to general fairness, which emphasises the need to grant participatory rights to individual victims. Therefore, the CLR casts a certain amount of doubt about its consistency with the victims' right to fairness. More generally, the ICC failed to send a message about effective and fair access to justice for those affected by international crimes.

8.10 Conclusion

The place of victims in proceedings at the ICC has proved to be a contentious issue, since neither the RS nor RPE have established a clear set of participatory rights for victims. The lack of an explicit normative basis has not prevented the Chambers from answering the question of whether victims can impact the scope and substance of the proceedings by way of placing material before the Chamber in a positive way. In this context, expressivism has emerged not only as one of the key foundations for international criminal justice, but also as a vehicle for effectively tailoring a meaningful victims' participation scheme at the ICC, seeking new ways to recognise victimhood.

The study of the ICC's case law concerning victims' participatory rights at the investigation, pre-trial, and trial stages illustrates that the arguments of the Chambers can be interpreted as advancing the expressive aims of the international criminal trial, shedding new light on the understanding of the possibilities for victims' involvement at the ICC. The grounds on which the Chambers' decisions have justified victims' participation reshapes victims' role in a way consistent with

265 ibid. See also Pierre Bourdieu, *Language and Symbolic Power* (Harvard University Press 1991) 119.

266 Bruno Latour, *Reassembling the Social: An Introduction to Actor-Network-Theory* (Oxford University Press 2007) 39.

267 Pues (n 135) 963.

expressivism, since they highlight victims' potential contribution to the norm-expression function of the international criminal trial, which entails conveying disavowal about the moral unacceptability of atrocity, crafting authoritative truths about the past atrocities and reaffirming the importance of human rights. The Chambers expressively included a reference to 'the determination of the truth' as continuous with the determination of the guilt or innocence of the accused, but not reducible to it. By acknowledging the substantial interests of actors, other than the parties, in the outcome and conduct of trials, the Judges advanced that victims' participation in the proceedings has the potential to contribute to producing more comprehensive, historically accurate trial records, ensuring that the truth is not subsumed by choices made by either party.

Victims' involvement has the potential to lead the ICC to embrace more effective modalities of participatory justice, as it increases options for consultation of victims at the different stages of the proceedings. The model of victims' participation in the processing of evidence designed by the ICC sends a strong message about fairness to victims, which should represent a genuine standard to assess the quality of the international criminal procedure. This can be an asset *per se*, which can provide a greater sense of justice to victims and, most importantly, afford a broader view of the prevailing ideas, standards and trends on victim-related issues on a scale beyond the criminal justice horizon.

In view of the foregoing, the overall conclusion to be advanced is that the recognition of victims as 'participants' in the proceedings has drawn attention to their capacity to bring about a potential qualitative enhancement to the messages the trial conveys. The expressivist conceptualisation of victims as crucial actors in the trial can offer an important added value for the practice of the ICC and, more generally, provide an influential and leading model for international criminal justice, since victims' narratives about charged criminal offences, their causes, and their consequences are read as constituent parts of the Prosecutor and Defence 'discursive battles' about how mass violence is best understood, explained and responded to.

References

Books and journals

Ambos K, 'International Criminal Procedure: 'Adversarial', 'Inquisitorial' or Mixed?' (2003) International Criminal Law Review 1

Amnesty International, *The International Criminal Court: Ensuring an Effective Role for Victims* (1999) <amnesty.org/en/documents/ior40/010/1999/en/> accessed 17 January 2022

Amnesty International, 'Democratic Republic of Congo – Mass Rape: Time for Remedies' (2004) AFR 62/018/2004 <amnesty.org/en/documents/afr62/018/2004/en/> accessed 24 January 2022

Annan KA, 'Letter Dated 16 July 2004 from the Secretary-General Addressed to the President of the Security Council' (July 2004) <un.org/en/ga/search/view_doc.asp?symbol=S/2004/573> accessed 24 January 2022

Assembly of States Parties, 'Report on the Activities of the Court' (2005) ICC-ASP/4/16 <https://iccforum.com/media/background/outreach/2005-09-16_ICC-Report_on_the_Activities_of_the_Court_(ICC-ASP-4-16-Eng).pdf> accessed 6 June 2022

ASF, Center for Justice and Reconciliation, DRC Coalition for the ICC, FIDH, HRW, REDRESS, and the Women's Initiative for Gender Justice, 'DR Congo: ICC Charges Raise Concern, Joint letter to the Chief Prosecutor of the International Criminal Court' (31 July 2006) <https://www.hrw.org/news/2006/07/31/dr-congo-icc-charges-raise-concern> accessed 6 June 2022

Bassiouni MC, 'Negotiating the Treaty of Rome on the Establishment of an International Criminal Court' (1999) 32 Cornell International Law Journal 443

Baumgartner E, 'Aspects of Victim Participation in the Proceedings of the International Criminal Court' (2008) 90 International Review of the Red Cross 409

Bischoff JL, Boas G and Reid NL, *International Criminal Law Practitioner Library: International Criminal Procedure*, vol 3 (Cambridge University Press 2011)

Boas G, Bischoff JL and Reid NL, *International Criminal Law Practitioner Library: Elements of Crimes in International Criminal Law*, vol II (Cambridge University Press 2008)

Bourdieu P, *Language and Symbolic Power* (Harvard University Press 1991)

Cassese A, 'The Statute of the International Criminal Court: Some Preliminary Reflections' (1999) 10 European Journal of International Law 144

Cohen M, 'Victims' Participation Rights within the International Criminal Court: A Critical Overview' (2009) 37 Denver Journal of International Law and Policy 351

Committee of Experts on an International Criminal Court, 'Draft Statute for an International Criminal Court: Alternative to the ILC Draft (Siracusa-Draft)' (1995) <legal-tools.org/doc/39a534/pdf/> accessed 2 March 2022

Cryer R et al., *An Introduction to International Criminal Law and Procedure* (Cambridge University Press 2014)

de Gurmendi Fernández SA, 'International Criminal Law Procedures: The Process of Negotiations' in Roy S Lee (ed), *The International Criminal Court: The Making of the Rome Statute: Issues, Negotiations and Results* (Martinus Nijhoff Publishers 1999)

de Gurmendi Fernández SA, 'Elaboration of the Rules and Procedure of Evidence' in Roy S Lee (ed), *The International Criminal Court: Elements of Crimes and Rules of Procedure and Evidence* (Transnational Publishers 2001)

de Gurmendi Fernández SA and Friman H, 'The Rules of Procedure and Evidence of the International Criminal Court' (2000) 3 Yearbook of International Humanitarian Law 289

De Hemptinne J and Jorda C, 'The Status and Role of the Victim' in Antonio Cassese, Paola Gaeta and John R Jones (eds), *The Rome Statute of the International Criminal Court: A Commentary*, vol 2 (Oxford University Press 2002)

Di Giovanni A, 'The Prospect of ICC Reparations in the Case Concerning Northern Uganda: On a Collision Course with Incoherence?' (2005) 2 Journal of International Law & International Relations 25

Donat-Cattin D, 'Article 68: Protection of Victims and Witnesses and Their Participation in the Proceedings' in Otto Triffterer (ed), *Commentary on the Rome Statute of the International Criminal Court: Observers' Notes, Article by Article* (2nd edn, Nomos Verlagsgesellschaft 2008)

Friman H, 'The International Criminal Court and Participation of Victims: A Third Party to the Proceedings?' (2009) 22 Leiden Journal of International Law 485

Glasius M and Meijers T, 'Trials as Messages of Justice: What Should Be Expected of International Criminal Courts?' (2016) 30 Ethics & International Affairs 429

Haslam E, 'Victim Participation at the International Criminal Court: A Triumph of Hope Over Experience?' in Dominic McGoldrick, Peter Rowe and Eric Donnelly, *The Permanent International Criminal Court: Legal and Policy Issues* (Hart Publishing 2004)

Haslam E and Edmunds R, 'Common Legal Representation at the International Criminal Court: More Symbolic than Real?' (2012) 12 International Criminal Law Review 871

Heikkilä M, *International Criminal Tribunals and Victims of Crime: A Study of the Status of Victims before International Criminal Tribunals and of Factors Affecting This Status* (Institute for Human Rights, Åbo Akademi University 2004)

Human Rights Watch, 'Commentary to the Second Preparatory Commission on Rules of Procedure and Elements of Crimes-Section II: Victims in the ICC' (1999) <hrw.org/legacy/campaigns/icc/docs/prepcom-july99.htm> accessed 17 January 2022

Human Rights Watch, 'Seeking Justice: The Prosecution of Sexual Violence in the Congo War' (2005) <hrw.org/reports/2005/drc0305/drc0305.pdf>

Kendall S and Nouwen S, 'Representational Practices at the International Criminal Court: The Gap between Juridified and Abstract Victimhood' (2013) 76 Law and Contemporary Problems 235

Kirsch S, 'The Trial Proceedings before the ICC' (2006) 6 International Criminal Law Review 275

Kress C, 'The Procedural Law of the International Criminal Court in Outline: Anatomy of a Unique Compromise' (2003) 1 Journal of International Criminal Justice 603

Latour B, *Reassembling the Social: An Introduction to Actor-Network-Theory* (Oxford University Press 2007)

Lewis P, 'Trial Procedure' in Roy S Lee (ed), *The International Criminal Court: Elements of Crimes and Rules of Procedure and Evidence* (Transnational Publishers 2001)

Leyh BM, 'Bridging the Divides in International Criminal Proceedings: An Examination into the Victim Participation Endeavor of the International Criminal Court' (2009) 21 Florida Journal of International Law 93

McDermott Y, 'Some Are More Equal than Others: Victim Participation in the ICC' (2008) 5 Eyes on the ICC 27

McDonald GK, 'Trial Procedures and Practice' in Gabrielle Kirk McDonald and Olivia Q Swaak-Goldman (eds), *Substantive and Procedural Aspects of International Criminal Law: The Experience of International and National Courts* (Kluwer 2000)

McGonigle Leyh B, 'Victim-Oriented Measures at International Criminal Institutions: Participation and Its Pitfalls' (2012) 12 International Criminal Law Review 375

McKay F, REDRESS on behalf of the Victims' Rights Working Group, 'Address to the Plenary' (1998) <legal-tools.org/doc/46e5ed/pdf/> accessed 17 January 2022

McLaughlin C, 'The *Sui Generis* Trial Proceedings of the International Criminal Court' (2007) 6 The Law & Practice of International Courts and Tribunals 343

Moffett L, 'Meaningful and Effective? Considering Victims' Interests Through Participation at the International Criminal Court' (2015) 26 Criminal Law Forum 255
Mouthaan S, 'Victim Participation at the ICC for Victims of Gender-Based Crimes: A Conflict of Interest' (2012) 21 Cardozo Journal of International and Comparative Law 619
Plevin AM, 'Beyond a 'Victims' Right': Truth-Finding Power and Procedure at the ICC' (2014) 25 Criminal Law Forum 441
Preparatory Committee on the Establishment of an International Criminal Court, 'Draft Statute of the International Criminal Court – Working Paper Submitted by France' (1996a) A/AC.249/L.3 <legal-tools.org/doc/4d28ee/pdf/> accessed 2 March 2022
Preparatory Committee on the Establishment of an International Criminal Court, 'Proposal Submitted by Egypt for Article 43: Proposal Concerning the Protection and Rights of Witnesses and Victims (Article 43 of the ILC Draft Statute)' (1996b) A/AC.249/WP.11 <legal-tools.org/doc/41a017/pdf/> accessed 2 March 2022
Preparatory Committee on the Establishment of an International Criminal Court, 'Decisions Taken by the Preparatory Committee at Its Session Held from 4 to 15 August 1997' (1997a) A/Ac.249/1997/L.8/Rev.1 <digitallibrary.un.org/record/243787?ln=en> accessed 2 March 2022
Preparatory Committee on the Establishment of an International Criminal Court, 'Proposal by New Zealand on Article 43' (1997b) Non-Paper/WG.4/No.19 <legal-tools.org/doc/658b45/pdf/> accessed 2 March 2022
Pues A, 'A Victim's Right to a Fair Trial at the International Criminal Court?: Reflections on Article 68(3)' (2015) 13 Journal of International Criminal Justice 951
REDRESS, 'Ensuring the Effective Participation of Victims Before the International Criminal Court Comments and Recommendations Regarding Legal Representation for Victims' (2005)
Röben V, 'The Procedure of the ICC: Status and Function of the Prosecutor' (2003) 7 Max Planck Yearbook of United Nations Law 513
Robinson D, 'Serving the Interests of Justice: Amnesties, Truth Commissions and the International Criminal Court' (2003) 14 European Journal of International Law 481
Roche D, 'Truth Commission Amnesties and the International Criminal Court' (2005) 45 British Journal of Criminology 565
Schabas WA, 'Sentencing by International Tribunals: A Human Rights Approach' (1997) 7 Duke Journal of Comparative & International Law 461
Sloane RD, 'The Expressive Capacity of International Punishment: The Limits of the National Law Analogy and the Potential of International Criminal Law' (2007) 43 Stanford Journal of International Law 39
Stahn C, Olásolo H and Gibson K, 'Participation of Victims in Pre-Trial Proceedings of the ICC' (2006) 4 Journal of International Criminal Justice 219
Tonellato M, 'The Victims' Participation at a Crossroads: How the International Criminal Court Could Devise a Meaningful Victims' Participation While Respecting the Rights of the Defendant' (2012) 20 European Journal of Crime, Criminal Law and Criminal Justice 315
Triffterer O (ed), *Commentary on the Rome Statute of the International Criminal Court: Observers' Notes, Article by Article* (2nd edn, Nomos Verlagsgesellschaft 2008)

Trumbull C, 'The Victims of Victim Participation in International Criminal Proceedings' (2007) 29 Michigan Journal of International Law 777

UN General Assembly, 'Report of the Preparatory Committee on the Establishment of an International Criminal Court – Volume I (Proceedings of the Preparatory Committee during March–April and August 1996)' (1996a) A/51/22 <legal-tools.org/doc/e75432/pdf/> accessed 2 March 2022

UN General Assembly, 'Report of the Preparatory Committee on the Establishment of ICC–- vol II (Compilation of Proposals)' (1996b) A/51/22 <https://digitallibrary.un.org/record/222882> accessed 3 June 2022

UN General Assembly, 'Report of the International Criminal Court' (2005) A/60/177 <https://www.icc-cpi.int/sites/default/files/NR/rdonlyres/EDBEBEC0-7896-46EC-9AD6-7C867F67CF1B/278503/ICC_Report_to_UN.pdf> accessed 3 June 2022

UN Office for Drug Control and Crime Prevention, 'Guide for Policy Makers on the Implementation of the United Nations Declaration of Basic Principles of Justice for Victims of Crime and Abuse of Power' (1999) UNDCP/ODCCP(09)/V642

Vasiliev S, 'Article 68 (3) and Personal Interests of Victims in the Emerging Practice of the ICC' in Carsten Stahn and Göran Sluiter (eds), *The Emerging Practice of the International Criminal Court*, vol 48 (Brill 2009)

Vasiliev S, 'Victim Participation Revisited: What the ICC Is Learning About Itself' in Carsten Stahn, The Law and Practice of the International Criminal Court (Oxford University Press 2015)

Walleyn L, 'Victims' Participation in ICC Proceedings: Challenges Ahead' (2016) 16 International Criminal Law Review 995

Women's Initiatives for Gender Justice, 'Statement by the Women's Initiatives for Gender Justice on the Opening of the ICC Trial of Jean-Pierre Bemba Gombo' (2010) <www.iccwomen.org/documents/Bemba_Opening_Statement.pdf.pdf> accessed 17 January 2022

Zappalà S, *Human Rights in International Criminal Proceedings* (Oxford University Press 2003)

Zappalà S, 'The Rights of Victims v. the Rights of the Accused' (2010) 8 Journal of International Criminal Justice 137

Cases

Prosecutor v Abdallah Banda Abakaer Nourain and Saleh Mohammed Jerbo Jamus, (Order inviting the Registrar to appoint a common legal representative) ICC-02/05–03/09, Trial Chamber IV (6 September 2011)

Prosecutor v Abdallah Banda Abakaer Nourain and Saleh Mohammed Jerbo Jamus (Decision on common legal representation) ICC-02/05–03/09, Trial Chamber IV (25 May 2012)

Prosecutor v Abdallah Banda Abakaer Nourain and Saleh Mohammed Jerbo Jamus (Proposal for the Common Legal Representation of Victims) ICC-02/05–03/09, Registrar (25 August 2011)

Prosecutor v Bahar Idriss Abu Gaiuda (Decision on Victims' Modalities of Participation at the Pre-Trial Stage of the Case) ICC-02/05–02/09, Pre-Trial Chamber I (6 October 2009)

Prosecutor v Francis Kirimi Muthaura and Uhuru Muigai Kenyatta (Decision on victims' representation and participation) ICC-01/09–02/11, Trial Chamber V (3 October 2012)
Prosecutor v Germain Katanga and Mathieu Ngudjolo Chui (Decision on the Set of Procedural Rights Attached to Procedural Status of Victim at the Pre-Trial Stage of the Case) ICC-01/04–01/07, Pre-Trial Chamber I (13 May 2008)
Prosecutor v Germain Katanga and Mathieu Ngudjolo Chui (Decision on Limitations of Set of Procedural Rights for Non-Anonymous Victims) ICC-01/04–01/07, Pre-Trial Chamber I (30 May 2008)
Prosecutor v Germain Katanga and Mathieu Ngudjolo Chui (Transcripts) ICC-01/04–01/07 (15 July 2008)
Prosecutor v Germain Katanga and Mathieu Ngudjolo Chui (Transcripts) ICC-01/04–01/07, (21 April 2011)
Prosecutor v Germain Katanga and Mathieu Ngudjolo Chui (Decision on the Modalities of Victim Participation at Trial) ICC-01/04–01/07, Trial Chamber II (22 January 2010)
Prosecutor v Germain Katanga and Mathieu Ngudjolo Chui (Transcripts) ICC-01/04–01/07 (24 November 2009)
Prosecutor v Germain Katanga and Mathieu Ngudjolo Chui (Closing Statement by Victim Representative) ICC-01/04-01/07, Trial Chamber II (16 May 2012)
Prosecutor v Germain Katanga and Mathieu Ngudjolo Chui (Decision on the implementation of regulation 55 of the Regulations of the Court and severing the charges against the accused person) ICC-01/04–01/07, Trial Chamber II (21 November 2012)
Prosecutor v Germain Katanga and Mathieu Ngudjolo Chui (Judgement on the Appeal of Mr Katanga Against the Decision of Trial Chamber II of 22 January 2010 Entitled 'Decision on the Modalities of Victim Participation at Trial') ICC-01/04–01/07, Appeals Chamber (16 July 2010)
Prosecutor v Germain Katanga and Mathieu Ngudjolo Chui (Directions for the conduct of the proceedings and testimony in accordance with rule 140) ICC-01/04–01/07, Trial Chamber II (20 November 2009)
Prosecutor v Germain Katanga and Mathieu Ngudjolo Chui (Corrigendum to Decision on the Conduct of the Proceedings and Testimony in Accordance with Rule 140) ICC-01/04–01/07, Trial Chamber II (1 December 2009)
Prosecutor v Germain Katanga and Mathieu Ngudjolo Chui (Transcripts) ICC-01/04–01/07 (30 November 2009)
Prosecutor v Germain Katanga and Mathieu Ngudjolo Chui (Transcripts) ICC-01/04–01/07 (23 June 2010)
Prosecutor v Germain Katanga and Mathieu Ngudjolo Chui (Order on the organisation of common legal representation of victims) ICC-01/04–01/07, Trial Chamber II (22 July 2009)
Prosecutor v Jean-Pierre Bemba Gombo (Fourth Decision on Victims' Participation) ICC-01/05–01/08, Pre-Trial Chamber III (12 December 2008)
Prosecutor v Jean-Pierre Bemba Gombo (Corrigendum to Decision on the participation of victims in the trial and on 86 applications by victims to participate in the proceedings) ICC-01/05–01/08, Trial Chamber III (12 July 2010)
Prosecutor v Jean-Pierre Bemba Gombo (Transcripts) ICC-01/05–01/08 (22 November 2010)

Prosecutor v Jean-Pierre Bemba Gombo (Decision on the supplemented applications by the legal representatives of victims to present evidence and the views and concerns of victims) ICC-01/05–01/08, Trial Chamber III (22 February 2012)
Prosecutor v Jean-Pierre Bemba Gombo (Order regarding applications by victims to present their views and concerns or to present evidence) ICC-01/05–01/08, Trial Chamber III (21 November 2011)
Prosecutor v Jean-Pierre Bemba Gombo (Decision (i) ruling on legal representatives' applications to question Witness 33 and (ii) setting a schedule for the filing of submissions in relation to future applications to question witnesses) ICC-01/05–01/08, Trial Chamber III (9 September 2011)
Prosecutor v Jean-Pierre Bemba Gombo (Decision on Directions for the Conduct of the Proceedings) ICC-01/05–01/08, Trial Chamber III (19 November 2010)
Prosecutor v Jean-Pierre Bemba Gombo (Decision on common legal representation of victims for the purpose of trial) ICC-01/05–01/08, Trial Chamber III (11 November 2010)
Prosecutor v Joseph Kony et al (Decision on legal representation, appointment of counsel for the defence, protective measures and time-limit for submission of observations on applications for participation a/0010/06, a/0064/06 to a/0070/06, a/0081/06 to a/0104/06 and a/0111/06 to a/012) ICC-02/04–01/05, Pre-Trial Chamber II (1 February 2007)
Prosecutor v Laurent Gbagbo (Decision on Victims' Participation and Victims' Common Legal Representation at the Confirmation of Charges Hearing and in the Related Proceedings) ICC-02/11–01/11, Pre-Trial Chamber I (4 June 2012)
Prosecutor v Thomas Lubanga Dyilo (Decision on the confirmation of charges) ICC-01/04–01/06, Pre-Trial Chamber I (29 January 2007)
Prosecutor v Thomas Lubanga Dyilo (Judgement pursuant to Article 74 of the Statute) ICC-01/04–01/06, Trial Chamber I (14 March 2012)
Prosecutor v Thomas Lubanga Dyilo (Decision on the Schedule and Conduct of the Confirmation Hearing) ICC-01/04–01/06, Pre-Trial Chamber I (7 November 2006)
Prosecutor v Thomas Lubanga Dyilo (Decision on the Arrangements for Participation of Victims a/0001/06, a/0002/06 and a/0003/06 at the Confirmation Hearing) ICC-01/04–01/06, Pre-Trial Chamber I (22 September 2006)
Prosecutor v Thomas Lubanga Dyilo (Decision on victims' participation) ICC-01/04–01/06, Trial Chamber I (18 January 2008)
Prosecutor v Thomas Lubanga Dyilo (Decision on the legal representative's request for clarification of the Trial Chamber's 18 January 2008 'Decision on victims' participation') ICC-01/04–01/06, Trial Chamber I (2 June 2008)
Prosecutor v Thomas Lubanga Dyilo (Opening Statement by Victim Representative) ICC-01/04–01/06 (26 January 2009)
Prosecutor v Thomas Lubanga Dyilo (Decision on the request by victims a/0225/06, a/0229/06 and a/0270/07 to express their views and concerns in person and to present evidence during the trial) ICC-01/04–01/06, Trial Chamber I (26 June 2009)
Prosecutor v Thomas Lubanga Dyilo (Prosecution's Document in Support of Appeal against Trial Chamber I's 18 January 2008 Decision on Victims' Participation) ICC-01/04–01/06, Office of the Prosecutor (10 March 2008)

Prosecutor v Thomas Lubanga Dyilo (Defence Appeal Against Trial Chamber I's 18 January 2008 Decision on Victims' Participation) ICC-01/04–01/06, Defence (10 March 2008)

Prosecutor v Thomas Lubanga Dyilo (Partly Dissenting Opinion of Judge G M Pikis) ICC-01/04–01/06, Appeals Chamber (11 July 2008)

Prosecutor v Thomas Lubanga Dyilo (Partly Dissenting Opinion of Judge Philippe Kirsch) ICC-01/04–01/06, Appeals Chamber (11 July 2008)

Prosecutor v Thomas Lubanga Dyilo (Judgement on the Appeals of the Prosecutor and the Defence against Trial Chamber I's Decision on Victims' Participation of 18 January 2008) ICC-01/04–01/06, Appeals Chamber (11 July 2008)

Prosecutor v Thomas Lubanga Dyilo (Decision on the defence observations regarding the right of the legal representatives of victims to question defence witnesses and on the notion of personal interest -and- Decision on the defence application to exclude certain representatives of victims from the Chamber during the non-public evidence of various defence witnesses) ICC-01/04–01/06, Trial Chamber I (11 March 2010)

Prosecutor v Thomas Lubanga Dyilo (Decision on the Manner of Questioning Witnesses by the Legal Representatives of Victims) ICC-01/04–01/06, Trial Chamber I (16 September 2009)

Prosecutor v Thomas Lubanga Dyilo (Decision on the defence application for disclosure of victims applications) Trial Chamber I, ICC-01/04–01/06 (21 January 2009)

Prosecutor v William Samoei Ruto and Joshua Arap Sang (Decision on victims' representation and participation) ICC-01/09–01/11, Trial Chamber V (3 October 2012)

Prosecutor v William Samoei Ruto and Joshua Arap Sang (Opening Statement by Victim Representative) ICC-01/09–01/11, Trial Chamber V(A) (10 September 2013)

Prosecutor v William Samoei Ruto and Joshua Arap Sang (Decision on Common Legal Representative for Victims' Request to Participate in Hearings and Examine Witnesses) ICC-01/09–01/11, Trial Chamber V(A) (20 November 2013)

Prosecutor v William Samoei Ruto and Joshua Arap Sang (Decision on victims' representation and participation) ICC-01/09–01/11, Trial Chamber V (9 October 2012)

Prosecutor v William Samoei Ruto et al. (Decision on the Motion by Legal Representative of Victim Applicants to Participate in Initial Appearance Proceedings) ICC-01/09–01/11, Pre-Trial Chamber II (30 March 2011)

Prosecutor v William Samoei Ruto et al. (Second Decision on the 'Request by the Victims' Representative to Access to Confidential Materials') ICC-01/09–01/11, Pre-Trial Chamber II (23 September 2011)

Prosecutor v William Samoei Ruto et al. (Decision on the 'Request by the Victims' Representative for Access to Confidential Materials') ICC-01/09–01/11, Pre-Trial Chamber II (21 September 2011)

Prosecutor v William Samoei Ruto et al. (Decision on Victims' Participation at the Confirmation of Charges Hearing and in the Related Proceedings) ICC-01/09–01/11, Pre-Trial Chamber II (5 August 2011)

Situation in Darfur, Sudan (Corrigendum to Decision on the Applications for Participation in the Proceedings of Applicants a/0011/06 et al) ICC-02/05, Pre-Trial Chamber I (14 December 2007)

Situation in Libya (Decision on Victim's Participation in Proceedings Related to the Situation in Libya) ICC-01/11, Pre-Trial Chamber I (24 January 2012)
Situation in the Democratic Republic of the Congo (Decision on the Applications for participation in the proceedings of VPRS 1, VPRS 2, VPRS 3, VPRS 4, VPRS 5 and VPRS 6 (Public Redacted Version)) ICC-01/04, Pre-Trial Chamber I (19 January 2006)
Situation in the Democratic Republic of the Congo (Corrigendum to the "Decision on the Applications for Participation Filed in Connection with the Investigation in the Democratic Republic of the Congo by a/0004/06 et al") ICC-01/04, Pre-Trial Chamber I (31 January 2008)
Situation in the Democratic Republic of the Congo (Judgement on victim participation in the investigation stage of the proceedings in the appeal of the OPCD against the decision of Pre-Trial Chamber I of 7 December 2007 and in the appeals of the OPCD and the Prosecutor against the decision of Pre-Trial) ICC-01/04, Appeals Chamber (19 December 2008)
Situation in the Democratic Republic of the Congo (Decision on Victims' Participation in Proceedings Relating to the Situation in the Democratic Republic of Congo) ICC-02/04, Pre-Trial Chamber I (11 April 2011)
Situation in the Republic of Côte d'Ivoire (Decision Pursuant to Article 15 of the Rome Statute on the Authorisation of an Investigation into the Situation in the Republic of Côte d'Ivoire) ICC-02/11–14, Pre-Trial Chamber III (3 October 2011)
Situation in the Republic of Kenya (Decision Pursuant to Article 15 of the Rome Statute on the Authorization of an Investigation into the Situation in the Republic of Kenya) ICC-01/09–19, Pre-Trial Chamber II (31 March 2010)
Situation in the Republic of Kenya (Decision on Victims' Participation in Proceedings Related to the Situation in the Republic of Kenya) ICC-01/09–24, Pre-Trial Chamber II (3 November 2010)
Situation in the Republic of Kenya (Decision on a Request for Leave to Appeal) ICC-01/09, Pre-Trial Chamber III (11 February 2011)
Situation in Uganda (Decision on victims' applications for participation a/0010/06 et al) ICC-02/04, Pre-Trial Chamber II (10 August 2007)
Situation in Uganda (Decision on Victim's Participation in Proceedings Related to the Situation in Uganda) ICC-02/04, Pre-Trial Chamber II (9 March 2012)

Legislation

Rome Statute of the International Criminal Court 1998 (2187 UNTS 90)
Rules of Procedure and Evidence of the International Criminal Court 2002 (ICC-ASP/1/3)

9 Conclusions

9.1 Introduction

This book has aimed to provide critical insight into the question of which criminal justice model provides a meaningful foundation for the participation of victims in international criminal proceedings and clarifies the nature and scope of their participatory rights. This was accomplished through an extensive analysis of the existing literature and body of jurisprudence on distinct approaches to victims' participatory rights, with a view to suggesting ways of operationalising victims' participation in international criminal proceedings. In doing this, the book has critically examined the challenges and limitations of the traditional theoretical frameworks of criminal justice, namely retributive, utilitarian, and restorative justice models, in dealing with victims' participation in proceedings before international criminal tribunals, and has investigated how such limitations can be addressed through the adoption of the framework envisaged by expressivism.

This concluding chapter commences with a discussion of the key points that have emerged from this book. It also discusses the book's contribution to the growing debate in international criminal justice scholarship about the need to develop a fairer and more effective procedure that affords a proper procedural role to victims of mass atrocities.

9.2 What is the appropriate avenue for justice for victims?

A central theme running throughout the analysis in this book is the idea that framing a model of participation for victims in international criminal proceedings without a broader reconsideration of the eligible justifications for justice within the international arena would fall short of providing an effective response to victims' need for justice. It is, thus, necessary to depart from the retributivist, deterrent, and restorative criminal justice models and adopt an expressivist approach, which has not only emerged as one of the key foundations for international criminal justice, but also as a vehicle for effectively tailoring victims' participatory rights as well as harmonising the diverging understandings of the role of victims, as recognised by the common law and civil law traditions.

Victimological studies did not produce a radical reform of the existing criminal justice models, informed mainly by the retributivist and deterrent paradigms,

DOI: 10.4324/9781003215448-9

which relegated the victims to a marginal role in the criminal process. Nor did victimology break down those mechanisms which prevent victims from exercising participatory rights, as its response to the calls for a better integration of victims into criminal justice systems has only resulted in a range of modest reforms. The victims-based approach, based on the victims' procedural rights, which involved victims' participation at the final stage of the criminal process in the form of victims' impact statements, reflected the sense of reluctance in common law countries to afford victims a greater say in the criminal process. The main concern was avoiding the potentially disruptive effects to the proceedings of victims' participation, which was considered to pose a threat to the expeditiousness and fairness of the trial. The victims' right to service approach, by justifying victims' role depending on the identification of their physical, psychological, and financial needs, tended to direct victims away from the criminal justice proceedings into alternative pathways to justice. Restorative justice practices have the merit of having placed new obligations on criminal justice agencies to make their practice more inclusive of victims' concerns. However, the negotiated process envisaged by the restorative justice model goes beyond the strict scope of the criminal process because the nature of the rights conferred on victims appears to be more similar to rights to service rather than participatory rights.

The same dynamics of retributive, deterrent, and restorative justice systems, which marginalised victims' role at the domestic level, have been transferred to international criminal justice, as the ICTY, the ICTR, and the ICC were established under the banner of these criminal justice frameworks. This transplant proved to be problematic not only because retributive, deterrent, and restorative justice models do not grant victims a meaningful role, but also because it downplayed the inappropriacy of those criminal justice theories in the context of mass atrocities in international law.

There are significant departures from domestic criminal law, which have called for greater attention to the impact that the specific features of international criminal law have on these criminal justice models. The high selectivity of those to be prosecuted lowers the chances of catching and punishing the perpetrators of gross violations of human rights and, therefore, decreases the deterrent effect of punishment as well as invalidating the imperative of retributivism, which requires that all persons deserving a punishment have to be punished. Furthermore, it is not possible for the international criminal tribunals to mete out a punishment commensurate with the extensive nature, seriousness, and recurrence of the atrocities committed. Indeed, this factor not only does not serve retribution, it also weakens deterrence as the benefits of the crime outweigh the seriousness of the punishment. Restorative justice has proved to be more attentive to the needs of victims; however, proceedings before international criminal institutions do not align with the core elements of restorative justice practices and its prioritisation of victims' participation. These elements, namely victim–offender encounter, offender's acknowledgement of responsibility and apology, collaborative conflict-resolution approach, healing and reconciliation of victims and communities, symbolic reparation, and material compensation, have been developed to address juvenile criminality, first-time offenders, and low-level crime and, thus, are not structured to operate in the particular context of the international criminal justice, characterised by grave harm caused to victims and communities by mass atrocity.

There is, thus, a critical need to reformulate the criminal justice paradigm that underpins the international criminal justice system. The book has built on expressivist theories to provide a well-grounded foundation for international criminal justice, since one of its virtues is its ability to explain some of the unique features and paradoxes as well as the limitations of legalism in relation to international criminal law. The normative claim underlying expressivism, according to which, by expressing valuable social messages, criminal law operates as a mechanism for altering social norms, holds greater importance in international criminal justice than in other models. Expressivism imposes a change in perspective: it advances a distinctive role for international criminal justice, continuous with, but not reducible to, the purposes of punishment. As opposed to punishing simply because the perpetrators deserve it or because potential perpetrators will be deterred, expressivism emphasises the symbolic meanings generated by the practices of the international criminal process as a whole, where the acts and perspectives of the different actors get voiced. In particular, the expressivist potential lies in the didactic function of the trial and its capacity to create historical narratives as representations of truth and their pedagogical dissemination. The communicative and performative features of the trial are as important as its outcomes or substantive findings, as they advance the idea of the proceedings being an attempt to craft historical records and create communal meaning. In the expressivist view, the trial is conceived as a communicative institution in post-conflict societies that is able to have an impact on present and future societal understandings of mass violence, peremptorily repudiating conduct amounting to international crimes, symbolically rejecting the acquiescence of the international community to those crimes and promoting human rights. The trial, thus, becomes a forum for dialogue and open possibilities, rather than a forum for the provision of closure, providing a new way of thinking about atrocities amounting to international crimes and stimulating processes of historical memory building, persuasion, and internalisation of values.

The expressivist model of international criminal justice, which draws attention to the performative and communicative dimensions of the trial, puts forward a cutting-edge understanding of what structure the criminal process should have and what type of performance and functions the individuals involved in the criminal process carry out. Through the adoption of the expressivist framework, it is possible to establish a common grammar that bridges the gap between the different concepts of the criminal process in the civil law and common law systems, contributing to harmonising the procedural understanding of the rights and role not only of the victims, but also of the other actors, such as Judges, Prosecutor, and Defence. Structuring the international criminal proceedings around key elements of expressivism, namely the performative and communicative features of the trial, through which the truth-telling and educative functions unfold, smooths the rough edges off the adversarial nature of the criminal process.

The expressivist understanding of the criminal proceedings as a forum for providing a narrative of the events and enunciating condemnation of the atrocities committed provides an important conceptual justification for victims' participation in international criminal proceedings. Victims become critical actors in international criminal proceedings, as their participation can potentially contribute to re-enacting the crime, constructing an authoritative acknowledgement of the events, and communicating the denunciation of those heinous conducts. The message to those who think they can engage with these criminal conducts that impunity will not be tolerated can be expressed not only through punishment, but also through the mechanism of victims' participation, which makes it possible to convey the repudiation of such crimes. In fact, within the expressivist paradigm, the victim's voice contributes to the enhancement of the quality of the narrative shaped during the proceedings and, ultimately, to the establishment of the truth, resulting in an effective prosecution of perpetrators and putting an end to impunity.

Tailoring the structure of the proceedings in a way that reflects the norm-expression function of the trial has required a loosening of the adversarial model and its characteristic of a contest between parties. This approach has meant a more active role for the Judges, who play an important role in enacting the performative and communicative dimensions of the trial. Judges operate as active fact-finders to determine the truth and as interpreters that give meaning to the narratives expressed by the parties in the application of the law. In a similar way, the Prosecutor plays a fundamental role for the enactment of the performative and communicative features of the proceedings as he/she carries out a narrative and educative function. The charges presented by the Prosecutor entail narratives which can be seen as a 'counter-performance to the crime', sending the message that the trial serves to overcome the criminal acts. Prosecutions are a means of teaching a lesson, which goes beyond the perpetrators and other actors involved in the proceedings. The Prosecutor's action seeks to educate society and the international community generally about the world's horrors and consolidate declared norms and shared beliefs about the way individuals ought to behave. While expressivism does not affect the Prosecutor's exercise of his/her prosecutorial discretionary powers, it requires that he/she acknowledges that victims represent one of the constituencies[1] they have to serve. The Prosecutor's direct 'antagonist', namely the defendant, whose role is to counteract the charges and contest evidence, presents his/her counter-narrative, which is an alternative to the Prosecutor's version of the events under adjudication. In doing so, the Defence has often used a set of practices, which includes political speeches as a means of maintaining a leadership role, the promotion of the defendant's persona, the delegitimisation of international criminal courts, and a challenge to their authority. Consequently, the Defence's narrative, which *per se* is the highest expression of the right to a fair trial, can represent a threat

1 M Findlay, 'Activating a Victim Constituency in International Criminal Justice' (2009) 3 International Journal of Transitional Justice 183, 187.

to the expressivist concept of the trial as a performance of justice, and also to the legitimacy of the whole international criminal justice endeavour.

By requiring international criminal courts to apply as secondary sources treaties, principles and rules of international law, consistent with internationally recognised human rights, Article 38 of the International Court of Justice Statute, and, at a more specific level, Article 21 of the RS provide an entry point to the reliance of the case law of the ECtHR and the IACtHR, as a source of principles and rules that can be applied for purposes relating to the participation of victims. The system of legal bases advanced by the ECtHR and the IACtHR to justify the role of victims can be interpreted as consistent with the framework of the expressivist function of the trial. These regional human rights monitoring bodies acknowledged that because of values that their respective conventions protect human rights violations involve breaches of rights that have a special status. Thus, the criminal proceedings should serve to reaffirm the importance that society places on those serious infringements. It can be maintained that the State's obligation to undertake an effective investigation is consistent with expressivist values, since criminal proceedings become the mechanism to express disavowal and condemnation of those conducts violating human rights, to reaffirm the importance of human rights and to educate the public to respect those rights.

The case law of the IACtHR and ECtHR also recognised the right of the victims, whose basic rights to life and to the prohibition to inhuman treatment are violated, to participate in related criminal proceedings to express their concerns. The IACtHR and ECtHR have articulated two basic rights of victims: the right to access to justice to obtain an investigation and the right to participate in criminal proceedings. In view of the seriousness of the infringements suffered by the victims, the system of criminal justice should not only seek to punish the perpetrators, but also to ascertain the truth, by providing victims' version of the events. The victim's right to access to and participation in criminal proceedings reflects the view of the ECtHR and the IACtHR that victim's voice enhances the quality of the narrative shaped during the proceedings, effectively contributing to the prosecution and punishment of those responsible.

Expressivism proved to be an important factor in the creation and operation of international criminal justice institutions. Specifically, the expressivist value of the IMT at Nuremberg, the ICTY, and the ICTR can be traced in the multiple goals underpinning their creation, such as promoting the national and international rule of law; ending the impunity of those who violate human rights; providing a mechanism for the transformation of social norms in developing democracies; conveying expressions of shame and apology; safeguarding basic standards of human rights; and communicating the denunciation and the disavowal of heinous conducts.

The analysis of the case law on victims' involvement in the proceedings before these international criminal tribunals demonstrated that there was an expressivist 'deficit' with regard to the way the procedural role of victims has been implemented. Due to the predominance of the adversarial procedural model, victims played the quite marginal role of witnesses, which prevented victims from having an effective right to access to and participation in international criminal proceedings. Although expressivism envisages victims as active agents in the proceedings, whose storytelling is fundamental to pursuing expressivist goals, in the proceedings before these International Criminal Tribunals, Prosecutors, Judges, and Defence counsels took control of victims' narratives and imposed a particular frame or stereotype to keep the perceived injustice of victims' suffering at bay. The concept of victims' procedural role before the Nuremberg IMT, the ICTY, and the ICTR has negated their potential for shaping the expressivist message of the international criminal trials. The practices of these tribunals have restricted the capacity of victims' narrative to present their perspective of the events and to bring about a potential qualitative change in the message the trial conveys.

On reviewing the existing case law of the ICC concerning victims' participatory rights at the investigation, pre-trial, and trial stages, this study has illustrated that the arguments of the Chambers can be interpreted as advancing the expressive aims of the international criminal trial, shedding new light on the understanding of the possibilities for victims' involvement at the ICC. The right of victims to participate at the investigation and pre-trial stages is perhaps the most controversial issue in the case law of the ICC. While, in the *Lubanga* case, the Pre-Trial Chamber I preferred to rely on the well-established adversarial approach, which sees the Prosecutor as the absolute *dominus* of the investigation stage, in subsequent cases, the Pre-Trial Chambers held a broader interpretation of the role of victims at the investigation and pre-trial stages. The Judges read the legal framework of the ICC on victims' participation emphasising the important contribution of victims to ascertaining the truth because, at the investigation and pre-trial stages, victims' rights serve as an important check on the prosecutorial discretion. The Chambers specifically attempted to harmonise the victims' right to participate in the investigation and pre-trial stages by introducing a set of rights for victims.

With regard to the right of victims to participate at the trial stage, the jurisprudence of the ICC has held as legal justification for victims' participatory rights values that reflect the expressivist account of the criminal justice system brought to light in this book. By expanding the modalities of participation to include those rights not explicitly contained under the ICC legal framework, the Trial Chambers have grounded their decision precisely on the assistance that victims can give the ICC in determining the truth and, thus, effectively contribute to the fight against impunity. Specifically, the Chambers' interpretation of victims' right to express views and concerns conceived the term 'views and concerns' as a means of empowering victims to contribute to crafting the narrative of the events at the trial stage and, thus, to forging the didactic message that the trial should convey. In this view, the right of victims to present views and concerns breaks the stiff bipolar structure of the proceedings, dominated by the Prosecutor and Defence, as such self-standing procedural action becomes a mechanism aiming at suggesting to the Judges how to orientate their fact-finding.

The most significant step forward in providing a meaningful model of victims' participation is represented by the mechanism that allows victims to introduce evidence based on Article 69(3) of the RS. The spirit of this mechanism presents elements and values that can be read as ingrained in the expressivist justice model because it demonstrated that the goal of international criminal justice is not only the determination of the guilt or innocence of the defendant, but also to seek to ascertain the truth and to give victims a voice. The ICC engagement with victims as 'third actors' in the fact-finding process can potentially bridge the gap between traditional models of international criminal trials and a broader expressivist aspiration of the ICC in terms of crafting a robust and permanent record of history and creating a useful narrative for post-conflict societies and the international community. The analysis of the case law of the ICC also uncovered the important limitation of a specific modality of victims' participation, namely the common legal representation. It is argued that to a certain extent the common legal representation negates the essence of the victim's right to participate in the proceedings. The common legal representation, which pools victims together for purposes of participation, overlooks the role of victims as a fundamental part of the criminal proceedings, in favour of a collective and rather abstract concept of victimhood.

9.3 Final observations

The analysis in this book has proceeded from the standpoint that the endeavour of providing a meaningful foundation for the participation of victims in the international criminal proceedings demands a great deal of rethinking of the understanding of the main purpose behind the entire enterprise of international criminal justice. The in-depth reflection on the goals and functions of international criminal justice has illustrated that it is crucial to adopt a new framework of justice, namely the expressivist model, which clarifies the scope and content of victims' rights in international criminal proceedings. This study has also argued a case for the need to adopt the expressivist framework in international criminal justice to radically reform the existing procedural model influenced by the civil law and common law systems and their respective inquisitorial and adversarial approaches. It has been suggested that, through the adoption of the expressivist justice model, it would be possible to establish a common grammar that is able to bridge the divide between the inquisitorial and adversarial languages, which have shaped victims' participatory rights in diametrically opposed ways, and harmonise the diverging understandings of victims' role.

This book has sought not only to explore the purposes and nature of victims' participatory rights, it has also offered critical insights into the limitations of the retributive, deterrent, and restorative model of international criminal justice. The critique of the deterrent, retributive, and restorative criminal justice models has been based on the distinct character of international crimes that are generally committed at times when law and order have largely broken down and grave crimes are committed against a large segment of the population by organised groups. The selectivity of prosecutions, a general dearth of proportionate punishment (relative to the crimes committed), as well as the overall lack of willingness on the part of offenders to make amends for their wrongdoings are shown to weaken such classical justice models. In proposing an expressivist model to international criminal justice, this book has demonstrated that such a paradigm responds to these structural obstacles in a more effective way than the above-mentioned criminal justice frameworks. This book, therefore, has sought to make a significant contribution towards a better understanding of the goals and functions of international criminal justice.

It is intended that this book will be valuable in highlighting the nature and purposes of victims' participation in international criminal proceedings. In particular, the study underlines the critical need to reformulate the criminal justice paradigm that underpins the international criminal justice system in order to implement an effective framework for victims' participation, which can successfully give a voice to victims in the proceedings. The objective is to create a fertile ground to put forward a core set of participatory rights for victims, which should be granted to victims systematically, rather than based on a casuistic approach. As the ICC's legal framework does not envisage a protected core of participatory rights, the analysis expounded throughout this book can provide some insight into a potential set of victims' rights and, thus, enhance an overall predictability for victims' participation. In particular, given that victims do not have the right to present evidence nor to challenge the admissibility of evidence, they can only be requested by the Chamber to do so, this book tried to shed light on the relationship between the participatory rights of victims and the truth-finding mandate of the court in light of the expressivist model of the international criminal justice.

In view of the foregoing, the overall conclusion to be advanced is that the analysis presented has sought to provide a model for international criminal justice, in which the recognition of victims as crucial actors in international criminal proceedings highlights their capacity to bring about a potential qualitative enhancement of the messages the trial conveys. Indeed, victims' participation in international criminal proceedings will continue to be a vexed question, as there is no one best way to incorporate victims' participatory rights. However, the expressivist justice model is a better response to the challenge of determining a proper role for victims in international criminal proceedings, since the assumption of the trial as a platform for framing the narratives of gross human rights violations encourages victims to express their independent voice and bring their story-telling about the complex and serious dimension of the atrocities suffered to the proceedings.

References

Book

Findlay M, 'Activating a Victim Constituency in International Criminal Justice' (2009) 3 International Journal of Transitional Justice 183

Index